Myth, religion and society

Myth, religion and society

Structuralist essays by
M. Detienne, L. Gernet, J.-P. Vernant and
P. Vidal-Naquet

Edited by
R.L. GORDON

Senior Lecturer in the
School of Modern Languages and European History,
University of East Anglia

With an introduction by
R.G.A. BUXTON

Lecturer in Classics in the
University of Bristol

CAMBRIDGE UNIVERSITY PRESS
Cambridge
London   New York   New Rochelle   Melbourne   Sydney

EDITIONS DE LA MAISON DES SCIENCES DE L'HOMME
Paris

Published by the Press Syndicate of the University of Cambridge
The Pitt Building, Trumpington Street, Cambridge CB2 1RP
32 East 57th Street, New York, NY 10022, USA
296 Beaconsfield Parade, Middle Park, Melbourne 3206, Australia
and Editions de la Maison des Sciences de l'Homme
54 Boulevard Raspail, 75270 Paris Cedex 06

First published 1981

Printed in Great Britain at the University Press, Cambridge

British Library Cataloguing in Publication Data
Myth, religion and society.
1. Mythology, Greek
I. Gordon, Richard L   II. Detienne, Marcel
292'.1'.308   BL790   80-40783
ISBN 0 521 22780 1 hard covers
ISBN 0 521 29640 4 paperback

Contents

Sources and acknowledgements

The following are the sources of the essays in this collection. The Editor and Publishers wish to thank the publishers mentioned for their permission to publish these essays. The translations have been made by the Editor or adapted by him from those listed.

1 'L'Union avec Mètis et la royauté du ciel', in M. Detienne and J.-P. Vernant, *Les ruses de l'intelligence: la mètis des grecs* (Flammarion, Paris, 1974), pp. 104–24 [= *Mélanges ... H. Ch. Puech* (Paris, 1974), pp. 101–16]. Published in English as *Cunning intelligence in Greek culture and society* (Harvester Press, Hassocks, Sussex; Humanities Press Inc, New York, 1978), pp. 107–30, translated by Janet Lloyd.

2 'La Corneille de mer', in *Les ruses de l'intelligence*, pp. 201–41 [= 'Le Navire d'Athéna', *RHR* 178 (1970), 133–77 considerably altered]. *Cunning intelligence*, pp. 215–58.

3 'Le Mythe prométhéen chez Hésiode', in J.-P. Vernant, *Mythe et société en Grèce ancienne* (Maspero, Paris, 1974), pp. 177–94 [= *Il mito greco: atti del convegno internazionale (Urbino 1973)*, edd. B. Gentili and G. Paioni (Rome 1977), pp. 99–106]. Published in English as *Myth and society in ancient Greece* (Harvester Press, Sussex; Humanities Press Inc, New York, 1980), pp. 168–85, translated by Janet Lloyd.

4 'Sacrifice et alimentation humaine à propos du Prométhée d'Hésiode', *Annali della Scuola Normale di Pisa* 7 (1977), 905–40, reprinted as pp. 37–71 of 'À la table des hommes' in Detienne and Vernant et al. *La cuisine du sacrifice en pays grec* (Gallimard, Paris, 1979), pp. 37–132.

5 'Valeurs religieuses et mythiques de la terre et du sacrifice dans l'Odyssée', *Annales ESC* 25 (1970), 1278–97 [= *Problèmes de la Terre en Grèce ancienne*, ed. M.I. Finley (Mouton, The Hague, 1973), pp. 269–92]. (With alterations and corrections here.)

6 'Orphée au miel', *QUCC* 13 (1971), 7–23 [= *Faire de l'histoire*, edd. J. Le Goff and P. Nora (Gallimard, Paris, 1973), 3, pp. 56–75].

7 'La Notion mythique de la valeur en Grèce', in Louis Gernet, *Anthropologie de la Grèce antique* (essays collected by J.-P. Vernant) (Maspero, Paris, 1968), pp. 93–137 [reprinted without

significant alteration from *Journal de psychologie* 41 (1948), 415–62].

8 'Le Chasseur noir et l'origine de l'ephébie athénienne', *Annales ESC* 23 (1968), 947–64, which appeared in the same year as 'The Black Hunter and the origin of the Athenian Ephebeia', *PCPhS* 194 (n.s. 14) (1968), 49–64 (translated by Janet Lloyd). (With extensive alterations and corrections here.)

9 'Le Cru, l'enfant grec et le cuit', in *Faire de l'histoire*, pp. 137–68. (With alterations and additions here.)

10 'Esclavage et gynécocratie dans la tradition, le mythe et l'utopie', in *Recherches sur les structures sociales dans l'Antiquité classique*, introduced by C. Nicolet (Colloques nationaux du CNRS, ed. CNRS, Paris, 1970), pp. 63–80. (With additions and corrections here.)

11 'Athènes et l'Atlantide', *REG* 78 (1964), 420–44. (With additions and corrections here.)

12 'Entre Bêtes et Dieux', in *Nouvelle revue de psychanalyse* 6 (1972), 231–46 (special issue 'Destins du cannibalisme') [reprinted with slight alterations as 'Ronger la tête de ses parents', in M. Detienne, *Dionysos mis à mort* (Gallimard, Paris, 1977), pp. 135–60.] Published in English as *Dionysos slain* (Johns Hopkins, Baltimore, 1979), pp. 35–67, translated by Mireille Muellner and Leonard Muellner.

Introduction, by R.G.A. Buxton

Writing in the *Bulletin of the Council of University Classical Departments* for 1977, M.L. West addressed himself to the question of how, if at all, the subject of Greek myth should be taught to undergraduates. While accepting that students ought to be aware of 'the stories themselves', he expressed scepticism about the introduction of more theoretical matters:

When it comes to interpretation of myths, the problems are much harder. Before we can think about teaching anything, we must believe we know something, and probably most university teachers feel a profound lack of confidence in this area . . . interpretation of myths is not a field in which soundness abounds . . . The sort of graduate we ought to be aiming to produce, in my view, is not one who knows what the Greek myths are all about (for none of us claims to know that), nor one who has mastered some glistening Method . . .

These remarks by one of the most gifted philologists of the present day would, I imagine, be received with approval by most classical scholars. And indeed it is hard to refrain from a certain sympathy with such a brisk refusal to be taken in. The history of the study of mythology has been dominated by good ideas carried to absurd lengths; and one may be pardoned for thinking that Euhemerus, say, or Max Müller, would have benefited from more frequent promptings by the voice of Empiricism. But it is unrealistic to expect of a theory, or even of a Method, that it explain everything; enough, surely, if it permits us to perceive new connections or, in the case of history, to cut fresh diagonals through the past. The essays collected by Dr Gordon in this volume offer, from their different but related perspectives, hope that Professor West's methodological reservations may be unduly defeatist.

What these studies have in common may, for better or worse, be summarized in the contentious word 'structuralism'. Unfortunately, to say that one is a structuralist is about as informative as to say that one is a democrat. The range of uses to which the term has been put in linguistics, anthropology and literary criticism — to name only three areas — is such as practically to rule out any workable definition covering all the available cases. Yet in relation to the four authors here represented the definitional problem is not insuperable. All are working within the same intellectual tradition; all see as at least part of their task the recovery of the implicit categories — the structures — in terms of which 'Greek mentality' was articulated. In the case of Vernant,

Vidal-Naquet and Detienne, who are all very much alive and active today, their own position *vis-à-vis* the structuralist movement is something which they themselves confront from time to time. In the case of Louis Gernet (1882–1962) we are dealing rather with one who is in certain respects a precursor of the structuralists, and in whose rich and many-sided output we can find the seeds of much that is occupying scholars at present.

Jean-Pierre Vernant, Pierre Vidal-Naquet and Marcel Detienne all teach or have taught at the École Pratique des Hautes Études in Paris.[1] To say that they form a 'school', with the magisterial Vernant at its head, would not be entirely misleading: Vernant and Vidal-Naquet have produced a joint volume on Greek tragedy,[2] while Vernant and Detienne have collaborated on a book (from which the first two pieces in this collection are drawn) about cunning intelligence in Greek thought[3] and, with others, on a study of sacrifice;[4] moreover, the footnotes in their works bear frequent witness to the respect which they have for one another. None the less there are significant differences between them, both in approach and in their areas of special interest.

Detienne works principally on mythology. In *The Gardens of Adonis*,[5] an analysis of a number of Greek myths and rituals involving spices, he made an important contribution to our understanding of how Greeks perceived the distinction between proper (wifely) and improper (excessively seductive) conduct by women, and how that perception received symbolic expression through myth and ritual. Characteristic of Detienne's approach here and elsewhere — characteristic, too, of Detienne's model in the book, the anthropologist Claude Lévi-Strauss — is the attention paid to 'empirical categories' as deployed in mythical narratives and ritual transactions: he shows repeatedly how contrasts between, say, types of animal or plant constitute one of the fundamental vehicles for the logic of myth. So in 'The myth of "Honeyed Orpheus" ' (pp. 95–109 below) he draws our attention to the rôle of honey in various traditional tales. Much of Detienne's work is concerned to illuminate the system of religious thought of the Greek *polis* (city), but he has also done complementary analyses of marginal types of religious activity which define themselves by contrast to the *polis*. A classic instance is the essay (pp. 215–28 below) in which he examines the different modes of deviance exemplified by Pythagoreans, Orphics, Cynics and followers of Dionysus, and in which, as usual, he pays close attention to the rôle of empirical categories — here those relating to the preparation and consumption of food — in the self-definition of these groups.

Vidal-Naquet is a historian of formidable range. His contributions in this collection cover the world of 'Homeric' society, rites of status-transition between adolescence and adulthood, ideological reflections of the rôles of women and slaves in Greece, and a discussion of a 'philosophical' myth in Plato. Elsewhere he has written on Greek tragedy, the Jewish historian Josephus, and a wide variety of problems in Greek social history, as well as on several contemporary historical issues.[6] He writes in a more condensed way than Detienne, is more diverse, and is certainly less easy to classify. If one were to isolate one thread which runs through his essays reprinted below it would be an interest in the relationship between social practices and institutions, on the one hand, and their ideological counterparts in myth and literature, on the other; perhaps the clearest example is the paper on the 'Black Hunter' (pp. 147–62 below), in which a myth and an institution are brilliantly confronted.

Like Vidal-Naquet, Vernant has tended to prefer the article to the book as his vehicle. His aim in the splendid *Les Origines de la pensée grecque* and *Mythe et pensée chez les Grecs*[7] — to recover the way in which the Greeks' mental universe was articulated, above all in relation to matters of religion — has been continued in his later writings. The two papers on Hesiod (pp. 43–56 and 57–79 below) are typical of his approach. Hesiod's tales about Prometheus and Pandora turn on the crucial distinction between men and gods: men must work and put up with misfortune; the gods are free of such trouble. Vernant explores the implications of the distinction by examining Hesiod's accounts in detail. Central to the analysis is sacrifice, the ritual which re-enacts, by the separation of the parts of the victim which it entails, the separation of men and gods. Hesiod, as Vernant presents him, is much concerned with boundaries; and that makes him a prime witness for the structuralists.

Having glanced at the three scholars individually we must return to 'structures'. Vernant's approach to Greek myth offers a convenient place to begin.

One common way of studying the Greek pantheon has been to select a divinity and trace his or her ancestry back to its 'origins' in natural phenomena, ritual, geographical or historical fact, the unconscious, or somewhere else.[8] This enterprise, like etymology, is a perfectly respectable branch of human enquiry. But, just as etymology needs to be complemented by research into the interrelationships of words within a language at a given time, so, argues Vernant, no single member of the pantheon can be properly understood in isolation from the rest: we must broaden our outlook and take in the pattern of interrelationships between the deities. Only then shall we be in a position to see how the conceptual universe of the Greeks was divided up, and how differentiations with respect to time, space, sovereignty, etc., were implicit in the way in which they conceived of their gods.

An illustration may help. The ancient traveller Pausanias (5.11.8) tells us that on the base of Pheidias's statue of Zeus at Olympia the goddess Hestia is linked with the god Hermes. In a long and brilliant analysis[9] Vernant suggests that the pair embody contrary but complementary aspects of the Greeks' experience of space: Hestia is the hearth, the fixed point, the centre around which human life within the *oikos* (household) is organized; Hermes operates in a context of change, transition, movement, the linking of opposed states. And the polarity has a parallel in Greek social life: As Hestia is to Hermes, so woman (who stays at home) is to man (who leaves home and has dealings with others). Neither Hermes nor Hestia makes sense if viewed in isolation; only when each is contrasted with other elements in the 'system' do the distinctive traits of the two emerge clearly. Moreover — and here is another characteristically structuralist gambit — the analysis points the way towards an identification of homologous patterns within different areas of experience in the given culture: as Hermes is to Hestia, so man is to woman. A third aspect of Vernant's study is its demonstration that something which is for us an abstract category — space — was perceived by Greeks as a function of the specific forms of divine activity represented by Hermes and Hestia. What is true of space is also true, for example, of work[10] and cunning intelligence:[11] the Greeks' way of classifying sorts of physical and mental behaviour by no means always corresponds with our own.

Of the articles reprinted below it is Detienne's piece on the 'sea-crow' (pp. 16—42) which matches most closely the account I have just given. He discusses the different forms of power exercised in relation to the sea by Athena (the sea-crow is a marine bird which figures occasionally as an epithet of Athena) and Poseidon. When Athena has to do with the sea it is, Detienne argues, in relation to navigation and the finding of a path across the treacherous deep. Her interventions show her to be the divine equivalent of the ideal human helmsman: quick-witted, deft, able to out-manoeuvre the tricky problems posed by the shifting sea. Poseidon, by contrast,

does not help the helmsman by opening up a route for him through the raging sea. His form of action is rather in keeping with his status as the elemental power of the sea: he calms its violence and restrains the anger of the waves which he himself has unleashed . . . In other words, the rôle of Poseidon in navigation is as passive as that of Athena is active (p. 29)

The argument widens to embrace other areas of activity in which Athena and Poseidon might appear to overlap; but the result is the same: Athena displays *mētis* (cunning intelligence), Poseidon does not. Once more we have an emphasis on boundaries, and a demonstration that the figures in Greek myth should be seen not as isolated individuals but as standing in a network of contrastive relationships with other comparable figures.[12]

Vernant, Vidal-Naquet and Detienne share an awareness of the essential seriousness of the myths, a sense that they are not 'just stories', but tales with a logic of their own and with a profound relevance to issues generated by Greek culture. The view that there can be a 'logic' or 'reason' of Greek myth[13] does not of course recommend itself to proponents of the idea that Greece witnessed the emergence of Reason from the fogs of (irrational) Myth; but it is none the worse for that. This last-mentioned idea contains, in fact, about equal measures of truth and falsity. It is plain that in certain contexts – philosophy, medicine, historiography come to mind – issues came to be debated in classical Greece in ways which constitute a radical break with traditional 'mythical' modes of thought. Yet it is equally plain that men such as Plato, Hippocrates and Thucydides were marginal in the influence which they had on the beliefs of ordinary Greeks. For hundreds of years after these and similarly gifted intellectuals had been applying principles of reasoned argument to their chosen field of enquiry, most Greeks will have carried on articulating their view of the world in terms far more traditional; and not surprisingly, since the myths were embedded in and supported by the ever-present ritual observances of the religious calendar. Moreover, even when individual thinkers did introduce 'rational' argumentation and the deployment of empirical evidence, these commonly existed side by side with inherited assumptions owing more to myth than 'reason'. In the case of philosophy and the sciences this has been brilliantly demonstrated by Lloyd in two major works.[14] For historiography we may cite Herodotus: on the one hand, he is a meticulous assembler of detailed empirical data, as in the account of embalming among the Egyptians (2.86ff.); yet, on the other, he will express views based on breath-taking *a priori* assumptions, asserting for example that the customs of the Egyptians are the reverse of those of the rest of mankind (2.35). In Greek thought there is a ceaseless *va-et-vient* between the 'mythical' and the 'rational', and he who would generalize in the matter needs to beware of the different situations obtaining in different contexts.

The paper by Gernet is devoted precisely to the complexities of the 'transition' from a mythical to a more positivistic mode of thought. Louis Gernet[15] was a specialist in ancient Greek law, but his interests in anthropology and sociology led him to explore other, wider aspects of Greek society. The result was a series of extraordinarily penetrating articles later collected under the title *Anthropologie de la Grèce antique*; the paper translated as ' "Value" in Greek myth' (pp. 111–46) formed part of this collection. To our own 'positivist' way of thinking, argues

Gernet, 'value' is an abstract notion which we perceive in terms of quantity. But for a society such as archaic, premonetary Greece 'value' is a product of a complex of symbolic associations 'combining categories which are for us distinct' (p. 111; compare Vernant on the mythical perception of space). The bulk of the paper consists of an attempt to identify this archaic sense of value by examining a group of stories about *agalmata*, objects of (usually) aristocratic wealth — tripods, gold cups, magical-royal rings, etc. — whose worth resides in their special talismanic numinousness as opposed to their 'external' value. The enquiry is a circuitous one (cf. Gernet himself at p. 140) but it has many telling points to make about the distinctiveness of mythical thought. He ends by explicitly confronting the mythical/rational opposition in the light of his particular theme:

Because [the 'external signs of wealth'] were no longer the exclusive property of a class within which the heritage of mythical kingship and its effective symbols had continued to flourish, economic value tended to eclipse the older complex image . . . The invention of money certainly makes possible the deployment of an abstract conception of value. (p. 145)

But Gernet is too subtle to miss the true complexity of the picture, recognizing that the 'symbolic' and 'external' conceptions of value coexist and interact long after the introduction of money (cf. p. 146).

Although Gernet predates the explosion of widespread interest in structuralism, his reference (p. 116) to Saussure (the linguist who must be seen in retrospect as one of the founding-fathers of the movement), and especially the unambiguous adoption of the myth-as-language analogy (*ibid.*), mark him out firmly as a forerunner of the approach later developed by Vernant. In fact, the analogy with language is basic to structuralism, and lies behind much of what is done in this book. It can be seen most clearly at work in 'Between Beasts and Gods' (pp. 215—28). Detienne looks at some mythical accounts of cannibalism, and then develops his analysis by locating the practice within a system of comparable terms designating other ways in which humans relate to food (see esp. p. 217); only when a grid or map of the contrasting possibilities has been reconstructed does it become feasible to consider the significance of any one of them. The area of linguistics which supplied the impetus for this approach is phonology: a phoneme only signifies in virtue of the contrasts between it and other phonemes. As critics of the myth-as-language analogy have observed, this does not apply rigorously to myth: one can hardly regard the isolated utterance 'Scythians eat human flesh' (cf. p. 220) as *entirely* devoid of meaning, however much more nuanced its import becomes by its being put back into its structural context. But surely we should be reasonable here. (1) To say that myth is like a language in certain respects is not to say that it is a language in every respect. (2) To speak of Greek myths as constituting a 'system' may err on the side of formality, but it is a vitally important counter to those who regard the stories as a random hotch-potch of the inherited conglomerate.

It may be useful to say something about how the selected articles have been grouped together. Section I consists of two pieces on the Greeks' perception of their gods. Vernant discusses how the sovereign power of Zeus was thought to operate; Detienne looks, as we mentioned earlier, at the relative provinces of Athena and Poseidon. In both studies the central theme is the extent to which divinities display or lack *mētis*. The concept is one for which we have no satisfactory equivalent, so the two papers cover a similar area to Vernant's analysis of Hermes/Hestia, viz. a demonstration of the way in which Greeks divided up their experience differently from ourselves.

From boundaries between divinities we turn in Section II to boundaries which externally delimit and internally structure the condition of humanity. In 'The myth of Prometheus in Hesiod' Vernant, after examining the 'narrative logic' of the two accounts, summarizes what is implied in them regarding the position of mortals: ' . . . the story locates humankind between beasts and gods, its status characterized by sacrifice, the use of fire for cooking and for manufacture, woman seen as wife but also as animal belly, corn as staple food and labour in the fields' (p. 50). Sacrifice, agriculture, marriage: these are the markers of human life, distinguishing men from gods and from beasts. (Compare the last paragraph of 'Sacrificial and alimentary codes in Hesiod', p. 79.) Sacrifice and agriculture also appear as central themes in Vidal-Naquet's fine essay on the *Odyssey*. This might just as well have been placed in Section IV, since it is much preoccupied with questions of deviation from social normality. Vidal-Naquet shows how accepted Greek conventions relating to land-cultivation and sacrifice are contrasted with a rich variety of alternative modes of behaviour found in lands with which the wandering Odysseus comes into contact. The last paper in the section, and perhaps the most methodologically radical (and contentious) one in the book, brings us to the third Hesiodic constituent of the human condition: marriage. In seeking to make sense of the Aristaeus episode in Virgil's fourth *Georgic*, and in particular that aspect of it which concerns Aristaeus's loss of his bees, Detienne goes right outside, or behind, Virgil's text. He starts from two facts: (1) Aristaeus is guilty of a sexual transgression — pursuit of Orpheus's wife; (2) Aristaeus loses his bees. The link is reconstructed by Detienne on the basis of associations which bees have elsewhere in ancient thought with sexual purity. The analysis broadens to incorporate more and more myths about bees and honey, especially those which in some way touch on the relations which should properly obtain between men and women in marriage. Some scholars will remain unconvinced that the key to *Georgic* 4 has been discovered here, feeling perhaps that what Virgil himself chose to convey disappears from time to time under the weight of mythological context. But there can be no denying that Detienne once again provides many insights into the way in which myths make statements about social reality through the deployment of an empirical logic.

The third section brings together three essays which show how myths reflect features of social organization. Gernet, as we have seen, uses a group of myths to illustrate the conception of value held by Greeks at a particular stage in the development of their society. Vidal-Naquet's two studies relate to the period of social adolescence, known in the case of Athenian males as *ephebeia*, through which young people passed before reaching adulthood: 'The Black Hunter' attempts, by reconstructing a little-known myth, to recreate the ideology of the *ephebeia*; while 'Recipes for Greek adolescence' — a slight departure from the French title, which translates literally as 'The Raw, the Greek child, and the Cooked' — involves initiation rituals outside Athens as well as in it, girls as well as boys. To any who remain sceptical about interpretations in terms of empirical logic I recommend Vidal-Naquet's account of the astonishing find in a necropolis at Eretria (p. 173) where the Raw and the Cooked differentiate childhood from adulthood in a manner clear enough to quicken the pulse of even the most algebraic of structuralists.

Sometimes Greek myths reflect social reality, but sometimes they distort or invert it. In the final three papers we meet a number of mythical narratives which tell of inversions of the norm. In 'Slavery and the rule of women' Vidal-Naquet assembles several 'world-upside-down' traditions in which it is imagined that power is in the hands of women and/or slaves; from the way in which slavery is projected ideologically, important conclusions are drawn about the differences between the Athenian and Spartan models of slavery. 'Athens and Atlantis' is about a rather special sort of myth, namely the one invented by Plato in his dialogue *Timaeus*. Vidal-Naquet's densely-argued analysis of the twin mythical cities, proto-Athens and Atlantis, demonstrates that they represent alternative imaginative models which contrast with each other and with the real Athens; *en passant* he disposes of a number of naively realist historical-geographical interpretations of the Atlantis story, a procedure which might well be extended to discourage comparably literalist readings of the more orthodox myths.

In the concluding paper Detienne offers us more alternative models. Taking as the norm the type of mediating sacrifice (*between* beasts and gods) usually practised within the *polis*, he shows the complementary and contrasting ways in which four sects circumvent this normality. The analysis is neat and formally satisfying — whether too neat is something for the sceptical empiricist to decide for himself — and the style is refreshingly direct.

It should be clear from what I have said that no one uniform approach will be found exhibited in what follows; rather, a variety of strategies, a number of which are common to many or most of the pieces. Needless to say, there is nothing sacrosanct about the order — the articles may be taken by date of composition, or grouped according to author. In the latter case what emerges is the individuality of the four scholars represented. If structuralism is 'some glistening Method', the quality of the reflected light is entrancing in its variety.

Notes

1 Vidal-Naquet and Detienne are still there; Vernant is now at the Collège de France.
2 Vernant and Vidal-Naquet, 1972.
3 Detienne and Vernant, 1978.
4 Detienne and Vernant, 1979.
5 Detienne, 1977.
6 One may cite *Torture: Cancer of Democracy*, Harmondsworth, 1963; *Journal de la commune étudiante* (with Alain Schnapp), Paris, 1969; 'La mémoire d'Auschwitz', in *Esprit* for September 1980, 8—52.
7 Vernant, 1962; 1971.
8 At this point I am adapting some remarks from my note in the *Bulletin of the Council of University Classical Departments*, 1977, 12—13.
9 Vernant, 1971: I, 124—70.
10 Vernant, 1971: II, 5—64.
11 Detienne and Vernant, 1978.
12 For another aspect of the Athena/Poseidon distinction see Vidal-Naquet at p. 206 below.
13 Cf. a chapter in Vernant, 1974, entitled 'Reasons of myth'.
14 Lloyd, 1966; 1979.
15 For an appraisal of his work see Humphreys, 1978: 76—106.

I: Myth and divinity

1. The union with Metis and the sovereignty of heaven

Jean-Pierre Vernant (1974)

Having consummated his marriage with Metis ('Resource'), Zeus takes the Titan Themis ('Order') to his second wife.[1] These two marriages complement one another, each helping to guarantee the supremacy of the new king of the gods, just as the two goddesses compose a pair both compound and contrastive. Each of them has oracular powers, her knowledge comprehending the whole sweep of time. Each, by virtue of her relation with earth and water, the primal elements, enjoys powers that antedate the reign, the very birth, of Zeus. Themis, born of Gaia ('Earth'), is patron of oracles on land; Metis, daughter of Oceanus and Tethys, represents — like various Old Men of the Sea — divination by water (Vernant, 1963: xvii–xviii; Detienne, 1967: 29–50). But the omniscience of Zeus's first two wives takes different forms; which accounts for his marrying Themis only after he has digested the special powers of Metis, and made himself *mētieta* ('metisized') — by swallowing her.

The omniscience of Themis relates to an order which is conceived as already inaugurated, once and for all settled and fixed. Her utterance has assertive or categorical force: she states the future as though it already were. Because she pronounces what shall be in the present indicative, she frames not advice but directives: she says 'Do this', 'Do not do that'. Metis on the other hand has to do with the future understood as a risk. Her utterance has a hypothetical, problematic cast: she advises what should be done so that things may turn out in one way rather than in some other way. She tells the future not as something already determinate but as a possibility — either good or ill; and at the same time she offers the use of her stock of wiles to make it turn out for the better rather than for the worse.

Themis represents, in the world of the gods, stability, continuity, regularity, the permanence of order, the cycle of recurring seasons (she is the mother of the *Hōrai*: Hesiod, *Theogony* 901–2), the fiat of fate (she is also the mother of the *Moirai* 'who distribute to mortal men good fortune and ill': *Theogony* 904–6). She it is who marks pro-

1

hibitions, boundaries which may not be crossed, the gradations which must be respected if everyone is to be kept always within his proper rank and sphere. By contrast, Metis makes her presence felt when the divine world is still fluid, or when its balance of forces is momentarily out of kilter — in disputes over succession, struggles for sovereignty, wars and rebellions, the rise of a new power. At these moments, things get dramatic and disconcerting in heaven; if they are to triumph, the powers that be in the world beyond must display not merely courage and strength, but intelligent planning, cunning and resource.[2]

In marrying Metis, Zeus — who has just overthrown Cronus and upset the old order — is not simply recognizing the services she rendered him; he is also providing himself with the wherewithal to establish an entirely new order. In marrying Themis, he renders permanent and sacrosanct the rules he has just decreed and his redistribution of honours and privileges. His double marriage both sets the seal upon the fall of Cronus and his own accession, and precludes the possibility of subsequent change.

Wily Metis is a threat to any established order. Her intelligence works in the realm of feint and disconcertion the better to turn the tables, to upset the seemingly most settled system. This comes out in the realm of myth in the motif that her children are dangerous: they inherit from their mother her devious cunning. Thus armed, her son is bound to challenge his father's supremacy, overthrow his sovereign, establish a new dispensation. By marrying, mastering and swallowing Metis, Zeus reveals that he is not a king like other kings; he becomes more than a mere king, he becomes sovereignty itself. All the *mētis* in the world, all the reserves of disconcertion hidden in cunning time, are now inside Zeus. And so sovereignty ceases to be the prize in a perpetual struggle; it becomes a stable, enduring state. The king of the gods may now celebrate his marriage with Themis, give her fine children, the Seasons and the Fates. He has fixed irrevocably both the pattern of things to be and the hierarchy of functions, ranks and honours. He has set them hard. Whatever now comes to pass, it will now always have been entirely foreseen and ordained in the beginning by the mind of Zeus.

Hesiod does not describe in detail the manner in which Zeus overcame Metis and swallowed her to make himself the 'Cunning One', ὁ μητίετα, ὁ μητιόεις.[3] He merely says that when Metis was about to give birth to Athena, Zeus 'deceived her mind by a trick, by dint of cunning words, and put her in his belly' (*Theogony* 889–90). It cannot have been easy: a scholiast on the passage tells us that Metis could transform herself into any shape she liked; Zeus swallowed her 'after confusing her and making her small', πλανήσας οὖν αὐτὴν ὁ Ζεὺς καὶ μικρὰν ποιήσας κατέπιεν (Scholiast on Hesiod, *Theogony* 886, p. 110

di Gregorio).[4] There is here an obvious folklore motif: a witch or magician has the power to change shape, thus becoming invincible. On the pretext of testing their power, the hero gets them to run through the repertoire until they turn into some creature small and weak enough to be safely overcome.

The story of Periclymenus and his fight with Herakles seems to draw on the same pattern. The story is known first from Hesiod's *Catalogue of Women*, in a passage quoted by the scholiast on the *Argonautika* of Apollonius of Rhodes [completed by a papyrus] and also known from the Iliadic scholia (frg. 33 a,b Merkelbach—West).[5] This account, which seems to have fixed the legendary tradition, presents Periclymenus as the most formidable of the sons of Neleus. His grandfather Poseidon has granted him the power to change into any shape during a fight. Periclymenus boasts that he will by such magic be able to worst great Herakles, the son of Zeus. As it turns out, Herakles kills him at the time of his sack of Pylos; but he has need of all of Athena's cunning when she offers him her sharp-eyed help to defeat this slippery customer. Periclymenus turns into an eagle, a lion and a gigantic snake, one after the other; on Athena's advice, Herakles waits till he turns into a fly, and then swats him with his club. There is a slightly different version which Hesiod develops (cf. Schwartz, 1960: 346—7), in which Herakles takes advantage of a moment when Periclymenus has turned into a bee and is resting right in the centre of his chariot-yoke: again following Athena's bidding, Herakles kills him with an arrow. In each case it is the goddess's *mētis* which creates the critical moment and brings the incident to a successful conclusion. It is her resourcefulness which causes his own power to recoil against the magical warrior, the power of metamorphosis that he has inherited from his forebear, the god of the sea. She does not merely tell Herakles the right moment to strike; she does not simply point his opponent out in whatever shape; she sets up the chance which Herakles siezes, for it is she who treacherously suggests to Periclymenus that he become a fly or a bee so that he can startle his opponent's horses.

So we can say that Athena in Hesiod's version turns on Periclymenus and his auto-metamorphic power the very same trick employed by Zeus against Metis in the *Theogony* to prevent her from giving birth to a daughter endowed no less than himself with her mother's terrible cunning.

A theogony mentioned by Chrysippus the Stoic philosopher (*SVF* 2, 256 [frg. 908] = Galen, *De Hippocratis et Platonis placitis* 3,8 [5, p. 351 Kühn]) differs somewhat from Hesiod's account in the *Theogony*.[6] For it places the marriage of Zeus and Metis not at the beginning of the god's matrimonial career but during a quarrel between him and his lawful wife Hera.[7] Yet the variant does confirm Hesiod in a crucial point: it mentions that Metis was swallowed by a deception. Zeus escapes to a safe remove from Hera in order to make love to Metis; and then 'deceiving her despite all her knowledge (or, by an alternative reading, 'for all her turning'[8]), laid hands on her and set her deep in his belly for fear that she might give birth to a child mightier than the thunderbolt; so the son of Cronus who sits enthroned on the peak of the aether in an instant swallowed her up. She was then carrying Athena to whom Zeus gave birth from his head on the steep banks of the river Triton. And Metis remained hidden within his belly.'

The scholiast to Hesiod links this theme of the transformations of Metis to her swallowing by Zeus.[9] But Apollodorus introduces it right at the start of their affair: according to him, Zeus 'had intercourse with Metis, who took on all sorts of shapes to escape him, and when she became pregnant he took her by surprise and swallowed her' (*Bibliotheca* 1.3.6). Marriage and absorption appear here as two aspects of a single encounter with Metis which Zeus must win: courtship, sex and total assimilation. Fly and fluid, Metis raids her magic-trick box to try and elude Zeus's embrace, making use of the self-same 'skilled trickery' (δολίη τέχνη) that Thetis employs against Peleus, Proteus against Menelaus, and Nereus against Herakles.[10]

The mythical setting in each of these incidents is essentially the same. Different they may be, but all these sea-gods share with Metis not only a metamorphic capacity but devious cunning and knowledge of the future. Those who confront them have always to surprise — by dodge, stratagem, ambush or disguise — someone of extraordinary cunning and wariness and vigilance; and hold him fast in an unbreakable grip come what may. His magic neutralized by this binding, when he has rung every metamorphic change, the monster must surrender to his captor: the trickster tricked, the cunning conned, the knotter knotted. The god who could pass through every shape finds his way barred and blocked; for his captor, this obscure and riddling being now becomes forthright and clear. The price these polymorphous divinities have to pay, fluid, ambiguous and contradictory as they are, is the compulsion to make known whatever route, solution or expedient their adversary is searching for.

It is nevertheless only Zeus who pushes the struggle against this creature of the waters embodying all the powers and privilege of cunning intelligence to the ultimate point: he does not merely grip Metis in his arms, as does Peleus to force Thetis to sleep with him, or Herakles Nereus and Menelaus Proteus to force them plainly to reveal a secret essential to an enterprise; he binds her in his belly so as to make her a prisoner for ever: he shuts her up inside him so that she may be part and parcel of him, and so provide him at all times with that fore-knowledge of future risks which will give Zeus control of the shifting and uncertain course of things.

The struggle with the metamorphic god dramatizes his captor's accession to the privilege of *mētis*, his acquisition of that nimble-wittedness which enables one to get out of hopeless predicaments. The struggle's reversed fortunes serve to highlight the transition from the fluid/mobile to the stable/static; from opacity to clarity; from the contrary to the direct; from uncertainty to good hope: in short and in plain Greek, from the hero's initial *aporia* ('helplessness') to a *poros*, an ingenious dodge that he learns in the end and which will enable him to carry out his ultimate purpose. The god is taken by surprise. To get free, he assumes the most disconcerting, disparate and frightening shapes, becoming by turns running water, burning fire, wind, tree, bird, tiger, snake. But the series cannot continue indefinitely: there is a repertoire of shapes; when one has run through it, one must come back to the beginning. If his adversary has been clever enough not to let go, the metamorphic god has to give up and go back to his usual, his original shape and stick with it. This is Chiron's advice to Peleus: Thetis may turn herself into fire, water or into some wild animal, but he is not to let go until he sees her return to her 'old shape', her ἀρχαία μορφή (Apollodorus, *Bibliotheca* 3.13.5). So also with Idothea's advice to Menelaus about her father Proteus's tricks:

> ... that will be
> the time for all of you to use your strength and your vigor,
> and hold him there while he strives and struggles hard to escape you.
> And he will try you by taking the form of all creatures that come forth
> and move on the earth, he will be water and magical fire.
> You must hold stiffly on to him and squeeze him the harder.
> But when at last he himself, speaking in words, questions you,
> being now in the same form he was in when you saw him sleeping,
> then, hero, you must give over your force and let the old man
> go free, and ask him which one of the gods is angry with you ...
>
> (*Odyssey* 4.415–23, tr. Lattimore)

And Proteus, surprised by the double ruse of ambush and disguise,[11] does indeed attempt to escape by running through all his dirty tricks, his ὀλοφώϊα (410, 460), by using all his *doliē technē* (455). He changes into a lion first, then into a dragon, a panther, a giant hog. He turns into running water and a mighty tree. All in vain. The grip never slackens. His range of magic exhausted (460), he comes back to his true form and turns into an Old Man of the Sea, truthful and explicit; the trial of strength and cunning turns into an open discussion in which both sides speak quite frankly, without evasion or deceit (*atrekeōs*, 486; cf. Hesiod, *Theogony* 233).

5

So one gets control over the deception embodied in the metamorphic god and his fluent variegation by suddenly laying hold of all his different forms, gripping him undaunted like a vice. The texts are quite explicit. Menelaus wonders to Idothea how a mere mortal like himself is to impose his will upon a god like Proteus; the sea-nymph tells him that the secret is to pounce on her father before he gets suspicious and hold him tight. So at the opportune moment, Menelaus and his friends rush the Old Man of the Sea, and Menelaus throws his arms around him and holds on (ἀμφὶ δὲ χεῖρας βάλλομεν: 419, 455). Chiron tells Peleus to get Thetis in a bear-hug (συλλαβεῖν) and hold tight (κατασχεῖν) (Apollodorus, *Bibliotheca* 3.13.5). Herakles gets Nereus into a bear-hug (συλλαβών) and grips him (ἔδησε) and will not release him (οὐκ ἔλυσε) until he is told the information he wants (Apollodorus, *Bibl.* 2.5.11). And representations of such scenes in art are even more explicit: the hero, whether Herakles versus Nereus or Triton, or Peleus raping Thetis, is always shown holding his opponent in a bear-hug, left hand locked in right.

But when the struggle is over, the arms open and the god capable by *mētis* of changing shape is released. By contrast, Metis 'hidden in the belly of Zeus' remains for ever locked in his belly-grip, the prize of treachery.

Zeus overcomes Metis by turning against her her own weapons, cunning, surprise, deceit. In the same way Menelaus, in order to overcome Proteus, must counter his 'tricks' with the *doloi*, ambush and disguise, which the god's own daughter has devised for his ensnarement. And even that does not suffice: it is only in his sleep, when his usual wariness fails and his vigilance nods, that the polymorphous god can be surprised and overcome; his *mētis* must momentarily have quit. Herakles jumps Nereus while he sleeps.[12] Idothea outlines to Menelaus her clever plan for delivering her father quite helpless: Menelaus must watch for the moment when Proteus falls into heavy sleep; the god has hardly got himself stretched on the sand for a snooze than he is all but strangled (*Odyssey* 4.414, 453).

Hupnos, Sleep, is a formidable and powerful god: he casts his magic net over all that breathes, over the fastest thought, the quickest mind. At whim, he fetters anything that moves with invisible chains like those his twin brother *Thanatos*, Death, locks round mortals and never unfastens.

The vitality and exceptional mobility of the gods do not permit them to elude this paralysing power of *Hupnos*: they too get trapped in his snares and stay there as long as he wishes, diminished, reduced, their erstwhile vigour dimmed, their silvery quickness dulled. In these moments of rest, during which their inherent *mētis* is clouded, they can be taken unawares. In Homer, *Hupnos* can modestly say that he can easily send to sleep any of the immortal gods, even the tireless circulation of Oceanus, the father who engendered all creatures (*Iliad* 14.243–6); against only one divinity is his power of binding useless, because his *mētis* never rests or fails: 'But Zeus the son of Cronus not even I can approach or put to sleep, unless he himself command me' (247–8). By virtue of his intestine *mētis* that sovereign god is perpetually wakeful; unfingered by sleep, his ever-open eye keeps him always on guard. No attack, no wile, no *mētis* can ever again surprise him. While Cronus, for all his cunning, for all his mastery of snares born of crooked *mētis*, fell into bondage; deposed from heaven's throne, he ekes out a life merely the shadow of a god's, the ghost of real sovereignty. And in that distant exile, now he sleeps for evermore.

The counterpart in the world of the gods of the human instruments of *mētis* – hunting-nets, fishing-nets, snares, ropes, pits, anything plaited, woven, cooked, engineered or fixed (Detienne and Vernant, 1978: 45–7) – is this invisible, irrefrangible, magical bond. Such a binding has several implications. First, the god loses one of his main privileges, the power instantly to change place, the gift of ubiquity which enables him to appear, faster than lightning or the swiftest thought, wherever in the universe he chooses to make manifest his power. The binding of a god dooms him to the very margin of the cosmos, or even to the impenetrable Beyond; the pit of Tartarus whose mouth is forever sealed; or a cave on an island lost to the world. Even when he is bound within the organized universe, his immobility – his range of action reduced to zero – so diminishes his power and his being that he is weakened, helpless, wasted in that demi-death sleep is for gods.[13]

An Orphic tradition can thus imagine Cronus snoring supine after munching the 'food of deception' which Zeus persuaded him to try after baiting it with honey (*OF* p. 190, frgs. 148–9); or his head nodding on his vast neck, snared by *Hupnos* who tames all creatures (Porphyry, *De antro nympharum* 16, p. 18 Arethusa).[14] Two passages in Plutarch also describe this state: in one, Cronus has been banished to an island where he sleeps guarded by Briareus (*De defectu oraculum* 18, 420a); and in the other, he lies fast asleep inside a deep cave (*De facie in orbe lunae* 26, 941f). But in both, sleep is 'the prison Zeus devised for him'.[15]

Between the somnolence of Cronus unthroned and almighty Zeus's unflagging wakefulness are many gradations. These degrees of divine stir and wakefulness are exploited by the myths of sovereignty to suggest the dangers which might at certain moments even threaten Zeus's own sovereignty: the struggle which Zeus has still to undertake against Typhoeus/Typhon after defeating the Titans is an especially apt example.

In Hesiod's *Theogony*, Typhoeus is a dire monster (*pelōr*, 856), the ultimate offspring of Gaia's coupling with Tartarus. Near-Eastern models there may indeed be for this Greek character (Vian, 1960: 17—37; Walcot, 1966: 9—16); but in Hesiod Typhoeus displays original features which warrant full description. Through Gaia his mother, he is a chthonic power set over against the gods in heaven. Through his father Tartarus, whom Hesiod calls ἠερόεις, 'dark and misty', he is related to Erebus and Night, the immediate issue of Chaos: he is an aboriginal power by double inheritance. Late-born, younger than Zeus, he carries on the line of the 'firstlings', the primal beings set by Hesiod at the roots of the world, into a universe now differentiated and reduced to order. By his ancestry Typhoeus is endowed with extraordinary force and fury; but the very character of his energy turns him into an agent of confusion and disorder, a minister of chaos. Hesiod mentions the strength of his arms, and a number of notable features besides: in particular, his feet are never at rest. The Hittite monster Ullikumi, with whom he has often been compared, is a threat to the King of Heaven because his monstrous bulk cannot be moved.[16] But Typhoeus is always moving: his feet are *akamatoi*, just keep on going (*Theogony* 824); whatever speed they move at, they never tire, never rest. The excessive violence of his nature also reveals itself in the heads milling monstrously on his shoulders: atop his trunk there writhe a hundred serpent heads, a hideous multitude of eyes darting their coruscating gaze at every point at once (826—7). He has, not one voice matched to his own self, but a thousand different proper noises: now he speaks with the voice of a god; now imitates animals — bull, lion, dog; now whistles like a kettle (829—35). This cacophony of voices, this kaleido-scope of noise,[17] replicates in sound his monstrous polymorphism, manifest also in Nonnus's quite traditional conception of him as fusing the whole gamut of animal species into composite form, or in the idea to be found in the scholiast on Aeschylus's *Prometheus Bound* that his hundred heads compose a gallery of all wild animals.[18]

Energy, movement, vigilance, flaming stare multiplied a hundredfold — all this makes Typhoeus truly in his essential chaos Zeus's fitting adversary. As Hesiod says,

> Surely that day a thing beyond all help
> Might have occurred: he might have come to rule
> Over the gods and mortal men, had not
> The father of gods and men been quick to see
> The danger . . .
> (*Theogony* 836—8, tr. Wenham)

Aeschylus is Hesiod's true heir in presenting Typhon's assault on Zeus as a struggle for mastery of the world, a struggle between the fire flashing from the monster's numberless eyes and the sleepless thunderbolt in the hand of Zeus, possessor of *mētis* (*Prometheus Bound* 356—8; cf. Detienne and Vernant, 1978: 78—9). The same theme, as we have seen, appears in Epimenides's version too: Sleep has closed Zeus's eyelids and Typhoeus seizes his chance to slip into the palace; he is all ready to make himself master of the throne when, just as everything seems lost, Zeus opens his eyes: the monster collapses, blasted (*FVS* 2, p. 34, frg. B8; cf. Detienne and Vernant, 1978: 79—80). It is only in Apollodorus that we find Zeus momentarily defeated, his sovereign power temporarily eclipsed.

Apollodorus's Typhon, like those of Plutarch and Nonnus of Panopolis, incorporates features which recall the Hurro-Hittite Ullikumi and the Egyptian god Seth. So it is all the more instructive that despite these influences the myth's logic and purport remain true to the Greek tradition as expressed in Hesiod. In Apollodorus, Typhon is the son of Gē and Tartarus, and he is the most powerful, most gigantic of all the creatures engendered by Mother Earth (*Bibliotheca* 1.6.3). Half-man, half-beast, he plants his feet on the earth that gave him birth; his head overtops the mountains to graze the highest heaven. When he extends his arms, one hand scrapes the sunset, the other sunrise. His bulk thus fuses high and low, East and West, confounding all the cardinal points, just as in Hesiod the most utterly different sounds meet in him, those of the wild beasts which inhabit the earth and those of the gods who dwell in heaven. And we may pursue the comparison.

In Hesiod's *Theogony*, Typhoeus's blasted body is hurled by Zeus to the bottom of Tartarus. From the monster are born the howling gales, the whirlwinds unleashed from dark Tartarus to spring surprise attacks by land or sea, blustering wildly here, there and everywhere, confounding all the rules of space in incoherent tumult. Evil would have come of Typhoeus's victory for universe and for gods, disorder restored, a world turbulent as Tartarus, the blank hollow beneath the earth, void in perpetual vertigo, no up, no down, no left, no right.[19] And the monster's children, the wild winds, stand henceforth for men on the face of the earth as symbols of that same 'incurable' evil: 'Mortal men have no remedy against this scourge' (*Theogony* 876). Hesiod contrasts these nocturnal, chaotic winds from below with the ordinary winds, Boreas, Notos, Zephyr, whose origin is heavenly, of the gods. They are the sons of *Eōs* (Dawn) and *Astraios* ('Star-strewn'), brothers of the Morning Star and of all those heavenly bodies that shimmer in the night and stud with beacons heaven's dark dome, night after night tracing their fixed and constant paths (378—82). These ordinary winds blow always in the same directions, scoring routes for ships across the sea's back; and they impart to the visible world direction and order by establishing bounds and granting coherence to its several parts.

The relation between Hesiod's Typhoeus and the whirlwinds, which reduce human space to a confusion reminiscent of primal chaos, both widens and specifies the burden of Apollodorus's description of Typhon, highlighting the monster's enduring character in Greek mythological thinking as a 'chaotic power'. And Apollodorus's text, in developing the *Theogony*, confirms the rôle of devious intelligence in the exercise of sovereignty in another respect also: the motif of *dolos*, of ruse or deception, is crucial to the whole story. Battle is first joined at a distance. Typhon shoots flames from mouth and eyes. He hurls incandescent rocks. Zeus from afar launches his thunderbolts. But Typhon advances on heaven — they struggle at close quarters. Zeus lands a blow with Cronus's sickle (*harpē*), and tackles his wounded foe hand to hand. But Typhon catches Zeus in his snake-coils, rendering him helpless, snatches away the sickle and cuts out the tendons from his arms and legs; then, slinging Zeus paralysed over his shoulder, he takes him to Cilicia, and leaves him in the Corycian cave, hiding the tendons in a bearskin. He sets a snake-woman, Delphynē, to guard them, just as Zeus once bade Briareus watch over the Titans, and Cronus *Kampē* ('Curve'), over the Hundred-Arms (cf. Detienne and Vernant, 1978: 85–6). All is apparently over. Zeus is defeated, is now in that very bondage to which he reduced Cronus. He languishes helpless deep in a cavern, robbed of the strength in arm and leg which made Typhoeus in the *Theogony* a match for the King of the gods, so long as he eluded the thunderbolt and escaped mutilation (cf. γυιωθείς: *Theogony* 858).

But Zeus is saved, and his royal power restored, thanks to the intervention of two 'tricksters',[20] cunning Hermes and his crony Aigipan, whose rôle in Apollodorus's story corresponds exactly to that of Metis in Hesiod and of Prometheus in Aeschylus. The pair manage to steal Zeus's tendons without being seen and to fit them back into his body. Re-equipped with arms and legs, Zeus regains all his native strength (τὴν ἰδίαν ἰσχύν). Suddenly he appears before the astonished Typhon, who turns and flees. Zeus, mounted in his chariot, pursues him with his thunderbolt. But even now neither would have been victorious had the Fates not devised a new trick, a second stratagem. They fool Typhon with the same ploy that Zeus used in the Orphic story to trap Cronus, the 'food of deception'. They persuade him to bite into a fruit which they promise will make him invincible. But the alleged 'invincibility drug' is in fact an *ephēmeros karpos* ('fruit of a day'), the opposite of a food of immortality: it inevitably brings upon any who eat of it exanimation and death. The monster's elemental violence is overborne by Zeus's allies, whose cunning succeeds in duping him.

This trick-motif is given an almost baroque treatment in the fifth century AD by Nonnus of Panopolis, who devotes the first two books of his epic *Dionysiaka* to the story of Typhon; but beneath the welter of fantastical detail lies the full range of the traditional language of *mētis*. Zeus is utterly preoccupied with his love-affairs, and leaves his thunderbolts lying around in a corner of heaven, where their smoke betrays them. Typhon takes the advice of Gaia, stretches his arm up to the aether's peak and steals the sovereign weapon. In his presumptuous brutishness, the polymorphous monster can be seen as an anti-Zeus, the lord of disorder; he is to true kingship what a bastard, *nothos*, is to legitimate children; he is the embodiment of the revenge of the Titans and Cronus, whom he declares he will re-establish with himself in heaven. All the Olympian gods become refugees from their heavenly homes. Zeus requests the help of Cadmus to put into action an astute plan he has worked out with Eros. Subtle and ingenious, King Cadmus disguises himself as a shepherd with the aid of Pan. Apart from this fancy-dress, the only weapon he takes when he sets out to face the young usurper, who has already succeeded in spreading confusion through the cosmos, is a mere flute, from which he draws the most beguiling notes. The violent Typhon is soothed by the music and he unsuspectingly approaches Cadmus, leaving the stolen thunderbolts in his cave. Cadmus shows every sign of terror. Typhon reassures him, suggesting that he should carry him up to heaven to live with him and sing the glories of the new régime. Whereupon Cadmus asks for an instrument more fitting than the flute to celebrate the discomfiture of Zeus. A lyre, he says; but has no strings. Oblivious to the trick, blind to the web spun for his downfall, Typhon produces the tendons lost by Zeus in an earlier battle. Cadmus carries on playing. While his enemy is off his guard, Zeus slips unseen into the cave, recovers his weapons, and disappears. Cadmus disappears too, smuggled away in a cloud by Zeus. The music stops. Typhon gathers his wits and his normal state of rage. He looks for the thunderbolts. Too late, he realizes he has been tricked. It is now dark, sleep enfolds all Nature's living things. Even Typhon lies stretched out on his mother Gaia's bosom, his snakes heads coiled for sleep deep in caves. Only Zeus watches. In the morning, the monster challenges Zeus to battle, attacks him with his pullulating arms, his gaping snouts, his snakey hair, with lumps of rock, mountains, even the waters which he flings at the sky. All in vain. For all his thousand metamorphoses, Zeus engulfs him in the glowing streak of his thunderbolt.

Stranger still, though less sophisticated as a piece of writing, is

Oppian's version (*Halieutika* 3.9–28). Although this has obvious similarities to the Hittite myth of Illuyankas, it is also related to Apollodorus's and so to the Hesiodic tradition which, in the myths of sovereignty, closely associates the motif of cunning with those of food and swallowing. Oppian's whole account is dominated by Hermes *poikilomētis* ('of variegated *mētis*'), who first devised the tactics used by skilled fishermen (βουλὰς δὲ περισσονόων ἁλιέων ... πρώτιστος ἐμήσαο) and revealed the arts of hunting and plotting the death of fish. Hermes entrusted the 'art of the deep-sea' (that is, fishing) to his son Pan, who is also reputed to have been the saviour of Zeus and the killer of Typhon: he tricked the horrid monster by tempting him with the offer of a fish-feast. Typhon was thus persuaded to leave his roomy cave safe in the depths of the sea and come ashore, where Zeus's thunderbolt in a trice set all his heads ablaze.

This Typhon destroyed by greed clearly owes a good deal to the earlier of the two versions of the Illuyankas myth known to us (Vian, 1960: 28–32; Walcot, 1966: 14–15). The dragon Illuyankas fought and defeated the Weather-god, who occupies in the Hittite pantheon a place that corresponds to that of Zeus in the Greek one. With the aid of an accomplice, a mere mortal called Hupasiyas, the goddess Inara then organizes a great celebratory banquet and invites Illuyankas. The dragon leaves his lair and comes to the feast, where he proceeds to stuff himself with so much food and drink that he cannot get back into his hole. Hupasiyas hobbles him and the Weather-god has simply to kill him. The resemblance between the two stories is beyond dispute. All the same, if Oppian has given Typhon characteristics taken from the Hittite Illuyankas, it is because they can be integrated almost unchanged into the Greek story of Zeus's adversary. Oppian's Typhon loves fish and lives on them; but he himself is not so much a dragon, like Illuyankas, as a fish. To overcome him, you have to go fishing; and that involves all the *mētis* of Hermes, all the snares of that cunning god, master of nets and traps, inventor of all those devices called even in Homer *doloi*. Zeus's supremacy among the gods is thus achieved by the same kind of cunning which is at a premium in hunting and fishing, and which enables men to get the better of animals as subtle as the fox or the octopus (cf. Detienne and Vernant, 1978: 27–54). Moreover, Oppian's Typhon is killed thanks to his greed. Like the bait which enables fishermen to catch fish — which hides death behind the pretty arras of life — the fish-feast offered Typhon is a lure, an *apatē* (deception), like Cronus's passion honey, which Zeus employs as an 'ambush' for his father to stumble into; and like the fruit offered Typhon by the Moirai in Apollodorus, which he expects to give him added vigour but which dooms him in fact to mortality.

The motif of a 'food of deception' turns up in another passage in Apollodorus, which also has to do with Zeus's struggles against his enemies, this time the Giants (*Bibliotheca* 1.6.1). So long as the battle between the Giants and the King of the gods remains in the balance, their status seems ambiguous: are they mortal and crushable, or immortal and invincible? From an oracle, the gods know that they will never win on their own; to succeed, Zeus needs the help of someone less great than himself. To kill the Giants he needs a mere mortal: Herakles, not yet a god, fits the bill. Warned of the danger to her off-spring, Gē takes counter-measures. She sets off to look for a *pharmakon* (philtre, charm, drug) which will protect the Giants from death even at the hands of a mortal. Zeus checks the appearance of dawn, sun and moon, anticipates Gē (φθάσας) and himself cuts and gathers the anti-death herb, just as he surprises (φθάσας) Metis in Apollodorus's other story and swallows her down before she can give birth to an invincible son (1.3.6).

Both the language and the structure of the story emphasize the close connection in Apollodorus between the various episodes of the conquest of sovereign power. Thus Metis tricks Cronus by getting him to swallow a *pharmakon* which instead of increasing his inner powers tenfold makes him vomit up those who are to defeat him; Zeus tricks Metis, swallows her and retains her inside him for ever; Zeus tricks Gē by plucking from under the Giants' noses the plant of immortality which would, had they been able to eat it, have made them invincible; the Moirai deceive Typhon by causing him to swallow what they allege to be an immortalizing drug, which is in fact a food which condemns him to defeat and death.

Apollodorus's text, in its description of Zeus's struggle for royal supremacy, thus lays decided emphasis on the motif of swallowing some kind of food, which is sometimes deceptive and sometimes genuine. Do we have simply here to do with a distortion of Hesiod's think-ing about the birth of the gods, or a true glimpse of one of its main structural elements?

The theme of swallowing appears in Hesiod at two decisive moments, which are clearly opposed to one another: Cronus swallows his children, but Rhea's *mētis* causes him to down a stone instead of Zeus, and he is soon compelled to vomit up all the children he has devoured; by con-trast, Zeus gulps Metis down and keeps her forever in the pit of his belly (*Theogony* 459–97, 888–900). Some other episodes in the *Theogony* allow us to interpret the significance of this double sequence in the myth. After Zeus has freed the Hundred-Arms and restored them to the light, he decides to summon their aid in a struggle which has raged indecisively for ten years, neither the Titans nor the Olympians being able to swing it in their favour (629–41). Before they enter the fray, the status of Cottus, Gyges and Briareus seems to have been comparable with that of the giants in Apollodorus — not mortal, yet without that unquenchable vitality and youth which is the particular attribute of the Immortals. It is only when the gods allow them to partake of their nectar and ambrosia — the food of immortality reserved exclusively to them — that the Hundred-Arms acquire their full strength and become the spearhead of victory: 'then a bold spirit swelled in all their breasts' (641). This nourishment feeds a divine energy in the Hundred-Arms which must have been etiolated by their earlier confinement: it is the exact counterpart of that *pharmakon* through which Typhon in Apollodorus expects to find the access of strength he needs to supplant Zeus, but which in fact reduces him to the common state of mortals.

In the *Theogony*, the effects of this immortality-food contrast with those of the waters of the Styx: Hesiod describes how, when a dispute takes place between two gods and one has to be shown to be in the wrong, Iris goes off to a subterranean arm of Ocean to fetch some of this primeval water (775–806). She brings it back in a golden ewer. The gods involved in the dispute pour on to the earth a libation of this water in support of their sworn claims, and it is natural to suppose that they also drank some (since that was usual in human contexts). The one who had falsely sworn at once fell to the ground and swooned, senseless and spiritless, for an entire 'great year'; as though wrapped in magic slumber, the sleeper is denied the divine nourishment while the stupor lasts: 'never does he draw near to partake of ambrosia or nectar' (796–7).[21]

It will now be easier to understand the signal importance in the *Theogony* of the division of shares of nourishment established between men and gods by Prometheus when he performed the first sacrifice. The story's structure is as follows (*Theogony* 535–57; *Works and Days* 42–50; cf. pp. 57–65 below). In the beginning, gods and men lived together and ate together at the same feasts. Prometheus was given the task of dividing the food appropriately to each group. He planned to use this opportunity to trick Zeus and cheat him for the profit of mankind. This was the origin of the duel of cunning and deception between the Titan with *mētis* and the sovereign god known as *ho mētioeis*; on either side, the weapons were *dolos* and *apatē* (deception). A great ox was killed in the presence of gods and men. Prometheus divided the carcass into two portions, each deceptive: one concealed under the most appetizing surface the bare bones stripped of meat, the other hid the choicest meat under the skin and the stomach, which cannot be eaten. With due deference to rank, Zeus was given first choice. The lord of Olympus, who 'had seen the trick and was not deceived' (*Theogony* 661), pretended to fall in with Prometheus's ploy; but in so doing, he turned Prometheus's snare for himself into a trap for men. The portion that was inedible, the white bones ever since burned by mortals on sacrificial altars in honour of the gods, is in fact the only genuinely wholesome portion; men reserve the meat for themselves and cook it to revive their failing strength. But what they keep is an 'ephemeral food', like the fruit treacherously offered to Typhon by the Moirai. Those who must live on it, and take pleasure in the eating, experience a hunger ever-renewed; their strength fades, they tire and die. By the same token, those who live only off the smoke from the bones, from the savour and the aromatics, enjoy the banquets of immortality and sit down at the tables where nectar and ambrosia are served.

Each category of animate creature has thus its proper food, the food it deserves: mortal men get the cooked meat of a dead animal; Typhon and the Giants have the 'ephemeral fruit' instead of the *pharmakon* of immortality; Cronus gets the 'food of deception' which confines him in the prison-house of sleep; the Olympians and Zeus's allies whom he has freed from their bonds, nectar and ambrosia. But Zeus, and he alone, gets the divine sustenance which his cunning gave him to swallow and digest, the goddess Metis — the drug that grants intelligence and cleverness beyond compare, the true *pharmakon* of unshakable sovereignty.[22]

2. The 'Sea-Crow'

Marcel Detienne (1970, 1974)

In most domains in which Athena operates we find a number of rituals, myths and pictorial representations that enable us to form an approximate idea of this divinity, whether in her guise as the terrifying warrior-goddess with the eye of bronze, as the tamer of horses who invented the bit, or the craftsman skilled in weaving. And at first glance an Athena *of the sea*, such as I suggest here, may seem both unlikely and impalpable: unlikely, in that the sea is not a place where Athena seems to have much chance of rivalling Poseidon (as she does to good effect in the case of horsemanship and charioteering); impalpable, in that there is no considerable ritual connected with a marine Athena, and no major myth about her. Nevertheless, if we look more closely, we find that a whole series of Athena's interventions occur in the context of the sea and of navigation. When Telemachus decides in the *Odyssey* to go in search of Odysseus, it is Athena who prepares the voyage and who guides the vessel. It is she who builds the Argonauts' ship, and who selects the pilot and helps him negotiate dangers. And, more generally, it is Athena who invented the first ship known to men — whether that was Danaus's or the craft of Jason and his companions. Finally, we learn in several places of an unusual Athena whose epithet is the name of a sea-bird, the *aithuia*.

Starting here, and trying to define the nature of this sea-bird, I hope to be able to give an account of this aspect of Athena's activity and to make clear the characteristic features of Athena of the sea. Early on in his *Description of Greece* (1.5.3) Pausanias refers to a promontory on the coast of Megara overlooking the sea from where Athena *aithuia* looks out over the sea. At the same spot is a tomb, the tomb of one of the kings of Athens, Pandion (Nilsson, 1951: 56–8). A brief note by the lexicographer Hesychius complements Pausanias's information: when the Metionidae had put Pandion to flight and expelled his children from Attica, Athena took the shape of an *aithuia* to carry the deposed king to Megara, hiding him beneath her wings (s.v. ἐν δ' Αἴθυια, 1 no. 2748 Latte). No other evidence from Attica or from Megara gives us any further information about this fragmentary royal myth. If we are to make any sense of this deity perched on the Megarian headland, we must therefore look at the evidence for this sea-bird whose name she bears and whose shape she takes.

Although we cannot precisely identify the species, the ancient naturalists, ornithologists and lexicographers have left us enough information of different kinds to allow us to be sure of its general type. Modern scholars continue to hesitate, as ancient writers did, between several different species of birds related to water ranging from the cormorant to the shearwater or 'sea crow', by way of the herring gull, the coot, the curlew, the puffin, grebe and diving-tern.[1] The uncertainty derives not merely from the character of the zoological evidence, which does not coincide with our own taxonomy, but even more from the likelihood that the distinguishing marks of species that are often closely related have been blurred by the imposition of a stereotype composed of an eclectic amalgam of behavioural traits characteristic of a whole series of water-birds, such as the *laros*, the *duptēs*, the *erōidios* and the *aithuia*.[2]

Now what are the *aithuia*'s essential behavioural traits? (I propose, for the sake of convenience, to call it the 'sea crow', *korōnē thalassios*, as do several lexicographers[3].) It is first of all familiar to men in two activities, fishing and sea-faring, because it works close to them. In some sources, sea crows are supposed to be men of former times who invented sea-fishing; when they became birds, they took to living close by ports and cities on the coast.[4] It is both a land and a sea bird, and therefore doubly ambiguous: it defies the opposition between land and sea just as it defies the opposition between air and water. It nests on promontories lashed by the waves; and walks slowly along the narrow strip of wet land that both separates and joins dry land and restless water. When it feeds, it dives for fish into the waves and seems to surge up from the swirling foam when it re-emerges carrying its catch.

'Semantically', the sea crow is a mediator at the centre of a triangle of elements, earth, water and air. As such, it is peculiarly well-fitted to symbolize a number of aspects of sea-faring. In that it is a sea-bird which leaves the land to launch out into the sea, and then returns to shore, it may be likened to the sea-farer. In his *Phaenomena*, Aratus compares sailors at sea to sea crows (καλυμβίσιν αἰθυίῃσιν) which settle on the waves and allow themselves to be carried by the swell (290—9 Martin; cf. Callimachus frg. 178.32—4 Pfeiffer; *Epigram.* 58.4 Pfeiffer). In Artemidorus's *Interpretation of Dreams* to dream of a sea crow means that one will become a navigator, with an intimate knowledge of everything to do with the sea; a person who has such a dream 'will never be unable to find his bearings' (5.74 [p. 319.6—15 Pack]). But if it stands for the navigator, it also may represent the ship that passes between the frontiers of earth, water and sky (Lycophron *Alexandra* 230). Its significance is to be understood in relation to these three elements: 'if the *aithuia* meets a ship and plunges straight into the water

17

in mid-flight, it foretells great danger. If, on the other hand, it flies over the ship, or goes and perches on a rock, this is a sign of a successful voyage' (*Cyranides* 3, περὶ αἰθυιας = Ruelle 2, p. 86). The point here is that the *aithuia* acts in two different ways. It plunges into the sea, and so brings *sky* and *earth* (i.e. 'here below') together (as several other texts state explicitly[5]). Or it alights on a headland, and so brings *water* and *land* together: this makes it the harbinger of an uneventful crossing from one point on land over the sea to another.

There is an episode in the *Odyssey* (5.285—464) which confirms the importance of the *aithuia* in the context of sea-faring. Just as the outline of Phaeacia becomes dimly visible on the horizon, Odysseus experiences the wrath of Poseidon — the winds blow wild, squalls gathering from all directions; night falls, mists cover the sea and the shore; water from above merges with the sea's waves. At the very height of this storm, when Odysseus has given himself up for lost, he is miraculously saved. Ino *Leucothea*, the 'white goddess', appears out of the spray, carrying the veil which enables Odysseus to reach Phaeacia. And in thus appearing before Odysseus, Ino has assumed the form of a bird — the *aithuia* (337, 353). So here in the *Odyssey* — at a point where the story depends upon a contrast between Poseidon and Ino *Leucothea* — the sea crow appears, a light in the storm, to save one in peril on the sea. The significance of this episode is highlighted by the talismanic quality of the veil which Ino *Leucothea* brings — which the Greeks later understood to be the purple fillet which the initiates into the Samothracian mysteries wore to protect them from the dangers of the sea (Scholiast on Apollonius Rhodius, *Argonautika* 1.917).

There are of course considerable differences between the ways in which Ino *Leucothea* and Athena work. Nevertheless, it is in this episode of the *Odyssey* that we are able most clearly to discern the general import of Athena *aithuia*'s relation to sea-faring. Two ancient interpretations by scholiasts help us to define it. Eustathius, in his commentary on *Odyssey* 1.22 (p. 1385, 64), says that the *aithuia* is *phôsphoros*, a 'bringer of light': like the Morning Star, it makes light appear in the midst of darkness. The scholiast on Lycophron, *Alexandra* 359 (p. 139. 28—30 Sheer), talking about Athena *aithuia* herself, says that she is called *aithuia* because 'like [that bird] she has taught men to sail in ships, crossing the sea from one end to the other'. Now it might seem that these three forms of activity, teaching men how to navigate, opening up a route across the sea, and bringing light in storm at night, have little in common with each other. Can they really be connected with one and the same Athena? And yet they are precisely the forms of activity evidenced in myth and epic for a marine Athena.[6]

In *Odyssey* 2.262—433 Athena takes over all the organization of

Telemachus's voyage: she chooses a ship and anchors it at the harbour-mouth; when they set sail she seats herself at the stern, where the helmsman sits, and summons up a favourable breeze (cf. Wachsmuth, 1967: 72—4). And she acts in rather the same manner in the epic of the Argonauts: through Tiphys, the outstanding helmsman she sends Jason, she steers the *Argo* for much of the voyage, at a discreet distance (Apollonius Rhodius, *Argonautika* 1.105—10; Valerius Flaccus, *Argonautica* 2.48—54). And at the most perilous point, when the ship has to squeeze through the Symplegades, she intervenes more directly. There are two different versions of this episode which enable us to describe what she does in greater detail. The first is that of Apollonius Rhodius (2.598—600). Just as the *Argo* is about to negotiate the 'tortuous path' (2.549) between the two massive cliffs which keep moving apart and clashing together, Athena seizes it, as it hangs between life and death, and shielding it with her left hand from the rocks propels it with her right at full speed the instant a way opens up through the wall of rock. In this version her intervention is merely an extension of the pilot's normal activity: she intervenes suddenly and to amazing effect, just like Ino *Leucothea*. But while the latter affords a salvation as absolute as it is magical, Athena simply extends the action she has already initiated through the helmsman by taking him under her protection. But at this juncture she no longer allows the steersman to mask her activity — she herself intervenes to open up for him a path which, without her, he never would have found.

In the second version, the *Argonautika* ascribed to 'Orpheus' (694—710 Dottin), Athena's intervention is apparently quite different. When the Argonauts reach the Black Rocks, Athena sends them a bird which alights on top of the mast. Suddenly the bird flies off and hovers by the rocks, waiting to find its chance. When it at last darts through, the two rocks, which have moved apart, dash together and catch its tail-feathers without preventing it from gaining the Black Sea. The Argonauts copy the bird and take the same route, and they too escape the Black Rocks, which — hopelessly outmanoeuvred — become immobile and take root in the sea. Now the bird which Athena sends to show the Argonauts the way, and which thus corresponds to the goddess's own intervention in Apollonius Rhodius, is a sea-bird, the *erōidios* (cf. *Iliad* 10.274; Thompson, 1936: 102—4). This is most probably some kind of shearwater — a bird of roughly the same type as the *aithuia* (Aratus, *Phaenomena* 913—15; Aelian, *Historia animalium* 7.7 [p. 173.23—5 Hercher]). We know from Homer that this bird was closely connected with Athena. When Diomedes and Odysseus are setting out on their night sally into the Trojan camp, an *erōidios*[7] appears, signifying that they will have Athena's help and protection in an enterprise necessitat-

19

ing a cunning and resourceful spirit.[8] But the bird does not have quite the same significance in each passage: whereas for Odysseus it is merely an omen, in the Orphic poem it operates on two complementary levels: it is first an effective warning, and then a model for navigation — when Athena's bird speeds through the rocks, only just escaping death, its flight-path indicates the *Argo*'s course. The episode is just like a passage in Apollonius Rhodius's version, where the Argonauts release a bird to test the route through the Symplegades (2.328–40). Following the advice of the seer, Euphemus holds a rock dove in the hollow of his hand and launches it forward from the ship's prow (2.555–6) — with very much the same movement as when, a little later in the same episode, Athena pushes the vessel forwards through the 'tortuous path' now opened up (2.599).

A detail in the story of the Argonauts indicates just how close are the affinities between ship and bird: just as the *erōidios* and the rock-dove lose a few tail-feathers as they fly through the rocks, so some of the stern-decoration is snapped off Jason's ship (2.601–2).[9] Whether it is sent by Athena, or foreshadows her intervention, the Argonauts' bird is in a sense the ship itself — or at least its double: just as the *aithuia* is. But this relationship between ship and bird can only be understood fully by looking at ancient navigation techniques: for the bird which finds a path for the Argonauts's ship is not merely an omen in the religious sense, it is also a means of navigation.[10] In ancient Greece, as in Mesopotamia or Scandinavia, the release of birds was a common method of navigation — in a period when there were no compasses, sailors took birds with them, and released them whenever they needed to know where land lay.[11] That technical point does much to account for the importance of certain birds in myths about the sea and sailing; and there is no doubt but that such a point is crucial in defining the nature of Athena *aithuia*. For it makes it possible to indicate more fully the parallel between *aithuia* and navigation. The bird Athena sends the Argonauts in the 'Orphic' version is much more than a mere sign from the goddess: its behaviour fits with the pattern I have indicated in Apollonius's version of Athena's intervention. In each case, its part is to pilot the ship and open a path for it through the sea.

I have shown that there exists a close connection between Athena and the art of the helmsman. But the connection can only take on its full significance if we understand Greek thinking about the sea, the frame of these interventions by Athena, daughter of Zeus and Metis. How did the Greeks view the navigator's skill in relation to their religious thinking concerning the sea?

Two sets of divinities come into question here, and we must consider their several properties and qualities. The first pair is *Pontos* and *Poros*, which belong exclusively to the world of the sea; the second is *Tyche* and *Kairos*, which have a wider sphere of reference but which are very important in the realm of navigation.

Pontos, the 'Salty Deep', is a primordial power of the open sea, the vast expanse limited only by sky and land. *Pontos* 'of the thousand paths' is a mysterious and disturbing realm, thought of as having paths that are constantly obliterated, routes never charted, tracks closed as soon as they are opened (Benveniste, 1966: 296—8). In this chaotic expanse, where every voyage is like breaking into an unknown land without any landmarks, movement pure and simple forever reigns. Whipped by the winds that blow across it, churned by the to and fro of the waves, the sea is the most mobile, changeable and polymorphous of spaces. Greek has a whole series of expressions for this fundamental aspect of the sea — which became, in an entire tradition of thinking, a symbol of coming-to-be and of generation: rolling like a cylinder (κυλινδεῖσθαι),[12] left, right, up, down (ἔνθα καὶ ἔνθα, ἄνω καὶ κάτω),[13] blowing wild, moving in opposite directions (ἄλλοτε ἀλλοῖος),[14] turning back, turning round, turning over (μεταβάλλειν, μετατρέπειν)[15] — all these metaphors are used to describe the nature of *Pontos*.

The counterpart of *Pontos* (which is termed *apeirōn*, 'limitless', presumably because it cannot be traversed from one end to the other) is *Poros*, which was known as a cosmogonic power at least since the time of Alcman (5, frg. 2 ii [*PMG* p. 24]; cf. 1.14 [*PMG* p. 2]). Originally, *Poros* meant a ford, a means of crossing a stretch of water; and thence it came to mean the route or path the navigator has to open up through the *Pontos*, over the sea. The relation between *Pontos* and *Poros* is revealed in Greek mythology in those dramatic accounts which describe Odysseus or the Argonauts steering through the Clashing or the Black Rocks, whether these be the *Planktai*, *Kuaneai*, or the *Symplegades* (Lindsay, 1965). These are all vast moving rocks which rear up out of the sea, shifting constantly both up and down and from side to side: they constitute an image of a realm in which there are no fixed directions, in which left and right, up and down, are interchangeable and ever-changing. It is not by chance that one of Athena's most important interventions is in the chaotic context of the *Symplegades*; just when the helmsman realizes to his horror that he has reached a part of the *Pontos* which *cannot* be crossed, Athena comes and opens a path for him — indicates a *poros*, that is, both a solution to and an exit from the *aporia* ('pathlessness' and so 'confusion') into which the sea plunges sailors and their helmsmen.

By contrast with these two cosmogonic powers, the complementary pair *Tyche* and *Kairos* serves to define more narrowly the realm of

21

navigation, and its specific type of human action. In Archaic Greek thought, *Tyche* ('Chance') is thoroughly ambivalent (Strohm, 1944). She is the daughter of Oceanus and Tethys — a sea-goddess in fact; and sister to Metis. Like the sea, she symbolizes change and mobility.[16] More exactly — and this is her negative side — she stands for one whole aspect of the human condition in a series of images of the individual buffeted by the waves, whirled by the winds, relentlessly eddied this way and that. But she does not merely reflect the sea's changeability, for there is a positive side to her: it is she who takes charge of the tiller and guides a ship unerringly to harbour. For several writers *Tyche* represents the chance of success, and so the aim achieved, success itself.[17] This is the *Tyche* of Pindar's *Olympian* 12, who comes aboard and takes over the helm from the pilot (Janni, 1965: 106–7); and the *Tyche* of Alcman's frg. 64 (*PMG*), who is the daughter of Prometheia and who can guarantee success thanks to her gift of foresight (*prometheia*), which gives one control over time and human affairs (cf. Ehrenberg, 1965: 145–7). Though these two facets appear quite contrary, they are as inseparable as the two faces of a double-herm.[18] Their complementarity can be appreciated by considering the link between the helmsman and the sea. Just as the human art of foresight develops against the background of a future both opaque and unpredictable, the art of the helmsman can be exercised only within the context of the uncertainty and unpredictability of the sea. The tiller's motions cannot be dissociated from the motion of the waves. *Tyche* allows the unpredictability of the future to be limited to certain possibilities. And here, the activity of this sea-goddess extends beyond navigation itself and becomes a means of organizing any form of human endeavour.

A similar extension of scope characterizes the second term of this pair, *Kairos*, 'Propitious Moment', whose ambivalence matches that of *Tyche* (Kucharsky, 1963: 95–105). Strictly speaking, *Kairos* is not a sea-divinity like *Tyche*; but it has special connections with that world. The Italian excavations at the ancient site of Elea (now Velia) have revealed epigraphic evidence from the fifth century BC for a trio of sea-divinities in which 'Olympian *Kairos*' occurs between *Pompaios* and Zeus *Ourios*.[19] Of these three, *Pompaios* is the most obscure: the word means simply 'Companion'. Easily the best-known is Zeus *Ourios*, the Zeus responsible for favourable winds (Cook, 1914–40: 3.140–55). One of his temples, said to have been founded by Jason (Polybius 4.39.6; Pomponius Mela, *De chorographia* 1.101), stood on the Asiatic coast of the Thracian Bosphorus.[20] Before trying to cross the Black Sea, the *Pontos Axeinos* ('unfriendly to strangers'), sailors would go there and offer sacrifice, in the hope that the sea would then deal kindly with them and become *Pontos Euxeinos*, the 'hospitable to strangers', thanks to a favourable wind sent by Zeus.[21] But the wind (*ouros*) sent by Zeus is not just a literal following wind; metaphorically, it may refer to the moment of departure,[22] the moment of launching out on to the sea.[23] That makes the association between Zeus *Ourios* and *Kairos* all the more significant. Aristotle (*Eudemian Ethics* 8.2: 1274a5—7; *Nicomachean Ethics* 3.5: 1112b4—7) says that in the art of navigation there can be no general knowledge applicable to every case — no certain knowledge of all the winds that furrow the sea. Even for the most experienced helmsman, *Pontos* remains always the Unknown. A navigator's excellence is not to be measured by the scope of his knowledge but by his capacity to foresee and anticipate the snares set for him by the sea — which are by the same token opportunities offered his skill. Alcaeus devoted an entire poem to the idea that the voyage is gained or lost not at sea but on dry land.[24] Zeus *Ourios* may blow favourably, but to profit from it the navigator must have foreseen its coming and expect it. *Kairos*, associated with Zeus *Ourios* (representing the opportunity itself), means the propitious moment which the good helmsman must seize — who has long foreseen the chance that will present itself for him to exercise his *technē*, his 'know-how'.[25] The marine *Kairos* of Velia, supported by Zeus *Ourios*, can thus be seen as a reflection of ambivalent *Tyche* within a single dimension, that of time. But whether they form a pair or not, *Tyche* and *Kairos* both emphasize one essential aspect of navigation, the necessary complicity between the helmsman and the element he confronts.

From *Pontos* to *Kairos*, from the ancient cosmogonic principle symbolizing the Salty Deep to the new-comer among divine forces symbolizing Time Used, all the religious imagery of the art of navigation focuses upon the type of man we have earlier seen to be related to Athena in her various manifestations. In Greek thought, the figure of the helmsman is of central importance; and he is characterized by his possession of one quality above all — *mētis*. Even in the *Iliad* it is already a cliché to observe that *mētis* alone enables the helmsman to steer a straight course despite the wind (23.316—17). In the chorus of Sophocles's *Antigone* devoted to man's triumph over Nature by means of his inventions, artifices and expedients (332—75), the poet places navigation first in the list of the enterprises of this 'resourceful' (*pantoporos*) creature.[26] Finding a *poros* — a way, a solution, a dodge — pitting one's wits against the wind, being constantly on the alert, anticipating the most favourable opportunity for action: all these are activities and manoeuvres — 'machinations' (*mēchanai*) as the Greeks called them — which demand a many-sided intelligence, the *gnōmē poluboulos* that Pindar ascribes to the helmsman (*Isthmian* 4.73—4). Faced with the sea, an expanse in which 'contrary winds from opposite quarters of the sky may contend in a single instant',[27] the helmsman can only control it if he shows an identical trickiness.

Foresight, vigilance and an ability to keep the ship on course, are among the essential qualities of the navigator's *mētis*.[28] Plato, *Epinomis* 976a—b, remarks that no sailor can 'know the secret of the wrath or favour of the wind'; so he must remain constantly on the alert, never allowing 'his eyelids to close in sleep'.[29] Elsewhere, he notes: 'The genuine navigator can only make himself fit to command a ship by studying the seasons of the year, sky, stars, and winds, and all that belongs to his craft' (*Republic* 6, 488d—489a, tr. Cornford). Like Danaus the first navigator, a helmsman both prudent and far-sighted (*pronoös*: Aeschylus, *Suppliant Women* 176—9, 970), the good pilot must weigh up all the chances. He must be like a good player of backgammon (*Suppliant Women* 13). He must foresee the sudden veering of the wind, meet cunning with cunning, espy the elusive chance to reverse the shifting balance of forces. Once launched out on to the *Pontos*, on to the shifting sea, the helmsman puts his whole mind to correcting the ship's course with deft adjustments of the tiller, and to navigating by the reference-points the stars trace out in the vault of heaven.[30] Steering, correcting, keeping on course (*ithunein*) — all these are ordinary expressions in the language of ancient seamanship; their very banality stresses that for a pilot the ability to maintain a set course is quite as important as the ability to keep in mind one's ultimate destination.[31] The shifting sea and the whims of the wind dictate a circuitous, tacking, tortuous route; but the navigator's intelligence can guide the ship true and never deviate from the course decided in advance.[32] And all of Athena's interventions here take place in the helmsman's sphere, in his active rôle as navigator, in the exercise of that cunning professional intelligence in which the daughter of Zeus can properly perceive a reflection of her own *mētis*.

Let us now leave the sea for a moment and come back to dry land, and in particular to that location in which competitive racing between the fleetest of men takes place. Here Athena's interventions are more discreet than anywhere else. She is not a divinity invariably associated with the gymnasium as are Hermes (Siska, 1933: 26—31) or Herakles (38—43). But it is in this area, of competition and agonistic rivalry, that Athena's peculiar mode of activity, which I have just defined in the area of navigation, finds an exactly comparable expression.

When Pausanias visited Sparta in the second century AD, he discovered archaeological evidence for an unusual rôle played by Athena in an athletic contest (3.12.4, 13.6). A track known as the 'Starting Line' (*Aphetaïs*) led out of the Agora. Close by was a sanctuary (*hieron*) dedicated to Athena *Keleutheia*; and Odysseus was supposed to have consecrated the statue in this temple (*agalma*) after his victory in the foot-race which decided between the suitors for Penelope's hand in marriage. Pausanias adds that Odysseus set up three separate temples to Athena *Keleutheia* at three different spots. Why three? And what services must Athena 'of the track' have rendered Penelope's successful suitor?

Now *Keleutheia* is an unusual epithet for Athena. Does it mean 'protector of the track', as the ordinary meaning of *keleuthos* ('path', 'track') would suggest? Or is she 'protector of the race' as the whole mythological context would urge?[33] Since etymology is of no help,[34] there are only two ways of interpreting this cult-title of Athena's here: either to define the specific nature of her relationship to this type of athletic contest, or to examine her special relationship to Odysseus. But the two questions are in fact inseparable: witness a passage in the *Iliad* (23.768–83) which reveals the complicity between Athena and Odysseus in an athletic competition which, as it happens, is a foot-race.[35] Its occasion is the games in honour of the dead Patroclus. When *polumētis* ('wily') Odysseus runs against Ajax son of Oileus, fleet of foot, he has to call upon Athena in order to win:

Hear me, goddess, be kind; and come with strength for my footsteps.
> (tr. Lattimore)

Athena responds at once: she gives Odysseus an extra spurt of energy and makes his rival slip:

Now as they were making their final sprint for the trophy,
There Aias slipped in his running, for Athena unbalanced him,
Where dung was scattered on the ground from the bellowing oxen slaughtered
By swift-footed Achilles, those he slew to honour Patroklos.
> (tr. Lattimore)

No one is deceived, certainly not Ajax:

Ah now! That goddess made me slip on my feet, who has always
Stood over Odysseus like a mother, and taken good care of him.
> (tr. Lattimore)

Odysseus and Athena are thick as thieves, as Athena herself reminds him when he lands on the shore of Ithaca without knowing it. She tests his *mētis* by assuming the guise of a young man and telling him the name of the place where he has just woken up (*Odyssey* 13.221–351). So as not to betray himself, Odysseus thinks up a string of lies: 'Never was his mind at a loss for cunning tricks' (13.255). Athena listens to him with a smile: 'What twister (*kerdaleos*), what thief (*epiklopos*), even if he were a god, could surpass you in cunning of every kind . . . You reach your homeland and still think only of the knavish tales and lies dear to your heart since childhood . . . Enough of these lies! *We are*

25

Marcel Detienne

two of a kind: you may have the sharpest mind and smoothest tongue among mortals, but what the gods all talk about is Athena's brains (*mētis*) and tricks (*kerdē*)' (291–9).

Exactly the same happened in the chariot race. Odysseus, like Antilochus, is less powerful than his closest rival; yet it is he and not Ajax who carried off the prize. Just so does Antilochus, primed with good advice, triumph over faster horses because he is able to foresee how the race will develop. Odysseus owed his victory to a combination of circumstances which seem in Homer's account to depend entirely upon Athena's intervention; but these circumstances are in fact an expression, in the context of epic, of the unpredictable nature of any competitive encounter – and of the profit that *mētis* inevitably derives from such unpredictability. For if fleet Ajax comes a cropper in the dung, it is because he does not anticipate an obstacle which Athena's favourite indeed does not help him avoid, and which he may even have encouraged to pop up under his feet. 'Athena made him stumble': to be sure, but the point is that if he has no *mētis* a man cannot anticipate the narrowing of the track which will give him the chance to take the lead, nor see the patch of mud ahead which may cause the man in front to slip. In setting up his statue in honour of Athena *Keleutheia* Odysseus had two things in mind: to mark the shared intelligence that made *mētis* their common badge (Stanford, 1963: 29, 39–40); and to stress the rôle of cunning in athletic contests.

It seems reasonably clear that this Athena, whose statue stood near the place known as the 'Starting Line', was not a deity of 'the good start', although we know of such an Athena from an Attic inscription,[36] who must have been the counterpart of the Athena of victory over rivals in the race whom Ajax speaks of in the *Iliad* passage I have just discussed. It is true that the place known as *Aphetaïs*[37] derives its name without any doubt from the starting-line (*aphesis*) of the classical gymnasium. But two points connected with religious cult suggest that there is no particular relation between Athena *Keleutheia* and the 'start' properly so-called. First, we know that at Sparta the starts of races were placed officially under the protection of different divinities, the Dioscuri, with the epithet *aphetērioi* (Pausanias 3.14.6): their statues probably stood at the entrance to the Spartan 'Campus Martius' – the *Dromos* – where in Pausanias's time the young men still went to train (Delorme, 1960: 74). Secondly, according to another tradition reported by the same author (3.13.6), the tutelary divinity of the start of the competition between Penelope's suitors was one *Aphetaios* – we might call him the divinity of the starting-pistol – whose statue was supposed to stand on the very spot where that race took place.[38] Although these facts show how important the start was in religious terms, they exclude any assimilation of Athena *Keleutheia* into a divinity presiding over 'good starts'.[39]

But in this act by which Odysseus showed his gratitude to Athena there is a detail which throws some light on the meaning of this cult-title of hers. We have seen that he dedicated three sanctuaries after his victory (Pausanias 3.12.4: ἱδρύσατο δὲ τῆς Κελευθείας ἱερὰ ἀριθμῷ τρία διεστηκότα ἀπ᾽ ἀλλήλων). Why *three*? Surely because on every race-track, every *dromos*, there are three points of special danger, three *kairoi* critical in both time and space, when/where all can change dramatically and the whole race be in doubt. First there is the start, the *aphesis*, when you have to make a dash to get the best position in the first few yards. Then there is the turn, the *kamptron*, where you have to take a hair-pin bend and come right round to enter the straight parallel to the outward one: the 'Horse Startler' (*taraxippos*) at the hippodrome at Olympia illustrates this perfectly (Detienne and Vernant, 1978: 191–2, 200–1). The driver has to squeeze round the turn, grazing the post; to do that he must keep a tight rein on the inside horse while giving the outside one its head, and at the same time avoid getting tangled up with another driver's chariot: manoeuvres which demand all one's skill. Thirdly, the last critical time/place is the *terma*, the finishing-line: the last few yards of a race can confound every prediction.[40]

Athena *Keleutheia* at Sparta is the patron of these three critical points/moments in a race. She is not content merely to be with Odysseus as he runs: she is regent of the very location of the race, dominating the entire contest. *Mētis* gives her, here as elsewhere, the privilege of anticipating how the race will develop and of directing it from start to finish. And there is further evidence of her rôle in agonistic sport to be found on a relief — the so-called 'Mourning Athena' (Stele 695 in the Acropolis Museum, Athens).

Athena is shown here helmeted and clad in the *peplos* (a long garment worn by women). She leans on a lance and is apparently 'meditating' with her head bowed, in front of a pillar. For many years this figure was supposed to represent Greek Reason.[41] More recently this humanist and aesthetic interpretation has collapsed in the face of the archaeological arguments advanced by Charles Picard (1939: 39–40; 1958: 95–8) and François Chamoux (1957: 143–59).[42] They are agreed that the interpretation of the relief depends upon the significance of the mysterious pillar in front of Athena; but they disagree over its identity. Picard saw it as a boundary-stone (*horos*) marking the city-boundary, while for Chamoux it is a *cippus*, one of the stones that mark the starting and finishing lines of the track in the *palaistra*. According to the first view, 'mourning' Athena is in fact Athena *Horia*,

(Apollodorus, *Bibliotheca* 1.9.27). According to a different tradition, to be found in Valerius Flaccus, *Argonautica* 1.188—98, Jason solemnly sacrifices before his departure to Poseidon, the Zephyrs and Glaucus a white bull adorned with purple headbands; he also slaughters a heifer in honour of Thetis. During the ceremony, Jason prays to Poseidon, and Poseidon alone, humbly offering him the first ship ever to cross the seas: 'Grant me your pardon, you who reign over the foaming waves, . you who surround the earth with the waters of the sea. I know that I am the first man to venture where it is forbidden to go; I know that I deserve to be made the plaything of the storms . . . ' He then ascribes the blame for his daring upon Pelias, and closes the prayer thus: 'Only receive this ship . . . upon your waves and do not cause them to swell in anger.' We have here an exact definition of Poseidon's mode of operation. As with horses, so with ships: before using them one must win Poseidon's goodwill and obtain his consent. In each case he displays the same characteristics. Just as he is Master of Horses, so he holds bridling sway over the sea and ships.

But the comparison may be pushed still further. And we may start with this same sacrifice offered by Jason to Poseidon. Just as Bellerophon presented Poseidon with a horse fitted with Athena's bit and tamed by her, so the ship which Jason offers Poseidon is Athena's work. This is clear from the whole Greek tradition. In Apollonius of Rhodes's account, the daughter of Zeus and Metis supervises every stage of *Argo*'s construction; the carpenter Argos works to her directions (2.1187—9), but it is the goddess herself who selects the trees from Mount Pelion (1188), who fells them with an axe, and who arranges the props (δρύοχοι: 1.723; cf. Chantraine, 1962: 258—9) to support the ship in building. And it is she, finally, who teaches Argos how to measure the wooden cross-beams with a rule (1.724). In other myths her rôle is equally crucial: when Danaus is credited with building the first ship, it is always upon Athena's advice and with her assistance.[48]

The parallel between horse and ship thus reveals a new aspect of Athena's interventions in the area of navigation. By the same token, her mode of operation in relation to the horse emerges more fully and clearly defined. I have earlier (p. 29 above) distinguished two categories, the riding-horse and the chariot and team, in which the separation of powers between Athena and Poseidon was identical. But if we take the horse-drawn chariot, it becomes clear that Athena's activity is more complex than we might have imagined, extending not merely to driving the chariot and horses but to the building of the chariot-body and the interlocking of the various sections of which it is made. The first *Homeric Hymn to Aphrodite* reminds us (12—13) that Athena was the first to teach carpenters to make chariots and wagons adorned with bronze.[49] With both chariot and ship, then, Athena clearly has a double rôle which includes the art of construction as well as steering or driving.

Now we are more likely to be aware of the differences rather than the similarities between these two activities; but the ancient Greeks saw many affinities between them. We can see this by looking at a number of different references to Athena. In the version of Apollonius of Rhodes, after the passage through the Symplegades, the Argonauts' helmsman Tiphys rejoices at having escaped the clashing rocks, giving all the credit to Athena who of course shoved the ship forward at the crucial moment. Curiously though it is not this aspect of Athena's intervention which he elects to celebrate: he gives thanks to *ship-building* Athena, to the Athena who firmly fixed the planks together with dowels (γόμφοισιν συνάρασσε: 2.612–14 [cf. *Odyssey* 5.248]) – just as though there were no differences between the two, as if they were simply identical. This identity is also asserted by an ancient source with whose help we earlier identified Athena *aithuia*: the scholiast on Lycophron's *Alexandra*. Before he explains that Athena was called *aithuia* because she taught men the art of navigation and to find a path through the sea, he offers a different interpretation (closely connected with this one, however). Athena is called *aithuia* 'because she is the prudence (*phronēsis*) by which ships are built'.[50] The implication is clear: the two activities, building and steering/driving, are connected with the same Athena of the sea because each depends upon the same type of Athena-intelligence, her *mētis*, her practical intelligence.

Woodcutters, carpenters and shipwrights are all craftsmen who enjoyed traditionally the favour and protection of Athena. In the *Iliad*, we hear of the great affection she has for *Tekton Harmonides*, 'Carpenter, son of Joiner', 'whose hands knew how to make master-pieces of every kind'; in particular, this Tekton was famous for having built (*tektēnasthai*) the ships of Paris/Alexander (5.59–64). If a carpenter is able to cut a ship's keel fair and straight with the aid of a line, he does so by the grace of Athena who has granted him skill in woodworking (15.410–12). If a plough needs to be made with the share-beam fixed to the pole with dowels, this too is a job for a 'servant of Athena' (Hesiod, *Works and Days* 430–1). And just as Athena has shown carpenters how to make ships or ploughs, she has taught them the art of constructing chariots and wagons.

Whatever it is, chariot, plough or ship, Athena presides over all the phases of working with wood – the felling of the timber, the planing of the planks, or the jointing of the parts of the frame. For all are operations which involve *mētis* in the same degree. As the *Iliad* has it (23.315): 'the woodcutter is far better for skill (μήτι) than he is for brute strength' (tr. Lattimore; cf. Chapot, 1887–1919: 332–6). Every carpenter is first a woodsman: he starts by taking his axe to trees he has selected himself in the forest (*Iliad* 12.390—1; cf. Hesiod, *Works and Days* 807—8). We have seen that when Athena decides to build the *Argo* her first care is to visit Mount Pelion to obtain materials. Once the trees are down, the planks have to be sawn up and adzed smooth.[51] A myth from the Homeric *Cypria* shows that this task too was performed by her: when the magical weapon which is to be the weapon first of Peleus and then of Achilles is being made, the centaur Chiron cuts the ash chosen for the shaft, and Hephaestus the blacksmith tips it with metal, thus making it a weapon of war. It is Athena who carefully planes or smoothes it (ξέσαι: frg. 3 Allen = frg. 5 Evelyn-White [Loeb]). After the timber has been prepared and smoothed, the carpenter who is building a ship, chariot or plough, begins to do the fitting and assembling of the parts, and fastening them together (ἁρμόζειν, ἀραρίσκειν, γομφοῦν, πεγνύειν). One of the most widespread methods of ship construction in ancient Greece was to build the shell *first* by fitting the planks with tongue and groove joints and then fastening each tongue with a wooden peg or dowel [the frame was then made inside the prepared shell] (Taillardat, 1968: 185—6; Casson, 1971: 201—23). Athena presides over this major phase in the construction of a ship in Apollonius of Rhodes's *Argonautika*: 'As Argos fitted the planks together with pegs, Athena breathed divine power into the ship' (2.613—14).

The different operations in wood-working are thus all combined into a whole in this mythical presentation of a marine Athena who is also a builder of ships. And they are so combined in their proper order by another figure who is as skilled in steering a ship as in building it — Odysseus, Athena's protégé and the hero whom the Greeks regarded as the perfect embodiment of all human *mētis*. Once the gods have agreed that he may leave the island where he is detained by Calypso, he sets about building himself a ship. He fells twenty trees and trims them skilfully with an axe; and then he cuts them carefully, using a line, and assembles the shell — tongue and groove joints secured by pegs (*Odyssey* 5.234—57).[52] Then the mast is up and the sail hoisted on this ship he has built 'like a master-craftsman' (εὖ εἰδὼς τεκτοσυνάων: 250), and

> taking his seat artfully with the steering-oar he held her
> on her course, nor did sleep ever descend on his eyelids
> as he kept his eyes on the Pleiades and late-setting Boötes,
> and the Bear, to whom men give also the name of the Wagon,
> who turns about in a fixed place and looks at Orion,
> and she alone is never plunged in the wash of the Ocean.
> (*Odyssey* 5.270—4, tr. Lattimore)

Even by night, which Aeschylus calls 'mother of care for the prudent pilot' (*Suppliant Women* 770), Odysseus steers his craft with the self-same *mētis* that built it.

But we can go still further in our attempt to define how the same intellectual model can be applied to activities as dissimilar as carpentry and steering. In summarizing earlier what the carpenter does, I said nothing of a crucial procedure in wood-working, the use of the line. This is used to saw beams and planks dead straight (cf. Blümner, 1875—87: 2.234—5). 'Straight down the line' (ἐπὶ στάθμην ἰθύνειν) is a traditional expression in the *Iliad* and *Odyssey* in referring both to a skilful carpenter,[53] and to a good shipwright (*Odyssey* 5.245; *Iliad* 15.410). One of the images for the idea of straightness is the

> ... chalkline [which] straightens the cutting of a ship's timber
> in the hands of an expert carpenter, who by Athene's
> inspiration is well versed in all his craft's subtlety.
> (*Iliad* 15.410—12, tr. Lattimore)

Now in Greek the verb *ithunein*, 'guide straight', refers to the way a line extends without deviating left or right.[54] It is also a technical term found in both our contexts: in navigation, it is used to refer to the ship's course which the pilot holds straight across the sea, despite winds and tide, thanks (as the *Iliad* has it) to his *mētis* (23.316—17; cf. Apollonius Rhodius, *Argonautika* 1.562 etc.); and it is also used for driving a chariot — a charioteer with *mētis* can steer straight for the goal without swerving.[55] This lexical point seems to confirm the suggestion that when a carpenter builds a ship or a chariot he employs the same type of intelligence as the helmsman when he steers his ship over the sea, and the charioteer, when he drives his team on the track.

In Greek thinking about Athena, then, there is no clear distinction made between building and driving/steering, between cutting out a ship's keel with the aid of a line and steering the ship on the sea. Being each so intimately linked with Athena's practical intelligence, ships and chariots both are seen to be as guidable as they are makeable. And this double aspect of Athena's activity can be confirmed by a semantic detail from the language of *mētis*.

Among the expressions in classical Greek for the idea of *plotting*, *planning*, or *thinking up schemes* is a group which employs imagery taken either from hunting or from fishing. Thus a plot may be *knotted* (μῆτιν πλέκειν) just as a fish-trap or hunting snare is knotted. A plan can be *woven* (μῆτιν ὑφαίνειν) just like a fishing or hunting net (Detienne and Vernant, 1978: 45). But there is yet another expression, 'to build a plot/plan': *tektainesthai mētin* (*Iliad* 10.19). The verb *tektainesthai* refers to wood-working and the activities of the carpenter. A cunning ploy is 'devised' or 'constructed' in the same way that one assembles the various bits from which a trap is made to produce the means of deception. A perfect example is the famous Trojan Horse, which was as much a stratagem devised by Odysseus at Athena's inspiration as it was a contrivance in wood built by Epeios — again with Athena's help (*Odyssey* 8.493—4; cf. Yalouris, 1950: 65—78; Schachermeyr, 1950: 189—203). The same goes for the ship and the chariot: both are the product and the instrument of Athena's intelligence, in which a single *mētis* is at work devising and producing tools to implement its plans. To quote an epigram on the invention of the ship (*Anthologia Palatina* 6.342 = 1, p. 411 Stadtmüller), Athena first conceived it (ἐμήσατο). In other words, she created it by an act at once intelligent and practical.

This comparison between Athena and Poseidon in the two contexts of the ship and the horse confirms Athena's twofold activity by contrast with the usually passive rôle of Poseidon, limited to a quite nominal sovereignty. But before we accept this distinction between these rival gods, I must discuss some mythological and ritual texts which might seem to provide evidence of varying weight against the hypothesis. First, Poseidon is surely represented by Homer as the great god who protects the Phaeacians, that people of sailors and carriers. Second, he is closely connected with a mythical helmsman named Phrontis ('Knowing One') in his temple on Cape Sounion in Attica. Finally, he is in the myth of the Argonauts the father of Ankaios, whose reputation as a helmsman was enough to make him the successor of Tiphys, Athena's protégé, at the helm of the *Argo* all through the second half of the expedition.

(1) The Phaeacian episode occurs just after the intervention of Ino *Leucothea*, the *aithuia*, thanks to whose talismanic veil Odysseus manages to reach Scheria, the land of the Phaeacians, and escape Poseidon's anger (p. 18 above). Now the Phaeacians, the subjects of King Alcinous, are presented as both marvellous sailors and protégés of Poseidon: Phaeacia is a city built right on the sea (*Odyssey* 6.262—9) with a population of sailors interested only in masts, oars and finely-wrought ships (270—1), and its streets filled with oarpolishers and tacklemakers, makers of sails and rigging (268—9). Their passion is betrayed in the very names: Topship, Quicksea, Paddler, Seaman, Poopman, Beacher, Oarsman, Deepsea, Lookout, Goahead, Upaboard . . .[56] They are a nation of ships' fitters and marvellous rowers. But apart from this single-minded passion for the sea, the Phaeacians are characterized by another peculiarity: they live in a spot so remote that no other people comes into contact with them. Unlike ordinary men they associate habitually with the gods, who come and sit amongst them on days of feasting and banqueting (7.199—206). But while any god may visit Phaeacia if he wishes, only one possesses his own temple there, in the agora (6.266) — Poseidon, the god who fathered the line of Alcinous and who grants the Phaeacians the privilege of crossing the seas. Poseidon's sovereignty over this land seems undeniable.

There is just one other god who could rival him, at least if we were to accept one interpretation of four disputed lines in praise of Poseidon's subjects:

> As much as Phaiakian men are expert beyond all others
> for driving a fast ship on the open sea, so their women
> are skilled in weaving and dowered with wisdom bestowed by Athene,
> to be expert in beautiful work, to have good character.
>
> (7.108–11, tr. Lattimore)

Does Athena's patronage extend to the weaving women only, as the last sentence seems to imply in its employment of a formula used elsewhere for Penelope, who is likewise, by the grace of Athena, as nimble of wit as she is at the loom (πέρι γάρ σφισι δῶκεν 'Αθήνη | ἔργα τ' ἐπίστασθαι περικαλλέα καὶ φρένας ἐσθλάς ~ τὰ φρονέουσ' ἀνὰ θυμὸν ἅ οἱ πέρι δῶκεν Αθήνη, | ἔργα τ' ἐπίστασθαι περικαλλέα καὶ φρένας ἐσθλάς | κέρδεά θ' ... : 2. 116–18)? Or does it extend also to the Phaeacian sailors, as might be implied by the affinities I have noted earlier between Athena and helmsmen?[57] But, attractive though it is, there are two reasons for rejecting such an interpretation.

First, Athena intervenes only at the very edge of Phaeacia: before Odysseus sets foot there, Athena makes a single appearance to block winds sent by Poseidon against his victim's ship — she stirs a brisk North wind for Odysseus to reach the shore (5.283–7).[58] Once he has done so, she behaves with immense discretion, refusing to show herself to him, unwilling to act openly, hanging back 'out of respect for her uncle' (6.329–31). She no sooner guides her protégé to the house of Alcinous than she disappears on her way back to Athens and the house of Erechtheus (7.78–87). And a topographical point betrays exactly the relation between her and Poseidon in Phaeacia: while his temple dominates agora and city, the one place dedicated to Athena is a modest grove (6.321) — and it is outside the town, on the edge of Alcinous's kingdom.

The second reason confirms that Athena scouts the Phaeacians, but it also gives the key to the relationship between them and the great god of the sea. They are seafarers and carriers, and they possess extraordinary ships — quite as extraordinary as Dionysus's: they travel without a hitch, faster than wings or thought — not even a falcon, the fastest thing that flies (13.86–7), can keep pace. But Poseidon has added to this gift of speed over the water the privilege of 'crossing the great abyss of the sea' (λαῖτμα μέγ' ἐκπερόωσιν: 7.35). These ships cross the chasm of the sea even when shrouded in mist and cloud 'without fear of damage or shipwreck': they themselves 'understand men's thoughts and purposes' (8.559; cf. 560–3). When ordinary men go to sea, they must constantly adjust the ship's course with the steering-oar, but on

Phaeacian ships there is 'no helmsman, no tiller' (8.557–8). Since Poseidon has granted them the freedom of the chasm of the sea, they do not have to cheat the winds or watch for bad weather. For them in fact the sea is not a 'chasm' that cannot be crossed: it has become familiar terrain stripped of mystery. And of course that is why Athena and her *mētis* have no place in the land of Phaeacia. The art of navigation is there useless, rendered superfluous by the very ships' privilege of knowing all the paths of the sea.

If 'the men of Phaeacia surpass all other men in rowing swift ships on the sea' (7.108–9),[59] they do so thanks only to Poseidon who gives their ships navel-knowledge of the chasm of the sea. But equally he may take away that knowledge all of a sudden in a fit of rage, metamorphosing hawk-swift ship into a dumb stone or some inert sea-rooted rock.[60] In other words, so far from undermining my earlier analysis of the proper modes of Athena and Poseidon, the case of Phaeacia offers precious confirmation. Even when Poseidon's power rules supreme, when it is as it were given free play, it operates on either side of navigation, outside the field of Athena's proper sphere.

(2) Here, then, Poseidon's character is revealed by the total exclusion of Athena. In the other two cases, the two gods are in more direct competition, and in contexts which do involve navigation and the steering of ships. The first is set at the very tip of Attica, at Cape Sounion. Here, facing the sea and dominating the site, stands a temple of Poseidon, 31.15 m long and 13.48 m wide (Kirsten and Kraiker, 1967: 163–7).[61] Sounion was famous even at the period of the composition of the *Odyssey*, for it was here that Menelaus's fleet on its way back from Troy lost its helmsman Phrontis, slain by Apollo's arrows as his ship was speeding along, as he sat with his hand on the steering-oar (3.278–81). He had to be buried, so Menelaus beached his ships and gave him a full funeral, probably on this headland sacred to Poseidon.

Some years ago Charles Picard, following up the excavations carried out by Greek archaeologists, found strong evidence for identifying a small building just outside the *temenos* of Poseidon as a *hērōön* [shrine of a 'hero'] of Phrontis (1940: 5–28). Sounion may therefore provide evidence for a particularly close association between Poseidon and a helmsman whose very name Phrontis ('Knowing one') indicates that he possessed navigating skill worthy of a protégé of Athena:

> [He] surpassed all the breed of mortals
> in the steering of a ship wherever storm-winds were blowing.
> (3.282–3, tr. Lattimore)[62]

The rest of this episode in the *Odyssey* tells us more about his skill. Once he loses Phrontis, Menelaus is caught unawares in a trap set by Zeus: rounding Cape Malea, the fleet is surprised by a storm which the

King of the Gods has devised (ἐφράσατο) for them (3.286—92).[63]
Several ships are destroyed; the rest are blown as far off course as Egypt,
where Menelaus finds himself stuck: a god holds him prisoner and
'binds his path' (ἔδησε κελεύθου: 4.380). It seems evident that by
losing Phrontis at Sounion, Menelaus has lost the *mētis* without which
ships cannot ride out bad weather (cf. Severyns, 1966: 119).

But must we therefore conclude that this skill in navigation has been
somehow confiscated by Poseidon, who otherwise gives the impression
of having no connection with any form of *mētis*? If we look more
closely at the evidence from Sounion, I think we will find that we
should not. For it is clear that the site at Sounion was not reserved
exclusively to Poseidon. We find in Pausanias (1.1.1 cf. Euripides,
Cyclops 293—4) that when sailors arrived within sight of Attica the first
thing they saw was a little temple perched right on the top of the headland (ἐπὶ κορυφῆ τῆς ἄκρας). This was the temple of Athena *Sounias*,
the foundations of which have been found about 500 m away from the
temple of Poseidon, on a level eminence. In their excavation of this
sanctuary, the Greek archaeologists came across more precise evidence
for Athena *Sounias*: a small painted clay plaque, a votive offering,
which shows a ship steered by a bearded man who is sitting with his
hand on the steering-oar (as described in Pausanias 10.25.2: a scene
painted by Polygnotus in the *lesche* of the Cnidians at Delphi). Even if
we do not go so far as to identify this with Picard as 'a memento of the
death of Phrontis', it is nevertheless clear that the helmsman heroized at
Cape Sounion was connected with Athena as well as Poseidon.

The relation between Phrontis and the two divinities of the sea may
be defined by analogy with the role of another legendary helmsman
who was also one of Menelaus's men. A post-Homeric literary tradition
has it that Phrontis's place was taken by a helmsman named Canopus or
Canopus. It was he who took Menelaus's fleet from Rhodes to Egypt
where he was accidentally killed and turned either into a star visible
only to sailors crossing from Rhodes to Egypt, or into the brightest star
in the constellation Argo (which represents the ship's steering-oar).[64]
The story of Canopus illustrates perfectly and concisely the relationship
between navigation and astronomy: the legendary helmsman is transformed into one of the brilliant beacons which help the good navigator
to find his way across the sea. And according to the Chronicle set up in
the temple of Athena *Lindia* at Lindos on Rhodes, the same Canopus
dedicated the steering-oars of his ship not just to the patron deity of
Lindos, who is also the protector of pilots but jointly to Athena and
Poseidon:

> Κανωπος ο [Μ]ενελαου κυβερνατας οιακας εφ ω[ν]
> επεγεγρα[π]το Κανωπος ται Αθαναιαι και Ποτειδανι

'Canopus the helmsman of Menelaus (dedicated) his steering-oars on which was inscribed "Canopus to Athena and Poseidon".'[65]

At Lindos as at Sounion this close association of Athena and Poseidon with the helmsman can mean only one thing: while the navigator's skills derive principally from Athena, no helmsman can effectively exercise them without also acknowledging that aspect of Poseidon's sovereignty which is represented in the banal image of the Lord of the sea carrying on his back ships men have made. It is not enough for Phrontis and Canopus to be Athena's protégés: they are necessarily also clients of Poseidon. He may do without Athena, but she cannot dispense with her powerful partner — precisely inasmuch as the navigator's skill cannot be deployed without the collaboration of the element which is at heart beneath Poseidon's sway.

(3) At Sounion as at Lindos, Athena and Poseidon are to be understood as twin powers, at once clearly distinct from one another but also collaborative; indeed their collaboration is both effective and necessary. In our third case, however, the two are found in more or less direct collision, again in the context of navigation. Nonnus's *Dionysiaka* describes a chariot race in which the competitors are Athena's charioteer and Poseidon's coachman (Detienne and Vernant, 1978: 204); just so a real opposition seems to be set up between the successive helmsmen of the *Argo*, between Tiphys, who is chosen and sent by Athena, and Ankaios son of Poseidon, who is entrusted with the helm on the sudden death of Tiphys.[66] It is true that strictly speaking Ankaios does not *compete* with Tiphys. But he is presented as his rival in the art of steering, as is evident from two passages in the *Argonautika* of Apollonius which praise his knowledge as a navigator and his skill in handling the steering-oars:

(Erginos and Ankaios) . . . ἴστορε δ 'ἄμφω
ἠμὲν ναυτιλίης ἠδ' ἄρεος εὐχετόωντο (1.188—9 Fränkel)

'both boasted their prowess in seafaring and war';

. . . περιπρὸ γὰρ εὖ ἐκέκαστο
ἰθύνειν (2.867—8 Fränkel)

'for he was especially skilled in guiding (ships)'.

We might expect that a comparison between them might cause us to modify in at least some respects the division of power we have sketched here. Let us see.

We may note first that the gods' relation to their protégés is very different. Athena encourages Tiphys to join the Argonauts and become the helmsman. She stands at his side and acts with him when they come to the Symplegades. By contrast, Poseidon never intervenes in favour of the man whom it is tempting to call 'his' helmsman: it is not Poseidon but Hera who prompts Ankaios to lay claim to the post left vacant by

Tiphys's death. And at points of high drama it is Argos, Jason, the Dioscuri or even Triton (a lake-god) and Apollo *aiglētēs* ('the dazzler') who come to his assistance and get him out of trouble. Ankaios never either receives or requests help from his divine father. Once this distinction is made, the contrast between the two helmsmen becomes transparent. Whereas Athena's pilot shows himself to be truly in control of the ship, even to the point of outshining Jason on occasion in front of all his companions, Ankaios seems a dim, insignificant figure, usually quite inadequate to cope with eventualities he has been unable to anticipate.

From the very beginning of Apollonius's *Argonautika*, Tiphys is presented as a masterly helmsman, quick to anticipate (προδαῆναι) changes in the weather and shifts in the wind, able to calculate his course (τεκμήρασθαι) by the position of the sun and stars (*Arg.* 1.106— 8; cf. Valerius Flaccus, *Argonautica* 1.481—3; 2.55—71). It is he who gives the signal for departure and who supervises the manhandling of the ship into the water (*Arg.* 1.381—91). All through the first part of the expedition he is up with the morning star, watching for favourable winds and urging the Argonauts to set sail (1.519—22, 1273—5). It is his *mētis* and his prudence (φραδμοσύνη) that decides the route (1.559—62). At the entrance to the Bosphorus only his skill in manoeuvring enables him to find a way through the gigantic waves which threaten to overwhelm the boat (2.169—76). But the supreme demonstration of his mastery is the shooting of the Symplegades, the Clashing Rocks. They follow the advice of the seer Phineus; Euphemus releases a rock-dove to test out the passage as Tiphys gives the order to row (2.555—67); the bird has barely cleared the rocks when he orders the Argonauts to haul on the oars and shoot between the two cliffs just as they begin to move apart again (2.573—4). When they are half-way through, he is quick enough to make a last-minute swerve to avoid a giant wave which threatens to swamp them (2.580—7); and then it is Athena's turn (see p. 19 above).[67] When they finally emerge into the Black Sea, Tiphys is filled with a great joy in striking contrast to the other Argonauts' terror. He encourages Jason and comforts the crew, declaring to their general surprise that henceforth the mission's success is assured: all Phineus's predictions have come to pass and now that they are through the Clashing Rocks the way is open before them (2.610—37).[68] Shortly afterwards, he suddenly dies (2.854—7).

Ankaios then comes forward (2.864—98). In him we have a radically different type of helmsman. No doubt he has some knowledge of navigation and can use the steering-oars. But he never anticipates anything, never makes a decision or truly *controls* the ship. At the very first difficulty they meet, when they have to leave the Black Sea to enter the

River Phasis which leads to Colchis, it is Argos who takes Ankaios's place to supervise the manoeuvre (2.1260–1; cf. 1281–3). On the return journey, it is again Argos who tells the Argonauts what course to follow (4.256–93). From then on, the voyage of the *Argo* is punctuated by a series of miraculous interventions. To show them the way to the River Istros (Danube), Hera traces out a great shining line in the sky (4.294–302). After the murder of Apsyrtus (Medea's brother), the prophetic beam built into the ship's prow reveals that the Dioscuri must pray the gods to open up the 'paths of Ausonia' which lead to the island of Circe (4.580–92).[69] On another occasion, when the wind looks like blowing the expedition off into mid-Ocean, Hera once again intervenes, this time more directly and energetically: she shouts at them and alerts them to their mistake (4.640–4). In all this, Ankaios might just as well not be there: he plays no part at all. Nor is he any more in evidence when they shoot the Wandering Rocks (the *Planktai*). It is Thetis and the Nereids who seize the ship and guide it through, taking advantage of a moment of calm brought about by the collaboration of Hephaestus and Aeolus, the Master of fire and the King of the winds (4.922–63). And the rest of the voyage simply confirms his impotence. With the Peloponnese already in sight, yet another storm forces them into the Libyan Sea and beaches them deep in the Gulf of Syrtis, on a desert coast (4.1245–9). This is too much: Ankaios tearfully tells the others that he is abandoning his post and that he refuses to be helmsman any longer (4.1261–76).[70] Henceforth we hear nothing more of him. The final part of the voyage is marked by two further divine interventions: Triton (the son of Poseidon) rises from the depths of the lake which is called after him and guides the ship by the keel to the point where the lake flows into the sea (4.1551–1619); and finally Apollo *aiglētēs* causes a bright light to shine out in the black stormy night, so saving the Argonauts from the perils of the impenetrable darkness (κατουλάς) (4.1694–1718).

Throughout the epic, Poseidon's helmsman is sharply contrasted with Athena's. Unlike Tiphys, Ankaios never shows that he possesses even a grain of *mētis*. As the expedition continues his incompetence becomes more and more evident until he is forced to resign. But of all the episodes in the story as Apollonius tells it there is one which spells out the limitations of this Poseidonian pilot better than any — that is when the Dioscuri are given charge of the Argonauts' ship.[71] When the *Argo* reaches the Stoichades, the Dioscuri, who have been designated by the prophetic beam, are confirmed in their new rôle by Zeus who entrusts them with responsibility in the future for saving ships in danger (4.588–9, 649–53). Their mode of intervention is markedly different from Athena's. The 'saviours of ships' appear in the sky, shining at the top of ships' masts: they are *phôsphoroi*, 'bringers of light', and they still the wind and calm the waves (*Homeric Hymn to the Dioscuri* 2.11–17; cf. Cook, 1914–40: 1.760–74). There was a ritual for causing them to appear: sailors sacrificed white lambs to them on the ship's stern when danger threatened (*Homeric Hymn* 2.9–11). This ritual is the exact converse of the one the Athenians performed to appease storm-winds: when a storm threatened they would sacrifice a black lamb to them on the sea-shore (Aristophanes, *Frogs* 847–8). The object here was to appease the dark clouds (τυφῶς), to avert the fury of the winds by the offering of a black victim, a colour reserved to the powers of the underworld. The first ritual is a request to the Dioscuri to make a light shine in the storm, whose dazzling brilliance is symbolized by the colour of the sacrificial victims. And Plutarch well describes the singularity of the way in which the Dioscuri operate: 'they do not sail [with men] and share their danger, but appear in the sky as saviours' (*De defectu oraculorum* 30, 426c).

This digression on the Dioscuri confirms that there is no rivalry between Tiphys and Ankaios that might reflect a rivalry between Athena and Poseidon in connection with navigation. The one helmsman who can claim to have any connection with Poseidon is obliged to entrust the safety of his ship to the good offices of the Dioscuri. In other words, the salient difference between Tiphys and Ankaios is precisely the point at which the difference between the action of the Dioscuri and the intervention of Athena is most evident. Ankaios is as neglected by Poseidon as the Phaeacians are blessed by him. He is a dreadful helmsman: he can only appeal for help to the Dioscuri.[72]

It cannot then be denied that Poseidon's power, which is limitless on the sea, applies neither to the helmsman nor to the art of navigation, but operates both 'above' and 'below' this technical level. It operates 'below' when the god at will unleashes or calms the forces of the sea; and 'above' when he grants the Phaeacian ships such perfect knowledge of the paths and the chasm of the sea as to render superfluous the whole art of navigation.

Marine Athena, a 'sea crow' like Ino *Leucothea*, affords the seafarer help as total as it is magical, yet which cannot be characterized by the opposition between black and white typical of the Dioscuri.[73] She may stand by the helmsman to open up a path for him over the sea; she may release a bird to find the way through the chasm of the deep; but always she manifests herself in the marine world in the exercise of a skill in navigation which can hold a course over the sea, outwitting the winds and the beating waves. But this same sharp practical intelligence is manifested also as technical skill, in the art of cutting the timbers straight with the line, and then in the equal art of fixing them together to build the very means whereby navigation becomes possible. In the area of activity which she shares with Poseidon, Leucothea and the Dioscuri, Athena is characterized against all other divinities of the sea by a dual capacity, both to make and to guide ships. And here lies her distinction, her special mode of action, in the world of navigation.

II: The human condition

3. The myth of Prometheus in Hesiod

Jean-Pierre Vernant (1974)

Hesiod devotes two long passages to the story of the theft of fire by Prometheus, one in the *Theogony* (535–616), the other in *Works and Days* (45–105). These two versions are not merely complements. They are formally interrelated by virtue of an allusion in each to an incident explicitly narrated in the other: *WD* 48 refers to the first section of the story in the *Theogony*, Prometheus's trick in apportioning the sacrifice at Mekone; while *Th.* 512–14, by way of introduction to the myth of Prometheus, mentions the acceptance by Epimetheus of Zeus's fatal gift to man in the shape of Pandora, which is the final section of the story in the *Works and Days*. The two versions thus constitute a single entity, and must be analysed as such.

I begin by presenting a formal analysis of the narrative, taking agents, actions and plot one by one, first in the *Theogony* and then in the *Works and Days*. I shall then attempt, by comparing the two texts, to bring out the overall logic of the narrative conceived as one.

Level 1: Formal analysis of the narrative

1.1 The agents

1.1.1 Theogony

In the presence of gods and men

on one hand Prometheus	on the other, Zeus and those who carry out his final decisions, Athena and Hephaestus

Characteristic of Prometheus are his *mētis*, his cunning, his wily intelligence (511, 521, 546, 550), and his skill in deceiving, his δολίη τέχνη (540, 547, 551, 555, 560); of Zeus, his sovereign *mētis* (520, 545, 550). Zeus is also described as 'father' (542), lord of the heavens and of the thunderbolt (558, 568, 602).

Jean-Pierre Vernant

1.1.2. Works and Days

on one hand Prometheus Epimetheus representing: men	on the other Zeus (assisted by Hephaestus, the Graces, Peitho, Aphrodite, Athena and Hermes) gods

Prometheus's *mētis*, a compound of anticipation, guile and deceit, is matched by Epimetheus's want of *mētis*, for Epimetheus never understands anything until it is too late, and is always the fall-guy. The twin-brothers are opposed but complementary, uniting subtle calculation with gross fatuity; and precisely that combination characterizes the human condition.

1.2. Actions (structural and literal)

The story as a whole is a duel of wits between the Titan of *mētis* and the lord of Olympus, the King of the Gods, who is *mētioeis* ('possessed of *mētis*'), to see which can outwit the other.

In the *Theogony*, the duel takes place in the presence of gods and men. They are still united; and the result of the contest is to determine the final distribution between them of honours and portions (*timai* and *moirai*). In *Works and Days* gods and men are already sundered, and the two sides confront each other as it were in the tussle between the two representative heroes, Zeus for the gods, Prometheus—Epimetheus for men.

In both texts there is a strict parallelism between the actions of Prometheus and those of Zeus. These actions can be presented as follows:

1.2.1.

Preparatory (premeditated) dispositions ($\tau i \theta \eta \mu \iota$ and its compounds; cf. for Prometheus, *Th.* 537–9, 541; for Zeus and his assistants, *Th.* 577–8, 583, 601; *WD* 61, 74, 80) which are designed to deceive, *apatān*, the opposition. On each side, this deception (*apatē*) or trick (*dolos*) involves the same recourse to 'hiding' or 'concealing from sight' (*kaluptein*, *kruptein*), and, in the case of Prometheus, 'stealing' without being seen (*kleptein*).

1.2.2.

A game of reciprocal giving of deceptive presents, trick gifts, which may be either accepted or rejected. The rules of this game follow the following formal pattern, which also sums up the logic of the stories:

44

giving | taking the gift = accepting
not-taking the gift = rejecting

not-giving | not-taking what is not-given
taking what is not-given = stealing

1.3. Plot

1.3.1. Theogony

This general grammar represents the organization of the narrative. The individual episodes can be expressed in the following terms, with each one introduced by a time-marker which gives it a particular relation to the other episodes in the sequence:

Episode 1 (535–61)
Time-marker: 535–6: καὶ γὰρ ὅτ ... τότ' ἔπειτα ('Now when ... , after this ... ')

In the presence of gods and men, and that there might be distinction between them (cf. ἐκρίνοντο), Prometheus 'secretly disposes' (539: κατέθηκε καλύψας; 541: εὐθετίσας κατέθηκε καλύψας) the two portions of the ox he has 'laid before' (537: προύθηκε) gods and men, and sacrificed and then cut up. Prometheus offers Zeus the appealing but in fact uneatable part of the ox; Zeus accepts this apparently preferable portion and finds he has been tricked — though all along the trick itself was part of the *mētis*, the cunning trap, laid on purpose by Zeus to encompass man's downfall. Zeus is angry.

This transaction establishes which share of the blood sacrifice is to be reserved in future to men (i.e. the meat and the entrails covered in their fat = the edible parts) and which to the gods (the stripped white bones, burned upon the alter after being scattered with incense).

Episode 2 (562–9)
Time-marker: 562: ἐκ τούτου δὴ ἔπειτα ('From that time on ... ')

Zeus cannot forget Prometheus's trick, and 'refuses to give' men the heavenly fire (the thunderbolt) which they used previously (οὐκ ἐδίδου). Unseen by Zeus, Prometheus steals fire (ἐξαπάτησεν ... κλέψας ... πυρὸς αὐγήν). Men are denied heavenly fire, but Prometheus's fire burns among them and enables them to cook food.

Zeus is angry at thus being tricked.

Episode 3 (570–84)
Time-marker: 570: αὐτίκα ('Whereupon ... ')

In recompense for the fire which he had denied and which Prometheus

45

stole, Zeus orders the manufacture for men of something which had not hitherto existed, an evil (*kakon*), Woman.

It is made ready by Hephaestus and Athena, who 'dispose' it as Prometheus did the portions of the ox in Episode 1.

Episode 4 (585—613)
Time-marker: 585: αὐτὰρ ἐπεὶ δή ('After this, when . . . ')

Woman, the 'beautiful evil' that is the recompense for fire, is put together and laid before gods and men, just as Prometheus had brought out the sacrificial ox. But she is a gift exclusive to men (570, 589), token of their misfortune. Woman is to men what hornets are to bees, a ravening belly (*gastēr*) gobbling the fruit of others' labour (590).

Henceforth, then, men must choose: either they do not marry, and have grain enough, since the female *gastēr* does not deprive them of it — but no children, since a female *gastēr* is needed to give birth; or else they marry, and even with a good wife, evil comes to counterbalance good (609).

Among human beings, goods and ills are mingled inseparably because Zeus, in the gift of woman, has given men a κακὸν ἀντ' ἀγαθοῖο, 'an ill to match a good'.

Conclusion (613—16)

Prometheus may have been able to steal (*kleptein*) fire; but it is impossible to 'steal the mind' (*klepsai noön* = to deceive) of Zeus. For all his ingenuity, the Titan comes to a terrible end.

The narrative-structure can be summarized thus:
    Prometheus offers Zeus a *dolos* (a false gift, a trick present)
        Zeus accepts it
    Zeus is angry, and denies men (heavenly fire)
        Prometheus does not accept this denial; he steals fire and gives it to men
    Zeus then constructs Woman (that is, a *dolos*) and gives her to men
    Gods and men are now sundered
    Prometheus gave men the flesh of sacrificial beasts to feed upon; to the gods he gave the bones, to be burnt
    Prometheus gave to men the fire he stole; Zeus reserved for the gods' sole use heavenly fire
    Zeus has given men, and men only, Woman
    The human condition, insofar as men are to be distinguished from the gods, thus involves (1) sacrifice, (2) 'Promethean' fire with its corollary cooked food, (3) marriage.

1.3.2. Works and Days

Preamble (42—8)

The gods have hidden from men (κρύψαντες) their means of life (βίον), i.e. grain. If they had not, there would be no need to till or plough; but Zeus 'hid' (ἔκρυψε) the means of life after Prometheus had tricked him (an allusion to the first episode in the *Theogony*).

Episode 1 (49—59)
Time-marker: 49: τοὔνεκ' ἄρ' . . . ('From then on . . . ')

From that day (when he was tricked) onwards, Zeus meditated (*emēsato*) bitter sorrows for men. He hid fire (50: κρύψε δὲ πῦρ). Prometheus stole it. Zeus was angry.

Zeus makes it known that to balance the account he will 'make men a gift' of an ill they will love to have (cf. 57: δώσω and contrast οὐκ ἐδίδου, *Th.* 563).

Episode 2 (59—82)
Time-marker: 59: ὣς ἔφατ' . . . ('Thus he spoke . . . ')

The seductive but dangerous gift is made ready by Athena, Hephaestus, Hermes, the Graces, Peitho ('Persuasion') and Aphrodite.

The ill is named Pandora, 'the gift of all the gods' to 'bread-eating' men (82; cf. the same term in *Th.* 512).

Episode 3 (83—9)
Time-marker: 83: αὐτὰρ ἐπεὶ ('But when . . . ')

Hermes brings the gift of the gods, δῶρον θεῶν, from heaven to the house of Epimetheus. Prometheus had warned his brother never to accept a 'gift' from Olympian Zeus, but to refuse it and send it back. But Epimetheus accepts the gift. By the time he realizes his mistake, the damage is done.

Episode 4 (90—104)
Time-marker: 90: πρὶν μὲν ('Before this . . . ')

Prior to this, there were no hardships in human life — no work, no sickness, no old age.

But Pandora lifted the lid of the jar, and all ills escaped among men, everpresent but ineluctable because unpredictable. For they are invisible — by contrast to the Woman, an evil visible enough but which disarms thanks to a parade of beauty. They are moreover inaudible, again unlike Woman, who uses her voice, her *phōnē*, all the better to disarm those foolish enough to listen to the untruths which it utters.

And thus the ills go unseen that men would avoid if they could but see them; and the ill which they can both see and hear deceives and seduces them in the specious image of the good.

Conclusion

It is then impossible to 'escape the mind of Zeus' (and men must pay heed).

The structure of this version can be summarized thus:
The gods have hidden from men the means of life
For Zeus, having fallen victim to an *apatē* (Prometheus's trick in hiding the portions of the ox), 'hides' fire
Prometheus steals this hidden fire unbeknown to Zeus and gives it to men
Zeus puts together the 'gift of all the gods' and offers it to Epimetheus, who is the counterpart of Prometheus. Instead of rejecting it, Epimetheus accepts
Consequently human life is full of ills. Some are hidden, invisible; others are quite visible, but camouflage themselves as desirable blessings.

1.4. Comparison between the two versions: the narrative logic

There are a number of divergences between the story in the *Works and Days* and that in the *Theogony*.

1.4.1. The matter of Prometheus's deception (*apatē*) over the parts of the ox gets only a passing mention; but Epimetheus's acceptance (i.e. the acceptance by men) of Zeus's gift of Pandora and its wretched consequences — the opening of the jar of evils — is fully treated (the motif is simply alluded to in the *Theogony* 511–12).

1.4.2. Pandora and her rôle as a 'gift' — a deceptive, baneful gift which might have been either accepted or rejected — are emphasized heavily (cf. the explanation of the name Pandora, and lines 57, 82, 85, 86). But the theme of the gift is present already in the *Theogony* version — and in fact determines its entire logic (note especially ἕλε' ('take', 'choose'), 549; οὐκ ἐδίδου ('he refused to give'), 563; and the 'ethical' datives ἀνθρώποισιν ('for mankind') in 570 and 589).

1.4.3. The act of 'hiding' (*kaluptein, kruptein*), which in the *Theogony* is attributed explicitly to Prometheus and implicitly to Zeus, appears in *Works and Days* explicitly in relation to Zeus. The notion actually acquires a general theological significance in the context of the relation between Zeus (the gods) and humanity.

1.4.4. The episode of the theft of fire is identical in the two versions. The two versions of the creation of the first woman and/or Pandora correspond exactly, though the account in the *Works and Days* is more detailed; in each case, the feminine creature made by the gods for humankind is presented as a *parthenos* (an unmarried but nubile girl) adorned for her wedding ceremony.

1.4.5. The two versions can thus be treated as the components of a single whole. Comparison between them helps to emphasize certain features of the narrative logic. I distinguished earlier between two kinds of action on the part of the agents in the intrigue: between (1) preparatory actions — arranging and concealing, and (2) actions which involve a relation to others — giving or not-giving; accepting or rejecting the gift/not-gift. If we now compare the two accounts, these two kinds of action may be seen no longer as merely superimposed or juxtaposed, but as in concert.

For 'not-giving' is identical with 'hiding' (cf. *Th.* 563 'Zeus gave no more fire'; *WD* 50 'Zeus hid the fire'). So far as the gods are concerned, no longer to give men a good hitherto freely available is to 'hide' it from them. From this viewpoint, 'hiding (the means of) life' (i.e. corn) and 'hiding fire' are two aspects of a single action. Originally corn grew on its own, a gift to men from the ἄρουρα αὐτομάτη ('the obliging earth': *WD* 116–17). All they had to do was to bend down, pick it up and eat. Afterwards, when corn was 'hidden', cereals — that is, plants that grow 'cooked' as opposed to 'uncooked' green vegetation, which grows on its own — involve agricultural labour (wearisome *ponos*): the land must be ploughed and the seed (*sperma*) buried in it to get grain. Likewise, in the beginning heavenly fire was freely available to men on the ash-trees where Zeus put it. Afterwards, it had to be buried 'in the hollow of a fennel-stalk'; or its 'seed' preserved by hiding it in the ashes (again *sperma*, cf. *Odyssey* 5.490: *sperma puros* associated with the words *kruptein* and *kaluptein*). Fire survived only when fed (Herodotus 3.16); it had to be nourished continually. Lastly, men originally sprang up spontaneously from the ground, just as corn did from the furrows and fire from the ash-tree. But henceforth men must toil for the female belly, which has to be fed like fire and ploughed like the land, so that they may be able to bury their seed (*sperma*) in it.

But if the gods' 'not-giving' to men means 'hiding' so also does their 'giving': since every gift from the gods is a *dolos*, an *apatē*, a trick or deception, and in fact withholds what it pretends to bestow; it looks like the gift of a good, but contains an unseen evil. In effect, since good things have been hidden (not-given) by the gods, men cannot have access to them except by way of the ills (*ponos*; women) in which they are wrapped. And conversely, the gods' gifts to men are ills disguised as goods.

The opposition giving versus not-giving which seemed to dominate the structure of the narrative thus resolves into two different forms of a single action 'hiding':
(1) 'not-giving' = 'hiding' a good so that it cannot be gained except by way of the ills in which it is wrapped
(2) 'giving' = 'hiding' an evil under the seductive appearance of good.

The narrative-logic reflects the ambiguity of the human condition, in which, thanks to the gods' action in 'hiding', goods and ills whether 'given' or 'not-given' are always linked indissolubly. At the same time, the story locates humankind between beasts and gods, its status characterized by sacrifice, the use of fire for cooking and for manufacture, woman seen as wife but also as animal belly, corn as staple food and labour in the fields.

1.5. The discussion so far has dealt with the organization of the text as a narrative, with its syntax and logic. We must now extend it, at a different level, by examining its semantic content, taking into account all the details of the architecture of each episode as well as the complex network of relations between their constituent elements.

This will enable us to set up a third level, the structural context, or more accurately the structure of the mental world (classificatory categories, the patterning and encoding of reality, the delimitation of semantic fields) within which the mythical narratives were produced, and which permits the modern interpreter to make them once again fully intelligible in all their density of signification.

Level 2: Analysis of the semantic components

For brevity's sake, I offer the results of an analysis of the significant elements in each episode in the form of general conclusions. The portions of the sacrificed ox, the stolen fire, the first Woman/Pandora, and cereals as the staple of life — all four are related to one another by homology and similarity in a number of different ways. These relations we may summarize as follows:

2.1. Pandora (at the story's end) corresponds to the parts of the sacrificed ox (at the outset).

2.1.1. She is an inviting gift offered by Zeus to men just as Prometheus had offered Zeus the inviting portion of the carcass.

2.1.2. She is a *dolos*, a trap, a deception, because her external appearance conceals a reality totally at odds with it. In the case of the ox, the eatable parts were concealed beneath the double covering of skin (*rinos*) and stomach (*gastēr*), both rebarbative; the inedible parts were camouflaged by an appetizing layer of white fat (*Th.* 541: καλύψας ἀργέτι δημῷ). As for Pandora, inside (*WD* 67: ἐνδέ; 77, 79: ἐν δ' ἄρα) she has the mind of a bitch, the habits of a thief and a voice (αὐδή) designed for deceit and subterfuge (*WD* 67, 78). But this inward 'bitchiness' — the 'evil', *kakon* — is concealed beneath a double layer of apparent attraction — the *kalon*, the 'fair': the physical looks of a girl no whit inferior to the immortal goddesses; and the clothes and jewels in which she is arrayed, especially her white robe (*Th.* 574: ἀργυφέη ἐσθῆτι; cf. 541) and the dazzling veil which hides her (*Th.* 574–5: καλύπτρην δαιδαλέην). The divine grace, the χάρις, that limns her person and her apparel makes her a snare (*dolos* cf. *Th.* 589; *WD* 83), concealing her true animality — just as the appetizing white fat made the preferable portion of the ox (*Th.* 544) offered Zeus into a snare (*dolos* cf. *Th.* 547, 551, 555, 560, 562) by covering over the uneatable bones.

2.1.3. She is a *gastēr* (*Th.* 599), a ravening belly that devours the *bios*, the staple food that men get by agricultural labour (see *WD* 374, 704 for this female voracity). The eatable portion of the ox which Prometheus set apart for men is likewise placed inside the animal's *gastēr* (here 'stomach'). *Gastēr* means a container, a vessel in which food is cooked (*Odyssey* 18.44–5; Herodotus 4.61); but it also has another semantic value: Prometheus's deception in hiding all the eatable parts inside the animal's *gastēr* condemns the human race henceforth to be unable to live without eating, without filling this 'paunch' which concealed its appointed diet of sacrificial meat. As slaves for evermore of this hateful, wretched, baneful *gastēr* — the source of all evils and worries, says *Odyssey* 15.344; 17.286, 474; 18.55 — men themselves are in danger of becoming 'just like bellies' (*Th.* 26: γαστέρος οἶον; cf. Epimenides, *FVS* 1, p. 32 frg. B1). Pandora embodies physically that 'bitch-belly' characteristic of the human condition, sundered now by Prometheus's trick from the gods. 'What is there', asks Odysseus, 'bitchier (*kunteron*) than the hateful *gastēr*?' (*Od.* 7.216). And within Pandora Hermes hides a *kuneos noös*, the 'soul of a bitch'.

But the voracity of the female belly is not merely directed towards food: it is also for sex. In high summer — the Dogdays — women's hunger for sex erupts in lascivious self-abandon (*WD* 586–7; cf. Alcaeus, frg. 347.4 Lobel—Page). Pandora's *kuneos noös* involves *machlosunē*, 'hot pants', no less than gluttony.

2.2. Pandora corresponds also to Promethean fire, whose counterpart, or reverse, she is at several semantic levels just as she is in the narrative-structure (cf. ἀντὶ πυρός: *Th.* 570, 585, 602; *WD* 57).

2.2.1. She is first a *dolos*. Promethean fire acts as a snare in just the same way as the portions of the ox and Pandora. It is hidden from view inside a fennel-stalk, the interior of which is not damp but dry and fibrous and burns in secret. Put inside the hollow fennel (ἐν κοίλῳ νάρθηκι: *Th.* 567; *WD* 53), the stolen fire is concealed within a green plant carried in the hand. But unlike heavenly fire, Promethean fire is a hungry fire: it dies when not fed. It is also an engendered fire: to light it you need a fire-'seed', like the one Prometheus hid in the fennel, just as the farmer hides the corn-seed in the belly of the earth, and the husband his seed in the belly of his wife.

2.2.2. Pandora also reveals herself as the counterpart of fire, as ἀντὶ πυρός, by being herself a fire which burns men, shrivelling them up with weariness and worry, by her two appetites and all the ills she brings them. However strong a man may be (*WD* 705: εὕει ἄτερ δαλοῖο), she burns him even without tinder; and in the flower of his youth (ὠμός, 'raw') withers him to old age (Euripides, frg. 429 Nauck²). As Palladas of Alexandria [late 4th cent. AD] put it, in a gloss on Hesiod: 'As the price of fire Zeus gave us another fire, women . . . Fire will go out, but woman is an inextinguishable fire, full of heat and ever flaring up . . . She burns man up with worries, eats him away, transmutes his youth into premature old age' (*Anth. Pal.* 9.165.1—4 cf. 166 [Stadtmüller]).

2.2.3. Pandora is characterized finally by her *epiklopon ēthos*, her 'thieving disposition' (*WD* 67), further noted in *WD* 375: 'Who trusts a woman trusts a thief.' To the 'stolen' fire which Prometheus cunningly filched from Zeus and gave to men there corresponds its 'reverse', the 'thieving' fire which Zeus in revenge palmed off on foolish Epimetheus — Prometheus's own 'reverse' — so as to ruin man.

2.3. Pandora corresponds to *bios*, the staple which Zeus 'hides' along with his heavenly fire; just as Prometheus hid meat in the *gastēr* of the ox, and the seed of stolen fire in the fennel-stalk. The belly of the woman, which man must till in order to implant his seed if he wants children, is like the belly of the earth which man must till if he wants corn — because Zeus has hidden *bios* within it. Plato observes that woman imitates the earth in pregnancy and childbirth (*Menexenus* 238a). Moreover, 'Pandora', 'All-gifts', is one of the names of Earth, because, we are told, she freely grants us all that is needful for life. That is why she is called *zeidōros*, fruitful; and why another of her names is *Anēsidora*, 'she who sends gifts up from below' (Scholiast on Aristophanes, *Birds* 972, p. 229 Dindorf [4.3]; Hesychius and *Etymologicon Magnum* s.v. Ἀνησιδώρα [1,5096, Latte; p. 108.31 Gaisford]). This rôle of Pandora–Anesidora as the giver of good things hidden in the earth is emphasized in painting and sculpture: her fruitfulness is no longer due to the spontaneous bountifulness of the 'obliging fruitful earth' (ζείδωρος ἄρουρα αὐτομάτη: *WD* 117–18) as in the golden age, but a fruitfulness which demands now agricultural labour, toil (*ponos*), ploughed fields (*erga*). At Phlius, near Corinth, the title Anesidora was given to Demeter, in association with Gē, Earth (Pausanias 1.31.2). Marriage, which entered human life with Pandora, is of course a sort of ploughing in which the woman is the furrow (*aroura*) and the man the ploughman (*arotēr*). At this level, the female belly adds to its appetitive and sexual meanings (what the belly does in consumption and consummation) an association, linked fundamentally to marriage, with the procreation of children and the production of grain – what the female belly first hides and then brings forth; and which cannot be produced except by way of this belly, which first 'hides' it.

It will be clear, despite the limitation of this analysis to the major aspects of the myth, that the grammar of the narrative (the logic of the actions) and the semantic content are closely linked. The narrative logic operates by a process of inverted equation: for the gods in their dealings with men, both 'giving' and 'not-giving' = 'hiding'. The grammar of the narrative also has a semantic function: for men good things are hidden in ills; and ills are either concealed within goods, or else invisible. The entire system of semantic relations is articulated about the same theme, which is illustrated and developed at several levels and in numerous directions by the network of correspondences. Their interaction gives substance to the underlying idea that, beneath all its forms and in all its diverse aspects, human life is set thanks to divine 'concealment' in a world of good and evil mixed, of ambiguity, of doubleness.

Level 3: The social-cultural context

Prometheus's trick set the seal on the sundering of men from gods by instituting the sacrificial meal in its usual form. Among the inevitable consequences and corollaries of this act are (stolen) fire, women and marriage (which imply birth through procreation, and death), the cultivation of corn and agricultural labour. These different elements form so close a texture in the myth that they compose an indivisible whole.

A number of points can be made:

3.1. This complex of relations was used throughout Greek paganism as a framework for a definition of the human condition in terms of features which distinguish it both from the gods and from the animals.

3.2. At the level of social institutions, sacrificial practices, the use of fire, marriage-rites and agricultural institutions are all multifariously linked. As a ritualized kind of cooking, the sacrificial meal involves fire: the portion given to the gods is burned on the altar, while the eatable parts must be boiled or roasted for men to eat. Sacrifice is also related diversely to agriculture: domestic animals (sacrificed) and wild animals (hunted) are at the same relative distance from men as are cultivated plants (seen as 'cooked') and wild plants (seen as 'raw'). This intimate connection between animals used for sacrifice and cultivated plants is emphasized in the ritual procedure in sacrifice, where barley-grains and wine are included as part of the process of killing and burning the ritual victim.

Links between marriage and agriculture are to be found in the organization of the pantheon, in marriage rituals, in religious festivals such as the Thesmophoria, and in a whole range of other myths.

3.3. Each of the characteristics selected by the myth so as to distinguish men from the gods is equally relevant to the distinction between men and animals. Two rules govern the choice of the food consumed at sacrifices: men do not eat meat of just any kind (above all, not human flesh); and they eat it cooked. Hesiod himself contrasts this with the carnivorous and cannibal habits of animals, which eat one another (*WD* 277–8). In one mythical tradition (to be found in Aeschylus's *Prometheus Bound* and Plato's *Protagoras*), the significance of the fire which Prometheus steals is not so much its sundering of heaven and earth as its education of mankind from primitive bestiality. Fire here is 'technology', the source of all the skills known to the busy mind of man. Marriage too marks a clear division between man and animals, who couple without rules, crudely, with any other member of the species which happens to be around. Again, the gods are immortal because they do not eat bread or drink wine (*Iliad* 5.341–2); and animals likewise are innocent of these cultivated foods: they are either carnivorous or they eat raw vegetation.

In both the *Theogony* and *Works and Days* Hesiod's narrative makes Prometheus the agent of the divorce between gods and men: he stresses the estrangement of each from the other. But distance from the gods implies as a corollary distance from the animals. What the myth of the institution of sacrifice defines is the very status of man between animals and gods. If we are to interpret the text at all its levels of signification, if we are to extract the entire gamut of its implications, we must set it in a much wider context: we must see its relation to the sources for other versions of the myth, widen our enquiry to include other groups of myths concerned with the origins of civilization, and take account of social practices.

3.4. If we do this, we shall better understand Pandora's rôle in the story. Pandora's double nature is virtually a symbol of the ambiguity of human existence. She betrays all the tensions and dualities which are inherent in man's status between animals and gods. In her beautiful exterior, rivalling that of the immortal goddesses, Pandora reflects the splendour of the divine; but her 'bitch-soul', her 'bitch-temper', reduces her to the level of the animals. Through marriage, which she represents, and through the articulate speech and force Zeus commanded she be endowed with, she is fully human (*WD* 61–2: ἐν δ' ἀνθρώπου θέμεν αὐδὴν καὶ σθένος). Yet this humanity which she shares with men as their companion (the inevitable reverse of maleness) is itself ambiguous. Because she speaks the language of men, because she can talk to them, she belongs to humankind; but she is ancestress of a γένος γυναικῶν, a 'race of women', which is neither identical with nor totally dissimilar from male mankind. The articulate speech which Zeus gave to her as well as to men is not, for her, a means of saying what is, of conveying truth to others; but of hiding truth in falsehood, of giving verbal existence to that which is not – a way of triumphantly ensnaring the minds of her male partners (*WD* 78).

3.5. Pandora's fundamental ambiguity is matched by that of Elpis, Hope, who remains behind in the house with her (*WD* 96–7) trapped in the belly of the jar (*WD* 97: ὑπὸ χείλεσιν), after all the ills have flown away among men. If human life were all pleasure, as in the golden age, if all ills were still safely shut up in the jar (*WD* 115–16), it would be meaningless to hope for anything other than what is; or if life were totally and irredeemably in the hands of evil and misfortune (*WD* 200–1), there would be no place for hope. But since henceforth ill is mixed inextricably with good (*Th.* 603–10; *WD* 178 cf. 102), so that we may not foresee exactly how things will turn out, we go on hoping: if men had unerring foreknowledge like Zeus they would have no use for Hope; if they lived entirely for the moment, ignorant of the future and indifferent to its wares, they would also be innocent of her. But

55

they are fixed between the clear foresight of Prometheus and the blank myopia of Epimetheus, oscillating between them without ever being able to disentangle them. They know beforehand that suffering, illness and death are inevitable; but ignorant of the precise lineaments of misfortune, they recognize it only when it has struck and it is too late.

Immortal beings such as the gods have no need of Hope; and she is not known to the animals, who do not know that they are mortal. Man is mortal like the beasts. If, like the gods, he could foresee all the future, if he dwelt entirely in the realm of Prometheus, he would not have the strength to endure, because he would not be able to face his own extinction. As it is, he is aware that he must die, but knows neither its time nor its manner. So Hope, which is foresight but blind (Aeschylus, *Prometheus Bound* 250; cf. Plato, *Gorgias* 523d—e), a saving illusion, both good and bad, Hope is the one thing that allows men to endure this ambiguous, divided existence, the consequence of Prometheus's deceit in the institution of the first sacrificial meal. Ever since, everything has had its dark face: no communication with the gods which is not also, in sacrifice, the acknowledgement that between mortals and immortals there lies an impassable barrier; no fortune without misfortune; no birth without death; no plenty without toil; no Prometheus without Epimetheus. And no Man without Pandora.

4. Sacrificial and alimentary codes in Hesiod's myth of Prometheus

Jean-Pierre Vernant (1977)

The significance of Greek sacrifice is defined for us in one particular myth. If we push the analysis far enough, the myth suggests an understanding both of the structure of ideas upon which the sacrificial ritual is based, and of the enormous range of evocations it carried. In one episode of the *Theogony*, parts of which are picked up in *Works and Days*, Hesiod describes how Prometheus set himself up as Zeus's rival, and how he tried by trickery, lies and deception to attain his own ends by thwarting those of the King of the Gods. The first outcome of this battle of wits between Titan and Olympian was the ritual distribution of those parts of the sacrificed domestic animal — here a large ox supplied, killed and dismembered by Prometheus — which were assigned on the one hand to men, and on the other to the gods: to the first, the meat and the entrails thick with fat — everything one can eat; to the second, the bare bones burned on the fire with a little fat and aromatic spices at the sacrificial altars.[1] The aetiological value of this sequence in the myth is explicitly stressed by the text: 'And thus it is that the race of men upon earth burn white bones to the immortal gods upon fragrant altars' (lines 555—6), and has been recognized by most commentators.

But only the narrowest implications have been elicited. Almost always it is understood as an explanation of a particular, indeed minor, aspect of the ritual, as a response to a kind of paradox supposedly presented to the religious consciousness of the Greeks by a detail in the blood sacrifice (which was also a meal) that later became incomprehensible. Sacrifice was supposedly an offering bestowed upon the gods to pay them honour and to gain their favour; how then to explain that it was not the best morsels that were set aside for them, but the parts of the animal that were inedible — the junk, as it were? But to confine the significance of the first part of the text to this one point is simply to condemn oneself to supposing that it is more or less gratuitous, and to misunderstand the links between it and the following sections which give the myth its meaning as a whole. If the figure of Prometheus, his rivalry with Zeus, his final come-uppance, the entire tale told by Hesiod in the long passage of the *Theogony* which deals with the children of Iapetus (507—616), only deals with sacrifice entirely by the way, in passing, then we have to admit that Hesiod's choice of Prometheus is pretty arbitrary. Prometheus would have been made responsible for a sacrificial ritual whose deeper significance Hesiod had no interest in revealing by placing it within a complex theological system; he could only have wanted to find an *ad hoc* explanation by inventing a fairy-story, as one makes up a fib to justify oneself after the event.

On this view, what relation could there possibly be between the first act in the Prometheus saga and those which follow it in Hesiod's version; between the cutting up of the ox and the ritual allocation of its parts on the one hand, and on the other, the theft of fire (Act the Second) and the creation of the first woman (which concludes the dismal drama)? Hesiod must have bundled together into the same text quite disparate elements; quite artificially have attached to the traditional theme of the theft of fire an aetiological myth designed to account for what seemed to him peculiar about sacrificial ritual, and off the top of his head a tarradiddle about the origin of women that betrays his own private antifeminist 'philosophy'. It would then be quite as vain to hunt in the myth for a coherence which does not exist as to expect to derive from it some understanding of the nature and function of sacrifice.

But this will no longer do. First, because it stems from a view of mythical habits of thought which belongs to the past. But more precisely — more concretely too — because the text contradicts it at every turn. Hans Schwabl (1966: 73—85) has shown that even at the formal level the Prometheus episode follows in its mode of composition strict rules which give the whole an undeniable unity, give it a strictly logical and unified character. This coherence is equally marked at the narrative level: Hesiod underscores in the logical relationship between the episodes the perfect continuity of the account, and makes quite evident the necessary dependence of each episode upon the one that precedes it. It is because Zeus never forgets for an instant the deception of which Prometheus has been guilty in granting men the meat from the sacrificed animal (*Th.* 562), that he determines henceforth to deny men his (heavenly) fire. And it is because he catches sight of the fire secretly stolen by the Titan (*Th.* 569) merrily blazing on earth, that in return for this new gift-by-deception that men enjoy he offers them for his part the third and final gift-by-deception: the first woman, 'fire's counter-gift' (*Th.* 570). The action proceeds according to an impeccable logic from start to finish, to constitute a drama whose successive stages take their strictly necessary places in the narrative sequence. Finally, I have shown in the previous study (above, p. 50—3) that on the semantic level there is a dense structure of symbolic relations between the themes employed in each section of the story of Prometheus: in the unfolding of the narrative, each event is linked with others; and by the end, they constitute as a whole a coherent composition whose every constituent part is related in a quite strict manner to every other. At the diachronic level of the account, the episode of the theft of fire has a mediating rôle: it is through it, and by means of it, that the link is made between the first section (the deception, *dolos*, of Prometheus in the assignment of the sacrificial portions) and the last (the deception, *dolos*, of Zeus in assigning to men the first woman). Again, it is through it that the reversal of the activity and of the relative position of the actors takes place: in the first episode, the initiative, the deception, is Prometheus's — Zeus appears to be tricked,[2] men receive from the Titan the gifts in which they rejoice; after the theft of fire, just the reverse: the initiative, the deception, become Zeus's — it is now he who 'gives' to men, but the happiness men experience at receiving the divine gift is nothing else than the trap in which they are about to be taken, and indeed, in a wider sense, the symbol of mortal man's misery.

From this perspective, the final episode is simply the inevitable consequence of those which came before. Here, as in a mirror, are reflected, arranged and ordered all the earlier events; through it, they illuminate each other to take on their true significance which can only be revealed at the very end. The 'trap' that is woman has then to make its entrance before the true nature of Prometheus's 'trap' for Zeus can be finally understood — when the Titan 'fiddles' the portions of the sacrificial animal so as to bestow upon men the benefit of all the meat: the good part, upon which men congratulate themselves (as they congratulate themselves on the 'beautiful evil' that Zeus bestows upon them in the person of the Woman), turns out in reality to be the bad. The petard set by Prometheus to hoist Zeus devastates mortal men as it blows up in his face; and fire itself, which Prometheus stole, for all its benefits, is a gift no less ambiguous than the first female human-being — all decked in perilous allure.[3]

These sequences are too intimately related within the narrative texture, and their symbolic values too overlapped, for it to be possible to isolate them and treat them separately. We must take the myth for what it is, not an assemblage of disparate episodes but a single story; and understand that in this coherent whole the relationship linking blood sacrifice, Prometheus's fire and the creation of woman can be the result neither of serendipity nor of an author's whimsy: they are necessary, necessary in the sense that they are of the very essence of the myth and fulfil the function Hesiod assigns them in the context of his *Theogony*. All through the struggle between Titan's supple cunning and the unbending intelligence of Zeus what is ultimately at issue is this: the rules which define man's estate, the mode of life appropriate for men now. The ritual of sacrifice is presented as the initial consequence and as the most immediate expression of the gulf opened between gods and men on the day that Prometheus entered upon his rebellious course. The myth links sacrifice to primeval events which have made men what they are, doomed to death,[4] dwelling upon the earth,[5] troubled by ills without number,[6] eating barley from the fields they work,[7] dwelling with female spouses[8] — all in all a tribe of creatures utterly cut off from those to whom in the beginning they were yet so close, living as they did in commensality with them, sitting at the same tables and sharing the same feasts[9] — those Blessed Immortals, who dwell in heaven, nourished on ambrosia, up to whom there now wafts the smoke of burnt-offerings . . . The sacrifice-episode is neither secondary nor an afterthought. It lies at the centre of the myth. It has nothing to do with 'explaining' an odd detail in the ritual, that bones were burnt; by pointing out the difference between those portions reserved in sacrifice for the gods and those for men, it highlights the gulf which ever after separates them — the fact that they belong to two distinct tribes. Just as the earlier closeness was expressed in myth by means of the image of a community of banqueters feasting together, so separation now is marked by the contrast between two alimentary modes. The opposition between these forms is written into the very heart of the ritual; and yet the ritual is a means of creating a link, a communication, between the sundered tribes — it tries, so far as it can, to build a bridge from earth to heaven.

The subject of diet is prominent in the myth then; and it resonates in many different ways. Sacrifice is presented as a meal at which one eats meat. But this eating of meat is hedged about with a whole series of constraints and restrictions. It is, first of all, limited to certain species of animals, excluding others. Precise rules govern how the beast is killed, cut up, divided out, prepared and eaten. Finally, the meal is partly religious in intention: it seeks to honour the gods by inviting them to join a feast which is thus, at least in theory, their own, a *dais theōn* — in some sense they are present, and they may either accept or reject the offering.[10] Sacrifice is an alimentary ritual; and as such it does not simply lay down the conditions under which an animal may be killed for consumption, under which men may licitly, and indeed with piety, eat it. It is directed towards the gods. It claims to link them with the banqueters in the joyful solemnity of the feast. And it therefore evokes the memory of that former commensality, when men and gods together passed day after day in happy common feasting. But though sacrifice looks back to the far-off days of the Golden Age when men still lived 'like the gods' and shared their food, without thought of ills, toil, sickness, old age or of womankind,[11] it is not the less true that in its very structure it registers that that blessed time when men and gods feasted together is over for ever. For it sets aside for the gods' attention the bones that cannot rot, that are consumed in the fire and reach them in the form of sweetsmelling smoke that drifts up to heaven; and leaves to men the carcass of a beast from which the life has already departed, a lump of dead flesh, with which they may satisfy momentarily their ever-gnawing hunger. Ordinarily, people ate meat only on the occasion of a sacrifice and according to its rules. By their presence the gods give their blessing to this feast of meat-eating. But they do so only to the extent that the ritual allocates to them what truly belongs to them — the very life of the animal, that pumps from the bones with its spirit as the victim slumps under the poleaxe, that flows out too in the blood that spatters the altar; and those parts of the animal which, just like the spices that burn with them, do not rot after death. In devouring what can be eaten, men simultaneously restore their failing strength and acknowledge the baseness of their human condition — confirming their absolute submission to those very Olympian gods whom the Titan Prometheus when he established the pattern in the first sacrifice once thought to trick with impunity. The alimentary ritual which establishes communication between man and divinity itself underscores the gulf which sunders them. That communication is founded upon a religious ritual which, by memorializing Prometheus's error, reaffirms on every occasion of its performance the existence of that uncrossable gulf. And it is the purpose of the myth, as told by Hesiod, precisely to lay bare the origins of the separation and to make plain its dire consequences.

Understood in this way, Hesiod's account confirms and extends Jean Casabona's conclusions, using an entirely different approach, in his study of Greek sacrificial language (1966). He observed that for us sacrifice and what goes on in the abattoir belong to different semantic areas. Not so for the Greeks. For them, from Homer to the end of the classical period, the same language applied to both areas. Greek has no verbs to express the idea of slaughtering an animal for human consumption other than those which mean 'to sacrifice', 'to slaughter for the gods'. *Hiereuō* can mean the one as well as the other. In Homer *hieréion* is used for an animal seen as 'sacrificial victim' and as 'meat for consumption'; later, opposed to *sphagion*, *hiereion* means a victim whose flesh is eaten — the term evokes simultaneously sacrifice and butcher's-shop. Again, *thuō*, which came to be used as a general term for the sacrificial ritual as a whole, and which never lost its associations with burnt offerings and sweetsmelling smoke, refers both to the ritual of killing and to the feasting upon meat which comes after; and it is associated with words meaning to entertain, to have a good time.

In distinguishing two, and only two,[12] portions of the ritually-slain animal, which are strictly opposed to each other in having reverse alimentary values, Hesiod is treating sacrifice as a form of consumption characteristic of men as opposed to gods. In doing so, he is linking this first section of the myth of Prometheus to the major tradition of religious thinking. So far from innovating here, or forcing the meaning of words, or making ordinary notions more sophisticated, his account rests firmly on the ordinary semantics of the language of sacrifice.

To understand that form of Greek sacrifice which involved the eating of meat, one has then to take Hesiod's account entirely seriously. We must study the text closely, without assuming that anything is non-significant. And we must compare the two versions, in the *Theogony* and in the *Works and Days*, taking note of agreements and divergencies.

First of all, what is the context of the Prometheus episode in each poem? And how does this context help to elucidate the status of the ritual? For the *Theogony* there is no difficulty. The work as a whole is devoted to the origins, the birth, the battles and the victory of Zeus, his forcible seizure of sovereignty by means of which he successfully establishes, over against the former régime, the foundations of a permanently viable authority which can never be overcome or shaken. Zeus's accession to the kingdom of heaven does not merely signify, as the text stresses at three separate points, the ordering of all things for the gods, a strict division between them of honours, powers and privileges;[13] along with the sovereign who founded it, this cosmic order is to exist henceforth unchanged and irrefrangible.

In a poem in which everything takes place at the level of the gods, among the gods, there is no place for an account of the origins of men in the proper sense. We learn how the gods came into being, not men. The *Theogony* does not say whether *Gaia*, the Earth, bore them, whether they were created by Zeus and the immortals, or whether they were born of the blasted Titans' ashes, as the Orphic tradition had it. Nevertheless men are present in the narrative. They appear all of a sudden during the course of a particular episode, that devoted by Hesiod to the descendants of Iapetus — more precisely, to his son Prometheus. There is no question of an account of the genesis of mankind, such as one might expect in a poem about the Creation. The text speaks of men as creatures already in existence, dwelling with the gods, still among them.[14] The result of Prometheus's action is not to give them an existence they already had, but to define their status as mortals over against the Blessed Immortals. This location of humanity, this circumscription of the modes of life appropriate to it and which make it a race apart, is achieved by means of a division between men and gods of what belongs to each. At Zeus's request, or at least with his agreement, Prometheus undertakes to make this decisive allocation. And the method he uses is precisely the cutting up and the division of the parts of the sacrificial victim (*Th.* 537 δασσάμενος; 544 διεδάσσαο μοίρας). The son of Iapetus cuts up the sacrificed animal and allots it in two portions, one for gods and one for men; and this determines the division between the two races — the dividing up of the animal both occasions and declares the opposition between their two statuses. In and through the sacrifice the gulf between mortals and Immortals opens and remains open; along this line of the division of the parts of the victim is set the frontier between the everlasting youth of the Olympian gods, masters of heaven, and this ephemeral sort of existence that men must evermore on earth shuffle on to become themselves.

Mankind then has become what it is thanks to a division analogous to that effected by Zeus in relation to the gods ever since his accession to the throne, when he established for each his proper domain and his privileges.[15] But in the divine realm this division follows two clearly contrasted principles. In the case of his enemies, his rivals for the sovereignty of heaven, the Titans and Typhoeus, it is effected by violence and repression (*Th.* 882: τιμάων κρίναντο βίηφι); exiled to Tartarus, the routed gods are put out of action — stripped of all honour (*atimoi*) they are excluded from the ordered world. By contrast, in the case of the Olympians and their allies, the division is harmonious and consensual. What then of the division from which men derive their status? It stems neither from brute violence nor from mutual agreement; not imposed by force yet not decided in common: it is effected by a process fundamentally ambiguous, multifarious, devious. On the one hand, the violence is disguised as its opposite — smiles, flattery, affability, paraded respect.[16] On the other, agreement and negotiation figure merely as subterfuges to conceal the real means by which one's opponent is constrained against his will. Instead of the overt struggle which effected the division between Titans and Olympians we have a guerrilla war, a trial by stealth and duplicity, in which the game is to catch the monkey by hoisting him on his own petard. Instead of an agreement in good faith between victorious allies to effect a fair division, we find deceit, a game of bluff in which public asseverations are always uttered with a forked tongue.

This negotiation by guile corresponds to the ambiguous status of men in relation to the gods: they are joined to them, and at the same time separated from them. Men are not sufficiently dangerous threats to Zeus to compel him to eliminate them in an all-out struggle, any more than they are equals with whom he has to forge an alliance by a straightforward division of privilege.[17] Along with all mortal creatures, such as the beasts of the field, they exist at another level than the gods, they are separate, strangers to the world of divinity. And yet, alone among mortal creatures, and by contrast to the beasts, their way of life implies a constant reference to and a special relation with the super-natural Powers. Each city, each community is linked to the divine world by means of an organized religious cult, and so in a sense has rights in that world.

This ambiguity of status, this separation in unity with the gods, nigh but far, is reproduced up to a point by Prometheus himself in the divine world. On every measure his status in relation to Zeus is equivocal. Though a Titan, he did not take his brothers' part in the Battle of the Gods against the Olympian. He is not Zeus's enemy: he even, according to Aeschylus, planned the victory. Equally, he was not to be utterly excluded from the world, shut up in the depths of Tartarus. But he could hardly be said to have been an absolutely trusted friend. At the very heart of Zeus's ordered world, there he is, a rival, a very present threat inside the circle of Olympian gods. His claim to recognition — almost a revolt — is also the voice of what the world contains, in contrast to the gods, of negativity, of gratuitous suffering, of inexplicable and arbitrary evil. And his challenge is the more dangerous in that it is deployed precisely where Zeus believes himself supreme — the realm of quick-wittedness, acuity, foresight, the domain of 'know-how' in which men also claim to have their share. The fruits of a subtle and fertile mind Prometheus employs to benefit humanity at the expense of the gods, trying to spare them the ills inseparable from mortality and to obtain for them the blessings the gods reserve to themselves.[18] If he secretly opposes Zeus's plans in carrying out what he was told to do, it is because he hopes, by closing the gap between gods and men so far as possible, to make men into creatures somehow like himself, truly Promethean creatures, who should be neither entirely separate, distant, inferior and suppressed (as Zeus wants them to be), nor yet quite inti-mate, close, equal and united (as the Blessed Immortals are one to the other); but at a half-way point, occupying a median status that recalls his own mediating function, his own ambiguous rôle as hostile ally, abetting antagonist, prisoner at large, pardoned sinner, redeemed and reconciled rebel.

Prometheus the Titan represents, in this episode of the *Theogony*, a questionmark — inscribed by a god sufficiently near to men to wish them close to the gods — against an Olympian order which has ordained for that special class of beings called human, with whom the Titan shares a special relationship, exhausting toil, the slow decay of physical strength, pain, sickness, death, all that evil which constitutes the radical inversion of what it is to be divine. If he had defeated Zeus in this trial by deceit upon which they entered over the division between men and gods, sacrifice would have guaranteed to men admission to that non-mortal existence for which they are always doomed to search. Failure means not only that the ritual of sacrifice becomes the act by which the absolute apartheid of the two is symbolized, but that the split is glossed with the character of a justifiable and irremediable Fall, whose legitimacy mortal men are forced to recognize each time they enter into communication with the powers above following the rules of Prometheus's sacrifice.

It is the location of this episode within the account as a whole, and a number of details in the text, that provide a thorough theological justification for the concatenation of evils which Prometheus unleashed. Paradoxically enough, Prometheus is himself said to be good, kindly (*eüs*: *Th.* 565; *WD* 50). But the favour he shows to men is merely the inverse, the mask, of his secret malevolence towards Zeus. His one-sidedness (*heterozēlōs*, *Th.* 544) in making the division betrays his desire to subvert the dispositions of Zeus's sovereign order. The ends he darkly purposes in performing the task of distribution allocated to him are an expression of his fundamental rivalry with Zeus (*erizeto boulas*: *Th.* 534). The Fall of man is thus linked directly to the spirit of competition, jealousy and strife — in a word, *eris*, dark daughter of Night — that slips, thanks to Prometheus, insidiously into the Olympian gods' aetherial world. That world is a stranger to *eris*. More precisely, with Zeus as king, it ought not to know any sort of *eris*. It came into being through open conflict; the victory of the Son of Cronus ended that conflict but it also relegated the time of conflicts between the gods to a time before the Olympian order, just as it relegated the enemy powers to a place beyond the sway of the Immortals.[19] A passage in the *Theogony* makes it clear that if nevertheless some conflict or discord (*eris kai neikos*) does arise between the Blessed Ones, there is a procedure laid down to expel the person responsible without debate or delay: he is first deprived of consciousness, breath, life, and wrapped in the sleep of death; and then he is excluded from the councils and banquets enjoyed by the Immortals.[20]

But if we take the episode of Prometheus as an account of an *eris* between a god and Zeus, the whole thing constitutes within the *Theogony* a narrative of a thoroughly paradoxical rivalry: paradoxical both because it is quite different from other such stories and because it involves, crucially, creatures who are not gods. Compared with the quarrel between Olympians and Titans, the differences are plain. Prometheus's *eris* is not an open war, duly declared. It is not aimed at seizing power, makes no claim to Zeus's throne. It does not take place before his victory, before his foundation of order and the division of privilege. It offers no threat to his sovereignty; it seeks to change it from within, by working underground. Neither is it comparable to that other *eris* among the Immortals to which the *Theogony* alludes, whose solution — in a divine society already firmly established and organized — is provided for in advance by the quasi-judicial procedure of expulsion. Nor yet does Prometheus's *eris* occur after the establishment of this order, any more than it antedates it: in the myth it occurs at the same time as the foundation of Zeus's order, coincidentally with his other organizational tasks. Or rather, it coincides with a particular aspect of his disposition, one which is not a mere formality, and which is problematic because it concerns ambiguous and puzzling creatures, whose status simply has to be the result of a botched compromise, some sort of deal, after a struggle between divine adversaries who block each other at every point, each outwitting the other until the whistle blows. Of course, at the end of the match, it is Zeus's version of the allocation which gains the day. But in order to win, he must follow the path laid down for him by the struggle with Prometheus; he has in each hand to accept Prometheus's bidding, keep tally of the points the wily Titan wins for men, and which Zeus, unable to expunge, has to turn against them.

Such an account explains the obliqueness of the Prometheus episode, which is a sort of parenthesis within the development of the *Theogony* as a whole. Indeed, it is doubly parenthetical, first in relation to the genealogical exposition, and second in relation to the sequence of events in the divine world. At line 337, Hesiod starts to describe the Titans' family-tree. He has already given us their names, in order of birth which runs, on the male side, from Oceanus to Cronus (oldest to youngest) by way of Koios, Krios, Hyperion and Iapetus. We are thus told the names of the children of Oceanus, Hyperion, Krios and Koios. But at line 453 we move to the descendants of Cronus when we expected those of Iapetus, and the genealogical account, through mention of the birth of Zeus, continues with the narrative of the mythical events which constitute the second set of divine legends of succession (the first set concerns the castration of Ouranos and the installation of Cronus as ruler) and enters on the central theme of the struggle for the sovereignty of heaven (the struggle of Zeus against Cronus, and the Olympians against the Titans). Cronus devours his children so that none of them shall supplant him upon the throne; Zeus escapes his father's gullet. The first thing he does is to cause his father to vomit up those whom he has swallowed; and then he releases the Cyclopes from their bonds. They provide him with the instrument of victory, the thunderbolt, in which Zeus henceforth 'trusts and rules over mortals and Immortals' (line 506).

It is at this moment that Hesiod breaks off the account of Zeus's struggles and goes back to the genealogical exposition — to the children of Iapetus, whose proper place would have been after the Titans older than Cronus. In fact, the real function of the genealogy of Iapetus is to introduce the story of the *eris* which pits Prometheus against Zeus, an *eris* that is no less marginal to the struggles for sovereignty (it has nothing whatever to do with the battle against the Titans) than to the ordering of the divine world under Zeus's sway (because that order knew no *eris*). Its logical place in the story is thus neither clearly before nor evidently after Zeus's victory. It is peripheral, circumstantial, just as the question of the status of humankind seems, in the *Theogony*, quite external to the grand conflict which sunders the world of the gods for the possession of power. Indeed the poem makes no mention whatever of the existence of men under Cronus.

So the Promethean parenthesis precedes the purple passage on the War against the Titans, the triumph of Zeus and the allocation of honours. But occurring as it does immediately after the freeing of the Cyclopes and the gift of the thunderbolt, and immediately before the freeing of Obriareus, Cottus and Gyes, who make possible the Olympians' victory, it is put into a context in which the reign of Zeus seems already secure even though the details of the fighting have not yet been properly narrated. The scene is Mēkōnē, the old name of Sicyon. So we know the precise location, human, on earth, where the contest took place. But we do not know exactly at what moment it took place in the sequence of events which divide up the divine calendar. In other words, Prometheus's *eris* — insofar as that confrontation between two gods has to do with the relations between gods and men rather than with the society of the gods itself — is aligned on a temporal axis which is not exactly the same as the gods'. In the narrative, the two time-axes seem to be contiguous without exactly coinciding; just as the *eris* of Prometheus is neither that of the Titans nor identical with that juridically regulated in advance by the Olympians, and so introduces into the world of the gods a dimension of being, a quality of existence, which is too nearly human to be perfectly integrable into the hierarchical order of divinity.

The counterpart in the *Works and Days* of the *eris* which, in the *Theogony*, though it uses divine machinery, is essentially concerned with, and directed towards, men, is that which takes place in Boeotia directly between Hesiod and his brother Perses.

There is a stricter parallelism between the relation of the two texts to their context than might appear. In the *Theogony*, Prometheus's trickery over the parts of the sacrificial animal is introduced by *gar*, 'for', which links the episode from which stems man's misfortune directly to the preceding line, which concerns the *eris* of Prometheus against Zeus. In the *Works and Days*, the second version of the Prometheus story also begins with a *gar*, which this time refers to the admonition which Hesiod has just given his brother concerning the *eris* which sets them against one another. Their *klēros*, their family plot of land, has been divided between them. This division was not achieved by force, by brute violence, as when one takes possession of enemy booty in war. Nonetheless, it did not take place by agreement between the two brothers, by a friendly arrangement, as it should. In order to obtain more than his share, Perses had stirred up rancorous quarrels (*neikea kai dērin*: WD 33). He had taken the matter to arbitration by the rulers of Thespiae, in principle the representatives of Olympian Zeus's allocatory justice. But the rulers were suborned, and gave judgement against justice. They handed down a crooked verdict, a prejudiced opinion. Taking the side that lacked justice, they apportioned the land unequally, granting the one much of what belonged to the other. And thus they displayed that same spirit of partiality with which Zeus ironically reproached Prometheus in the *Theogony*. There seems to me to be a clear analogy between the two situations, divine and human, which introduce in each poem the myth of Prometheus, with its harsh implications for mortal men. Moreover, Hesiod does not simply remind his brother of the grievous wrangle he had provoked, of the fraudulent division he had cleverly obtained at Hesiod's expense: he enlarges the significance of the private quarrel to universal justice and order; he makes it the basis for what one might well call a veritable theology of *eris* — inasmuch as the firstborn daughter of Night impresses all human existence with her seal. And this theology, right at the beginning of *Works and Days*, contains an explicit allusion to the *Theogony* on the subject of *eris*, which is here taken up and specified.

To the gods there might appear to be only one kind of *eris*: the Immortals knew only that violent struggle during which Zeus triumphed over his rivals and which his victory caused to become extinct in the divine world.[21] But at the level of mankind, things are quite different. There is there not one *eris* but two; and this bifurcation of the daughter of Night corresponds to her sovereign power over men's lives, to her continuous presence in and for the good as well as in and for the worse. In her double, bifurcated, ambiguous form *eris* has now two aspects just as there are two kinds of wicked division between men: war against an enemy from without, on the battlefield, and faction within a single community, in the public place of assembly (*WD* 29 and 30). The first relies on force of arms, the second employs the tongue and tricky deviousness (*WD* 321–2, with an opposition between χερσὶ βίη and ἀπὸ γλώσσης). But whether they use violence or deceit, both have the same object, to grab booty, to make oneself rich at the expense of another by taking from him what belongs to him. Ill-gotten gains do not last. Zeus himself makes haste to pay the guilty the grim reward of their crimes (*WD* 325–6, 333–4), just as he crushed the brute violence of the Titans, and as he punished the crooked trickery of Prometheus. This wicked *eris*, extinct among gods, punished among mortals, men do not love. And, Hesiod goes on, if they do honour it, it is against their will, under constraint of the decisions of the Immortals (*WD* 15).

But before she gave birth to this rancorous *eris*, which the will of the gods has given men against their will to be their companion, Night bore another, similar, but of different disposition, whose praise the wise man should sing. It is she who stirs, by emulation, every man who sees prosperity abounding in the fields and in the house of a neighbour whose application to hard agricultural toil is greater than his. This *eris* of competition, of energetic rivalry in work, Zeus, sat on high in the lambent aether, has established below as the foundation for all well-gotten gain. He has set her in the roots of the earth (*gaiē*: *WD* 18–19, with the opposition αἰθέρι ναίων – γαίης ἐν ῥίζηισι), where men live and from which they draw their sustenance. The Son of Cronus desired that by means of this *eris* they should find the path to wealth in accordance with the order instituted by himself. There is then no way in which men can escape *eris*, to whom their whole lives are subject: they may only choose the good rather than the evil one. It is not by bandying words in the agora, listening to disputes and avoiding work in the fields (*ap' ergou*: 28), that Perses can hope to set himself on the path to success. To earn the means of life (*bios*), the fruit of Demeter (*Dēmēteros aktē*: 31–2), which Gaia bestows on men in plenty when she is worked, a man has to get down to it, water his furrows with the sweat of his brow, compete with someone else in toil. How could it be otherwise? Zeus exacts a harsh penalty for profits which are the fruit of violence or trickery by means of wicked *eris*; and the goods that he has granted to men, the wealth that gives them life (*bios*) and which is hidden in the earth, he does not wish that they should be able to gain without labour (*kai aergon eonta*: 44), without appealing to good *eris*. That might have been the case once, in the Age of Gold, when the earth herself, without having to be turned or seeded, caused the life-giving ears to sprout in such profusion that plunder, nor theft in the dark, nor competition in work – no sort of *eris* – had any place here on earth any more than in heaven. Man could live and eat without lifting a finger.[22] But the gods hid the means of life from men; they sunk it deep in the soil on the day that Zeus found himself tricked by Prometheus Crookedthought. And since that day human life has been what we see: the victim of a twofold struggle, endlessly pulled between each, now mercilessly punished by the gods if one follows the worse to escape the harsh demands of labour, now chained to the wheel of grinding toil if, obeying Zeus's command to enjoy in peace wealth punctiliously gotten, one determines to choose the good.

These two versions of Prometheus's trick, that which is set in the *Theogony* in the context of the Acts of the Gods, and which involves mankind only incidentally, and that in the *Works and Days* which was prompted by the bitter experience of Hesiod's quarrel with his brother, are thus complementary and mutually illuminating. If men, unlike the gods, cannot escape *eris*, that is because the human condition owes its inception and its rationale to that *eris* which Prometheus initiated against Zeus. Conversely, if Prometheus occupies in the divine world an ambiguous status which marks him out as the architect of a ritual of sacrifice whose ultimate consequence is to distance man from god and to deliver him into the hands of the daughter of Night, that is because the affinity between Titan and mankind is expressed primarily in the shape of this dark *eris* which he stirs up in the bright world of Olympus by rebelling against Zeus. The faltering equilibrium of sacrifice itself corresponds to this same tension between opposing terms: as the central act of cult, it links men with gods, but it does so by opposing their respective rôles. Men cannot have more than what was granted them in the trial of strength between the rival divinities. In conforming, in the consumption of meat, to a ritual order which reflects and resumes this first *eris* between the two powers on high, sacrifice takes on the rôle of mediator between gods and men, just like its mythical architect, Prometheus, and in many ways equally ambiguously. It acts as an intermediary between the two tribes. But it allows them to communicate only by recourse to a procedure involving a division which sets them against one another. It unites them, not so that they may meet again in social intercourse (as Prometheus hoped according to the *Theogony* to achieve; or as it was in the Age of Gold, as the *Works and Days* has it), but to reassert their necessary distance.

Another point becomes clear through comparison of the two accounts. The *Works and Days* does not repeat the first episode described in detail in the *Theogony*, the dismemberment and deceitful division of the pieces of sacrificial meat. The text simply refers to it, as one would to something familiar, by alluding to Zeus's anger when 'Prometheus Crookedthought deceived him' (48). Hesiod proceeds at once to the second episode of the myth, the theft of fire. There might then be some question whether the *Works and Days* version of divine rivalry which is the cause of man's present condition has not forgotten all about the alimentary aspect which I have argued to be fundamental to the *Theogony*. I said then that sacrifice, for which Prometheus's trick provides the template, both stimulated and expresses the gulf between gods and men because it implies for each a sharply different kind of nourishment. How then can it be that in the *Works and Days* Hesiod makes no specific reference to this act of division which founded the ritual and not only instituted the Fall but continues to symbolize, in its double character of religious ritual and form of consumption of food, the ambiguity of a humanity linked with the gods in cult but separated from them by the misfortune and misery stemming from the portion of sacrificial meat which men alone may consume?

In point of fact the alimentary aspect of the myth of Prometheus is no less in evidence in the *Works and Days* than in the *Theogony*. The theme of a kind of food reserved for men and intimately linked to their specific kind of existence is central in each account. It is simply that the theme is displaced. And that displacement, which is intelligible if we take account of the difference in perspective between the two texts, illuminates some essential aspects of the myth, in relation to sacrifice. In the *Works and Days* it is the products of the cultivation of the earth, Demeter's corn, cereal-consumption, which have a status analogous to that of the ox which is sacrificed, the portions of meat and meat-eating in the *Theogony*. The interest of the author of the *Erga* (that is, *Agricultural Work*[23]) is in man as cultivator. Man is understood and first defined as 'eater of bread'. The interest of the author of the *Theogony* is in man understood from the perspective of the gods: man is defined as one who consumes that portion of the sacrificial victim offered to the gods which is ritually reserved to him. But in each case human consumption of food is marked by Prometheus's *eris*. Ever since Zeus hid away the food that keeps him alive (*bios*), man can only eat bread if he has paid the price in labour, if he has won it by the sweat of his brow. Cereal food can be had only by dint of rivalry in labour, and it recalls the Titan's spirit of rivalry no less than does the sacrificial animal. Besides, it is not that the grain was simply itself hidden during the struggle with Zeus: that alteration of status, by which food was made to disappear beneath the earth whereas previously anyone could make use of it freely, constitutes Zeus's response to Prometheus's trick in concealing beneath the ox's hide the edible portions of the victim, so as to give them to men (*WD* 47–8). The cultivation of cereals is thus the counterpart of sacrificial ritual, its inverse. For henceforth, thanks to Prometheus's trick, men have the ox's meat to eat; and, thanks to Zeus's will, they will no longer have within easy reach, at their own convenience, the corn they must have to live.

Again, just like the sacrificial victim, cereals are eaten at the end of a negotiation conducted with the gods. The eating of corn establishes between men and gods a form of ritual communication while, in its very essence, it underscores the separation, the distance, the disparity between their statuses. For Hesiod to cultivate the earth for corn is a true cult which the peasant owes to the powers that be (Vernant, 1971: 2.19–20; Detienne, 1963: 34–51). For him, work is a sort of daily office, careful to perform every task at the appropriate moment and respectful of traditional forms. If the farmer's barn is stocked with corn, if he has bread enough and to spare, it is the result of a laborious and strictly regulated life whose punctiliousness has been rewarded ritually by his becoming dear to the Blessed Ones, by his becoming a kinsman, a *philos*, of Demeter (*WD* 300–1, 309: καὶ ἐργαζόμενοι πολὺ φίλτεροι ἀθανάτοισιν; 826–8). But to become a friend, a kinsman of the gods and to escape *limos*, hunger, presupposes that he recognizes and has accepted by his life of labour the harsh fiat of the fields (*WD* 388: πεδίων νόμος) ordained by Zeus, that marks with the passing of the Age of Gold the loss of that time when men grew not old, and dwelt in ignorance of hardship and toil, feasting with the gods. To eat corn implies that if he is to avoid hunger man, poor child of *eris*, can only devote himself heart and soul to grinding work, to *ponos*, that second child of *eris* (*Th.* 226–7: *Eris* gives birth to *Ponos* and *Limos*). To escape the evil born of *eris*, he must pass by its brother.

One final point of similarity. I have argued that, in the logic of the myth, all the edible parts of the sacrificial victim come to men, because these pieces of dead meat, which satisfy man's endlessly demanding hunger and restore his strength that without nourishment would consume away, constitute the proper food of fully mortal creatures, whose life-force is not, like that of the gods, free from any taint of the negative but uncertain, unstable, unsettled, prejudged to death. Now the very expression *bios* (life), used by Hesiod to refer to the ear of corn which is man's specific food, stresses a relationship between cereal-eating and the life-force typical of man which is so close that we might speak of consubstantiality: the fabric of man's life is woven of the same material as the food which sustains it. It is 'because they do not eat bread' that the gods are not mortal; innocent of barley, fed on ambrosia, they have no blood.[24] The *ichōr* in them has no irregularities of flow, no falls in pressure, no ups and downs, which are for men the stigmata, as it were, of their ephemerality, adumbrations of the death which eating can only stave off. In the *Iliad* there is a formula describing human-beings (21. 464–5):

> Men flourish on the ripe wheat of the grainland,
> then in spiritless age they waste and die. (tr. Fitzgerald)

To pick up the expression of the *Odyssey*, barley and wheat, the food of men, make up the *muelos andrōn*, the marrow of men, the very substance of their lifeforce (*Od.* 2.290 and 20.180: ἄλφιτα, μυελὸν ἀνδρῶν).

By means of these relationships and correspondences, which are so clearly marked, the myth of Prometheus connects sacrifice closely with the cultivation of corn. It presents them as phenomena of two different types which are yet interrelated and have the same value. This relationship is made clear by the explicit indications in the text which I have noted; but perhaps even more strikingly in what the text does not say, in its silence. The disconcertingly abrupt allusion in the *Works and Days* to Zeus 'hiding *bios* away' would be absurd, inept, incomprehensible if the text did not presuppose, written as it were tacitly into the myth-frame, a positional symmetry, a complete complementarity, between *bios*-by-corn and the sacrificial victim. The ritual of sacrifice plays the same rôle in relation to meat-eating as the cultivation of corn in relation to the eating of plants. In that case, the existence of an episode linking Prometheus's trickery at the sacrifice to the necessity of working the land in order to obtain the *bios* on which men subsist has no need of any justification other than its mere presence in the text. Moreover, the ox killed and dismembered by Prometheus, at the first sacrifice, is the domestic animal which is closest to man, most nearly integrated into his sphere, above all when yoked to the plough to cut the furrows. As such, it occupies the opposite pole to the wild animals which men hunt like enemies and do not sacrifice. The ox is sacrificed in principle with its own consent, as an animal which, by virtue of its closeness to man, is able if not to represent him directly at least to offer itself as a sort of delegate. The otherness of wild animals in relation to the world of men is revealed particularly in what they eat: they eat one another, without rules or restrictions, and without keeping back any part of the prey they consume for the gods. Their world knows no other laws than appetite. Indifferent to justice and to ritual, the act of eating on the part of animals cannot reflect, either in its modes or in its technique, a divine order on high: it expresses merely the relations of naked violence in that internecine war upon which wild animals are engaged in order to eat (*WD* 276–80).

What the ox is to wild animals, corn in turn is to wild plants. Of all the fruits of the earth, it is the most humanized. Wild plants grow by themselves, wherever conditions are favourable. Wheat can only be harvested at the end of a year of careful attention, rather as one educates children to turn them into men.[25] In the harvest the interplay of human effort and divine blessing produces an equilibrium of regular exchanges. Non-carnivorous animals feed off the plants which nature produces without cultivation, off the wild grass and vegetation which grows outside the fields and orchards worked by the hand of men, beyond the sphere of the domestic (Detienne, 1977: 12–14). Bread is peculiar to man; the mark and guarantor of civilized life, it separates mankind from the animals, and from the gods. Men live on cultivated domestic plants and sacrificed domestic animals. These two complementary aspects of human diet, locating as they do the human race midway between animals and gods, which are two kinds of beings simultaneously distanced from yet near to men, establish the latter in this median status which defines their proper condition (Vidal-Naquet, pp. 80–4 below).

Perhaps it is now easier to understand the full implications of the link established in the myth between the theft of fire and the division of the sacrificial victim on the one hand, and the hiding of grain in the earth on the other. According to the *Theogony*, it is because he is constantly mindful of the trick played on him by Prometheus in allocating the portions in such a way as to bestow on men all the edible parts, that Zeus decides no longer to provide them (*ouk edidou*, 563) with his celestial fire, the lightning, that they had previously enjoyed, and which had been freely available from ash-trees so long as they dwelt and feasted together with the gods.

Why this response? What does it signify? Obviously Zeus wishes first of all to prevent men from making use of the gift which men have received after the first round. By depriving them of fire, he prevents them from cooking the meat, which they could not eat raw. So the primary value of Prometheus's fire is alimentary. The Titan's ruse in hiding fire, concealing it within a fennel-stalk to carry it off to men, is intended to provide them with the means of sacrificial cooking. But to cook meat before eating it is by that very act to point up the contrast with animals, who eat raw flesh. The culinary fire of Hesiod's Prometheus thus has a quite general significance: it represents culture in opposition to primitiveness. In that sense it adumbrates the theme of 'civilizing' fire, 'master of all arts', developed in Aeschylus's *Prometheus Bound* (110–11 and 254). But the adumbration is idiosyncratic, with all the additional complexities and ambiguities demanded in the myth by the median status of humanity.

Prometheus's fire is not that of the gods, is not the fire of heaven, the lightning omnipotent in the hands of Zeus, immortal as its master. It can perish: it is engendered, grows hungry, falters, like all mortal creatures. To produce fire one must have a seed, preserved in the ashes or carried inside a fennel-stalk as was Prometheus's.[26] For it to stay alive, it must be fed; it dies if not fuelled.[27] Fire's unquenchable greed, which causes it to consume all that falls into its path, makes it like a wild beast, as several formulae in Homer already suggest (see p. 76 below, and Graz, 1965: 108–16, 183–93). Or would, if, once in the hands of man whose mastery it ensures, it were not at the same time domesticated. This cultural aspect, which is equal and opposite to the unleashing of a violent, animal nature, is clearly apparent in Prometheus's fire, associated as it is with clever artifice, subtle invention. No mere consequence of a cunning which eluded Zeus's sharp eyes and made it possible for men to have what god denied, it involves a technique for transporting fire, keeping it alight and starting it afresh, an aspect of the knowledge indispensable for human life.

But the *technai* at the disposal of men are quite as ambiguous as the Titan who made them available. Fire is a *dolos*, a tricky ruse, a trap, directed from the outset against Zeus. It allows itself to be taken, but may on occasion turn against men, not merely because the 'might of unwearying fire' is possessed of a power within, which passes human control, but, more precisely still, because this might is somehow mysterious, has something of the supernatural in it: its name is Hephaestus, after the god. And this quality adds a new dimension to what I have just said about the animal world and the acquisition of human civilization.[28] Fire exists in three different modes, animal, human and divine, and it can therefore act, at the very centre of sacrifice, as a mediator. When it is lighted on the altar, it does not merely pass between earth and heaven in its ascent to the gods with the burden of sweetsmelling smoke. It completes Prometheus's act of division because it separates, by the act of cooking, what is simply roasted or boiled, and which belongs to man, from what is entirely consumed away and, together with the animal's life itself, restored to the world beyond. In eating what has not been turned into ashes, but simply cooked — that is, softened and made tender to allow it more easily to be digested by weak human bodies — men retain only, as it were, the sacrificial left-overs, the gristle from a divine feast in which what really matters can only be had by being consumed entirely, caused to disappear utterly from this world below, devoured in the roar of the flames.

In this connection there is an instructive set of parallels and contrasts between sacrificial cooking and the ritual cremation of the dead. According to Walter Burkert (1972b: 66–76), the two practices are actually identical in function and structure, and he stresses the significance of the feast at funerals as well as at sacrifices. But the fact that there were feasts at funerals does not mean that they had the same character as the sacrificial feast. At the celebration of Patroclus's funeral, Achilles makes ready a banquet beside the corpse; they killed bulls, ewes, she-goats and pigs, and cooked the meat 'in Hephaestus's fire'. The victims' blood was collected in jars and poured as a libation all round the body (*Iliad* 23.29ff.). The dead man is thus the recipient of the lives of the animals whose edible parts are to be eaten; and it is with him that the sacrificial ritual which opened the funeral celebrations establishes a kind of contact. But the fire which is lit a little later on the pyre to burn the corpse (*Iliad* 23.110), and with it the animals and the Trojans which are to be burned up entirely (holocaust), is not a fire for cooking at all: the corpse is not *eaten*.[29] The point of burning the body is to open to the dead man's *psyche* the gates of Hades (23.71 and 75—6), to effect its passage from the visible world, where it is detained so long as the body has not received its 'portion of fire', into the invisible world beyond.[30] Here again fire plays the part of mediator, by shooting up and causing the dead man to disappear from human sight (*ap' ophthalmōn*), tearing at his flesh like a wild beast. The words Homer uses for this funerary fire-feast are *nemomai, esthiō, daptō* (23.117, 182, 183). Their alimentary connotations are reinforced by the explicit relation that Achilles sees between the honourable treatment of Patroclus's body which is burned in the fire, and the inverse, insulting, treatment which he means to accord Hector's — to be eaten by the dogs (23.180—3; cf. Graz, 1965: 213—17). There is not simply an opposition between honour and dishonour. For the corpse to be consumed by fire is for it to be volatilized, as a complete human body, and so to pass integrally into the other world. By contrast, to be devoured by the dogs, means, as the text makes explicit, that the flesh will be allowed to 'be torn apart raw by the dogs' (*kusin ōma dasasthai*). If Achilles were to carry out his intention, Hector's body would be dismembered in its natural raw state; which would not merely dishonour him in this world but ensure that he was for ever denied that invisible existence which can only be attained by cremation by fire on the funeral pyre.

There is one further point here. The part of the human corpse which the fire consumes without trace is precisely that part which in the animal victim comes to human beings for them to eat: the flesh, the tendons and the internal organs, all that which is perishable and which putrefies after death.[31] But the funerary fire is not allowed to consume the corpse so completely that one cannot distinguish between human ashes and those of the pyre. While the fire is still alight, it is extinguished with wine, especially where it had burned most fiercely (*Iliad* 23.237 and 250; 24.791). The remains — the bones, or rather the white bones (*ostea leuka*: 23.222, 224, 239, 252; 24.793) clearly discernible among the ashes (*tephrē*: 23.251) in the midst of which, though carbonized, they remained quite visible — were carefully gathered together.[32] They were then enclosed in a double covering of fat (23.243: δίπλακι δημῷ) and put into a *phialē*, an urn, or a small coffer, which was wrapped in cloth and put into a hole in the ground, the underground habitation of the dead man. The cremation of the body in the funeral ceremony, so as totally to consume, to disperse into the invisible world, that part of the body which constituted in sacrifice the portion reserved for men to eat, thus makes possible the separation, the segregation, of the 'white bones' which, again wrapped in fat, constituted in the sacrifice the portion of the gods — the portion which the *mageiros*, by dismembering the animal in such a way as to expose completely the major bones, set on one side right at the beginning to be put on the altar and burned.

The two practices are structured in a similar way, therefore, but their objectives are different, and each constitutes the inverse of the other. In sacrifice, the part that does not decay, the white bones, are cut out from the very first, and offered to the gods in the form of smoke. In cremation, the fire is required to separate the white bones, as it burns, from every particle of perishable flesh encumbering them, so that men may preserve them as the mark — set here on earth, as the guarantor to the kin — of the presence of the dead man in his tomb. In sacrifice, the part that really matters, the true vital life-force of the animal, returns to the gods with the burnt bones, while man eats the half-raw, half-cooked left-overs of the divine feast. In the funerary rite, the object of purifying the corpse by fire of all its corruptible parts, in which life and death are inextricably intertwined, is to restore the body to its essentials, to reduce the remains, through which men will continue to keep in contact with the dead man, to nothing but the white bones.

The *Works and Days* introduces the episode of the theft of fire in an allusive, abrupt and apparently illogical manner. Hesiod explains to Perses that 'the gods have hidden from men the means to life *(bios)*. If they had not you could live without lifting a finger, without work. But Zeus hid your *bios* away when he found himself tricked by Prometheus. Ever since, he has ensured harsh cares for men; he hid the fire from them.' One might be puzzled about the rôle of fire here if we did not already know, from the *Theogony*, that Zeus's refusal of the gift of fire was grounded in Prometheus's trick over the portions of the sacrifice. But the sequence still seems quite incoherent. The fact that Zeus was angry at being duped by the Titan is used to justify the necessity of agricultural work. Furious at allowing himself to be caught out, he hides the means to life by sinking corn into the earth. In the context, 'hiding fire' seems quite gratuitous, without any intelligible relation to what comes before. Unless there were, in archaic Greece, so intimate and evident a relation between hiding *bios* and hiding fire that the one has to go with the other.

Let us note first that in the beginning the same situation held for both fire and grain. In the Age of Gold, before the sundering of gods from men, that is before what happened at Mēkōnē, barley and fire were both directly and openly available to men. The latter used them as 'natural' goods bestowed upon them, with no need to hunt for them, the objects neither of care nor quest. For the gods, 'hiding' grain and fire means, in a material sense, that corn has first to be buried, hidden in the ground in the form of seed so as to germinate and then ripen above ground.[33] And that fire has to be buried, hidden in the ashes or in a fennel-stalk, in the form of seed, to shoot up and then dance on the hearth. Morally and metaphysically, it means that these two kinds of good hitherto naturally at the free disposition of men must henceforth be gotten, striven after, paid for; will be accessible only through the integument of evils in which they are shut; through grinding effort, toil, unceasing attention and reflection. Such evils, the necessary counterpart of blessings formerly dispensed with an open hand, turn barley and fire into the victories of human civilization rather than the natural products they once were.

Again, corn and more generally all cultivated plants were opposed by the Greeks to wild plants as the cooked against the raw (Detienne, 1977: 11—14). There are two aspects of this cooking. Species of plants which lend themselves to being cultivated are those in which the process of internal 'cooking' goes further than is the case with the wild species, where the raw humours predominate. In addition, the intervention of man, in opening and turning the soil so that the sun may penetrate, allows a still further improved and elaborate cooking of domesticated plants. And to this double cooking, the one natural, the other achieved by cultivation, we may add a third, which brings the process to completion: by transmuting flour into bread and pancake, oven-cookery makes corn fully digestible. It cuts the last link with nature and the raw, a link which made flour a hybrid, a muddle, neither raw nor cooked, neither wild nor civilized. Once out of the oven, bread has become something quite different: it is now *sitos*, human food, just as, once roast or boiled, a lump of raw, bloody meat is transmuted into a civilized dish.[34]

Now in the Age of Gold earth spontaneously bestowed on men products which possessed naturally all the characteristics and qualities of cultivated plants. These products grew already cooked, as though the soil, albeit unworked, had been cultivated and turned by the plough. They were moreover eatable at once; they did not have to be transmuted and humanized by the action of fire in cooking. The Age of Gold has nothing to do with the opposition between savagery and civilization: it cancels their difference by presenting civilized food as the spontaneous product of nature, which man once upon a time found without any bother, already cultivated, harvested, cooked and ready for eating. In this respect, the corn-harvests of the Age of Gold are like the meat-harvests of the blessed Ethiopians, which, according to Herodotus, they found close by the Table of the Sun: each morning, scattered over the plain which had produced them unaided overnight, the cuts of meat lay waiting, all carved, served-out and ready-boiled, for their patrons to come and dine. They just *grew* there cooked (Herod. 3.18).

The close of the Age of Gold means three things simultaneously: the necessity of sacrificial fire to cook meat, the necessity of agricultural labour to cook corn, the necessity of cooking-fire to render corn fit to eat. The anger of Zeus, to make men pay for the meat they obtained from Prometheus, hides both fire and corn from them in the selfsame gesture. If that is all that had taken place at Mēkōnē, men would not have been able, from that moment, to eat the fruit, now raw, of domesticated plants, any more than they would have been able, in the version of the *Theogony*, to eat uncooked the flesh of domesticated animals.

Prometheus's trickery did not simply establish, for all time, the rules for the division of the sacrificial victim. It brought in its train, no less inevitably, the constraint of labour, of *ponos*. Henceforth men, that they may eat as men eat, are doomed to the cultivation of corn as they are doomed to cook in the sacrifice.

5. Land and sacrifice in the Odyssey: a study of religious and mythical meanings

Pierre Vidal-Naquet (1970, 1976)

To J.-P.Darmon

This is an essay about land. Perhaps paradoxically, I begin with some details taken not from Homer, but from Hesiod. Contrary to common opinion, both the *Theogony* and the *Works and Days* can be used to elucidate, not merely works composed after them, but also those which antedate them or which are more or less contemporary with them — as is perhaps the case with the *Odyssey*.

I believe that the 'myth of the races' and the myth of Pandora in the *Works and Days*, and the myth of Prometheus in that poem and in the *Theogony*, justify a definition of the human condition which could be termed both anthropological and normative, both exclusive and inclusive. The exclusion is twofold. Hesiodic man is the man of the age of iron; which means in the first place that he is *not* the man of the age of gold — the mythical time when men 'lived like gods', knowing neither old age nor true death: 'They had all good things, and the grain-giving earth unforced bore them fruit abundantly and without stint. They pastured their lands (ἔργ' ἐνέμοντο) in ease and peace, with many good things' (*WD* 112—19).[1] The distinction between the age of gold and our own which I wish to study here — there are others — is that of work versus non-work (agricultural work, of course).[2] As compared with the age of iron, the age of gold — the age of Cronus — is an absolute model; it is a condition which the other other ages can never hope to attain. The lot of the race of the age of gold during their lives is enjoyed by the race of heroes, or at least by some of them, after death: Zeus places them 'apart from men' (δίχ' ἀνθρώπων), and apart from the gods, 'under the rule of Cronus', 'at the ends of the earth'. 'And they dwell untouched by sorrow in the islands of the Blessed along the shore of the deep swirling Ocean, happy heroes for whom the grain-giving earth bears honey-sweet fruit flourishing thrice a year.'[3] The age of gold in 'time' is succeeded here by an age of gold in 'space', in the islands of the Blessed, which are characterized also by the richness of the earth.

Elsewhere, in the myth of Pandora,[4] Hesiod summarizes in advance as it were the lesson of the myth of the races: 'Before this the tribes of men lived on earth remote and free from ills and hard toil (χαλεποῖο

80

πόνοιο) and heavy sicknesses which bring the *Kēres* upon men: for in misery men grow old quickly' (*WD* 90–3).[5]

To have been excluded from the age of gold means that man is not a god.[6] But he is not an animal either; and the second exclusion bars him from *allēlophagia*, cannibalism: 'For the Son of Cronus has ordained this law for men, that fishes and beasts and winged birds should devour one another, for Right (*dikē*) is not in them' (*WD* 276–8). The practice of *dikē* is what enables man to escape from the animal state: man is the creature which does not eat its fellows.

The inclusions are closely related — simultaneously inverse and complementary — to the exclusions. The *Works and Days* itself is about the working of arable land and all that is implied by it — the planting of trees and the rearing of animals, especially for ploughing. *Dikē* is a means of regaining — perhaps not the age of gold, for men are obliged to labour — but at least prosperity and fruitfulness in humans, land and flocks: 'The earth gives them (i.e. those who practise *dikē*) a life of plenty, and on the mountains the oak bears acorns on high, and in the midst, bees. Their fleecy sheep are laden with wool; their women bear children resembling their fathers. They flourish continually with good things; and do not travel on ships, for the grain-giving earth bears them fruit' (*WD* 232–7).[7]

This human work is linked in turn to the possession (thanks to Prometheus) of fire for cooking, that fire which had previously been concealed by Zeus (*WD* 47–50; see Vernant, pp. 74–9 above). In revenge for the theft of fire, Hephaestus made at Zeus's command Pandora, who is both earth and woman (*WD* 59–105).[8] The hints of the *Works and Days* are filled out by the *Theogony*. The quarrel between gods and men at Mekone has two episodes which are carefully paralleled.[9] There is first the primordial sacrifice of an ox and its unequal division, the gods receiving the smoke and men the flesh: which results in the confiscation of fire by Zeus and its theft by Prometheus. Secondly, men are given the ambiguous gift of woman, to make up for the gods' acceptance of the state of affairs brought about by Prometheus. Arable land, cooking, sacrifice, sexual and family life within the *oikos* — even, at one extreme, political life — form a complex, no element of which can be separated from the others. These are the terms which define man's estate, in between the age of gold and *allēlophagia*, cannibalism.[10]

The limits we find marked out here by Hesiod, with their characteristic features (which are also features of the crisis of his period) are repeatedly employed throughout the subsequent history of Greek thought. From the end of the sixth century BC in particular, these patterns were taken up in the violent political disputes which divided the

Greek world and led theorists to adopt contrasting 'positive' or 'negative' views of primitive man; the age of gold jostles against the theme of the misery of primeval man. One might be tempted — and some scholars have not resisted the temptation — to trace these disputes back to the time of Hesiod, and portray Hesiod as himself an opponent of progress.[11] It is not perceptibly more plausible to make him both a supporter of 'chronological primitivism' (because he starts with an age of gold) and an opponent of 'cultural primitivism' (in that he contrasts civilization with cannibalism), as does one useful anthology (Lovejoy and Boas, 1935: 35). For these two positions are in fact one.

It is not my intention to discuss this post-Hesiodic literature here.[12] I note simply, for reasons which will shortly become clear, that Hesiod's age of gold, the age of Cronus, the 'vegetarian' age before cooking and before sacrifice, which is described for us in so many texts,[13] is also the period of cannibalism and human sacrifice, in at least part of the tradition. Some of the texts which make this association between opposites may seem very late.[14] But we should not forget that as early as the fourth century BC the Cynics developed a theory of a 'natural' way of life which both condemned the eating of dead flesh and cooked food, and championed raw food, cannibalism and even incest, the opposite *par excellence* of culture.[15] And it would be wrong to see this as merely a view held by theorists: Euripides's *Bacchae* oscillates between the atmosphere of paradise described by the messenger early on in his speech, and the orgy of flesh-eating which culminates in the quasi-incestuous murder of Pentheus by his mother (*Bacchae* 677—768, 1043—147). Hesiod's Cronus is also a god who eats his own children (*Th.* 459—67).[16] From this perspective, it is Plato who is 'theorizing', when in the *Politicus* he chooses to define the age of Cronus as the time when cannibalism was unknown — a choice which happens to be the same as that made by Hesiod in his version of the myth of the races.[17]

If we begin from the other end, we find agriculture intimately linked with cooking, as for example in the Hippocratic treatise *On Ancient Medicine*, 3 (ed. Festugière), where it is shown that the cultivation of cereals, which replaced the eating of raw foods, is founded upon a form of food which has to be cooked. An association between agriculture, family life and the origin of civilization similar to that implied by Hesiod also occurs in the Athenian myths about Cecrops, who, guided by Bouzyges ('Ox-team Man'),[18] invented agriculture, and invented also the monogamous patriarchal family (Pembroke, 1967: 26—7, 29—32; and see pp. 215—28 below). The purpose of this essay is to see whether such associations exist already in Homer.

When Odysseus realizes that he is at last on Ithaca, his first action is to 'kiss the grain-giving earth in a greeting to his native land': χαίρων ᾗ γαίῃ, κύσε δὲ ζείδωρον ἄρουραν (*Odyssey* 13.354).[19] Now this is not merely the act of a man returning to his native land: it contains a fundamental point which deserves close analysis.

In talking about the *Odyssey*, we have to make further distinctions: not between the compositions of different bards detected by 'analytic' critics in the light of criteria that differ with every scholar and produce results at once predictably divergent and fatally untestable; but between units which have a significance in the poem as we have it. To put it crudely, we cannot discuss Cyclops or Calypso in the same manner as we discuss Nestor or Telemachus. In effect, as has often been recognized,[20] the *Odyssey* contrasts a world we may term 'real', essentially the world of Ithaca, but also Sparta and Pylos to which Telemachus goes, with a mythical world which is roughly coterminous with that of the stories in Alcinous's palace (Segal, 1962: 17). Similarly, Shakespeare's *Tempest* contrasts Naples and Milan on one hand with Prospero's magic island on the other (Marienstras, 1965: 899–917). Odysseus enters this mythical world after his stay with the Cicones, a perfectly real Thracian people, known still to Herodotus (7.58, 108, 110), in whose territory he eats, fights and plunders just as he might have done at Troy; and after a ten-day storm[21] which he encounters while rounding Cape Malea, the last 'real' place on his travels before he gets back to Ithaca.[22]

Proof that this contrast is indeed relevant is supplied by the text itself. Telemachus's route never crosses that of Odysseus. There are two points of contact only between the two worlds. One is plainly magical: Menelaus tells Odysseus's son how he was informed by the magician Proteus, in Egypt, the land of wonders, that Odysseus was detained on Calypso's island (4.555–8; 17.138–44).[23] The other is the land of the Phaeacians, those professional seamen who have been shown to occupy a strategic place at the junction of the two worlds (Segal, 1962).[24] I need hardly press the point. Odysseus's travels have nothing to do with 'geography'; and there is more geographical truth in the 'untrue' stories he tells Eumaeus and Penelope (14.191–359; 19.164–202)[25] than in all the stories in Alcinous's palace.[26] Crete, Egypt and Epirus are real enough.

For Odysseus to leave this fantasy world means to leave a world that is not the world of men, a world which is by turns super-human and sub-human, a world in which he is offered divinity by Calypso but also threatened by Circe with reduction to the condition of an animal. And he must leave it to return to the world of normality. The *Odyssey* as a whole is in one sense the story of Odysseus's return to normality, of his deliberate acceptance of the human condition.[27]

There is therefore no paradox in saying that, from the Lotus-Eaters to Calypso by way of the land of the Cyclopes and the Underworld, Odysseus meets with no creature which is strictly human. There is of course sometimes room for doubt: the Laestrygones, for example, have an agora, the mark of political life; but physically they are not as men are but giants (10.114, 120). Circe causes us to wonder whether we are dealing with a woman or a goddess: but finally, just as with Calypso, the humanity is merely in the outward form, in the voice. She is in truth δεινὴ θεὸς αὐδήεσσα, the 'terrible goddess with a human voice' (10.136; 11.8; 12.150, 449; cf. 10.228). Twice Odysseus asks himself what 'eaters of bread' he has landed among — that is, what men. But in each case the point is that he is not among 'bread-eaters' but among the Lotus-Eaters and the Laestrygones (9.89; 10.101).[28]

There follows from this a signal implication, that the 'stories' rigorously exclude anything to do with working the land, or with arable land itself insofar as it is worked.[29] The Thrace of the Cicones is the last cultivated land Odysseus encounters: there he eats mutton and drinks wine; and there he obtains the wine he later offers the Cyclops (9.45ff., 161–5, 197–211).[30] Euripides's Odysseus, when he lands in an unknown land, asks Silenus, 'Where are the walls and the city towers?' The answer comes: 'Stranger, this is no city. No man dwells here' (Cyclops 115–16).[31] Here it is fortifications which are the symbol of the presence of civilized humanity, or indeed of humanity at all. But Homer's Odysseus looks for cultivated fields, for the sign of human labour.[32] When the Achaeans reach Circe's island, they search in vain for the erga brotōn, the 'works of men', that is, for crops. But all they see is scrub and forest, where stag-hunts can be organized (10.147, 150, 157–63, 197, 251). In the land of the Laestrygones, the sight of smoke might be taken as evidence of domestic hearths and the presence of human-beings (10.99).[33] But there is 'no trace either of the work of oxen or of the work of men': ἔνθα μὲν οὔτε βοῶν οὔτ' ἀνδρῶν φαίνετο ἔργα (10.98). The Sirens live in a meadow, as do the gods elsewhere (12.159; cf. Homeric Hymn to Hermes 72; Euripides, Hippolytus 73–4). Although Calypso's island is wooded and even possesses a vine, this is never said to be cultivated (5.63–74).

There is one specifically human tree present in the world of the 'stories': the olive, the tree of whose wood Odysseus built his bed, the fixed point of his home (23.183–204). And in fact the olive is on a number of occasions the means of Odysseus's escape from danger, in several different forms. It provides the stake with which he bores through the Cyclops's eye; and the handle of the axe with which he builds his boat (9.319–20; 5.234–6; cf. Segal, 1962: 45, 62, 63). And although it is true that when he is with Aeolus, Circe or Calypso,

Odysseus has plenty to eat, and that the poet playfully draws attention to the vast difference between the gods' meals and those of men (5.196–9), we are never told where it comes from or who produced it.

A second exclusion is entailed by this exclusion of cultivated land: that of the sacrificial meal, which we saw from Hesiod to be so intimately related to the first. One could almost, in a sense, extend to the entire world of the stories the remark Hermes jokingly makes to Calypso when he arrives on her island: 'Who would choose to cross this waste of salt-water? There is not in these parts a single city of mortal men to offer rich hecatombs to the gods' (5.100–2). But only in a sense. For the sacrifice which Odysseus offers to the dead in accordance with Circe's instructions and with lambs she has provided is performed in a trench, and is intended to provide blood for the feeding of the dead (10.516–40, 571–2; 11.26–47) – it is the opposite of a sacrificial meal, whose purpose is to feed the living. And the same is true of the victims which Odysseus promises the dead and Teiresias that he will offer on his return: a barren cow and a black ram (10.521–5; 11. 29–33).

In the land of the Cyclopes, Odysseus's companions offer sacrifice (9.231: ἐθύσαμεν), as Polyphemus himself does not. But it is not a blood-sacrifice, for they are living on cheese (9.232; see below, p. 88). And the sacrifice they offer on the island just across from that of the Cyclopes – which is abnormal because the victims are the sheep belonging to Polyphemus, animals not reared by man – is rejected by Zeus (9.551–5): even when a human community does sacrifice in non-human territory, the sacrifice is improper.

We should now go back over Odysseus's journey and examine more or less in sequence the several types of non-human creature he meets with. I take it for granted that Scylla, and the inhabitants of the Underworld, are not human: Achilles has made the point so that we shall not forget (11.488–91). Likewise, the Lotus-Eaters are not bread-eaters: they eat flowers, and the food they offer Odysseus's companions deprives them of an essential facet of their humanity, memory (9.84, 94–7). Except during the encounter with Scylla (12.227), it is Odysseus who constantly remembers in the poem, the true man who stands out from his forgetful companions.

Much more difficult are the problems presented by the Cyclops episode. For here the mythical aspects with which I am here concerned are conflated with a quasi-ethnographical description of pastoral peoples (non-humanity may be just a different sort of humanity: savages)[34] and with an overt, quite realistic reference to colonization. If these men had been sailors 'they would have made their island a well-built place. The land is not bad; it would bear crops in each season. By the shores of the grey sea are soft, well-watered meadows, where vines would never wither, and there would be rich harvests every year, so rich is the soil under the surface' (9.130—5). This vision remains unfulfilled. The land of the Cyclopes is divided, it will be remembered, into two different areas. One is the 'small island', which is utterly wild and where hunting is quite unknown. There Odysseus's companions find memorable sport (9.116—24, 131—5). The other is the land of the Cyclopean shepherds. Such a division implies a hierarchy, cultivators—hunters—shepherds; and it may be relevant to note that the same series recurs later in Aristotle (*Politics* 1.8, 1256a30—40). But the Cyclopes are not merely barbarous herdsmen who lack political institutions and are ignorant of planting and ploughing (9.108—15). Their land is very close to Hesiod's age of gold: 'They do not plant or plough, but the earth provides them with all things: grain, vines and wine from heavy clusters of grapes, which Zeus's rain swells for them' (9.109—11; cf. 123—4). Although they have sheep, they have no true draught-animals: there are 'no herds or ploughs' on the island (9.122). So it is, even if we may suspect that the vintages of the golden age lacked breeding (9.111, 357—9).

But the real point is that the counterpart of the age of gold is cannibalism.[35] The details are so curious that it is impossible to believe that they are not intentional. Polyphemus brings in wood to make a fire for supper. But he does not use it: he is not an eater of bread, and even the humans he eats he does not cook as we might expect. He devours them raw, like a lion: 'entrails, flesh, bones, marrow — he left nothing' (9. 190—2, 234, 292—3).[36] Equally, he performs none of the actions characteristic of a sacrificial meal, for example the setting aside for the gods of the bones; and in any case the relations of these golden-age cannibals with the gods are fundamentally ambiguous. Homer stresses both that the Cyclopes trust in the gods (πεποιθότες ἀθανάτοισιν: 9.107) — which allows them not to plough or to sow; and Odysseus will later have cause to rue the kinship of Polyphemus and Poseidon (1.68— 73), and that Polyphemus treats Odysseus's appeal in the name of Zeus Xenios [who protects strangers and guests] with total indifference: 'The Cyclopes have no regard for Zeus who bears the aegis, nor for the blessed gods' (9.275—6). This detail bears a little further attention. The author of the *Iliad* seems to know of good Cyclopes, the *Abioi* ('without-food'), who milk mares and live on the milk, and are 'the most just of men' (*Iliad* 13.5—6). These men, now called *Gabioi*, reappear as Scythians in the *Prometheus Unbound* of Aeschylus (frg. 196 Nauck[2] = 329 Mette; see Lovejoy and Boas, 1935: 35).[37] They too are 'the most just of men and the most generous to strangers. They possess neither the plough nor the hoe, which break the earth and score the plough-land. Their furrows seed themselves (αὐτόσποροι γύαι) and give men food which never fails.' Later, Homer's literary heirs elaborated the theme of the Cyclopes' way of life as part of the picture of the 'noble savage'.[38] But the inheritance was not solely literary. When Ephorus (*FGrH* 70 F 42) contrasted two types of Scythians — actually referring to Homer's *Abioi* — one of them cannibal, the other vegetarian (τοὺς δὲ καὶ τῶν ἄλλων ζῴων ἀπέχεσθαι: 'they reject (all) living things'),[39] he was rationalizing and locating geographically a mythical opposition which is also an equivalent. The vegetarian is no less inhuman than the cannibal.[40]

The island of Aeolus offers us another type of the non-human which is no less classic. The details are worth lingering upon for a moment. It is a 'floating island' with bronze walls. There is naturally no cultivated land, although there is a *polis*, in perpetual banquet. But the feast is not a sacrificial one, and the bull in whose hide the winds are imprisoned is not offered to the gods (10.3—19). But it is of course incest which is the oddest thing about Aeolus's island: there is no exchange of women. The six daughters of Aeolus and his wife are married to their brothers (10.6—7). This is a closed world, where one banquets by day and sleeps at night (10.10—12). It is not a human *oikos*.

The Laestrygones look in some ways like another version of the Cyclopes, though the metaphor here is not hunting but fishing — they harpoon the Greeks like tuna-fish and then eat them (10.115—16, 121—4). On Circe's island, nature presents itself at first as a hunting-park. Odysseus kills an enormous stag (10.168: δεινοῖο πελώρου; 10.171: μέγα θηρίον; cf. 180; on Circe, see Segal, 1962: 419—42). Non-humanity is here revealed in two forms, that of divinity and that of bestiality. The latter is itself twofold: Circe's victims are changed into wild animals, lions and wolves, which nevertheless behave like domestic dogs (10.212—19). Circe has a drug added to the bread[41] served to Odysseus's companions, which turns them into pigs, although they retain their memory (10.239—43). Odysseus escapes this fate by taking with him a plant, the famous *moly*, which itself perfectly symbolizes the theme of reversal: 'its root is black, its flower the colour of milk' (10.304).[42] And whereas Odysseus's companions regain their shape, the men who had been turned into wild animals do not. The episode thus contains a clear hierarchy: men—domestic animals—wild animals. This last category has no connection with humanity and cannot be restored to it even by magical means.[43]

The Cimmerians, whose land borders on the country of the dead, are non-human, in spite of possessing a *dēmos* and a *polis*, in that they never behold the sun, just like the dead (11.14—19). The Sirens are a fiercer version of the Lotus-Eaters. To surrender to their seduction means never to return home (12.41–5); but, like the Lotus-Eaters, they can be foiled. These two of Odysseus's passages alone does he endure without harm. But if the Cyclops is to humanity what the raw is to the cooked, the Sirens belong to the rotten: their victims' corpses rot un-eaten in the meadow (12.45–6).

The episode of the herds of the Sun, heralded in advance at the beginning of the poem (1.8–9), merits closer attention. The cattle and sheep are immortal, that is, they do not share the condition of the animals humans use for farm-work and for sacrifice. Just as Calypso and Circe appear to be human, and just as the dead can pass as beings of flesh and blood at first sight, the herds of the Sun appear domestic: they are protected only by the prohibition against sacrificing them. While Odysseus and his companions have bread and wine, they respect the interdict (12.327–9), but with their supplies exhausted they must make a choice, between wild nature — to hunt and fish (the legitimate alternative, which Odysseus chooses: 12.330–2) — and the forbidden herds, which involves the sacrifice, the classification as 'domestic', of animals which they have to capture, to bring in from the wild. This latter is the choice of Odysseus's companions (12.343–65). We should note how Homer emphasizes the sacrificers' lack of the essential requisites for proper sacrifice: the barley-corns (*oulai* or *oulochutai*) for sprinkling on the animal before its throat is cut are replaced by oak-leaves (12.357–8),[44] the 'natural' substituted for the 'cultural'; the wine for the libations is likewise replaced by water (12.362–3).[45] The manner in which they perform the sacrifice itself also renders it an anti-sacrifice; and later, the flesh, both raw and cooked, begins to groan (12.395–6). But of course: these herds are immortal; man's share of the sacrifice is the meat of the dead animal, the remainder passing to the gods. The herds of the Sun are utterly unsuitable for sacrifice; and the companions of Odysseus do not escape with their sacrilege.[46]

The last stage of the hero's travels in the land of myth — he is now quite alone — sees him on Calypso's island, the navel of the sea (1.50). He is here offered the possibility of becoming immortal, by marrying the goddess (5.135–6; 23.335–6). Now the point of this, as I have said (p. 85), is that on Calypso's island the normal means of communication between men and gods — sacrifice — is unknown. Calypso can indeed dream of a code-breaking union; but she herself recalls that earlier attempts ended disastrously, Eōs (Dawn) and the hunter Orion and Demeter and the farmer Iasion (5.121–8). And although the ancient allegorists understood the island as a symbol of the body, of the matter from which man's soul must free itself (Buffière, 1956: 461–4), Homer's text scarcely supports such a reading. When he quits Calypso,

Odysseus is deliberately choosing the human against all that is not-human (Segal, 1962: 20).

By contrast to this world whose features I have just sketched, Ithaca, Pylos and Sparta belong undoubtedly to the 'grain-giving earth'.[47] Although Ithaca, the 'island of goats', is unable to support horses like Sparta (4.605—6), it is nevertheless a grain-producing land, and a land where the vine grows: 'It has grain and wine in quantity beyond telling, rain in all seasons and heavy dews, a good land for goats . . . a land good for cattle.'[48] As a famous, and archaizing, passage affirms, it is for the king that 'the dark earth bears wheat and barley, and the trees are heavy with fruit; the flocks bear without fail; the friendly sea brings forth fish under his good rule, and the people thrive under him' (19. 111—14).[49] Odysseus's wheat, barley, wine and livestock are no less than Penelope the prize in his dispute with the suitors. To return to Ithaca is thus to return to a land of grain. But Ithaca is not sufficiently land-locked: it is not here that Odysseus will one day meet death 'far from the sea'; he will have to go beyond Ithaca, pressing on inland until men mistake an oar for a winnowing-shovel (11.127—8; 23.274—5). And there a threefold sacrifice to Poseidon will call a halt to his wanderings; stability will prevail over movement.

Nor do I need to stress that Pylos and Sparta are corn-raising and stock-breeding countries (3.495; 4.41, 602—4, etc.). But this fact does not make the three different places all of a kind. Pylos is the land of perpetual sacrifice, the model of a religious country: Nestor is sacrificing to Poseidon when Telemachus makes his appearance — all the ritual details are mentioned (3.5—9); and a little later it is Athena's turn (3. 380—4, 418—63).[50] At Sparta, things are a little different, and we find features belonging to the world of myth. Menelaus's palace is different from Odysseus's but like that of Alcinous; with its decoration of ivory and amber, it is a residence worthy of Zeus (compare 4.71—5 and 7. 86—90). At Sparta, as on Scheria, there are objects made by Hephaestus (4.615—19; 15.113—19; 7.91—4). Sacrifice at Sparta is retrospective: Menelaus mentions a hecatomb he ought to have made during the journey when he learned that Odysseus was on Calypso's island, which thus connects with the world of myth (4.352—3, 472—4, 477—9, 581—3). Again, unlike Odysseus, Menelaus's future destiny is not death, but that other golden age, the Elysian fields (4.561—9).[51] And there is another respect in which Pylos and Sparta contrast with Ithaca: they are orderly kingdoms, where the sovereign, and his wife, are present; where the treasure-house is not looted; where the ordinary rules of social life are respected. When Telemachus arrives at Sparta, Menelaus is celebrating the marriage of his son (4.3—14). By contrast, on Ithaca we find a society in crisis: the three generations of the royal family are represented by an old man (whose exclusion from the throne becomes slightly mysterious when we compare him with Nestor), a woman, and an adolescent youth who is portrayed as slightly backward (1.296—7; cf. Finley, 1977: 76).[52] A society upsidedown, a society in a crisis symbolized by the revolt of the *kouroi* [the young aristocrats], waiting for the re-establishment of order.

Sacrifice here turns out to be both the sign of the crisis and the means of its resolution. Who makes sacrifice on Ithaca? If our sole criterion is the use of the verbs *hiereuō* and *spendō* and related words, the answer is everyone — both the suitors and Odysseus and his followers.[53] But if we examine the texts in which sacrifice is specifically addressed to the gods, we find that the suitors do not sacrifice. More precisely, one of them does suggest a libation to the gods: but this is Amphinomus, the one suitor whom Odysseus attempts to exclude from the coming massacre.[54] Antinous suggests a sacrifice to Apollo according to the rules, with the thighs burnt; but he is unable to fulfil his promise (21.265—8).[55] By contrast, on Odysseus's side, sacrifice either retrospective or immediate, is perpetual; Eumaeus's piety is stressed. 'The swineherd did not forget the immortals; he had a good heart' (14.420—1).[56] The comparison certainly suggests that we have to allow that *hiereuō* sometimes has a meaning which is not specifically religious.[57] More importantly, sacrifice is a double criterion in the *Odyssey*: of humanity, between humans and non-humans; and of social and moral values, between human-beings.

But there is in the human world of Ithaca at least one place directly connected with the world of the myths — the complex consisting of the harbour of Phorcys, named after Cyclops's own grandfather (1.71—2; 13.96—7; cf. Segal, 1962: 48), and the cave sacred to the Nymphs, the divinities of nature and of water. This cave has two entrances, one for gods, the other for mortals (13.109—12); and appropriately enough, just near it is a sacred olive-tree, under which Athena speaks to Odysseus (13.122, 372). And it is here that the Phaeacians leave Odysseus and his treasures.

Charles Segal (1962: 17) has observed that the Phaeacians are 'between the two worlds': they are placed at the intersection of the world of the tales and the 'real' world; and their main function in the poem is to transport Odysseus from the one to the other.[58] When Odysseus comes ashore in Phaeacia, naked, after completing, or almost completing, his return journey home 'without the help of gods or mortal men' (5.32),[59] he takes shelter under an olive-tree. But this olive-tree is quite remarkable: it is double, ὁ μὲν φυλίης, ὁ δ' ἐλαίης, both wild and grafted, oleaster and olive (5.477).⁶⁰ The very land of Scheria is double, comparable at once both with Ithaca, Pylos and Sparta and with the lands of the stories. Phaeacia contains all the characteristic elements of a Greek settlement in the age of colonization, physically framed as it is by the 'shadowy peaks' which can be seen from afar (5.279—80). It has arable land distributed by a founder (ἐδάσσαι ἀρούρας: 6.10).⁶¹ Its fields are beyond doubt the 'works of men': ἀγροὺς ... καὶ ἔργ᾽ ἀνθρώπων, 'fields and human tillage' (6.259) — exactly what Odysseus has looked for in vain in all his travels. It has a fortified citadel, distinct from the fields: *polis kai gaia* (6.177, 191; also 6.3: δῆμόν τε πόλιν τε). The country has in abundance wine, oil and corn; Alcinous has a flourishing vineyard of his own (6.77—8, 79, 215, 259, 293; cf. 7.122—6). In sum, the Phaeacians are men just like other men: they 'know the cities and rich fields of all men' (8.560—1). When Odysseus lands in Phaeacia, he is returning to humanity. As he draws near to Nausicaä, he is likened to a lion which descends from the hills and kills livestock or deer; but when he leaves Phaeacia to return to Ithaca, he is likened to a tired ploughman returning home (6.130—3; 13.31—5).

But at the same time, Phaeacia is sharply contrasted with Ithaca. There are no seasons in the magic garden of Alcinous (7.113—32).⁶² The West wind blows there perpetually; the vine bears blossom, unripe and ripened grapes all simultaneously. In effect, it is no ordinary orchard, but a golden-age land in the heart of Phaeacia. By contrast, Laërtes's garden is quite normal: 'each vine had its own time to be harvested, and the clusters of grapes were of every colour, as the seasons of Zeus caused them to change' (24.342—4; cf. Segal, 1962: 47).⁶³ On the one hand, the age of Cronus; on the other, the age of Zeus.⁶⁴ The contrast can be developed. The dogs guarding Alcinous's house, the creations of Hephaestus in gold and silver, are immortal, and naturally possess eternal youth; but everyone remembers the story of the dog Argo, whose life is exactly commensurate with the period of Odysseus's absence (7.91—4; 17.290—327).⁶⁵

And what of sacrifice here? They are performed in Phaeacia much as they are at Pylos or on Ithaca. 'We shall offer choice victims to the gods', declares Alcinous (7.191; cf. 7.180—1). Before Odysseus's departure an ox is sacrificed in the proper manner (13.24—7; cf. 50—6, libations to Zeus). And when the Phaeacians are threatened with destruction by Poseidon and Zeus combined, their fate turns on the result of the sacrifice which Alcinous decides to offer them: 'and they prepared the bulls' (ἐτοιμάσσαντο δὲ ταύρους: 13.184). This is the last act by the Phaeacians in the *Odyssey*, and we never discover their fate — the only case of a fate left in the balance. And yet, even here, the Phaeacians are not as other men. Alcinous can say: 'When we sacrifice

Pierre Vidal-Naquet

our magnificent hecatombs to the gods, they come and sit by us and eat with us' (7.201—3).[66] That sort of sharing has nothing in common with normal sacrifice which, in contrast, separates men from the gods. The Phaeacians are of course men: Alcinous and Odysseus remind each other of their mortality (7.196—8; 13.59—62), and the Phaeacians' last appearance in the poem clearly shows them facing the precariousness of the human condition. But they are also *ankhitheoi*, 'relatives of the gods' — not merely a polite epithet, for Homer uses it twice only, and both times of them (5.35; 19.279). They were once neighbours of the Cyclopes and suffered from their attacks until Nausithoös set them 'apart from men who eat bread' (ἑκὰς ἀνδρῶν ἀλφηστάων: 6.4—8). And in one sense they are indeed the complete reverse of the Cyclopes (Segal, 1962: 33): all their human virtues, the practice of hospitality,[67] piety, the arts of feasting and gift-giving, are the inverse of Cyclopean barbarism. Moreover, the present disjuncture and previous proximity of the Phaeacians and the Cyclopes is a sign of a more subtle relation: 'We are intimates [of the gods]', says Alcinous, 'like the Cyclopes and the savage tribes of the Giants' (ὥς περ Κύκλωπές τε καὶ ἄγρια φῦλα Γιγάντων: 7.205—6) — those same Giants whom the Laestrygones are said to resemble (10.120). Proximity and kinship: surely an invitation to search in Phaeacia for both the pattern of the world of fantasy and its reverse.

After landing in Alcinous's country, Odysseus meets a girl washing clothes, who invites him to come and meet her father and mother (7.290—307). He had met another girl, elsewhere, drawing water from a spring, who gave him a similar invitation; but she was the daughter of the king of the Laestrygones. Both in the cannibal and in the hospitable kingdom Odysseus meets the queen before he meets the king (10.105—15; 7.139—54; cf. 7.53—5). And is Nausicaä a girl or a goddess? A cliché, of course; but we must realize that she is a girl who looks like a goddess; while Circe and Calypso were goddesses who looked like girls (6.16, 66—7, 102—9; 7.291; 8.457). Alcinous, and very discreetly Nausicaä herself, entertain a marriage to Odysseus, parallel to these goddesses' more energetically prosecuted plans. The seductive Sirens sing like bards of the Trojan war (12.184—91), just like Demodocus at the court of Alcinous, who brings tears to Odysseus's eyes (8.499—531). The first represent the perilous, Demodocus the positive, aspect of poetry (Detienne, 1967).

It will no doubt be objected that there is a limit to the number of utterly different situations a man like Odysseus can encounter. That is true; but there is one coincidence which is perhaps more than usually curious. Before meeting with his eventual carriers, the Phaeacians, Odysseus encounters another, who brought him to the neighbourhood of Ithaca — Aeolus, master of the winds (10.21), who spends his time, like the Phaeacians, in feasting. In the course of both 'returns' Odysseus falls asleep; disastrous, after his sojourn with Aeolus, fortunate after Scheria (10.23—55; 13.78—92; cf. Segal, 1967: 324—9). Now it will be recalled that Aeolus's family practise incest; and, if we are to accept the lines which introduce the genealogy of Alcinous and Arete, the same is true of the Phaeacian royal couple:

> Ἀρήτη δ᾿ ὄνομ᾿ ἐστὶν ἐπώνυμον, ἐκ δὲ τοκήων
> τῶν αὐτῶν οἵπερ τέκον Ἀλκίνοον βασιλῆα
> Arete is the name she is called, and she comes of the same
> parents as in fact produced the king Alkinous
> (7.54—5, tr. Lattimore, slightly altered)

The rest of the text as we have it (56—66) corrects the inevitable impression by claiming that Arete is not Alcinous's sister but his niece; but in this case there is some justification for invoking the hypothesis of interpolation.[68]

All the same, the 'mythical' aspect of Scheria is counterbalanced by what I have termed the 'real' world. I have already shown this for land and sacrifice, but the point can be extended to its entire social organization. The social institutions of Pylos, Sparta, and of Ithaca particularly, are to be found on Scheria,[69] and the details of palace organization are identical between Ithaca and Alcinous's court: is it an 'accident' that there are fifty servants in Alcinous's house, and the same number in Odysseus's (22.421—2; 7.103), and the same with everything else?[70] But these identities do not produce identical societies. For example, although there is at least one 'angry young man' on Scheria, Euryalus, who insults Odysseus, he is compelled to apologize (8.131—415, esp. 396—415). One could hardly find a swineherd, a cowman, or a goatherd in Phaeacia; and there would be no chance of finding on Ithaca those professional sailors, who steer infallibly without the aid of pilots (7.318—28; 8.555—63, 566; 16.277—31; compare 16.322—7): Ithaca is an island whose men once went in ships, but it is in no sense a country of sailors, for all that Odysseus has acquired the necessary skill. Once back in harbour, he puts to purely static use the equipment of his ship — as when the ship's cable is used to hang the faithless servant-girls (22. 465—73).

And yet Phaeacia is an ideal and an impossible society: Homer, at the height of the Dark-Age crisis of monarchy, pictures a king who can restore peace, who rules over twelve obedient vassals (8.390—1), over docile sons, over a wife whose rôle, despite claims to the contrary, is limited to intercession;[71] and over old men whose sole function is to give advice (7.155—66 [Echeneus's speech]), and who are neither discarded like Laertes nor embittered like Aegyptius.[72] In this sense,

Alcinous's palace constitutes a perfect *oikos*; and yet it is impossible, as I have stressed. The Phaeacians are ignorant of physical struggle (8. 246), and of political struggle too: the stormy *agora* ('political assembly') of Ithaca (2.6—336) should be compared with the agora in Phaeacia (8.24—49). On Ithaca, even a youth as inexperienced as Telemachus earns the label *hupsagorēs*, 'assembly loudmouth' (1.385; 2.85); and there can be little doubt but that we have here a direct glimpse of historical reality. Both Pylos and Menelaus's Sparta, it may be argued, escape the crisis of monarchy; but both are orderly states, and the historical reality of crisis makes its appearance only when the logic of the story demands it. The crisis is on Ithaca, not necessarily everywhere in the world of men.[73]

But in that case, where lies the difference between Phaeacia and Pylos or Sparta? The answer lies unhesitatingly in the land-based character of the latter. And this is the paradox: at the very moment at which a few Greek cities were embarking on the maritime adventure of colonization in the West, the poet of the *Odyssey* describes a city of sailors as something wildly utopian. In a sense, what Odysseus would like to restore on Ithaca is a system comparable to that which exists among the Phaeacians: but he cannot succeed. He can never reproduce the perpetual feasting of the men of Scheria, with or without the gods' participation; in Book 24 he must seek a reconciliation with the families of the slaughtered suitors. The Phaeacians have cast him back into the world of men; their departure causes to vanish the images of anti-humanity which he encountered at every stage of his travels. Scheria may be the first utopia in Greek literature (Finley, 1977: 100—2, 156), but we have not yet reached the point at which political utopias are to be distinguished from images of the golden age (Finley, 1975a: 178—92).[74] For the age of gold remains present in Phaeacia, and it is that element which distinguishes this ideal society from another representation of the perfect city — that portrayed both in peace and in war by Hephaestus on the Shield of Achilles in Book 18 of the *Iliad*: every scene here, from the ambush to the law-suit, is taken from the 'real' world. The golden age must disappear; Odysseus's journey must culminate in his return to Ithaca.[75]

6. The myth of 'Honeyed Orpheus'

Marcel Detienne (1974)

In the middle of the nineteenth century there started a debate between classical scholars and anthropologists on the nature of mythology. Both sides were agreed that myths rested on a 'basis of rude savage ideas' (Lang, 1885: 28), but there the agreement ended. The classical scholars, led by Max Müller and full of the recent discovery of comparative linguistics, regarded mythology as an unexpected product of verbal misunderstanding, a sort of 'disease of language'. The anthropologists, from Tylor to Mannhardt, treated the mythical stories of the Greeks and Romans as evidence of a 'savage intellectual condition' through which the civilized races had had to pass and which could still be seen in primitive peoples such as the Australian aborigines, the Bushmen and the Red Indians (Lang, 1885: 83).

Then Max Müller died, and the classicists tidied up, here and elsewhere. Since they regarded classical mythology as inseparable from the values of which they, as heirs of Graeco-Roman civilization, were the appointed guardians, they thought it best to check this talk of its 'savage basis'. They did this by restoring the myths to history. They had a number of methods. They insisted that the stories belonged to a society of which they were the appointed interpreters. Or they detected traces of fact in the myths, but sufficiently obscured to send the mythologists chasing after the mythical narratives, tracking them across Greece from the first cities which could have been their original sites to the last to which waves of migration might have brought them.[1] But most effective of all was their third method, the handing over of mythical narrative to literary history. Ever since, classical scholars have used the written status of classical mythology to justify their prior claim to it, and until quite recently they did no more than select from it the elements compatible with the dominant ideology of the bourgeois society whose interests and aims so-called 'classical' philology has always so faithfully served.

A century after Tylor, social anthropology is taking the initiative in re-opening the dialogue with the classical fraternity by proposing that one of the most famous myths of the Graeco-Roman world should be re-examined in the light of data from Latin America. Claude Lévi-Strauss's suggestion (1973: 403 n.17) that the adventures of Orpheus, Eurydice and Aristaeus should be looked at afresh in conjunction with

95

the myths of the 'girl mad about honey' was made in full awareness that he was proposing to tackle one of the most vigorous myths of the West, one which had become firmly rooted in history in at least two ways. One of these is the metamorphosis into literature guaranteed to it by its possession of a hero with a voice sweet enough to charm all nature and a love strong enough to conquer death. Long before Virgil's fourth *Georgic*, Orpheus stood for the mythical figure of the poet, the master of the incantation in which words merge with music. And, just as his legend was transformed into musical narrative (cantata, oratorio, opera) so it developed into a major myth of literature, one of the extreme forms of which can be seen in the 'aesthetic mysticism' of Valéry and Mallarmé (Desport, 1952; Juden, 1970: 137—246). On the other hand, the myth of Orpheus is not merely the vehicle of a succession of literary ideologies; as it appears in the *Georgics* it refers to a factual history explained in detail by Servius in his commentary on the works of Virgil. According to Servius, the episode of Aristaeus and the myth of Orpheus and Eurydice was inserted in the second edition of the *Georgics* to replace an original section in honour of Gallus, a poet-friend of Virgil's and prefect of Egypt who was forced to suicide after losing favour with Augustus. It has been quite plausibly deduced from this that, obliged by his position of literary dependence to alter his poem, Virgil chose to tell the story of this myth rather than another, not only because of Aristaeus's affinities with bees, which are the subject of the fourth *Georgic*, but because the adventure of Orpheus gave him an opportunity to make a discreet allusion to his departed friend and, in particular, to Gallus's conviction that passionate love was a central element in human life (Brisson, 1966: 305—29). Paradoxically, however, with such an eminently 'literary' myth, coloured by so many precise references to history, it is the failure of a purely philological and historical approach to account for it satisfactorily which justifies a structural analysis. The first advantage of this approach, banal though it may seem, is that it takes a mythical narrative seriously, takes account of all its episodes, and explains even the most unlikely details.

Summary of the myth of Aristaeus, Orpheus and Eurydice

In the fourth book of the *Georgics*, after describing how bees can be generated from the rotted flesh of an ox, Virgil goes on to tell the story of Aristaeus, from whom men first learnt this technique of *bougonia*.

Aristaeus has lost his bees. He is desolate, and goes to see his mother, the nymph Cyrene, who advises him to consult Proteus, since only he can tell Aristaeus why the bees have deserted his hives. During the dog-days Aristaeus lies in wait. He surprises the sea-god as he is about to take his siesta in the heat of the day, surrounded by his seals. Unable to escape from a grip which holds him in spite of all his changes of shape, Proteus reveals to Aristaeus that his bees have left him to punish him for a serious offence he has committed. Aristaeus had pursued Eurydice, who, in trying to get away from him, had fallen on a monstrous water-serpent. In desperation, her husband Orpheus went to look for her in the underworld. Persephone had given Eurydice back when Orpheus suddenly forgot his instructions, turned round to look at his wife and lost her for ever. Orpheus himself then died, torn to pieces by furious women who took his obliviousness to anything except the memory of his wife for contempt of womankind.

After making these revelations Proteus disappears, leaving Aristaeus deeply repentant. Cyrene then tells Aristaeus how he can appease the nymphs, the companions of Eurydice: he is to offer them a sacrifice of four bulls, whose flesh, when rotted, will produce new swarms.

The main element which ancient mythology preserved from the myth of Orpheus and Aristaeus was the death of Eurydice and the tragic passion which drove Orpheus to go down to the underworld. This tradition emphasized the exemplary fate of the lovers precisely because it was incapable of accounting for the relation set up by the myth between the beekeeper Aristaeus and the couple Eurydice–Orpheus. Two series of questions arise immediately from the story in the *Georgics*. In the first place, why did Aristaeus chose to pursue Eurydice rather than another nymph? And why does his action result in the disappearance of bees which, apparently, have no special connection with Orpheus's young wife? Secondly, Orpheus is only brought into the myth because of Eurydice; is not his connection with the bee-keeper purely fortuitous and therefore gratuitous? In a famous study, the German philologist Eduard Norden set out to demonstrate the arbitrary character of the myth told in the *Georgics*. He argued that Virgil had latched on to the insubstantial figure of Aristaeus and simply invented his adventure with Eurydice and his rivalry with Orpheus (Norden, 1966: 468–532). The fact that the author of the *Georgics* was apparently the only authority for a connection between two separate myths, at least as far as their immediate significance was concerned, seemed to support his claim. The only objections were from those who attributed Virgil's inspiration to a Greek version of the Hellenistic period,[2] a mere question of 'sources' which did nothing to challenge the myth's status as the product of individual imagination. The reason for the persistent failure of ancient myth analysis to understand the meaning of the triangular relationship Aristaeus–Eurydice–Orpheus to which the *Georgics* bear witness is not simply that the method has an implicit tendency to select

97

from the myths values which legitimate a particular ideology of the eternal man. At a deeper level, its own definition of the literary work makes it incapable of recognizing the double context of this story, the mythical context and the ethnographic one. Only the first of these can account for the unexpected presence of Eurydice and Orpheus in the story of the inventor of honey, and the second is essential if any meaning is to be given on the level of myth to Aristaeus's misfortune in losing his bees.[3] Virgil's story begins with the disappearance of Aristaeus's bees. Three reasons are given for the disappearance of the bees, all equally explicit. First, there is a statement which derives from the experience of the peasant bee-keepers to whom book 4 of the *Georgics* is addressed: the bees died of hunger and disease (4.251ff., 318—19). This is followed by two complementary explanations of a mythical character, Orpheus's grudge and the anger of the Nymphs (4.453 and 533—4). Orpheus does not himself exact vengeance for the death of Eurydice; the only ones who have power over the bees are the Nymphs who brought them from their wild state in the oaks to the hive which they placed under the protection of Aristaeus. Conversely, only they can remove them from the half-wild, half-domesticated state in which agriculture has placed them. But the irritation of the Nymphs, as companions of Eurydice, is not enough to account for Aristaeus's misfortune. We must go further back; it is the offence committed by the first bee-keeper himself which compromises his special relationship with the bees.

From Aristotle to the Byzantine treatises such as the *Geoponica* and the *De animalium proprietate* of Philo, the Greek conception of the bee (*melissa*) was based on a model which, in essential features, remained unchanged for over fifteen centuries. The *melissa* was distinguished by a way of life which was pure and chaste and also by a strictly vegetarian diet. In addition to its rejection of hunting and the carnivorous life, and its possession of a 'special' food which it helped to prepare and which was part of itself, the bee showed a most scrupulous purity; not only did it avoid rotting substances and keep well away from impure things, but it also had the reputation of extreme abstinence in sexual matters. The same insistence on purity was also visible in the bee's distaste for smells, whether very pleasant or highly rebarbative; in particular it detested the scent of aromatics.[4] This last characteristic seems to have been sufficiently striking to make bee-keepers take various precautions, which are mentioned in Graeco-Roman treatises on bee-keeping; some recommend the bee-keeper to shave his head before going near the bees in order to be absolutely sure of not having any trace of scent or aromatic ointment on him.[5] The extreme olfactory sensitivity of bees is not the only reason for this behaviour; the bees' detestation of perfumes arises out of their hatred of effeminacy and voluptuousness and their particular hostility towards debauchees and seducers, in other words, for those who misuse ointments and aromatics.[6] Plutarch even, in one of his treatises, stresses the infallible discernment with which bees single out for their attacks only those users of perfume who are guilty of illicit sexual relationships.[7] He also emphasizes, in a chapter of the *Coniugalia praecepta* (44, 144d), that bee-keeping requires exemplary marital fidelity of its practitioners: the bee-keeper must approach his bees as a good husband does his lawful wife, that is, in a state of purity, without being polluted by sexual relations with other women. If he does not, he will have to face the hostility of his charges as the husband has to face the anger of his partner. This ethnographic context explains why Aristaeus lost his bees. While Virgil has no more than a discreet reference to the flight of Eurydice and her nymphs before the Thessalian bee-keeper, other less squeamish writers say plainly that Aristaeus desired Eurydice, that he wanted to seduce her and attempted to assault her (*stuprare, vitiare*).[8] It was because the inventor of honey had the smell of seduction on him that he was deprived of his bees. Orpheus's bitterness and the Nymphs' anger are therefore reactions to a sexual offence. This, by accidentally causing the death of Eurydice — who was bitten by a serpent in her flight — drove to despair a lover passionately devoted to his new wife, and deeply disappointed Aristaeus's protecting powers, the bees, who had chosen him for his exemplary conduct and his good upbringing — for which latter they had also been largely responsible.

The ethnographic context, which reveals a close relation between the conduct of the bees and the sexual behaviour of the bee-keeper, now sends us back to the wider mythical context to which the meeting between Aristaeus and Eurydice belongs. There are two immediate problems here. What can be the significance of the misconduct of a figure whose reputation as a virtuous husband is solidly established by the rest of the mythical tradition? And why does he pick on Orpheus's wife when no other myth puts them in direct connection or makes any reference to their possible affinity? A full answer would require a detailed analysis of the early sections of the myth of Aristaeus, for which there is no room here, but two things can be said. First, all the education given to the 'master of honey' was a preparation for a solemn marriage with the eldest daughter of the king of Thebes, and the bridegroom sealed the alliance with his father-in-law with the honey he brought as one of a number of useful presents. Secondly, one of the main results of Aristaeus's activity — in the episode which takes place on Ceos — is the establishment of harmony in conjugal relations; the sweet honey seems to produce a married life untroubled by either adultery or seduction. But what about the madness which came over Aristaeus when he came in contact with Eurydice? To explain this the sociological status of this young woman has to be examined and defined in relation to the mythology of honey, particularly since, as a nymph, Eurydice is one of the powers to which some traditions ascribe the invention of honey. Two myths, which dovetail closely, make an association between two groups in Demeter's entourage, the Nymphs and the Bee-Women, the *Melissai*. According to the first of these stories, it was a nymph called Melissa who discovered the first honeycombs in the forest, ate some and mixed it with water and drank it, and then taught her companions to make the drink and eat the food. This was part of the nymphs' achievement in bringing man out of his wild state; under the guidance of Melissa, Bee, they not only turned men away from eating each other to eating only this product of the forest trees, but also introduced into the world of men the feeling of modesty, *aidōs*, which they established by means of another invention, intended to reinforce the first, the discovery of woven garments. Since then, explains the myth finally, no marriage takes place without the first honours being reserved to the nymphs, the companions of Demeter, in memory of their part in establishing a way of life ruled by piety and approved by the gods. The purpose of the second story is to explain the association of Demeter with the nymphs connected with honey and bees. There is nothing unusual in the presence of Demeter in a myth centred on a 'cultivated' form of life consisting of dietary prescriptions and a sexual code, but it is given even greater justification by a ritual feature mentioned explicitly in the second myth. After the kidnapping of Persephone, the sorrowing Demeter entrusted to the Nymphs the basket (κάλαθος) which had held Persephone's weaving and went to Paros, where she was welcomed by King Melisseus, the king of the bees. When she was leaving the goddess wanted to thank her host, and so she gave Melisseus's sixty daughters the cloth Persephone had been weaving for her wedding, and at the same time told them of her sufferings and revealed to them the secret ceremonies she wished to institute. Ever after, the women who celebrate the Thesmophoria — the feast of Demeter reserved for lawful wives — were known as *Melissai*; their ritual name was *Bees* (cf. Detienne, 1977: 79—80; Detienne and Vernant, 1979: 211—12).

The emphasis now is no longer on dietary rules, which slip into the background, but on two different female statuses. The daughters of Melisseus move between the two first receiving the cloth woven by Persephone, which stands for the state of the *numphē*, the young girl thinking of marriage, and then giving their name to the married women, lawful wives, who meet to celebrate the mysteries of Demeter Thesmophoros. Nymph woman, Thesmophorian woman: this duality of the daughters of Melisseus is only fully exposed when placed in the setting of a series of images in which the bee is the animal symbol of certain female virtues. The description given above of various unique features in the behaviour of bees relied on the evidence of Plutarch in a long comparison between the bee and the lawful wife. When Plutarch included in the *Coniugalia praecepta* the advice that the husband should have the same regard for his wife as a bee-keeper for his bees, he was in agreement with a tradition as old as Hesiod, in which the bee stands for the good wife in the same way that the fox symbolizes cunning. In the minds of the Greeks, the *melissa* is the emblem of female domestic virtue; faithful to her husband and the mother of legitimate children, she watches over the private area of the house, taking care of the couple's possessions, always reticent and modest (*sōphrōn* and *aidēmōn*), so adding to the functions of a wife those of a housekeeper never greedy or fond of drink or inclined to doze, who firmly rejects the romantic chatter that women in general enjoy.

It is this model of the bee-woman which determines the distribution of attributes between the two female statuses possessed by the daughters of Melisseus, who are at one stage nymphs and at another *thesmophoroi*. Since only the women who celebrate the Thesmophoria are given the explicit title of *Melissai, Bees*, it is with their rôle that we will start.

The structure of the Thesmophoria is most clearly shown by contrast with the ritual of the Adonia. A comparison of the two rituals (see fig. 1) reveals a series of fundamental oppositions: between Demeter and Adonis, between cereals and aromatics, and between marriage and seduction (Detienne, 1977: 60–98). Analysis of the mythology of aromatics has produced two results which are relevant here, the contrast between the legitimate wife and the courtesan and the distance between the former, with her faintly unpleasant smell, and the pungent perfume of the latter. Whereas the festivals of Adonis display the licence of which women are capable when abandoned to themselves, the Thesmophoria always took place in a serious, almost severe atmosphere. The worshippers of Adonis were often courtesans; the followers of Demeter Thesmophoros were always the legitimate wives of the citizens, and the festival was strictly reserved for them; ceremonies were closed to slave women, the wives of metics and foreigners, and of course courtesans and concubines. The opposition between the *thesmophoros* and the devotee of Adonis was most sharply marked in the sexual behaviour prescribed for the participants in the two rites. In the Adonia men and women behaved as lovers, on the model of the relationship of Aphrodite and Adonis, but in the Thesmophoria not only were men carefully excluded but even the married women were

	ADONIA	THESMOPHORIA
Divine powers	Adonis and his mistress Aphrodite	Demeter Thesmophoros and her daughter Persephone
Sociological status of women	Courtesans and concubines	Lawful wives
Status of men	Invited by women	All (including husbands) barred
Sexual attitude	Seduction	Continence
Associated plants	Incense and myrrh	Abraham's balm
Smells	Abuse of perfumes	Slight smell of fasting. Hatred of the Bee-women for those who wear perfume
Food	Feasting	Fasting

Figure 1

bound to continence for the duration of the festival. The prohibition of sexual activity was reinforced in two ways, by the use of branches of Abraham's balm, chosen for its anti-aphrodisiac reputation, to make litters, and also by the faintly unpleasant smell which accompanied the fast kept by the worshippers of Demeter. In contrast to the perfumed courtesans who took part in the Adonia, the *thesmophoros* gave off a very faint smell of fasting which had the same function as the garlic eaten by the women at the Skiraphoria, namely — according to Philochoros of Athens — to keep their breath from being sweet-smelling and so enable them the more easily to avoid sexual activity. In short, the sexual and dietary abstinence practised by the women taking part in the Thesmophoria marked them out as exaggerated versions of the model of female domestic virtues represented by the bee. Furthermore, in ritual terms the *thesmophoros* is the sociological counterpart of the bees angered by the scent of aromatics.

Determining the status of the Nymph, who in this case is the *numphē*, necessarily involves the definition of her name. In the Greek classification of female ages, *numphē* denotes a status between those of the *korē* and the *mētēr*. A *korē* is often an immature girl, and always an unmarried woman (*agamos*); the *mētēr*, on the other hand, is the matron, the woman who has given birth to children. *Numphē* stands at the intersection of these two categories, and applies both to the young woman just before her marriage and to the bride before the birth of her children finally commits her to the alien home of her husband. This ambivalence makes the *numphē* an *ambiguous* bee and so very different from the *thesmophoros*. In her ritual dealings with the nymphs, who are the patrons of marriage, preside at the *Hydrophoria* (one of the marriage-rituals), receive the 'pre-nuptial sacrifices' (*proteleia*), and supervise the weaving of the long bridal veil, the *numphē* represents a type of woman who fully deserves the description 'bee', not just because she submits to purificatory procedures which qualify her for the most emphatically ritual part of marriage, but also because she displays *aidōs* and *sōphrosunē*, the modesty and reticence which are the mark of her new state. Nevertheless, before emerging as a *thesmophoros*, before becoming a Bee in the ritual sense, the *numphē* must necessarily pass through another state. In the days immediately following the marriage she will lead the life reserved for young married couples, the *numphiōn bios*. Crowned with aphrodisiac plants such as myrtle and mint and gorging themselves with cakes spiced with sesame and poppy seeds, the bridal pair need think of nothing else but leading a 'life of pleasure and voluptuousness', a life of *hēdupatheia*. This is a way of life symbolized by honey, for the Greek proverbial tradition makes an equation between the expressions 'to sprinkle oneself with honey' and *hēdupatheia*, which is the search for excessive pleasure and satisfaction. At this time of 'honeymoon' the young bride, the *numphē*, runs the risk of no longer being a bee but becoming a hornet (*kēphēn*), turning into the reverse of a bee, a carnivorous bee, brutal and at the mercy of excessive desires, driven to gorge without measure on honey and condemned to roll in what Plato describes as 'hornet honey', all the pleasures of the belly and the flesh.

So the status of *numphē* is an ambiguous one in a woman's life, since while society, by ritual procedures, invites the *numphē* to behave like a good bee, it nevertheless cannot prevent the new bride, who has access to the pleasures of love (*aphrodisia*), from automatically giving off a scent which makes her desirable and so, momentarily, even dangerous. This detour by way of the honeymoon was necessary to understand how Eurydice, the young girl who had become Orpheus's bride, could, quite involuntarily, have transformed the first bee-keeper into a vulgar seducer. In rushing after Eurydice, Aristaeus gave way for an instant to the seduction exercised by the honeymoon, to the seduction within marriage which threatens most of all someone whose whole life has been passed within the area of marriage. To see that the nymph Eurydice was particularly fitted for the part of the young bride on honeymoon, we need only remember that the mythical figure of Eurydice is entirely swallowed up in her love for Orpheus, the Thracian enchanter. All that remains to complete our analysis is to show that his intrusion into the story of Aristaeus is neither fortuitous nor unmotivated.

Orpheus has a double claim to a place in the mythology of honey, for the excessive love with which he surrounds Eurydice and for the contrast he offers in a number of respects with his ephemeral rival, Aristaeus the bee-keeper. In all the descriptions of their relationship, Eurydice and Orpheus appear as a pair of lovers who cannot bear to be separated, even by death. When Orpheus exploits the charm of his honeyed voice to get permission to leave the underworld with Eurydice, the gods of those regions impose a triple prohibition, oral, visual and tactile (Virgil, *Georgics* 4.487; *Culex* 289–93). He is not to speak to Eurydice, not to look at her, not to embrace her. These are three forms of distance which the gods of the underworld impose on lovers too violently in love with one another to put off the moment of meeting. The 'too great love' (Virgil's *tantus furor*, *Georgics* 4.495) which precipitates the destruction of both Eurydice and Orpheus is the sign of their inability to live the relationship of marriage outside the honeymoon. The story of Orpheus and Eurydice is not a story of tragic love or unhappy passion; it is the failure of a couple incapable of establishing a conjugal relationship which allows for the proper distances.

Nevertheless, Orpheus's propensity to 'roll in honey' is not the only feature of his which justifies the connection of his story with the mythology of honey and accounts for his involvement with the master of the bees. Honey is connected with the figure of Eurydice's lover in two ways. First metaphorically: from his melodious mouth come honeyed sounds which — according to the whole Greek tradition — enabled him to charm all nature and drew after him fish, birds and the very wildest animals. Secondly in matters of food, where he is the legendary initiator of a particular way of life, a diet of cakes and fruit coated with honey adopted by those who call themselves his followers, who also offer them to the gods in sacrifice in order to avoid shedding the blood of domestic animals. However, to fix more exactly Orpheus's position in the mythology of honey, he must be contrasted, not only with Aristaeus, but also with Orion, a savage hunter whose adventures, prefigured in the exploits of Aristaeus's son Actaeon, develop in constant contrast with those of the bee-keeper. A triangular relationship between Orpheus, Aristaeus and Orion is established in three areas, animals, women and honey, three areas in which Orion and Orpheus correspond as two extremes situated on either side of Aristaeus, their mutual mediator. Orion, a brutal, violent, club-wielding figure, appears throughout the mythical tradition as a savage, for ever pursuing fierce animals, which he loves to slaughter, and even going so far as to boast that he will wipe off the face of the earth all the animals which Gaia bears and nurtures. Orpheus is the opposite of Orion. Where Orion shows an excess of savagery in setting no limits to his hunting. Orpheus's distinctive characteristic is a perverse gentleness which makes him gather round him all the animals of the earth, even the fiercest, which like all the rest are drawn by the charm of his voice and the sweetness of his song. Aristaeus is hunter and shepherd, *agreus* and *nomios*, both at once, and his uniqueness lies in his ability to maintain an equal distance from each of these extremes; he tames some animal species (cattle, goats, sheep) and inaugurates their husbandry, but also uses traps to hunt the wild creatures (wolves and bears) which are a direct threat to his activities as a shepherd and a bee-keeper. The same relationships between the three figures reappear in their attitude to women. All that Orion can do is rape them; almost as soon as he sets eyes on his host's daughter on Chios he lusts after her and wants to have her; as soon as he catches sight of the Pleiades he chases after them. His violent desire even tempts him to lay hands on Artemis while she is taking part in one of his extermination hunts. At the opposite extreme from this brute, Orpheus is a young husband passionately attached to his wife; his honeymoon with her is excessive, and prevents him — like Orion — from becoming either a good son-in-law or a perfect husband, but in his case from an excess of attachment rather than violence. Both Orion and Orpheus, by opposite excesses, are excluded from the status attributed by the myth to the bee-keeper Aristaeus, the husband who keeps a proper distance between himself and his wife and who uses honey as an instrument of alliance with his father-in-law.

It is however honey which illustrates most clearly the function of Aristaeus as mediator between Orion and Orpheus. Aristaeus is a model bee-keeper. He receives from the nymphs the task of caring for the bees and obtains from his protectors the secret of the process which will establish honey and bees permanently in the world of men. Aristaeus's honey is the basis of a form of civilized life from which both Orion and Orpheus are excluded, though for directly opposite reasons. The giant Orion, because of his excessive brutality and violence, is unable to escape from a state of primitive savagery which he betrays most obviously by trying to violate the Pleiades — the Dove-Women counterparts of the Bees who nurtured Zeus. Orpheus, through an excess of honey, is likewise excluded from a civilized world which bee-keeping has begun, tentatively, to define. It is because he is 'all honey' that Orpheus obliterates the boundaries between the wild and the cultivated and mixes marriage and seduction together. In the presence of Orpheus lions and bears live alongside roe and fallow deer, and the fiercest animals are gentler than lambs. Just as he is all honey for the whole of nature, by his excessive attachment to his young wife Orpheus cannot prevent himself from being the lover and seducer of a woman whose lawful husband he also is.

The tragic death of Orpheus is the final event which confirms his

105

inability to establish himself in the area defined by the action of Aristaeus (fig. 2). Once Eurydice is gone for good, her distraught husband goes from improper closeness to excessive distance. Orpheus cuts himself off from women, who, furious at their rejection, behave towards him like wild beasts, and by so doing seem to take the place left empty by the beasts themselves, whom Orpheus has chosen as his closest companions and friends. This spatial pattern is illustrated in Ovid's *Metamorphoses*. When the women launch the attack which ends in the dismemberment of Orpheus, the man with the honeyed voice is in the middle of a circle of animals, and it is these who are the first victims of the enraged bacchants, who are armed with hoes, sickles, earth-pounders, spits and two-headed axes, all tools belonging to the cultivated life from which they now finally exclude Orpheus.

The hatred of bees for seducers, the social status of the bee-keeper, the social position of the bride, the definition of honey in relation to hunting and not-hunting, all these are aspects and dimensions which fill out the mythical background without which the misfortune of Aristaeus and Orpheus remains shut up inside a literary narrative. In the field of classical mythology the methodological contribution of social anthropology is as much to establish mythical language as an autonomous object as to work out the basic rules for deciphering it. The mythical narrative in Virgil's story only acquires definition when placed within its double context of ethnography and mythology. To identify the different levels of meaning, the different codes, which form the texture of the myth, all the cultural associations of honey must be explored, which involves areas as diverse as techniques of collection and the symbolism of the bee, institutions such as marriage and various ritual practices. Similarly, in order to interpret the Orpheus myth we need to explore its connections with other myths such as those of Aristaeus and Orion which with it form a group within which a number of 'transformations' take place. The result of this double analysis is a grid on which levels of meaning are distinguished along the vertical axis and correlations with other myths along the horizontal. All the elements of the myth now have a place, and decipherment can continue until the full richness of the logic of mythical statement is laid open.[9]

It is, of course, possible to interpret the Orpheus myth differently, but alternative interpretations achieve plausibility only by destroying the structure of codes which underpins the honey myths (in this case sociological, dietary and sexual codes). In such approaches Orpheus's glance at Eurydice, isolated from the other prohibitions (oral and tactile) revealed by a structural analysis, becomes pure impatience or, as in Monteverdi's opera, inability to control his urges, or again — this is Rameau's version — a breach of romantic conventions.[10] The climax of

	ORION	ARISTAEUS	ORPHEUS
Animals	Destroys all by savage hunting	Tames some (goats, sheep, cattle), hunts	Captivates all, even the fiercest
Women	Rapes and assaults. Detested 'son-in-law'	Model husband. Perfect son-in-law	Lover-husband. Incapable of becoming a good husband and *a fortiori* a proper son-in-law
Honey	Pursues Dove-Women (= Bee-Women)	Bee-keeper. Protector of bees, protected by Bee-Nymphs	'All honey'

Figure 2

this process is humanism's discovery of it as 'the most marvellous symbol of love ... which, stronger than death, triumphs over everything, except itself' (Bellessort, 1920: 145). All these are fragmentary interpretations, dazzled by the glitter of a single detail, but all still able to find support in the *Georgics*, where Virgil, without breaching the conventions of the myth or engaging in major distortion, gives Orpheus's glance an importance which makes it reveal the ideological bias of his story.

This detail also gives us a preliminary criterion by which to determine the level of mythical thought represented by Virgil's mythology; it is a reminder that, although most of the mythical discourse produced by ancient societies is embedded in literary narratives, often influenced by various forms of ideology, this does not necessarily mean that the development of the literary settings has distorted or destroyed the myths. This characteristic may be combined with another, which was recognized as a result of an investigation of a group of myths centred on aromatics and seduction; it was found that the categories and logical relations revealed by structural analysis of mythology are very largely the same as those used by the Greeks in a series of explicitly 'rational' works composed at the same time as the literary works which contain the myths. Provisional though they are, these conclusions on the type of mythical thought found in Greece suggest that we should not seek to press the very close connections between the honey myths centred on Aristaeus and the corresponding mythology of Latin America which seem to be indicated at first sight by the affinities between two mythical complexes of clearly unequal dimensions, but both centred on a pathology of marriage in which the mythical operator is honey. Our

107

Marcel Detienne

aim is no longer, as in Tylor's day, to recover the half-vanished traces of a 'savage stage of thought' revealed to us by archaic societies. The first, and essential, task is to construct the grammar of the way of thinking expressed in the myths, without prejudging the question whether mythical thought is a privileged expression of an image of the world immanent in the structure of the mind, or whether structural resemblances are to be attributed to a palaeolithic heritage on which both the Old and the New worlds have drawn. More urgent tasks confront the mythologist. The myths have to be grouped by means of an exhaustive analysis of their ethnographic context in ways which go beyond the cycles and classifications of the ancient mythographers. In addition, since the classical myths are deeply embedded in different literary forms, the analysis of the semantic field in which myths operate must be developed, and linguistic structures related to mythological ones (Sperber, 1968: 200—6).

All these tasks will help to comprehend a history inseparable from mythical statement throughout Graeco-Roman civilization. Until very recently, isolated myths tempted the hellenist's curiosity with the prospect of an institutional residue or the scarcely discernible lineament of some archaic practice. In future the business of the student of myth will no longer be to extract an institution or a social practice from a mythical narrative like a kernel from its splintered shell. What the mythical statements of a society reveal is its total mental universe, since, as we know, the only possible basis for structural analysis is a thorough acquaintance with the ethnographic context of each myth and each group of myths. Ritual practices, economic techniques, forms of marriage, legal institutions, classifications of animals, descriptions of plant species, all are aspects of a society which the mythologist must classify. Only then will he be able to judge the relevance of each term in its sequence and each sequence in its narrative, and go on to place the narrative, by reference to its various codes or levels of meaning, within a major or minor mythical complex. All this whole ethnographic context is nothing other than history, the history whose rhythm, chronology, changes, flux and reflux have been the objects of the historical study of ancient societies since the nineteenth century. The mythologist's structural models cannot do without the analyses of the historian; without them their coherence and logic would have no foundation.

Antiquarians and other believers in a history of 'events' wander through mythology with their spikes, triumphantly winkling out of corners a fragment of archaism here or the fossilized memory of some 'real' event there. Structural analysis of myth rejects this approach. Its discovery of invariant forms underlying variety of content enables it to

108

design an alternative total history moving on a slower and more fundamental time-scale (Burguière, 1971: v—vii). Structural analysis pen-
etrates below conscious expressions and, beneath the superficial movement of things, traces the deep, slow currents which flow in silence.
This is one of its contributions to modern historical technique, but
there is also another. By examining the myths in themselves, in their
own organizational forms, the historian of the Greek world is enabled
in his turn to isolate various general properties of mythical thought,
confronted as he is by the problem of coming to grips with a society in
which the appearance of a totally new form of thought, philosophy,
had a definite effect on the functioning of myths, but did not immediately induce a process of decay.[11]

III: Myth and social order

7. 'Value' in Greek myth

Louis Gernet (1948)

It is rather easy to forget that some fields of human activity, such as law and economics, are aspects of the human mind. For in our own world they operate apparently without any reference to man himself. If we are to see them for what they are, products of mind, we must look in the first instance not at their modern form but to their past, whose rich complexity can so easily be misunderstood by an unthinking application of attitudes stemming from Enlightenment philosophy; and it is this past which has brought about their present high degree of elaboration. Indeed, it is in the task of reconstructing those past conditions in which the products of the human mind can more clearly be grasped, wherever it proves possible, and to the degree that it is possible, that history finds one of its surest justifications. And that is, before anything else, a psychological enquiry.

The notion of 'value' in particular, I think, deserves some attention. For us today it is an entirely abstract notion, because we all conceive it necessarily in terms of quantification. But this is not the case in societies which, for want of a better term, we call 'archaic' or 'primitive': for in such societies the value of possessions or goods for consumption is determined by a whole range of conceptions and feelings — thinking about 'value' involves a consideration of all manner of relationships and associations. Such a field of enquiry may seem at first sight quite bewildering: which is yet another reason for studying it. For these societies present us with a 'total' notion of value, combining categories which are for us distinct: it is the object of respect, even of religious fear; the focus of interests, loyalties or pride; the leitmotif of that 'capacity for wonder' which according to Descartes is the first 'primitive passion'. Moreover, it involves or denotes a psychological 'pitch' at once higher and more diffuse than is the case with us.

We have here to do with true 'complexes', that is, with forms in which all the classic 'faculties' of mind are implicated and combined to an equal degree. The very idea of value may involve an uneasy balance between a generalized disquiet and a physical shrinking from something dangerous — both mental and physical behaviour is involved. Social

111

rules, such as those regarding reciprocal exchange of gifts, both give the notion content and intensify it. It is shot through with affective considerations, which are expressed in images whose rôle and character have to be taken into account. And deep down we can see the guiding principles — hard to discern but in control — the society's collective representations, which help to define it and which constitute the ineluctable framework for all its mental activity. I hardly need to make the point: all this provides the ideal conditions for a study of man's capacity to create symbols.

It can only heighten the interest of such an enquiry if it focuses upon that stage of historical development which borders upon the era of 'positive' value — chronologically that is — a stage at which psychological attitudes deriving from the remote past nevertheless persist. And it is that possibility which is offered by an archaic civilization which provokes such questions at almost every turn; a consideration which inspires the following remarks.

1

The problem of the origin of money is particularly important in relation to ancient Greece, where for the first time in human history the use of money in the strict sense (that is, of certified money) became widespread (Laum, 1924). One aspect of the problem is this. If we distinguish between 'symbol' and 'sign',[1] in such a way that the first remains charged with immediate affective meanings, whereas the significance of the 'sign' is limited, or apparently limited, entirely to its *function*, it is clear that what we mean by 'the origin of money' is the transition from 'symbol' to 'sign'; we are moreover aware that in many societies which do not make use of money as such there are to be found characteristic expressions of 'value', which fulfil functions more or less similar but seem essentially concrete by comparison (cf. Mauss, 1970: 17—45; Simiand, 1934: 1—58 with the discussion on pp. 59—86).

We may note that a parallel development is discernible in the case of law, where ritual precedes and adumbrates legal process. And the comparison is the more instructive in Greece in relation to an institution of evident social significance, the public games: in those legendary competitions (*athla*) which provide one of the favourite epic themes, the behaviour and attitudes by which individuals lay claim to prizes pave the way for the stereotyped acts and gestures characteristic of ancient law (de Visscher, 1931: 353—7). More specifically, one may see in them an antecedent of *mancipatio* (Gernet, 1948: 177—88). This is the act of laying claim to something by placing one's hand upon it; and it has a special relationship to the object towards which it is directed. In what might be termed the marginal instance, where it involves laying hold of the horn of a bull which a man has won, it is merely an extension of a properly religious act, and the object claimed, which is in principle a sacrificial offering, has a religious value. Although their significance is obviously more profane, the other objects given as prizes are no less 'charged' — the idea of 'owning' them cannot be separated from the conception of the value attached to them. The way in which these objects are conceived, the conception of rights over them and the behaviour demanded both in order to gain those rights and to protect them, all of these are tightly related to each other. Moreover, the very objects, the institutionalized prizes, themselves adumbrate money: one could almost say that in the case of the funeral games in the *Iliad*, for example, we are as far from money as we are from legal process. And that is a very interesting kind of relationship.

The objects distributed as prizes, especially cups, tripods, cauldrons, weapons and so on, can then be classified among the 'premonetary tokens' to which Bernhard Laum has drawn attention (1924: 104–25: 'die prämonetären Geldformen'). These objects are often evaluated by reference to their quantity: objects offered in ransom, gifts between guest-friends, involve considerations of number, which proves that there were relevant norms and traditions. In the case of an institution like the Homeric games, where all the contestants are given prizes, there must have been some hierarchy of value that governed them. Furthermore, many of these objects have a direct relation to the origins of money. In Crete, as late as the fifth century BC, fines are expressed in terms of tripods and cauldrons. Whether or not we are to understand them as monetary tokens (the point is disputed), the token itself and its function remain instructive. The iron sickles presented as prizes at the games at Sparta have been identified by some modern historians as a Spartan currency; conversely, agonistic types are commonly found on ancient coins, which were sometimes struck to commemorate games.

The objects given as prizes belong to a category both extensive and definite, relatively at any rate. Such objects or their analogues occur in several different but parallel contexts: traditional presents, gifts between guest-friends, offerings to the gods, grave-goods and objects placed in the tombs of princes. As a class of goods, they are the medium of aristocratic intercourse. They are classified implicitly as different from another sort of goods which are both inferior in nature and distinct in function. In the language of Roman law — though there, in an essentially peasant world, the distinction is formulated at a quite different level — we should say that they are pre-eminently *res mancipi*. By the same token, they constitute a special form of property — private property in the narrow sense, which, in the case of the warrior caste we are shown in the epics, is defined both in terms of the behaviour and customary rules which regulate it and by contrast with other property held on a juridical or quasi-juridical basis (such as ownership of land or livestock). Its owner enjoys absolute rights of disposal. The best proof of that is the institution of grave-goods: such objects follow the prince into his tomb. And finally, it is precisely this notion of private possession which is stressed in the vocabulary: the term *ktēmata* is normally used to refer to objects of this kind, emphasizing the idea of acquisition — acquisition in war, through the games, by gift; but never, in principle, by mercantile trade.[2]

This group of preferences, exclusions and norms serves to define a particular aspect of 'value'. Historians have usually thought it appropriate to focus upon objects that are clearly premonetary tokens; within that context, I propose to study those which possess two characteristics: goods in circulation (whereas livestock used as 'money' must have functioned chiefly as a method of payment)[3] and the product of human labour — metal-work in particular (and sometimes textiles). Such a restriction of the notion of value is intentional: it was ideas connected with cattle, with their specifically religious value and their ritual uses, that provided the major theme of Laum's essay on 'sacred money', and the basis for his theory concerning the religious origins of secular money. I do not intend to discuss this theory; but it is clear that, beyond religious cult — sacrifice, to be exact — where such a theory is quite legitimate, there exists this whole series of objects which Laum could account for only by special pleading, and whose character and functions I have just discussed: in an enquiry into the origins of money, this class of objects has its place; in a study of judgements about 'value', it must be considered independently.

We have of course to do here with economic value, or at least with its earliest forms. I shall however normally speak simply of 'value': as soon as one speaks of 'economic value', there is a tendency to suppress the idea of value itself, to substitute the idea of measure (which is nevertheless essential) for the idea of that which is measured. Moreover, I am not talking about some minimal, abstract sense of 'value' but of a highly-charged value embodied in certain objects which pre-exists that other sense and indeed conditions it.

To treat the different aspects of 'value' as a homogeneous reality requires no justification nowadays: one is free to recognize in them a common 'intention'; and they all involve a process of idealization. In this particular case, there is evidence for such a process at several different social-psychological levels.

The first is to be found in linguistic habits. The word *agalma*, in its earliest usage, implies the notion of 'value'. It can be used of all kinds of things, even, on occasion, of human beings thought of as 'precious'. It usually expresses some idea of opulence, and above all of aristocratic wealth (horses are *agalmata*). And it cannot be divorced from another notion which is insinuated by an etymology which the word itself makes evident: the verb *agallein*, from which *agalma* is derived, means both 'adorn' and 'honour'. Now the word *agalma* is used especially in relation to the class of movable objects which concerns me here; and it is highly relevant to add that in the classical period it became specialized in the sense 'offering to the gods', and above all that kind of offering which statues of gods represent.[4]

The objects I am concerned with are 'industrial objects'; but it must be stressed that they are products made for a luxury market. One indirect proof of their outstanding, extraordinary, 'value' is the quantities of imitations of them, the reproductions in cheap materials, whose use as *anathēmata* ('offerings') is, as it were, a symbol of a symbol; and great masses of them are known from excavations. But archaeology has also revealed a considerable upsurge in the proto-historical period of the production of jewellery and its dissemination by trade. Nevertheless, Karl Bücher's remarks on the special character of Greek industrial production remain true for the 'Archaic' period.[5]

If we now turn from technical and economic considerations to religion, we may start from my earlier observation that *agalmata* are characteristically 'offerings'; in Homer, where the word does not yet have this specialized sense, we find something even more telling: it denotes 'precious objects' which are spontaneously used as offerings. We have here a kind of religious 'trade' which is of special interest for my purposes: the notion of 'value' is here heightened, and specialized,[6] but it is evidently at the same time associated with the idea of lavish generosity — that is, aristocratic generosity (which Aristotle in the fourth century still takes to be characteristic of a class to which the tag 'noblesse oblige' remained appropriate).[7] And we should remember that this category of 'wealth', manifested as the property of the gods, remained a category well-defined in the classical period: in criminal law, sacrilege (*hierosulia*) is quite different from the crime of theft or malversation of a god's revenues. It is a quite special and unpardonable offence. And it involves laying hands upon a more revered category of 'sacred goods', which are to be identified precisely as our *agalmata* — tripods, vases, precious jewels and so on.[8]

2

But there is yet another level at which we can examine the mental activity through which 'value' comes into being, that is, becomes 'objective': the level of myth.[9]

We can see that precious objects occur in legends — even that they play, so to speak, a central rôle — because in them they are always endowed with a peculiar power. What I want to stress is that this way of thinking is particularly evident at the very stage at which I am studying the notion of 'value', that is, in the pre-monetary stage which is the immediate precursor of a period in which it was conceived abstractly. Perhaps we can learn something from that; at the very least, there is a problem to examine more closely.

There is no 'method' by which to conduct such an examination. We must read the stories, nothing more. But the stories presuppose or imply particular human attitudes: we should take them into consideration if we wish to read aright. The stories, moreover, are interconnected: there are similarities which we would do well not to overlook *a priori* because we are terrified of making arbitrary connections. I need really be granted only one thing: that mythology is a kind of language. We know the function of *'signifiants'* in a language (de Saussure, 1966: 122–7); taking my cue from linguistics, I would say that we have to take into account two kinds of connections. First, those between the constituent elements or 'moments' of a single tale (which we may take sometimes as the more significant in that their rationale is not immediately obvious and even seems on occasion not to have been understood by those who told them); and second, the associations by means of which one episode, theme or image evokes a similar group. Such connections and associations are of some help. But we must not be in too much of a hurry.

The tripod of the seven sages

There are advantages in taking first a story which looks historical — a story whose characters are historical persons, which is probably not earlier than the sixth century BC, and which moreover has just that reasonable and edifying tone which is typical of the period. It would be difficult to believe that it is a legend: the story seems simply to have been made up to illustrate an ideal of wisdom. But it is a legend in the sense that one keeps finding in it certain traditional ideas or images; and because throughout the tradition it compliantly retains a mythical base, without which the story would lose its minimum of affective or poetic interest that it always contains. It allows us at any rate now to pick out certain features, certain elements, which we may come across again later: a very proper introduction.

Our best source is Diogenes Laertius, who merrily gives us several versions (*Lives of the Philosophers* 1.27—33; cf. Plutarch, *Life of Solon* 4). The tradition goes back quite a long way, but it seems clear that large numbers of variants continued to circulate until pretty late: most of the authors Diogenes cites by name are fourth-century; but their building-blocks seem to be old, and even if these were made up to suit the tale, they were made up in keeping with the habit of mind that created legends: we need no more. The story goes something like this. It concerns the prize to be awarded 'to the wisest'. Each one of the seven 'sages' to be found in the constantly-varying list that was trans-mitted all through antiquity is accorded the prize in succession. The prize is sometimes a tripod, and sometimes a golden cup or goblet. Usually it is awarded first to Thales, and Thales relinquishes it in favour of another whom he deems wiser; who in turn gives it to a third. And so it goes on until it is given back by the seventh to Thales, who conse-crates it to Apollo.

Let us look first at the company (or perhaps 'at the luminaries'). The first thing to notice is that the tripod or vase is conceived as a prize awarded after a competition, a competition in wisdom, even happiness (Kuiper, 1916: 404—29), by a transposition of the underlying idea of rivalry. This feature is more or less explicit and is not demanded by the situation itself. A model comes at once to mind, that of the games, which we know to have been one of the preferred social contexts for the deployment of the precious object *quâ* charged image. Another model too, equally social, and perfectly compatible with the first: we have here a succession of gifts — the object goes from hand to hand; and the text of Plutarch is especially suggestive concerning those who have rights in the gift, and the gift-ethic: note especially the words 'cede' (which implies a certain respect), 'noble generosity', 'circu-lation'.[10] Above all we should notice how Plutarch gives concrete, pleonastic, expression to the idea of circular transmission. The seven sages form a group (the number itself is significant); the tradition else-where brings them together at a banquet; and the banquet, in the society of the legends, is the privileged locus for acts of generosity, for agree-ments and for challenges. But above all it is the place where things circulate — the cup and, with it, the toasts, which are so many offer-ings.[11] Beneath the story of the Seven Sages, there lies a traditional structure of ideas.

The object itself has a quite special value which is linked to religion: in the end, the tripod is consecrated to a god (as if its value had increased through its being passed from hand to hand). And even before, in one very interesting version (Diogenes Laertius 1.33), it already appears as a well-known type of religious object: an oracle ordered that it be sent 'to the house' of a wise man.[12] And that makes us think of the cult-practice whereby sacred objects are held by a number of appropriate people one after the other.

These models and associations intimate the existence here of a myth-structure. In a number of versions, the object has a history — almost an identity card — such as we often find in Homer for valuable items: it is divine right from the start, because it was made by Hephaestus. That is quite boring — practically a commonplace in the heroic tradition. But there are one or two more interesting points. When the object is a tripod, it is usually said to have been found in the sea, and to have been caught in a fishing net. And here there surely is a connection to be pointed out — which has indeed already been pointed out, and which is quite inescapable. Not only is the sea the element which conveys or carries off the god, the dead man translated into a hero, the infant hero and, above all, the chest in which he has been put;[13] but divinities and objects endowed with magical power are discovered or miraculously saved in fishing nets — as were the infant Perseus and his mother Danaë in the chest in which they had been cast away;[14] similarly in the parallel legend of Telephus and his mother Augē (Glotz, 1904: 51—2), the shoulderblade of Pelops, the most important of the bones of the hero, which were needed so that the Greeks might take Troy (Pausanias 5.13.4—6 Rocha-Pereira), and a famous moving statue [of the athlete/ hero Theagenes], now accursed, now imposed upon the credulity of popular religiosity (Pausanias 6.11.8). And we may also note that in the story which concerns us this mythical motif is related to another, which is its counterpart — at least in one rather full version in the tradition:[15] the tripod was originally a wedding-gift from the gods, and as such passed down in the family of the Pelopidae until it came to Helen, and was by her thrown into the sea 'in accordance with an ancient oracle'; and was miraculously recovered once the predicted period of time had elapsed.

The mythic connections of the precious object are then at once discernible — they almost leap out at one — in this moralizing story of the seven sages. But that does not mean that it is not also conceived as the repository of that social 'value', as involving that social manipulation, which are characteristic of the pre-monetary phase. The tripod and the cup are among the most typical examples in the list that I gave earlier. They can be substituted for each other; and they are treated as equivalents in the legends, except that, while the tripod is normally the carrier of mythical associations, the gold cup tends to be treated slightly differently. For it is not merely a rare object which is a privileged sign of wealth in a mainland economy that was still poor (Kuiper, 1916: 424): in the version given by Eudoxus of Cnidus (Diogenes Laertius 1.29),[16] the King of Lydia's organization of the competition presages the use of this kind of object — and the cup in particular — in the earliest contractual trade.[17]

The story of the tripod of the seven sages suggests, I think, that in the presentation of the *agalma* in the legends there are, as it were, two contrasted poles.

This discussion of the mythic density to be found in one and the same story would be incomplete if I failed to point out one element that might seem utterly adventitious.

Before it is awarded to one of the sages, the tripod is usually the focus of a dispute which turns into a war between cities. The episode is not essential; the story could have dispensed with it. Yet it fits neatly with the tale, as is revealed by one very interesting detail (Diogenes Laertius 1.32): as Helen threw the tripod into the sea, she foretold that it would be much fought over (περιμάχητος). That makes it sound as though it were endowed with a mysterious power: it exercises, exactly, a baneful influence. I incline to think that the persistence of this theme which has no bearing on the story derives from the fact that it is a constituent of the very idea of the precious object.

There is one other matter that I shall simply call to the reader's attention in the same way: the versions in which the cup figures do not include this feature. There must then have been a special connection between the symbolism associated with the tripod and an essential element of the mythical conception of 'value'. Indeed, the theme of the 'dispute over the tripod' is illuminated itself by a famous legend which pits Heracles against Apollo. The tripod is the one at Delphi: and so we can relate the possession of an *agalma* to the establishment or the repossession of some religious authority. And it is only to be expected that it might at the same time have a 'political' significance: a tripod given by the Argonauts to the Libyans or the Hylleans [or the people of Euesperis/Berenice] assured these nations of their right to undisputed possession of their land (Herodotus 4.179; Apollonius of Rhodes, *Argonautika* 5.522—36; Diodorus Siculus 4.56.6).

For us of course the symbolic implications of a single motif may well seem to diverge in different directions. But in myth they are bound tightly one to the other.

Eriphyle's necklace

Rather similar connections in relation to the precious object seem to have existed in the minds of those who created legends inspired by it; and they are revealed by other stories connected with conflict.

According to the tradition describing the oldest games, the things which were offered as prizes were truly impressive and in their own way very valuable; and among them we occasionally find arms and armour. Not of course to be used: these objects belong to a class well known to anthropologists — 'ornamental armour'. Our most interesting example is the 'shield of Argos', which gave its name to one of the contests in the great festival of Hera: as a synonym, Pindar uses the expression 'the bronze in Argos', thus stressing that aspect of the value of the metal object which is socially of greatest importance [Pindar, *Olympian* 7.83 Snell]. But there are resonances here too. This shield was connected with the one which King Danaus carried in the days of his youth and later consecrated in the temple of Hera (Robert, 1920—6: 1.273). And the prizes annually awarded seem to be a sort of *coinage* derived from this shield (Reinach, 1910: 221). In the legendary tradition, moreover, the shield is a bit like a talisman — it figures in relation to the installation and transmission of royal power in one case: on Danaus's death, his son-in-law takes it down and gives it to his own son (who is the proper representative of his maternal grandfather). On the other hand, the shield also possesses the power — manifested miraculously in time of war — of protecting the city to which the temple belongs. One glimpse of the shield of Danaus is enough to make its enemies turn and flee (Servius, *in Vergil. Aeneid. 3.286* [3, p. 115.20 Harvard edition]). We come across the same motif of magical armour, and in exactly the same form, in the story of Aristomenes's shield, which had also been consecrated, and which gained the day for the Thebans at Leuctra (371 BC) when it was placed on a trophy set up in full view of the enemy (Pausanias 4.32.5—6).

But it is in the context of specific behaviour in a given social situation that we can best understand the ambiguity of the precious object.

At just about the high point of the drama, there is a scene in Aeschylus's *Agamemnon* which even today provides a special frisson, is strangely powerful. Agamemnon has come back to Argos the conqueror of Troy. His wife Clytemnestra is about to murder him. But she is clever: she welcomes her husband with stentorian hypocrisy. What happens is this: she presses Agamemnon to enter the palace by walking over rich purple stuffs; he is hesitant, he is afraid; and finally gives in. And when the great door of the palace closes upon him we know that he is done for (*Agamemnon* 905—57 Page).

In the dialogue between the two characters, we find themes at once very old and extraordinarily vital: they surface in allusions in an urgent rhythm in which the apparent fracture of the discourse perfectly betrays the bartered resonances of the thought. Clytemnestra requires of the king that he should make manifest his divine power.[18] The King must never set foot directly on the earth (a well-known taboo). But the magnificent stuffs that he is going to set foot upon are also the focus of an actual ritual: it is by setting one's foot on the skin of a sacrificial animal, or on a tomb, or on one's ancestral land that one affirms a religious claim, one's assumption of power, one's right of ownership. Again, what Agamemnon walks on has here its own intrinsic quality — a quality that must be respected. What gives Agamemnon pause, what inhibits him from at once acceding to his wife's desire, is the thought of the hostile forces he might rouse up by so portentous a parade — condemnation by the gods to whom alone such processions are reserved and who will be angered to have their honours usurped; 'envy' in the form of human criticism (τὸν ἀνθρώπειον . . . ψόγον: 937), which he well knows is but that impersonal divine force (numen in Latin), all-powerful at certain moments, which emanates continually both from gods and from men and whose concrete form at any instant is the magical notion of the evil eye. But what orchestrates all these plaited themes is a conception of wealth: the object to which all these considerations of power and of danger are attached is something precious, a possession. The question is shall he despoil it — shall he precisely tread it — or shall he not? For on the one hand, wealth is, in itself, the object of religious awe (aidōs). Against that, it can be sacrificed intentionally, and Clytemnestra forces Agamemnon to admit that, under exceptional circumstances in which one would have a duty to run the risk involved in exceptional offerings, he could himself have vowed such an offering.

Female treachery triumphs: Agamemnon accomplishes his own doom by assimilating himself to divinity, by acquiescing in the fatal consecration brought about by setting his foot upon the purple stuffs;[19] and if his last utterance before he admits himself beaten expresses shame at the waste of such opulence, that may indeed be a testimony to bourgeois meanness; but it is also something entirely different.

The most typical example of the malefic power of the precious object is provided by the necklace which figures in the Theban cycle.[20]

Seven Argive heroes have undertaken to make war upon Thebes to restore to Polyneices, son of Oedipus, his proper rights after he has been driven out by his brother Eteocles. One of the seven, Amphiaraus, takes part only with extreme reluctance. To obtain his co-operation, his wife Eriphyle has to be employed as intermediary, for a consideration: a peplos and a golden necklace. A series of disasters ensues. Amphiaraus loses his life on the expedition. His son Alcmaeon avenges him by killing his mother. Polluted by his mother's blood, he too comes to a terrible end. He gives the peplos and the necklace to two wives, one after the other; and they are fatal. Their evil power persisted even into historical times: after the Phocian sack of the temple at Delphi, where they had been consecrated, the wife of one of the Phocian generals wanted to wear these treasures. They burned her to death.

We would do well to note in the initial story one or two links with social reality. The *peplos* and the necklace had a long history: they had been given to Harmonia, forebear of the kings of Thebes, on the occasion of her marriage to Cadmus; and they were handed down through the royal family until they reached Polyneices (who, interestingly enough, according to one source, received them when the inheritance was divided up, in exchange for allowing Eteocles first turn as king: Hellanicus, *FGrH* 4 F 98 [= Scholiast on Euripides, *Phoenissae* 71]). So they belong in principle to the category of marriage-gifts, itself part of the category of customary prestations and as such subject to social rules. We should also note that such things are found in pairs elsewhere too: in Euripides's *Medea*, the daughter of the king of Corinth is given a crown and a *peplos* by Medea — an association which recurs in the first century AD in the case of an imperial offering [by Nero] at Delphi: gold crown and purple *peplos* (Pausanias 2.17.6); Amphitrite gives Theseus a crown and a tunic, more or less as a present for his bride-to-be Ariadne; Alcmene is given a necklace and a cup by Zeus, who has taken the form of her husband.[21]

Some traditional prestations, in particular those given on the occasion of a marriage, certainly became heirlooms. And one could say that it looks very much as though, in our story at least, their alienation from the family brought about by Polyneices's action initiated the terrible career of the *agalmata*. But it is worth thinking about the manner in which their power is, at that decisive moment, let loose. Why did Amphiaraus have to go on the expedition? The legendary tradition on this point is at once opaque and complex. Now we find the idea of 'persuasion', now of 'obligation'. But all the sources agree that when Amphiaraus goes he is aware of what has happened and yet still has to go. Why must he go? One explanation invokes the idea that his wife has been granted beforehand the right to decide. The philologists rightly observe that this renders the motif of the inducement — the gift — superfluous (cf. Robert, 1915: 1,208). The duty is without explanation, the persuasion ineffectual; and anyway, they are mutually contradictory. When the legend was created in the epic poem to which our sources refer, it seems that an attempt was made, by dint of clumsy prosthesis, to explain this central element away because it was no longer fully understood. But in truth it is itself the explanation; and sometimes we can just glimpse that it is all the explanation needed: for example, when we look, in the figurative representations, at the scene of Amphiaraus's departure, where Eriphyle stands before her angry husband, clearly wearing the fatal necklace;[22] or when we are told that Amphiaraus, precisely so as not to have to go, forbade his wife to accept Polyneices's gifts (Apollodorus, *Bibliotheca* 3.61); or when Homer tells us that the hero's death was brought about by 'gifts to a woman' (γυναίων εἵνεκα δώρων) — an expression even the ancients found difficult, but which in its other occurrence in a different context refers to a legendary motif (*Odyssey* 15.247; 11.521). In each case we can see the underlying notion of the 'coercive force of the gift': Amphiaraus has to go off to his death once the gift has entered *his own house*.

That idea cannot in principle be separated from the notion that there inheres in the object given a mysterious power (Mauss, 1970: 8–12, 63–9); and we should note that the two do become separated in the usual run of legends about *agalmata*. That more or less obscures both the origin and the point of the motif in the myth — yet the motif endures, and the object of value cannot be represented socially without it.

But it does of course have other aspects: and they appear stereotyped in legendary tradition.

3

Polycrates's ring

Wealth is the focus of religious awe. Can it be got rid of? Sometimes it must — witness the scene in the *Agamemnon*: where we also saw that even to vow to destroy it involves facing terrible danger.

Polycrates was tyrant of Samos during the second half of the sixth century; for all that, the legend associated with him incorporates a number of instructive themes. In the form it takes in Herodotus (3.40–3), it has of course been adapted in the interests of a moralizing piety of the kind often to be found in that author: the unmarred prosperity of Polycrates stirs the gods' envy; he is advised to divest himself of some portion of his wealth — precisely, 'the object which is most precious to him'. And so he throws into the sea, during what can only be described as a ritual,[23] the famous ring which is the thing he values most. But strange to tell, the ring turns up again. Polycrates is unable to renounce that which he had accepted he must renounce. And he must be destroyed: only utter ruin can expiate obdurate prosperity.

Though it has come to dominate the unfolding of the story, the metaphysical idea of *nemesis* has not, in general, done too much violence to the traditional elements that we can glimpse even through the folk-tale motifs. Scholars have tried to define these elements by dint of parallels which are not exactly irrelevant, but too general to explain anything in a proper manner: for instance, the invocation of the ceremony in which the Doge of Venice was married to the Adriatic, to symbolize the Venetian claim to rule the sea. It is more appropriate to treat the myth as a myth, to break down its constituents, and pick up the associations it suggests in the Greek legendary tradition.

The first point is that the throwing of a ring into the sea also occurs in the legend of Theseus. The context, to be sure, is rather different: but that simply makes the presumption of the act's ritual character the more natural. While the ship carrying the victims destined for the Minotaur to Crete is on its way, Minos and Theseus quarrel — it does not here matter why, because quite independently of the reason (which is anyway later forgotten), it is clearly in itself a struggle for prestige between the two kings. Minos is granted by his father Zeus a favourable sign which confirms his divine descent; Theseus has to obtain a similar sign from his father Poseidon — and get it he does, after diving into the water. Such an ordeal of diving into the sea is well known elsewhere and might have done perfectly by itself. But it is motivated in the story by a quite extraordinary challenge by Minos which was not indispensable — indeed so dispensable that it does not even figure in our primary source — and which for that reason advertises itself the more loudly: Minos throws his ring into the sea and bids Theseus find it.[24]

So one first element to note is the rôle of the ring in a situation involving a competition in royalty: the test is unilateral in Polycrates's case, bilateral here; but there is a test in each: it is the power of a tyrant that is in the balance as it is the authenticity of royalty that is in question, the same act and the same object are the substance of a ritual.

But it is another story about a marvellous ring which enables us to approach nearer to the import of the symbol in the tyrant's tale: the story of Gyges's ring in the form which Plato is the first to give us (*Republic* 3, 359d–360c).[25] A shepherd in the service of one of the kings of Lydia, Gyges gets into an underground cave by way of an opening which suddenly appears; and there he discovers inside a brazen horse a naked corpse wearing a ring on its finger. He takes the ring and makes his way out. He discovers that if he turns the collet towards him, he becomes invisible. He takes advantage of this to murder the king and take the throne.

The ring here is the means of obtaining royal status by force, in a story which even in Plato preserves its most traditional elements (murder of one's predecessor and marriage to the queen). But granted that we are in the kingdom of Lydia, which is often believed to have issued the first money,[26] and where the incident itself is generally regarded as having taken place in the quasi-historical period of the seventh century, the really significant element is what gives the narrative its peculiar flavour. The essential part of Gyges's ring is the collet. The collet is what holds the seal in place (cf. now Cassin, 1960: 742–50); and Polycrates's ring, and even Minos's sometimes, is called a 'seal'. The ring fitted with an engraved stone is an important object in Greece from Mycenaean times, the sort of thing a prince takes with him to his tomb (Bruck, 1926: 8). We know that the seal was employed from very early times in Near-Eastern civilizations. Both facts allow us to infer that the seal was used relatively early in Greece; it is at any rate certain that the seal is directly related to the earliest coins — it is the antecedent of the struck coin (MacDonald, 1905: 43–52). It signifies, or rather *marks*, ownership, and as such is endowed with a special aura that was originally magical.[27]

It was in an underground cave — what the Greeks though of as a 'treasure-house' — that Gyges found his ring, his magic carpet to wealth and power; and, masked by a rationalizing context that ultimately makes it look a little childish, Polycrates's ring seems to be a charged 'sign' of wealth held and used by a tyrant. For what is special about this precious object in the Samian tale is that it can be used as a bet in an enormous wager in which all the power of its owner is at stake: Polycrates throws it into the sea — 'so that it can never more return among men', as Herodotus has his adviser say. But will the gift be accepted? — it is not, Polycrates fails to secure the favour or legitimacy that he wanted. It was not inappropriate for the legend to have interpreted this failure as a manifestation of *nemesis*: essentially, it is the outcome of an ordeal. The test is closely related to divination (so, Saintyves, 1912: 68–76).[28] For in divination (where the use of the ring persisted) it is a bad sign when an object thrown into the water does not sink to the bottom but is 'sent back' (cf. Pausanias 3.23.8 on the method used by an oracle at a shrine in Laconia).

The ordeal is of course also closely related to sacrifice. I need simply remind the reader of the fact that, at a ritual point which is roughly equivalent to sacrifice, the practice of making ex-voto dedications by throwing coins into a spring or well was carried on in the worship of healing gods and heroes. But what interests me at this juncture is the custom, apparently a properly royal custom, of sacrificing one of these characteristic objects, whether gold cups or other precious containers, by hurling them into the sea. There is an instance of this in the historical account of Alexander the Great (Arrian, *Anabasis* 6.19.5): when he reaches the Indus-delta, Alexander sails out into the sea,[29] sacrifices some animals and flings into the sea a gold cup that he has used to pour a libation, and some wine-mixing bowls, also of gold. Herodotus ascribes the same ritual to Xerxes after he has crossed the Hellespont

(7.54.2): after being used to pour a libation, a gold cup is flung into the sea together with a golden mixing-bowl (*crater*) and a scimitar.[30] The parallel is close and worth remarking: it is quite unlikely that Alexander should have been imitating Xerxes deliberately.

It must be clear that in such a case a theory of sacrifice, understood as an intellectualist justification for the religious act, would be quite wrong. The divine beneficiary can be entirely indeterminate. To be sure Xerxes is supposed to have been appealing to the Sun to give him a prosperous issue in his campaign in Europe; but Herodotus wonders whether it was really 'consecration' to the Sun, rather than an offering to the Hellespont which Xerxes had had lashed and to which, repentant, he might have wanted to offer a gift in compensation. As for Alexander, he sacrifices bulls to Poseidon; but the hurling of the cup and the craters into the Ocean — after a libation which takes place *after* the sacrifice of the animals, and quite independently — is an act which seems quite self-sufficient.[31] The purpose of the offering remains ill-defined, not only in the case of Xerxes, but in that of Alexander, where it is a matter simultaneously of giving thanks for the success of one expedition and praying for the success of the next. To the extent that the act is the product of conscious reflection at all, all we can say is that such reflection justifies *a posteriori* — after the event — and rather uncertainly a practice which the legend of Polycrates interprets as a royal test: that is, the total consecration of a precious object by throwing it into water.

Insofar as the rituals described by Herodotus and by Arrian are to be considered sacrificial, they are not to be classified as ordinary sacrifice, which is a contractual act; and just as this form is not as sharply delineated as that of sacrifice proper, so the underlying attitude to which it conforms is different. And there are quite a number of practices to which *agalmata* seem as it were to be spontaneously attracted which can give us some idea of that underlying attitude, at least in the context of religious or cult usage. For there are some sacrifices in which the object given up is entirely destroyed, in which that destruction is effected — exclusively, in the cases we might call 'ostensive' — by fire or by water, and whose essential feature is that one can see in them not so much a traditional idea, or even the notion of 'getting rid', as an intense need to destroy. And what is destroyed is not only animal victims, but sometimes deliberately and evidently intentionally precious things and symbols of wealth. That is the case with one of the rituals connected with the institution of annual ceremonial bonfires (cf. Nilsson, 1951–60d: 348–54): at one spring festival in Phocis, animals from the flocks and herds, clothes, gold, silver, images of the gods, were all thrown into the flames (Pausanias 10.1.6; cf. Nilsson, 1906: 222–3). Rituals which involve throwing things into the sea can be understood in the same way: here we find the chariot and team as the focus of the 'sacrifice' (Festus, s.v. *October equus* [p. 190, 28–30 Lindsay: Rhodes]; Pausanias 8.7.2 [Argos]; Servius, *in Vergil. Georg.* 1.12: [3, p. 134. 10–12 Thilo: Illyrians]) — that is, the special sign of superabundant wealth: the chariot itself, whose mythical 'charge' I scarcely need to recall; and the horses (sometimes still in harness), which only figure in sacrifice in the classical period on a small number of special occasions as everyone knows, but which are reserved in the legendary tradition for the most sumptuous sacrificial occasions which have no doubt lost nothing in the telling.[32]

Whether we take flamboyant sacrifices of an exaggerated kind or the ring, cup, or tripod cast into the sea; whether the sacrifice be a holocaust or focus upon a single symbolic object, it signals, in a whole gamut of rituals and legends, the destruction of wealth. But I have a feeling that at the level of myth the word 'destruction' is only a gesture towards the truth. It means, among other things, that the act is not necessarily *directed*: one might even argue that it does not in principle involve the idea of a god to whom it is offered; in the legendary tradition at any rate it excludes that notion almost *ex hypothesi*: there can be no question of it in the extreme case of Polycrates (cf. Stengel, 1920: 113), any more than in the story of Helen's tripod. But if the act is not directed, it has a purpose. And it is here that the mythical view is most plainly to be apprehended.

Polycrates's ring was not supposed to return to the human world; but such a thought opposes the human world to some other. One might even say that it presupposes it.

It is a constant theme of religious thinking that to destroy something can never mean that it simply ceases to exist. Of course we have to consider that point in relation to its concrete consequences. And for my present purposes, a rather odd story told us by Herodotus could be at least suggestive. Note that it too comes from a legend concerning a tyrant: the legend of Periander of Corinth (Herodotus 5.92η.1–4). Periander consults an oracle of the dead (it is perhaps not immaterial that he should have consulted it about a lost hoard which cannot be found); his dead wife, Melissa, appears but refuses to tell him where it is hidden because she is cold and naked: for the clothes that were buried with her are useless because they had not been consumed in the funeral flames. Hearing this, Periander calls all the townswomen, decked in their finest apparel, to a shrine, whither they proceed 'as though they were off to a festival'; once there, he has them stripped by his guards. All the clothes are burned, and Melissa's ghost gives him the information he wants.

The imaginative focus is clear from the story itself. We know that the institution of grave-goods was not done away with by the practice of cremation; indeed, for the dead to remain in possession of the goods he takes with him because they are 'part of him', they *must* be burned with him:[33] the very fact that they are destroyed by the flames means that they are guaranteed to the dead man. But in Herodotus's story this idea is slightly altered: its purpose is in some degree novel, less well defined in intention, especially with regard to the substance of the offering. No doubt Melissa is the beneficiary; but the sacrifice — monstrous, as befits a tyrant, and quite out of proportion to its immediate purpose — is, actually, directed towards the world of the dead which was the only consideration in the beginning and of which the ghost of Periander's wife is only one member. Moreover the act itself — and this is basic to the story — has the character of a gigantic holocaust whose particular object is these typical symbols of opulence, and for which the finest clothes of all the townswomen are not excessive. Tyrants by definition amass goods in the largest quantities; and they excel at making their subjects' property their own. But these goods, and above all these valuables, can be used to some purpose if their conspicuous destruction serves another world. Periander has his models: a tyrant in legend must follow the rules laid down by myth.

Those rules can be pieced together, by pursuing the different stories: we have several ways of getting at them. Somewhat differently, the theme of things not consumed but which disappear from view reveals its original significance in the legend about the early history of Cyrene. It does not concern an *agalma*, a focus of 'value', but an object which is simply possessed of magical power and nothing else. But it too is related to a typical *agalma* in terms of its functions, I think.

In the course of their voyage the Argonauts reached North Africa; they were received hospitably by the marine divinity Triton, to whom in exchange they gave a tripod (Herodotus 4.179.2) or in another version a gold crater. But we are also told that Triton himself gave one of the Argonauts, Euphēmos [Euphamos in Pindar], a clod of earth, *bōlos* (Pindar, *Pythian* 4.20—3 Snell). At first sight these two facts seem quite unrelated even though they are both given us by old versions: if we find that in the later tradition the gifts are reciprocal and related to each other (Apollonius of Rhodes, *Argonautika* 4.1547—63), that is surely not accidental; gift and counter-gift have a reciprocal relation. The tripod, whose thematic undertones are suggested by the golden crater which is its equivalent, is here a guarantee of security for the land where the recipient dwells (see p. 119 above). The *bōlos* (perhaps the legend made it precisely parallel) guarantees to its recipient the right to the land from which it was taken: we find it in this familiar significance in several stories in Greece containing some trace of a ritual of *traditio per glebam* (Nilsson, 1951–60c: 330–5). In the story about Euphēmos, the *bōlos* contains a magical power (*mana*) to help its owner. And to make this magical power effective, the *bōlos* has to be thrown into the sea (Apollonius of Rhodes, *Argon.* 4.1755–7). Pindar is more precise (*Pythian* 4.40–8): the proper time for their taking possession of the land was delayed by the imprudence of Euphamos's companions, who dropped the clod of earth into the sea in the wrong place; they should have dropped it off Cape Taenarum, in *one of the entrances to the underworld.*[34]

When you throw a magic object into the sea, you know what you are up to. It is a persistent theme: but its recurrence in legends about *agalmata* does not mean that a Greek had to have a specific awareness of the imaginative 'field' which they once occupied. It is enough for an imaginative scheme to endure. And their value in myth is revealed again in another set of motifs, which are, as it were, the mirror-image of the preceding one.

Polycrates's ring came back. Now to be sure, in the particular form in which our narrative presents the motif, it is folk-tale. But that does not mean that we have to suppose that it is merely a casual invention stitched on to a myth about ordeals. For we find it again in a quite different context; and the parallel makes it certain that it is not a unique idea in the legendary tradition. We know that Helen's tripod, which she threw into the sea, had one day to come back: she was herself perfectly aware of that. And come back it did: it was 'found' in the way that mythical objects are found.

Agalmata can come directly from the other world: there is one legend that tells us about one that the sea itself threw up (Antikleides [= *FGrH* 140 F 4, =] Athenaeus, *Deipnosophistae* 11.15, 466c, 3rd century BC; Plutarch, *Convivium* 20, 163b). Lesbos was settled by seven kings who, at a particular spot on the coast, had to offer a sacrifice ordered by an oracle, a foundation sacrifice, involving a human being. The daughter of one of the kings was thrown into the sea. Enalos, a young man who was in love with her, dived in with her. After a good while, he reappeared: his story was that the girl was living with the Nereids, the Sea Nymphs, and that he himself had been pasturing the horses of Poseidon. Then he allowed himself to be carried off by a wave; but soon emerged bearing a *gold cup* 'so magnificent, that human gold by comparison was just copper'.

129

Certainly the tale could have acquired its present shape thanks to some Alexandrian. But the love story should not distract us from its fundamental elements. One or two connections first. In Plutarch's version, which is fuller on this point, there is not just a human sacrifice: a bull was also thrown overboard; and this kind of total offering, particularly when it stands by itself (not preceded by the ritual killing in the usual fashion), is as we have seen characteristic of some unusual but enduring rituals analogous to those involving the throwing of horses into water (above, p. 127). And perhaps I am not entirely mistaken in thinking that this parallel may help us to understand the end of the story;[35] the people involved remind us of several things we already know. Moreover, the girl is thrown in decked in rich clothes and gold jewellery.

By contrast, the main character, Enalos, bears a name which obviously makes him into a hero of the sea. He is similar to a figure who occurs rather more commonly, namely Glaucus (practically a synonym indeed), and who is associated with the ritual of jumping into the sea — itself apparently linked to a memory of 'prophets' who specialized in such ritual dives: Glaucus obtained immortality by magical means. The truth is that it is an image of a paradise under the waves that is at least alluded to by the story of Enalos as it is in that of Theseus, for all that the idea is less well-known among the Greeks than among the Celts: the presence of Nereids in each certainly suggests the idea of immortality (Picard, 1931: 5—28), especially their rôle in the Enalos story. And Theseus, having gone down to the bottom of the sea under the circumstances I have described (p. 124 above), is given by Amphitrite, the Nereid who is married to Poseidon, two sumptuous *agalmata*: a costly gown and a crown whose purpose and meanings vary from version to version of the legend of Theseus, but which in this instance is conceived as a magnificent piece of jewellery.

In this group of stories, where the image of the other world is given firm shape, we can see that it is imagined above all as the place from which the *agalma* comes. The story of Enalos and of the gold cup brought up from the waves illustrates the notion of a free gift that comes from the world beyond. And this is not the only such instance in the tradition: it appears in another form on two occasions, and the analogy is the more striking in that the objects involved are not the same.

For all that it belongs to what is generally called history, the 'second Messenian war' is myth-stuff: Aristomenes, the national hero, is known by virtue of a tradition of popular epics. We have seen that his shield was supposed to be able to destroy the enemies of Messenia several centuries after his death (p. 120). This shield has a history.

Aristomenes lost it in a battle — rather mysteriously (it was taken by the Dioscuri). The Delphic oracle advised him to go down into the underground shrine of Trophonius in order to get it back. And Aristomenes did indeed get his shield back; and with it he performed mightier feats of arms than ever (Pausanias 4.16.7). Trophonius was a hero who ran an oracle. How was his intervention supposed to have worked?

The same question might spring to mind in an episode in the Bellerophon legend — this time, in connection with an *agalma*. Pindar tells us that the hero tried in vain to break in Pegasus, until Pallas Athena gave him a golden bit; and immediately afterwards, we find mention of a *dream* — or rather a dream which is reality — in which the goddess gave him the bit (*Olympian* 13.63—86 Snell). And where it all happened there was a shrine of Athena *Khalinitis* ('of the bit') as whose foundation-legend this story serves (Pausanias 2.4.1); while Bellerophon's experience is treated as a story of divination by dream. But it was not just a sign or an insight that the goddess gave: it was the bit itself. And that helps us to understand what might have seemed odd about the story of Aristomenes: Aristomenes 'got his shield back from Trophonius's cave'; the gift of a god is given directly. The thing comes from a world beyond which is as well the land of dreams as it is the subterranean cave of an oracular hero.

For Bellerophon, it is a matter of an object that is magical in that it acts in a marvellous way. But horse-harness, especially bridle and bit, is one of the most important items of warrior wealth; age-old tradition demanded that it be buried with its owner; fine examples were found at Olympia in the Roman period during construction work (Pausanias 5.20.8); Cimon of Athens, that perfect 'knight', solemnly and symbolically made an offering of one on the Acropolis on the eve of the battle of Salamis in 480 BC (Plutarch, *Life of Cimon* 5.2).

Like other mythical objects which are related to them in the Greek imagination, precious objects, traditional symbols of opulence, are ineluctably related — indeed, in a way especially related — to that other world presupposed by the religious mind: now they go down to it, and now they journey back.

4

The golden fleece

Quite deliberately I have so far confined myself to more or less late stories or fragments of legend whose interest lay in their revelation of the mythical imagination at work at a period immediately prior to the dawn of so-called positive thought. One feels that it should be possible to get back to older forms, much richer, and in which the scattered ideas that I have put together step by step might be found in direct relation to the general, yet more profoundly mythical, notion of wealth. Of that, the golden fleece could be a typical illustration. It is represented to us by different terms which amount to the same,[36] with rather different characters, in two groups of legends which are not related to one another: in the story of the Argonauts, and in the story of the house of Pelops.

The second of these is quite explicitly dramatic; and perhaps thereby easier to penetrate. We find it in Euripides — one of the few poets in antiquity to be interested in legend — and above all in a lyric passage in the *Electra* (699—746).[37] Let me say in passing that we could be lucky in finding a mythical theme in lyric; for Greek lyric proceeds by allusion, intimation or 'snapshots' of scenes or fragments of scenes, which can thus retain their proper significance and which the poets, Pindar especially, order without respect for chronology to suit their own ends. Quite different in character is continuous narrative; in our case, it is Pherecydes, one of the earliest mythographers, who provides us, through the medium of Apollodorus, with a classic instance. Each mode has its own interest. It is obvious that the second always involves some degree of reconstruction; but the linkages are not a matter entirely for the discretion of the narrator or of his literary sources: we can decipher a tradition in them, even in the connections which must be invented. All the same, it is best to begin where possible with the dramatic perspective, and we return to the *Electra*.

A marvellous lamb, a golden lamb, is born to a sheep belonging to Atreus, one of the claimants to the throne of Mycenae. The god of the flocks comes down the mountains of Argos and brings it into the city to the strains of his pipe. The public herald, from the agora-block, bids the people gather to behold the 'wonder', presage of a prosperous reign. All over the city, the shimmer of gold, and the bright altar-fires; the music of flutes and hymns to the gods. All of a sudden it is discovered that Thyestes, Atreus's brother, has stolen the golden lamb: he vaunts his new possession before the assembled crowd. And Zeus turns the sun and the stars from their bright course.

A poet obviously has the right to proceed by allusion; but it should be of interest to us that for all his elliptical manner, which forces us to supply certain facts from outside, for all his indifference to narrative or psychological motivation, yet Euripides has stressed the elements of spectacle, and above all the imagery of processions. Whether consciously or not, he gives us a scenario. And in this scenario the role of the lamb is quite clear: it is a talisman which grants its owner the right to be king, because it guarantees prosperity to the people; as such, it is made known during a festival[38] — and the very incoherence of what we can hardly term an account serves merely to highlight this point. That is Act I; Act II, still more Act III, are simply alluded to; but we might wonder whether they are not both also memories of a scenario. And that means that we need to understand the link between the two miracles.

The continuous narrative that we find in Apollodorus (*Epitome* 2.10–12) makes explicit the point which the chorus in the *Electra* makes synthetically. Atreus has made a vow to sacrifice the finest animal born among his flocks; whereupon the golden lamb 'appears'. An analogous motif is to be found in the legend of Minos, whose brothers dispute his right to succeed to the throne, and who explicitly requests, as a mark of favour which cannot be denied, that an animal, which he promises to sacrifice, shall miraculously be sent him (Apollodorus, *Bibliotheca* 3.1.3).[39] Both kings are false to their oath (though their right to the throne remains unaffected): the golden lamb is suffocated by Atreus and hidden by him in a chest (*larnax*). But Thyestes steals it;[40] and then he comes before the assembly and persuades it to decree that he who possesses the marvellous animal shall become king; and so produces the golden lamb. Atreus intervenes. He gets Thyestes to permit a repetition of the process: he is to become king again if the sun turns back in its course. And so it happens.

Artificial though the homology between the two episodes may be — indeed, precisely because it is so — it is quite clear that the second is the exact counterpart, with the same structure, as the first. It would not perhaps be excessively daring to see here two constituents of an investiture ceremony: at all events, they represent two successive aspects of royal power. Power over the elements is one of the essential attributes, familiar from Greek mythology in particular, of 'magical kingship': in our case, in a form and with evocations I need not analyse, this power is exercised over the course of the sun and the stars. What is the origin of the sort of fusion evidenced by the legend between this power and the power signalled and guaranteed by possession of the talisman? Euripides gives us a clue when he evokes, in a single phrase in relation to the golden lamb, the traditional theme of beneficent and prosperous rule. The two aspects of power are related.

But the significance of the talisman becomes more dense — or more extensive — in the myth which lies behind the Argonaut legend.

It is of course more complex than in the story of the house of Pelops; or rather it contains a number of shifts and so a number of different aspects. The golden fleece belonged to the ram which saved Phrixos when he was in danger of being sacrificed as a result of the intrigues of his step-mother, who had engineered a famine which could be brought to an end only by the sacrifice of the king or of one of his sons. Phrixos, the king's son, has been chosen as the victim: the golden ram miraculously appears and carries him off through the air. The plot, in the legend, is too bizarrely complicated for there not to be an essential connection between the marvellous animal and real ritual facts which even the legend hints at: in order to bring the famine about,[41] the stepmother persuades the local women to roast the seed-corn; one suggestive variant makes her give them roasted seed-corn herself. In truth, we have here a memory of very old agrarian rituals; and also the memory of ceremonies, which persisted in certain traditional festivals, in which the King, as here the Queen, distributes corn. The counterpart of royal beneficence is the king's responsibility, for he may be sacrificed, or be obliged to sacrifice his son, if the community's prosperity is endangered. It is in this institutional and mythical context that the legend itself sets the motif of the Golden Ram. In the end, the ram — which, in the story, is soon sacrificed — becomes a substitute victim:[42] a victim duly embellished, like all other marvellous animals, but also because of his relation to the god who caused him to 'appear', and to the royal figure for whom he substitutes.

The golden fleece itself appears in a different mythical connection, which relates nevertheless to the symbolic value of the marvellous animal. Its conception as a royal talisman is a kind of precondition of the Argonaut legend, in that Jason cannot obtain the throne he claims unless he first goes in quest of the golden fleece. But that point is made also more concretely. When he arrived in the far-eastern land of Colchis, land of the Sun, Phrixos gave to king Aiētēs the fleece of the animal which had saved him and which he had sacrificed. And it is from Aiētēs that Jason asks it back. Of the many dramatic exploits to which this claim gave rise, the clearest is one told us by Pindar (*Pythian* 4.224—43 Snell). The golden fleece is the stake in an ordeal which its claimant has to undergo: he has to yoke two terrible bulls to a plough and with them plough a piece of land. Aiētēs did this himself first; and when Jason in his turn performs the exploit he obtains the right, under the rules of the game, to take possession of the precious object. That is all; but for this brief drama to stand independently in Pindar, the poet must comply with a traditional mode of thinking by linking, as it were by an obligatory synthesis, two elements in the story: the heroic ordeal of ploughing, and the marvellous fleece. Athenian tradition perpetuated the institution of sacred ploughing, the exclusive right of the religious clans (*gentes* in Latin); these ceremonies included sowing the seed (just as Jason had to do); and in the rituals which accompanied the sowing, the fleece of a sacrificed ram, called the ram of Zeus, played a part. The mythical version associated in exactly the same way peculiar privilege in relation to agricultural work and possession of a talisman which must be the hide of a sacrificial victim.

The two legends I have taken — and matched — are evidence for a relation between the symbol of opulence and the themes of confirmation or investiture of a king. They also enable us to glimpse, in the mythical imagination, how this symbol works. It is associated, in the story of the sons of Pelops, with the magical power of a form of kingship characterized by its authority over the Sun. In the story of Jason, it is associated with the agrarian prosperity guaranteed by the exercise of a sole right to perform certain religious functions. And through these stories, it is associated with a mythical and ritual background involving the idea of an effective concentration of agrarian wealth and pastoral wealth in the person of the king, and under his control: the enduring rituals of the *Boukoleion* at Athens, of the Cattle Byre beside which was celebrated each year the marriage of Dionysus and the Queen [Aristotle, *Constitution of the Athenians* 3.5], the special power attributed to the sacred flocks, the special value — and the multifarious implications — that one finds in the image of the sacred or royal field (which is actually where Aiētēs performed his exploit); all of this is evidence for a way of thinking which I will here simply state, because the really important question is this: if the way in which the golden lamb or the golden fleece are represented is closely linked with the theme of agrarian wealth, which is itself also connected with royal responsibility, is not this form of representation simply the spontaneous and meaningless elaboration of a religious object which had a fundamental place in the scenarios?

The composite character of the image itself is quite instructive. Why a *golden* fleece, and even more, why a *golden* animal? We do not need to discuss the imprecisions and the contradictions of the legend: the important point is the fusion of two elements connoting wealth, wealth in flocks and herds, and wealth in precious metals — the very same elements which make up the mythical theme studied long ago by Usener, and whose relationship and fusion, in the legend of Atreus and that of Phrixos, he noticed (1899: 182–5). The theme is sufficiently amenable to particular intentions to free it from the narrowing and the coherence which it would have required if it were to stand by itself: it plays in the midst of a set of cultural forms and purposes from which it cannot be extricated. Following the path of mythical thinking, it will travel in this direction or in that. Atreus locked the golden lamb in a chest, as he would have done with some metal object; in the case of the image of the golden fleece, it is once again the idea of precious metal which seems to dominate. Conversely, it is the animal aspect which is

135

highlighted when the talisman of kingship is conceived particularly as coming from the royal flocks. But in truth the two elements, in the golden fleece, cannot be separated. It is odd to find, in a late descendant of ancient myth — a modern folk-tale from Epirus (Cook, 1914—40: 1.412—14) — how, more or less unconsciously, the associations of gold and its proper power have insinuated themselves into a context with whose framing they might have seemed to have had nothing to do. A king's daughter has been shut up in an underground palace: she must be found before anyone can marry her; a young man has himself sewn into a sheepskin, sold to the king as a sheep, and succeeds in getting to the girl. The skin he covers himself with is a golden fleece: the echo, or the reminiscence, might seem forced. But the king's daughter is shut up just like Danaë and Zeus got to her in the guise of a shower of gold; since the folk-tale speaks of a fleece, no doubt it was a golden fleece; and a golden fleece naturally goes underground, because that is where something valuable belongs. Even within a context in which imaginative products are simply for pleasure, the traditional associations continue to play their part.

The term 'composite image' is really only a label. It is not a matter of different images coming together; rather, of several meanings of a single collective representation which is, in the true sense, as 'plastic' as necessary. I cannot here analyse all these meanings; but I ought to sketch them at least in outline, because there is no better way of understanding the constituents of the notion of the *agalma*, which lies deep behind the idea of the golden fleece.

I start with something extremely old: one of the cults most palpably archaic is that of Zeus Akraios on Mount Pelion — close by the land of Phrixos;[43] his ministrants each year wound their way in procession up the mountain, wrapped in the skins of freshly-sacrificed rams; the ritual was performed at the time of the (heliacal) rising of Sirius, a crucial date which was the focus of meteorological magic in cases other than this. Ritually, the hide of the sacrificial animal has special powers of all kinds (Pley, 1911); but the miraculous fleece has a special relation to a class of objects in myth whose meaning is fairly apparent. Insofar as the animal-hide can be used as defensive armour, it is magical armour when it is the famous *aegis*: when used by Zeus, it spreads panic like a supernatural force. But Zeus may use it differently: when he shakes it like an Arcadian 'rain-maker' (cf. Virgil, *Aeneid* 8.351—4), it influences the sky and the atmosphere. It also, even when wielded by Athena, has the power to make things fertile. The *aegis* is a goat-skin: the goat Amalthea, which suckled Zeus, is usually a beneficent creature; one of her horns became the horn of abundance (the *cornucopia*), and provides a mythical name for a number of other symbols of agrarian prosperity; but it is sometimes a terrifying beast, and had to be 'hidden': its hide provided Zeus with a weapon when he undertook the famous war against the Titans after whose conclusion he founded a new monarchical order ([Eratosthenes], *Catasterismi* 13, pp. 98—100 Robert). But the Chimera, the monster defeated by Bellerophon, is also, as its name reveals, the Goat: it seems that, in its homeland Lycia, the Chimera was a *shield-device* (Radermacher, 1938: 97; cf. Malten, 1925: 125—9). The lamb at Argos may have been one (Frazer, 1898: 3.187): a stone ram stood on a tomb in the plain of Argos which was known as the 'tomb of Thyestes' (Pausanias 2.18.1).

These observations, few as they are, suggest at least a context of imagery: the notion of 'royal' potency which I have shown to have been associated with the representation of the fleece in myth may seem multifarious and almost endlessly ramified. It has nonetheless, far back in time, a sort of unity which the symbol's very plasticity sometimes enables us to glimpse. The link between gold and the Sun — which indeed specially sanctifies royal power — is particularly close in the legend of Aiētēs, king of a mythical East: it appears somewhat differently, more opaque but more suggestive, in the story of Atreus. Further-more, the fleece is not always 'golden'; sometimes it is purple: in Etruscan divination, the appearance of an animal of this colour [or of gold] in a flock or herd is the presage of a new dispensation which will be an age of prosperity and fertility (Macrobius, *Saturnalia* 3.7.2). Amid all the variations produced by the working of the imagination, this fact, which takes us back to a tradition of 'Aegean' beliefs, fits perfectly, even in its expression, with the idea revealed directly in the legendary history of Mycenae.

But there is an interesting shift. Pindar, one of our sources with the most highly developed sense of myth, mentions 'the shimmering fleece with tassels of gold' (*Pythian* 4.231; imitated by Apollonius of Rhodes, *Argonautika* 4.1142 Fränkel). 'Tassels of gold' is a detail Homer notes in a description of Athena's *aegis* (*Iliad* 2.447—9). And Homer tells us how many there were, and how much they were worth. It is a descrip-tion of a ritual vestment, this; borne by the goddess herself, the object is the locus of all manner of qualities, including beauty and 'value'. The manner in which the fleece is presented in myth is evolving into an image of an *agalma* even while it preserves, as it were, its material substance.

This imaginative shift which is nevertheless qualified by a relative persistence of the mythical symbol is a quite general phenomenon: we can see its analogue in relation to real objects or when real actions are

137

performed. Kings in legends or in epic carry a sceptre (Deubner, 1933: 85) which is both sign and instrument of their authority: as Homer puts it, there resides in it something of the power of Zeus, the fount of royal power. There is actually a necessary connection between the bearing of the sceptre and the power of uttering *themistes*, pronouncements and judgements, like those of the oracles: the sceptre is certainly derived from the prophet's staff, itself cut from a tree set apart by its natural capacity for divination. But the king's sceptre came to be made by a craftsman: the sceptre given by Zeus to the house of Pelops was fashioned by Hephaestus, the divine smith. And it of course ended up made of gold. Yet in that object made of metal — costly metal — there endures a magical quality akin to that once stored in a quite different material. Conversely, the practice of making offerings sometimes reveals a continuity of function in which one can observe the same transition: for example, the *anathēma* comes to replace the offering which is destroyed. The *anathēma* is a reproduction of the offering in precious metal: a typical example is the sheaves made of gold consecrated by a number of cities at Delphi (Plutarch, *De Pythiae oraculis* 16, 401f–402a; [Strabo 6.1.15: 264C]; Rouse, 1902: 66 n. 3); one, Metapontum, was to keep the symbol on its coins. And of course it is sacrificial animals that we find represented, especially in gold: and it is quite predictable that the legendary tradition should happen to preserve a parallel substitution in the case of the golden lamb of the house of Pelops (Antikleides, *FGrH* 140 F 8 [= Scholiast on Aristophanes, *Clouds* 144, p. 88.39–45 Dübner]).

All this is evidence for what, failing a more satisfactory term — because in reality there is continuity too — I will call 'displacement' (*transfert*): the same thematic field, sometimes the same states of feeling and the same attitudes, are evoked or intimated by an object which is deemed identical but which nevertheless is characterized by fundamentally new aspects. And it is of course here that we can see the transition to the full notion of value taking place: we find evidence of this in the case of one of the objects employed in religious 'trade', and which we also find as the object of human exchange as an *agalma*, with the kind of evocations we saw in the motif of the golden fleece; and it is not what we might have expected. In temple-inventories we sometimes find mention of a 'golden vine' (Homolle, 1882: 146 [from the Artemision at Delos]). The displacement here is of the same order as that in the case of the golden corn-ears, for example. The ordinary vine-stock is to be found in a number of rituals and myths, linked itself to a dense group centred upon the motif of the fruit-tree planted or created by a god or a hero; and the entire group is related to myths about kingship, and indeed to the memories of scenarios which persist in enduring rituals. This thematic complex extends into the golden analogue. It is a golden vine-stock which ensures the recognition of two heroes [Thoas and Euneōs], sons of Jason and grandsons of Thoas; and Thoas received it from Dionysus god of the vine. It has, at a decisive moment, to be 'shown', to be 'set forth'; it operates as a hereditary talisman.[44] Yet we also find the same object as an *agalma* proper. One of the clearest illustrations of the coercive force of the gift is offered by an episode at the end of the Trojan War: in order to obtain military assistance from his nephew, his sister's son, Priam sends his sister a vine with golden leaves and silver grapes made by Hephaestus; it had been the payment for the rape of Ganymede (Robert, 1920–6: 3.2.1, 1222–3). It is a fine example of the theme of 'gifts to a woman' (*Odyssey* 11.521); and the story unfolds in the same manner as that of Eriphyle's necklace (p. 121 above).

The object created by labour that *represents* a thing endowed with magical properties, and which we have seen to have acted as a talisman, is here the same as the object in which economic value inheres.

We have to do with a sort of projection of the ideal notion in the other world on to the plane of human life: treasure is real enough socially — an institution indeed; but it is also real enough in myth. It is both a social reality and a mythic reality. And the notion of 'treasure' involves also the place in which it is kept.

Hermann Usener quite rightly pointed out the link between the legend of the golden fleece and the motif of the storehouse. And of course, since its double significance as talisman and as 'value' is quite apparent, the object is kept by Aiētēs in his palace, by Atreus locked in a chest. By definition the symbol of opulence is something more or less concealed: its magical properties cannot be divorced from a degree of necessary secrecy. Certainly it must on some occasions be 'let out', unlike *palladia*, which are ultra-secret; but that does not mean that they are not related to objects which guarantee protection just as *palladia* do and which are, conversely, represented in legend from time to time in a way which recalls an object kept in a treasury. The bronze *hydria* which contained a lock of Medusa's hair, the guarantee of a royal city's safety, suggests a whole range of associations, in which the notion of opulence alternates or combines with that of magical power (Apollodorus, *Bibliotheca* 2.7.3 [cf. Pausanias 8.47.5]).

Precious things are often underground: a hoard at Delphi, which was discovered by miraculous means, had been buried. But it is things endowed with a power which is now 'political', now religious, that are buried in the earth: the knife used in the sacrifice which sealed a pact (Euripides, *Suppliant Women* 1205–9); the arrow of Apollo, hidden in the land of the Hyperboreans and made of gold, but also a sign of the

139

legitimacy of the prophet Abaris ([Eratosthenes], *Catasterismi* 29, p. 154 Robert; cf. Delcourt, 1938: 89 n. 1);[45] the Argonauts' tripod; the goat Amalthea; the thunderbolt of Zeus granted him on his accession as the symbol and as the guarantor of his authority (Hesiod, *Theogony* 503—6 Solmsen).

Even the denotations of the word treasure-house (*thēsauros*) are instructive. The earliest *thēsauros* is the underground pit in which agricultural produce is stored. It remained a place to store things; and jewels and clothes of value were kept there along with things that were to be eaten. The word came, however, to have a technical sense in the religious sphere, but interestingly enough was simultaneously in some degree 'secularized', in that the idea of a secret store in the end disappears; but we should remark one kind of temple-*thēsauros*, the offertory-box, which takes the form of a hollowed stone with a cover on top; an identical shape and arrangement is known with different purposes: for keeping cult-objects in — objects of extreme sanctity in an archaic religion (Pausanias 8.15.3); and in legend, for keeping hidden objects used for the investiture of kings (the stone of Theseus: Plutarch, *Life of Theseus* 3.6—7 Ziegler).

The chamber in which the ancient hoards of princes were kept was called a *thalamos* (the same word, interestingly enough, was used for the wife's or the daughter's apartments). It is usually thought of as underground; the story of Danaë suggests to us its associations in myth. We find the same associations stated explicitly in relation to the *thalamos* of Aiētēs (cf. Pindar, *Pythian* 4.160) — the owner of the golden fleece: Mimnermus calls it a *golden thalamos* 'where dwell the rays of the Sun' (frg. 11.5—8 Diehl [= *IEG* frg. 11a (2, p. 86)]). And Euripides speaks of the *thalamos* where the king, Phaethon's supposed father, keeps his gold locked up, and where the dead body of Phaethon, who is in reality the son of the Sun, is laid at the end of the drama (frg. 781 Nauck² = lines 222—3 Diggle). The Queen, says Euripides, keeps the keys; just so does Athena, daughter of Zeus, keep the keys of the treasure-house in which the thunderbolt of Zeus is locked away (Aeschylus, *Eumenides* 826—7; cf. Radermacher, 1938: 277—9).

The notion of the royal treasure-house, store of riches, store of *agalmata*, is founded upon the notion of the protective, powerful sacred objects kept safe in his stronghold by a legendary king or by a high god, lord of all.

5

I am afraid that in legend-land we seem to keep wandering off the path. The tortuousness will have been worthwhile if it has enabled us to perceive parallels and even one or two constants in some degree explanatory. It has moreover been unavoidable, because of course the social construction of 'value' and of the precious object is evidenced in social behaviour — a banality, but there is nothing like testing it in a particular civilization and even, as here, in the prehistoric antechamber of civilization: the functioning of gift-exchange at particular moments in social life; the consumption and if need be the destruction of wealth to acquire prestige, at the moment of entry into a special status, or in expiation; the mechanics of a form of power characterized by the obligation 'magically' to promote the prosperity of the collectivity: unless we know the principles which organize behaviour, unless we know the very lineaments of that behaviour, we cannot possibly understand the special status in myth of objects which are at once the substance and the means of human and religious intercourse, within a context of ideas which we have to reconstruct. Now, if legend helps in that reconstruction, the evidence it provides is assuredly diverse, wayward: we must take note of palpable variants; we must stop and think about the implications of each story, even if we are more interested in the psychological processes they display than in their institutional content.

If an ancient notion of 'value' is evidenced for us in the legendary tradition, it is for a good reason: it is mythical itself in terms of the way in which it is conceived. That means above all that its different rôles — or rather what subsequently turn out to be differentiated rôles — are in some degree fused: it tends to be global, involving economics, religion, politics, law and aesthetics all at once. That does not mean that we cannot recognize in it a form of thought,[46] since we have in some degree now understood its orientations. We may now attempt to specify the notions related to the idea of the *agalma* and the nature of their relationship.

There is a word in Greek, *teras*, which may be interesting, because it is sometimes used in relation to the objects I have discussed and because the structure of thought to which it points can be seen in the group of ideas with which I am mainly concerned (cf. Osthoff, 1905: 52—68). Roughly speaking, it denotes something extraordinary, mysterious — often for that reason frightening: its etymological doublet *pelōr* in Homer means a monster, such as the Gorgon; and after Homer, who uses *teras* rather in the less specific sense of a marvellous vision, it is in this sense that *teras* itself is quite often specialized. On the other hand, the word is associated — one could say is usually associated in the oldest usage — with the idea of 'sign': I should add that this 'sign' reminds us sometimes of the mark or emblem on a weapon, shield or breastplate (where, indeed, we often hear of monstrous animals being represented: let me in passing mention the particular connection there seems to be between such notions as 'monster' or 'omen' and shield-devices). Finally, its etymology is in this case of crucial importance: it has enabled Osthoff to trace behind the idea of the marvellous the idea of the 'magical' (*zauberisch*): its root, $*q^wer$, is the one which in Indo-European expresses the idea of 'doing', but especially in the magical sense.[47] There is then, in this group, the notion, latent or overt, but all the same central, of supernatural power attached to a sign, the idea of a religious force which can be concentrated in the thing which is specially denoted by the word *teras*. So it is appropriate, if hardly unexpected, that the golden lamb should itself also be termed *teras* (Euripides, *Orestes* 999 di Benedetto; cf. *Electra* 716); and that the bit which Bellerophon was given by Athena (Pindar, *Olympian* 13.73 Snell) — and which the goddess herself calls a 'charm' (*philtron* [: 68 cf. *pharmakon*, 85]) — should be too.

In the last analysis, it is surely the idea of religious force which we should take to be fundamental in the mythical displacement of the *agalma*. Even more important, the *agalma* is normally linked with the realm of the sacred. It is in accordance with the structures of religious thought that it is socially 'represented'. Although the associations of *thēsauros* are to some degree ambivalent, the notion of the 'concealed object' is based in the case of precious things upon that suggested by cult-practice. Their to-and-fro between the world of men and the other world, so characteristic of them in the legends, is an idea insistently imposed by the religious life, and the parallel is sometimes as clear as one could wish: as it is in a Boeotian cult in which the sacrificial animals which had been cast into pits were believed to reappear at Dodona (Pausanias 9.8.1) — which is simply a concrete and naively spatial interpretation of a practice familiar in 'chthonic' cult. On the other hand, the idea of the *agalma* is often linked to things properly religious; it can be associated with that of cult-apparatus, and derives some of its prestige from that association. The cup, which turns up again and again in legend, is usually termed there *phialē* — a libation-cup. Woven stuffs, which are included among the *agalmata*, have a very ancient place in worship: it may be that the games, in which in historical times they occasionally still were used as prizes, are the remote descendants of tribal jousts, and in any case the transvestism which remained a special feature of a number of festivals is instructively archaic; the offering of the *peplos* to various female divinities, a practice apparently institutionalized at a very early date, is also that in which the specialization of the object for cult purposes is most pronounced.[48]

There is then as it were a specific character of a religious nature inherent in the class of precious objects. But the psychological representation of *agalmata* follows a definite path: there is a principle of selection, and of 'freedom', at work there. It has its own 'space', in that the objects evoked at the level of mythical imagery are all equally objects in current use and which to some extent are in circulation. A particular notion of 'value' — a predominantly aesthetic one, it must be said — is evident: in a story such as that of Enalos, it moves into the foreground. Our task has been made easier by the 'displacements'. Sometimes myths permit us to perceive them; social institutions occasionally allow us to say how they work and something of their special quality: to the giving of food, the foundation of intercourse between peers or between 'prince' and his followers, is added the giving of *agalmata* (a gold cup is the magnificent postscript to a health) — which may even be a substitute for the first.[49] Conversely, we may stand this relation to the religious world on its head: not merely because an object is used in a religious context because it has value, but also because the fact that it is precious makes it worthy to be consecrated.[50] Hence we find in myth a number of objects which are essentially symbols of opulence and nothing more. The *larnax*, the chest in which Atreus locked the golden lamb, is a piece of furniture used to store valuable clothes and precious objects; and it is also the characteristic means of 'exposing' infant heroes or even gods (Glotz, 1904: 45).[51] The tripod did not apparently itself have ritual associations originally: we have the sequence something given as a gift → something given as an offering; it must have been only secondarily associated with Apollo's prophetic power[52] and then, as that god's proper symbol, have been able to pursue its mythical career in the divine iconography.[53]

In this ideological frame, it is a small but interesting point that the adjective *timēeis* is, for instance, the Homeric epithet for Eriphyle's necklace: in relation to a characteristic object in the legendary tradition, the complex notion of *timē* (honour, exclusive social right, special religious quality) becomes specialized, even standardized, in the sense 'precious'. That is a decisive moment: the very same objects which remain even in quasi-historical contexts charged with power derived from myth appear as what we would call external signs of wealth. Yet that notion is much less abstract than we might be inclined to think: both its origins and its enduring associations attest a conceptual stage in which wealth is not the only significance of such objects — they also embody a mysterious power; and it is by no means irrelevant that attitudes towards treasure and its accumulation even in the classical period are still characterized by traditional affects (cf. Athenaeus, *Deipnosophistae* 11.14–16, 465c–66d + 781c–d Kaibel).

6

I am trying to get the measure of a mythical notion. But the essential feature of mythical thinking is that it is not merely a way of thinking associated with images: the images are its indispensable mode. In this particular case, we can discern in the creation of the images a special character.

Legends about precious objects have as it were a raw material: they originate more or less directly in the thematic of magical kingship. The magical quality that inheres in the *agalma* is above all that of a special kind of social 'power': the well-spring of the construction of these images seems to be the very earliest social understanding of the different aspects of authority. It may be asked whether this continuity is not simply a matter of tradition; ought we not to think of it merely as a re-use? But it must have some rationale, because we can show that it endures in the unconscious long after the mythical period.

The conception of 'value' intimately linked with objects made of precious metal is related to the very earliest notion of 'wealth' and tends, like it, to gravitate towards an ideal core. In the mythical representation of kingship, in the scenarios that found and sustain it, the king, who bears the weight of the group's collective life and is the key to its agricultural and pastoral well-being, is marked out also as the keeper of that form of wealth betokened by the golden fleece. The possession of precious things is both sign and precondition of beneficent power; so too, the possession of the sacred field, of the sacred tree, of the sacred flock, which are all enduringly connected with it. This conceptual heartland, in which the talismanic object — in some degree already 'coined', insofar as it is a precious thing — is at once the expression and the guarantor of 'value', to a degree endures into the historical period in Greece. A temple treasure, belonging to a god, and which is also a city's treasure, a city's reserve fund, like that of Athena in Athens, does not include simply the official coins which the state is free to borrow in case of need: the ultimate safeguard is the more sacred property, the apparel of the goddess (*kosmos*) and all the precious objects whose most valued element was viewed in the financial dispositions of Pericles, and of Lycurgus a hundred years later, only as a last resort (Thucydides, 2.13.4–5; pseudo-Plutarch, *Vitae X oratorum*, ψηφίσματα γ΄, 852b). And this idea emerges later still in mythical form. Callimachus's *Hymn to Demeter* ends with a litany (6.119–38 Pfeiffer) in which the poet lists the different kinds of meaning he can find in the ritual procession which is his subject, all done with the most exemplary symmetry: the four horses that bear the sacred basket tell the blessings of the year and its four seasons; the ministrants' garb signifies the prayer for health; and finally, 'as the *liknophoroi* ('corn-basket-bearers') bear the baskets filled with gold, so may gold be given us in endless profusion' (126–7 Pfeiffer). In this Ptolemaic monarchy, whose pretty synthetic political-religious ideology yet remains rooted in deep pre-history, a dilettante court-poet manages to catch once more the feeling of the splendid pomp of kings blended with striking ritual: the parade of objects made in gold testifies to an effective power whose beneficiary is the social group and which works in just the same manner as the magical power of the kings in mythic time.

The collective memory at work in the legends which concern *agalmata* does not work arbitrarily: inside a conception of 'value' which is becoming independent, *sui generis*, traditional habits of thought ensure continuity with the magical-religious idea of *mana*.

In the earliest period of social history of which we have any direct evidence, the symbolism has already in large measure ceased to be polyvalent. It is certainly telling that when Homer describes or alludes, as he often does, to a precious article 'value' is attached to objects whose religious or legendary connotations are stressed by the poet himself or are easily supplied by his audience (for example, *Iliad* 16.220–4; 11.632–5); but I would also point out that an item of harness which might remind one of Bellerophon's exploit – and which in fact is suggestive *poetically* because of the legendary undertones – is in Homer essentially an example of an industrial product, on display for its market worth.[54]

Such an alteration in habits of thought presupposes social conditions (of which indeed we know almost nothing) which we may suspect to have encouraged in some degree the spread of 'external signs of wealth'. Because they were no longer the exclusive property of a class within which the heritage of mythical kingship and its effective symbols had continued to flourish, economic value tended to eclipse the older complex image; the well-known tag 'Money makes the man' is already apt for the pre-monetary period: it occurs, *sotto voce*, in the story of the tripod of the seven sages.[55] Thus gathered the revolution that brought about the invention of money, a revolution that occurred simultaneously in social life and in habits of thought. But as I draw to a close, it may not be unprofitable to touch on the evidence for continuity even within this sea-change, evidence which men of the time may have been the first to fail to recognize.

The invention of money certainly makes possible the deployment of an abstract conception of value. With the new state of affairs there comes the use of an instrumental agent whose substance (in the philosophical sense; whose material composition) might seem of little interest or importance: it was left to Plato and Aristotle, neither of them friends of the mercantile economy, to construct a theory of money-as-sign and money-as-convention. That was a logical theory, since of course these philosophers were interested only in the aspect of exchange and circulation (and they forgot or failed to understand that metal money had been very early used in a kind of religious 'trade' to settle debts — *ex-votos*, traditional offerings, expiations). And there can be no doubt that the instrumental agent once invented was admirably fitted to circulate. Circulate it did in Greece, both early and widely. But in the historical milieu in which money-as-sign first appeared, the religious, aristocratic and agonistic symbols stamped on its first specimens were attestations of origin: a mythical way of thinking endured right to the very moment at which the invention of coinage became possible. By which I mean to say that there is, in 'value' and so in the very token that represents it, a core which cannot be reduced to what they call rational thought.

8. The Black Hunter and the origin of the Athenian *ephebeia*[1]

Pierre Vidal-Naquet (1968, 1979)

To M.I. Finley
> *We have seen nothing;*
> *We are beastly-subtle as the fox for prey,*
> *Like warlike as the wolf for what we eat;*
> *Our valour is to chase what flies . . .*
> Shakespeare, Cymbeline 3.3.39—42

Before, and even more since, the discovery of Aristotle's *Constitution of the Athenians* the Athenian *ephebeia* has been a subject of controversy. This two-year 'military service' is described by Aristotle in chapter 42 of his little treatise. But was it an entirely artificial creation resulting from Lycurgus's policies, as Wilamowitz maintained, or was it rather an extremely ancient — even archaic — institution, of the kind likened by nineteenth-century scholars to the Spartan *krypteia*?

The argument has grown rather stale now, and as a result of the analyses and discoveries of the past thirty years it is easy enough to reach agreement on two points.[2] First, no one would now claim that the *ephebeia* in Lycurgus's time was in every respect an ancient institution: the Athenian politician re-ordered and rationalized whatever existed before his time. Second, everyone would now agree that the *ephebeia* of the fourth century BC had its roots in ancient practices of 'apprenticeship' whose object was to introduce young men to their future rôles as citizens and heads of families — that is, as full members of the community. I need hardly remind the reader of the rôle played by comparative ethnology in the realization of the significance of initiatory rituals in the ancient world: as early as 1913 Henri Jeanmaire based his own work on such studies (1913: 121—50), and only a little later Pierre Roussel commented upon a text of Aristotle (*Constitution of the Athenians* 42.5) in similar terms (1921: 456—60). We know that the ephebe 'cannot go to law either as a defendant or as a plaintiff unless it is a matter of upholding an inheritance, arranging the affairs of an heiress, or a priesthood related to the *genos*'. Aristotle's own explanation is simple: the ephebes must not suffer any distraction from their military service. But this sort of explanation is valid only for Aristotle's own time; Roussel observed, 'the *ephebeia* is much more than a period of military service. It is the period of transition between childhood and

147

complete participation in the life of the society . . . There is so much evidence from other societies, including Sparta in Greece itself, that young people led a life apart for a period of time before their definitive admission into the social group, that one is inclined to see an example of this practice here' (p. 459).

'Definitive admission' meant for the young citizen essentially two things: marriage, and entry into the hoplite phalanx (or later, becoming a sailor in the Athenian navy). So long as these two conditions remained unfulfilled — and the second was especially important in classical Athens — the young man's relation to the *polis* is ambiguous. He both is, and is not, a member.

This ambiguity is strikingly illustrated at the level of topography — remembering that the organization of symbolic space does not always coincide with actual geography. When Aeschines the orator mentions his own ephebic generation (around 370 BC), he says that he served for two years as '*peripolos* of this land' (*On the Embassy* 167) after childhood. When Plato came to copy the institution of the *ephebeia*, he makes his *agronomoi* circle round his city on the frontiers, first in one direction, then in the other (*Laws* 6, 760b; cf. Vidal-Naquet, 1981) thus taking literally the etymological meaning of *peripolos*, 'one who circles round'. In the fourth century BC the ephebic *peripolos*[3] was normally stationed in the frontier forts: Panacton, Deceleia, Rhamnus and so on. That might perhaps be entirely natural for lightly-armed young men[4] who were only called upon to fight under exceptional circumstances,[5] and would then obviously be used on patrol (which is another possible translation of *peripolos*). And yet these young men are associated with foreigners and with citizens of recent date: Aeschines served as a *peripolos* with young men of his own age and with mercenaries (*On the Embassy* 168); Thucydides mentions *peripoloi* twice, first in association with Plataeans (Athenian citizens of recent date) at a night-ambush near Nisaea in 425 BC (4.67—8), and later he says that the man who murdered Phrynichus in 411 was a *peripolos*, his accomplice being an Argive (8.92.2). Other sources too state that Phrynichus's murderers were foreigners (Lysias, *Against Agoratos* 71; *Sylloge*[3] 108 = Meiggs and Lewis, 1969: 260—3, no. 85).[6]

The same word could then designate both the young men of Athens and foreigners in her service. Both are marginal to the city (though the ephebe's marginality is temporary). But the ephebe's relation to the world of the frontier is complex. As young soldiers, they occupy the frontier-zone of the city which is expressed physically in the ring of fortlets (just as in Crete, where there is epigraphic evidence for a clearcut distinction between the young men, who occupy the *phrouria*, the *oureia*, the frontier-area, and the full citizens);[7] when they take the oath which makes them full hoplites, they mention the boundary-stones which separate Athens' territory from her neighbours'. But with these stones are associated wheat, barley, vines, olives, fig-trees — in a word, the world of cultivation (Daux, 1965: 78—90; cf. J. and L. Robert, 1966: 362—3 no. 165).

A short discussion of a non-Athenian poetic text may make it easier to understand this. The finest evocation of the duality of the Greek ephebe is no doubt the Jason of Pindar's fourth Pythian ode. Pelias, the old king of Iolcus, was appointed to 'die by the hands of the noble sons of Aeolus or their unrelenting schemes':

ἐξ ἀγαυῶν Αἰολιδᾶν θανέμεν χεί-
ρεσσιν ἢ βουλᾶς ἀκνάμπτοις (72—3 Snell)[8]

He had been warned to beware 'at all costs the man with one sandal' who should pass from 'a lofty retreat' to 'the sunny plain' — 'stranger be he or townsman' (ξεῖνος αἴτ'ὦν ἀστός: 75—7). And indeed Jason comes from afar off where he had been brought up, in wild nature, by Chiron the centaur and his daughters. He is a foreigner, and received as such, but also a citizen, speaking of himself as such to his fellow-citizens: κεδνοὶ πολῖται, φράσσατέ μοι σαφέως (117). He is a qualified ephebe twenty years old, ambiguous, with two javelins, and dressed both in the clothing of Magnesia but also in the leopard-skin of the wild man:

ἐσθὰς δ᾽ ἀμφοτέρα μιν ἔχεν,
ἅ τε Μαγνήτων ἐπιχώριος ἀρμό —
ζοισα θαητοῖσι γυίοις,
ἀμφὶ δὲ παρδαλέᾳ στέγετο φρίσσοντας ὄμβρους. (79—81)
. . . and a twofold guise was on him.
A tunic of Magnesian fashion fitted close his magnificent limbs,
and across it a panther's hide held off the shivering rains.
(tr. Lattimore)

The hair which the Athenian ephebe cut as a mark of entry into manhood still hangs down his back (82—3).

This prolonged adolescence takes us away from the world of social reality and into the realm of myth. Let us return to Athens, where the ephebe's ambiguity — at the level now of its institutional reality — can be seen as double. As Jules Labarbe saw (1953: 58—94), there were really two ephebic structures: the official *ephebeia*, which was a civic military service, and a more archaic one through which one gained admission to the phratry. Hence the expression *epi dietes hēbēsai*, which means (1) to be an ephebe in the civic sense, that is, to have reached the age of eighteen; and (2), as the literal sense suggests, to have attained the *hēbē*, to have been an ephebe for two years (cf. Labarbe, 1957: 67—75; Pélékidis, 1962: 51—65). Labarbe showed that the first *ephebeia* was marked ritually by the sacrifice of the *koureion* (the young man's long hair) at the age of sixteen. I may add that in one case at least admission to the phratry was not ratified until one year had elapsed from the date of the offering of the hair (*Sylloge*³ 921, lines 27–8 [= Sokolowski, 1969: no. 19, with bibliography — the so-called 'Ruling of the Demotionidae']).

The sacrifice of the hair took place at the time of the *Koureōtis*, the third day of Apatouria, the great festival celebrated by the phratries of the Ionian world, which took place in the month Pyanepsion (September–October). This month was marked by a series of festivals which have been shown, by Jeanmaire in particular (1939), to have been festivals celebrating the return of the young men from the campaigns of the summer. And it was through studying the aetiological myth connected with the Apatouria that I was led to formulate the ideas presented here.

The myth is known from a large number of texts dating from the fifth century BC right down to the Byzantines Michel Psellos and Johannes Tzetzes, who are of course simply resuming older sources. The texts do not for the most part come from the principal an ;ient works of literature or history; though alluded to by Strabo and Pausanias, it is recounted only by Konon (an extremely obscure Hellenistic mythographer), Polyaenus and Frontinus; otherwise it is a matter of scholiasts' remarks and entries in ancient lexica.[9] In view of the state of the sources, it is hardly possible to define an 'ancient' and more recent versions of the story, and I will therefore try to indicate the most important variants.

The scene is the frontier between Athens and Boeotia: an *eschatia*, mountainous areas that are the 'end' of a city's territory, and whose inhabitants are always at loggerheads with their neighbours over the border. Such places existed on the borders of all Greek states (Robert, 1960: 304–5, esp. 304 n. 4). They were the terrain of hunters and shepherds, frontier zones constantly in dispute. And they were necessary to Greek cities if only for training the young soldiers for war (the ritual nature of which training has been demonstrated by Brelich, 1961; cf. Garlan, 1975: 29–31).

A conflict broke out between the Athenians and the Boeotians. In some versions, over Oenoe and Panacton, in others over the frontier deme Melainai. The fourth-century historian Ephorus (quoted by Harpokration) says that the dispute was *huper tēs Melanias choras*: 'over an area called Melania'. I will observe simply that at Panacton there was an annual sacrifice to mark the Apatouria (*Sylloge*³ 485). The Boeotian king was Xanthos (or Xanthios, or Xanthias), which means 'the fair one'. The Athenian king was Thymoites, the last of the descendants of Theseus. It was agreed to settle the dispute by means of a duel, a *monomachia*. But Thymoites stood down, according to a scholiast on Aristophanes's *Frogs* and another on Aelius Aristeides's *Panathenaicus*, because he was too old. Another warrior came forward and was, according to some versions, promised the succession in return. His name was Melanthos (or Melanthios), 'the black one'. So the Black One was to fight the Fair One.

As they were fighting, Melanthos suddenly cried out, 'Xanthos, you do not play according to the rules (συνθῆκαι) — there is someone at your side!' — and as Xanthos looked round in surprise, Melanthos took his chance and killed him. The sources differ over details of what happened. Polyaenus and Frontinus say it was a ruse pure and simple; Halliday compares it to Tom Sawyer's trick when he cries out 'Look behind you Aunty' and thus escapes the beating she was about to administer (1926: 179). The *Lexica Segueriana* makes Melanthos pray to Zeus *Apatēnōr* (Zeus 'of wiles'). Most mention Dionysus's intervention — Dionysus *Melanaigis*, 'of the black goatskin'; and Plutarch (*Quaestiones conviviales* 6.7.2, 692e) says that Dionysus *Melanaigis* and *Nukterinos* ('of the night') was worshipped at Eleutherae (that is, not far from Panacton).[10] Afterwards, the victor Melanthos became king of Athens.

In every source, the Apatouria is explained by paronomastic etymology. The festival is supposed to commemorate this *apatē* ('wile', 'deception'), whether the inspiration of the deception is ascribed to Dionysus, to Zeus or to Melanthos himself.[11] The sources offer this explanation even though the scholiast on Aristophanes's *Acharnians* 146, as well as the grammarian quoted by the Suda s.v. Ἀπατούρια, knew an explanation which is more or less correct: *Apatouria* = *Homopatoria* (Ὁμοπατόρια). Nowadays we would say that the α of Ἀπατούρια is a copulative: the festival of the Apatouria is the festival of those who have the 'same father' — in other words, the festival of the phratries.

Over the years, there have naturally been many attempts to explain this myth. First of course historically — many such, from Johannes Töpffer's *Attische Genealogie* (1889: 225–41) to Felix Jacoby's great commentary on the Atthidographers, the historians of Attica. We are assured that Melanthos was a historical personage, a Neleid, the father of Codrus who, thanks to another *apatē* (disguising himself as a peasant), managed to get himself killed and thus ensured the safety of Athens in accordance with the oracles' prophecy. Melanthos is also described as the 'ancestor' of the phratry of the Medontidae. Attempts have even been made to pinpoint the story's date — Wilamowitz put it not earlier than 508 BC, because the frontier was only established then (1935–7: 5.1, 22 n. 2). And Jacoby, while not denying the mythical nature of the

151

story, envisaged the possibility of a real frontier skirmish (*FGrH* 3 b Supplement 2: 50 [on 323a F 23]).

But it was Hermann Usener who first attempted to provide an overall explanation of the myth.[12] He pointed out that this was a duel between the *Black* and the *Fair*, as a few ancient authors realized: Polyaenus quotes, or invents, an oracle given before the encounter, which runs: τῷ ξάνθῳ τεύξας ὁ μέλας φόνον ἔσχε Μελαίνας 'Having wrought the death of the fair one the black one seized Melainai.' [*Melainai* means 'the black country'.] Usener saw the duel in symbolic terms, as a ritual combat between winter and summer, an interpretation welcomed by, among others, Lewis Farnell (1909: xlvii; 1896–1909: 5.130–1), A.B. Cook (1914–40: 1.689) and Herbert Rose (1961: 131–3).[13] But it fails to explain what needs to be explained: the link between the duel and the festival itself. The same applies to Nilsson when, in a variant of the theory, he suggested that this *agon* ('contest') linked with the worship of Dionysus was one of the earliest forms of tragedy (1951–60a: 1.61–110, 111–16).

Many years later, in *Couroi et Courètes*, Henri Jeanmaire offered an entirely different view (1939: 382–3). He saw the duel between Xanthos and Melanthos as a ritual joust, perhaps followed by a procession, through which a claimant to the throne declared himself master of the territory. The name of Melanthos is replaced in Pausanias 9.5.16 by that of Andropompos ('the Leader of the procession'); and according to Plutarch (*Quaestiones graecae* 13, 294b–c) it was in a similar way – a duel involving a trick almost identical with ours – that Phemius, king of the Aenianians, established his claim to the valley of the Inachus. It also recalls the famous – legendary – battle between Pittakos and Phrynon at the time of the war over Sigeum between Athens and Mytilene (Will, 1955: 381–3).

But to my knowledge only Angelo Brelich has really attempted to explain the possible relationship between this myth and the Apatouria, the festival of the phratries during which the ephebes were received into the phratry after consecrating their hair (1961: 56–9).[14] In particular, he stresses the frequency with which duels between young men take place in frontier-districts and observes that Dionysus (whom he identifies with Dionysus *Melanaigis*) is described sometimes as *hēbōn* ('with his beard starting to grow'). But he fails to push his interpretation much further than this.

For my part, I was struck by three points which require explanation. First, that the story takes place in the frontier region, just as it is to the frontier that the Athenian ephebes are sent, and that in their oath they swear to protect the boundary-stones of their country. The second point is the story's stress on the *apatē*, the trick. Why should the ephebes have been offered a model of behaviour quite contrary to that which they swear in their oath to observe? We have single-handed combat (*monomachia*) and trickery, contrasted with fair hoplite-fighting on even terms. (Let it be noted in passing that the very name Melanthos was probably evocative for a reader of Homer: just as Dolon is the cunning wolf in the *Iliad* (Gernet, 1968b: 154–71) so in the *Odyssey* Melanthios or Melantheus is a treacherous goatherd (17.212, 22.159, 161, 182 etc.) and his sister Melantho is a treacherous servant (18. 321–2). Their father is called Dolios, 'the cunning one'.)[15] Thirdly, I was struck by the stress on black in the story (*melas* (adj.), stem *melan-*). We find the name Melanthos, the location, which in some texts is called Melainai, and Dionysus of the Black Goatskin (*Melanaigis*). And this is not the only occurrence of an association between the Athenian ephebes and the colour black· at least on certain solemn occasions, they wore a black *chlamys* (a short cloak) which was replaced, thanks to the generosity of Herodes Atticus, by a white one in the second century AD.[16]

In his discussion of the inscription which provides us with this last item of information (*IG* II² 3606), Pierre Roussel showed that the black *chlamys* was supposed to commemorate Theseus's forgetfulness: that ephebe of ephebes forgot to change the black sails on his ship for white ones on his return from Crete (after killing the Minotaur). But aetiology is not explanation; and George Thomson understood this black garment as a sign of ritual exclusion (1941: 107). And there is certainly something very peculiar about this predominance of black — we have only to refer, for example, to Gerhard Radke's conscientious catalogue (1936; cf. Moreux, 1967: 237–72) to understand just how startling, indeed shocking, a ritual victory for black might be in a festival celebrating the entry of young men into the community.

It may help to formulate these problems more precisely if I now digress in order to discuss the Spartan *krypteia*, an institution which has often been compared to the Athenian *ephebeia*, and which, though it involved a much smaller number of young men, was indeed parallel to it in some respects. It is well known that we have a very small number of sources for the *krypteia*.[17] But the scholiast on Plato's *Laws* 1, 633b says explicitly that it was a preparation for the military life. And Köchly argued as early as 1835 [following Karl Otfried Müller] that this training was to be compared to that of the Athenian *peripoloi* ([Müller, 1844: 2.302]; Köchly, 1881–2: 1.587–8); a point made even more clearly by Ernst Wachsmuth, who lucidly observed that this military apprenticeship took the special form of a helot-hunt (1846: 1.252; 2.304).[18]

A brilliant article by Henri Jeanmaire (1913: 121–50) elucidated the fundamental characteristics of the *krypteia* by means of comparison with certain African societies: compulsory isolation of certain young men around the time of puberty; living in the bush; even the killings of helots — all of these can be paralleled in black Africa, in the initiation-ceremonies and secret societies of Wolf-men and Panther-men. But if that is so, what of the military rôle of the *krypteia*? Jeanmaire's reply was unequivocal: 'the whole of Spartan military history cries out against the idea of turning the Spartiate hoplite into a tracker in the bush, clambering over rocks and walls' (p. 142). And he added wryly that if the *krypteia*, with its camping-out by night in the mountains, had really been a training for military life at the time of the battle of Thermopylae (480 BC), Ephialtes's path (by which the Persians surprised the Spartans) would have been discovered and guarded.

To my mind Jeanmaire was both profoundly right and profoundly wrong. What he failed to understand was that the *krypteia* was by no means completely unrelated to the life of the hoplite: for *krypteia* and the hoplite life were symmetrical opposites. If we make a list from what the sources tell us, we get the following result:

(1) The hoplite is armed to the teeth; the youth in the *krypteia* is *gumnos*, which means either that he carried no arms at all (Scholiast on Plato's *Laws* 1, 633b) or that he had only a dagger (Plutarch, *Life of Lycurgus* 28.2).

(2) The member of the *phalanx* is opposed to the youth on his own or living in a small group.

(3) The fighter in the plain is opposed to the youth who runs wild in the mountains.

(4) Plato's youth in the *krypteia* did his training in the middle of winter; the hoplite, according to Thucydides, fought in summer (cf. καλοκαίρι in Modern Greek).

(5) The trustworthy hoplite cheered on by Tyrtaeus (7th cent. BC) is opposed to the cunning killer of helots.

(6) The man who fights in the light of day is opposed to the youth who fights by night.

(7) The Scholiast on Plato's *Laws* says that the youth in the *krypteia* ate whatever he could find, living from hand to mouth, probably without ever finding time to have anything cooked; whereas the hoplite is above all a member of a common mess, the *syssition*.

(8) The members of the *krypteia* stayed in the areas which became, in a sense, the frontiers of enemy territories — for the Ephors annually declared war on the helots in a ritual comparable to the Roman declaration of war by the *Fetiales*.[19] [By contrast, the full hoplites were obliged to remain, in peacetime, close to their *syssitia*, that is, close to Sparta itself.]

In sum, with the hoplite order (*taxis*) reigns;[20] in the *krypteia* there is nothing but cunning, deception, disorder, irrationality. To borrow Lévi-Strauss's terms, one might say that the hoplite is on the side of Culture, of what is 'cooked', while the *krypteia* is on the side of Nature, of the 'raw', bearing in mind of course that this 'Nature', the side of non-culture, is itself to some degree socially organized.[21] And we might apply this point more widely: for example, in Crete we find *agelai* of young men, which Pierre Chantraine interprets as the 'herds of animals that are driven along' (1956: 32—3), opposed to the *hetaireiai*, the 'brotherhoods' of mature men. And I could go on, but I have said enough to indicate how, by a procedure which Lévi-Strauss would term a logical inversion, the *krypteia* dramatizes the moment when the young élite Spartiate leaves behind him forever his childhood.

In his *Polarity and Analogy* (1966) Geoffrey Lloyd has brilliantly shown how the principle of polarity played a fundamental rôle in the reasoning of Greek thinkers in the Archaic period — indeed I believe that his conclusions could easily be extended to include the Classical period itself: how can we understand Thucydides, for example, without using the notion of polarity?[22] And my intention here, as must already be evident, is to detect evidence of polarities expressed not in book-thinking but in social institutions; and I propose to do that without entering upon the question of whether 'thought' and 'institutions' are the effective consequences of one single entity, the Lévi-Straussian 'human mind'.

I think we may generalize and extend what I have already said in discussing the Spartan *krypteia*: for we must recognize that in Athens, and in many other parts of the Greek world — above all in Sparta and Crete, where very archaic institutions were preserved until well into the Hellenistic period — the transition between childhood and adulthood (the period of marriage and fighting) is dramatized both in ritual and in myth by what we might call the 'law of symmetrical inversion'. Indeed, since the publication of Arnold van Gennep's *The Rites of Passage* in 1909 (van Gennep, 1960), many rituals of status-transition have been analysed in these terms.[23] I may remind the reader, for example, that in Argos young women sported a (false) beard when they got married (Plutarch, *De mulierum virtutibus* 4, 245f); and that in Sparta, when a girl was to be married she 'was handed over to a *numpheutria* who cut off all her hair, dressed her in a man's clothes and shoes, and made her lie down all alone on a mattress in the dark' (Plutarch, *Life of Lycurgus* 15.5). The two cases are quite parallel, as is obvious when we remember that, according to Herodotus (1.82.7) adults in Argos had to be entirely bald, while in Sparta, they had to let their hair grow long. We have here then a kind of double inversion.

155

But we must return to Athens, and look again at the festivals connected with the young men's 'return' that are so marked a feature of the month Pyanepsion (September—October). In these festivals the ephebes played an important part; and they are all the more significant for me inasmuch as they also marked the end of the period of 'apprenticeship' — for this was probably the point at which the ephebes took their famous hoplite-oath in the Aglaurion and when they received their arms from the city.

Very shortly after the *Apatouria* occurred the festival known as the *Oschophoria* (held on the seventh day of Pyanepsion).[24] This is a particularly interesting festival because its aetiological myth is concerned precisely with Theseus's return from Crete after killing the Minotaur, and the conflicting emotions he feels — glad because he has been victorious, filled with grief at his father's death (Plutarch, *Life of Theseus* 22.4). And it was precisely this death which the ephebes' black *chlamys* was believed to commemorate.

The traditional sources for the Oschophoria diverge markedly from one another. I do not propose to analyse them exhaustively,[25] but will simply emphasize some points which have sometimes been neglected. First of all an essential rôle in the Oschophoria is played by an outlying *genos* [a group of relatively wealthy families claiming descent from a single ancestor], that of the Salaminians who had moved to Attica. It was this *genos* in particular which provided the youths (*neaniai*) who carried the vine-branches complete with bunches of grapes (*ōschoi*) — who were in consequence called *ōschophoroi*.[26] Secondly, the first event of the festival was a procession (*parapompē*) from Athens to the shrine of Athena Skiras at Phaleron. Now the word *skiron* means 'lime' and so 'badlands'; and Felix Jacoby has shown that the names *Skiras*, *Skiros* and *Skiron* were generally given to outlying districts which either were, or had been at some time in the past, frontier-areas.[27] Thus 'Skira' is another name for the offshore island of Salamis; Skiron is a village on the old boundary between Athens and Eleusis, and so on. The procession to the shrine of Athena Skiras was made up of boys (*paides*) led by two boys *disguised as girls* carrying the *ōschoi*; these boys are referred to as *paides amphithaleis*.[28] Plutarch explains the transvestism by saying that among the seven maidens whom Theseus took with him to Crete there were two boys disguised as girls.[29] I cannot here venture to tackle the very complex problems presented by the festivals connected with Athena Skiras: the sources are so confused that it is hard to tell which of the various festivals they refer to. I will simply point out that Athena Skiras seems to have been linked significantly with the custom of dressing-up: it is during her festival that Praxagora and her friends decide in Aristophanes's *The Assembly of Women* to dress up as men and wear false beards (and it so happens that one of the characters has a husband who is a Salaminian [18–25, 38]).[30] Plutarch, *Life of Solon* 8, gives two versions of how the Athenians seized Salamis (otherwise known as Skiras) from the Megarians; and in one of them the beardless young men disguise themselves as women. And he says that a festival was established on the promontory Skiradion after the seizure (though he links its details to the second story, which, though involving a deception, contains no transvestism) (9.4).

Besides the procession and the boys' transvestism, the Oschophoria featured a race (*agōn, hamilla*) between ephebes carrying *ōschoi*. Most of our information about this is derived from Proclus's *Chrestomathia*.[31] The course ran from the temple of Dionysus to Phaleron. The competitors were either two representatives from each of the ten tribes, each pair running separately; or else twenty youths, two from each tribe, all running against each other. The victor drank the 'fivefold cup', a mixture of oil, wine, honey, cheese and flour. After the ceremonies at Phaleron, and in particular the rituals of seclusion and the *deipnophoria* ('food-carrying'), there were libations, followed by a revel (*kōmos*) which brought the participants back to Athens. It is evident from Plutarch (*Life of Theseus* 22.3) that this revel was accompanied by a herald, and that the return journey too was explained by reference to Theseus's return from Crete (he was supposed to have stopped at Phaleron in order to sacrifice). In the story, Theseus's herald precedes him with the news of success, and discovers the death of Aegeus, which he reports to Theseus, who is still outside Athens. Theseus's party then entered Athens loudly lamenting, but still the bearers of happy news. And for this reason, says Plutarch, it is not the herald himself who is crowned at the Oschophoria, but his staff (*kērukeion*); and cries of joy, 'Eleleu', alternated with keening, 'iou, iou', in commemoration of Aegeus's death.[32]

The structure of the Oschophoria is thus marked by a series of oppositions. The most blatant is that between male and female, which is clear in the procession itself (boys dressed as girls versus the youths), but also in the contrast between the procession (boys dressed as girls) and the race (*dromos*) between the ephebes (the race of course is nothing if not virile: in Crete, the *dromeus* is a mature man (Willetts, 1955: 11–14), and in Lato, in particular, the word for leaving the *agela* to become a man is 'running out' (ἐγδραμεῖν: *IC* 1.16 [Lato], 5.21); according to Aristophanes of Byzantium an *apodromos* was a young boy not yet allowed to take part in the public races).[33] The race during the Oschophoria is indeed exactly parallel to the *staphulodromia* during the Spartan festival of the *Carneia*, which was also a festival of the phratries: it was a race in which five unmarried young men ran against each other (Harrison, 1927: 234 cf. 321). Thirdly, joy is opposed to grief, as is shown by Plutarch's *Life of Theseus* 22.3 — which has been considered, wrongly I think, to be a later interpretation.

It is well known that in archaic Greek societies, as well as in other societies, dressing up as a woman, as in the procession at the Oschophoria, was a means of dramatizing the fact that a young man had reached the age of virility and marriage. The classic example in Greek mythology is the story of Achilles on Skyros (Jeanmaire, 1939: 354–5; Delcourt, 1961: 1–16; cf. Bettelheim, 1962: 109–21). But it can be demonstrated that it is not the *kind* of disguise which is important, rather the *contrast* which it underscores. The opposition between light and dark for example is no less significant: young men not yet adult are known sometimes to have been called *skotioi* ('of the dark': Scholiast on Euripides, *Alcestis* 989); the *neaniai* ('youths') of the Oschophoria are called *eskiatraphēmenoi*, 'brought up in the dark' (Plutarch, *Life of Theseus* 23.2; Proclus, *Chrestomathia* 89 [p. 56 Severyns]).[34] Both Malla and Dreros in Crete seem to have held ceremonies of admission to the adult age-classes, which involved ritual nudity before the conferring of hoplite arms. The young men are called *azōstoi*, which Hesychius defines as 'those who are without arms'. At Dreros they were called *panazōstoi* and *egduomenoi*, 'those who have no clothes' — the latter term occurs also at Malla.[35] There was likewise at Phaestus a festival called the *Ekdysia* ('Clothes off'): the aetiology here is a story about a girl who turned into a boy — which forms a link between the two sets *boy : girl* and *naked : armed* (Antoninus Liberalis, *Metamorphoses* 17 [Leukippos]; cf. Papathomopoulos, 1968: 109–10; Willetts, 1962: 175–8).

It is perhaps worth noting finally that the sexual inversion of any young man about to become an adult is quite clearly related to these facts: it is enough to mention Ephorus's well-known story about the rape (*harpagē*) of a young Cretan boy, who is taken by his lover into the country (of course!) for two months, for a life of relaxation and *hunting*. It is on his return to the town that he receives the arms which make him a hoplite (*FGrH* 70 F 149 [from Strabo 10.4.21: 483C]).

I come now to the theme of the hunt, which appears in the title of this paper, and which I still have to explain and, if possible, justify. Pierre Chantraine has noted (1956: 40–65) that hunting is linked fundamentally with the *agros* in Greece, the land which lies beyond the cultivated area, that is, with the *eschatiai*, the borderlands of Greek cities. Plato calls his ephebe, the person who defends the frontier area, an *agronomos* (*Laws* 6, 760e–761a). More generally, hunting was so normal for heroes, whom the ephebes emulated, that F. Orth remarked that 'heroes are hunters and hunters heroes' (1914: 559).[36] In a sense, hunting is firmly on the side of the wild, the 'raw', of night;[37] and the skills employed in the Spartan *krypteia* were those of hunting. But only in a sense: we have to make certain distinctions.

My starting-point is a well-known text on education, from the end of Plato's section on education in the *Laws* (7, 822d–824a). Using the method demonstrated in the *Sophist*, Plato introduces here a whole series of distinctions. Each time he speaks of a left side, the side of evil, and a right side, that of good. Fishing depends upon the use of nets: it therefore falls squarely on the left. One ought then to restrict oneself to the hunt and the capture of quadrupeds (θήρευσίς τε καὶ ἄγρα: 824a). Here too, though, he makes a distinction: one is not allowed to hunt by night with nets and traps. All that seems to be permissible is that type of hunting which conforms to the ethos of the horseman and the hop-lite: coursing the animal, or killing it with a lance - both of them kinds of hunting which involve the use of one's bare hands (though bird-catching is tolerated *en agrois*, 'beyond the area of cultivation'). 'But as for the man who hunts by night, the *nuktereutēs*, with only nets and traps, let no man allow him to hunt anywhere' (824b).

When faced with a text of this kind, we must of course allow for Plato's dichotomizing method, and for his moralizing tone. Perhaps we should allow for a similar tone when Pindar describes Achilles killing deer without dogs, and without guile or nets, but simply by running faster than they (*Nemean* 3.51–2) – even though it reminds us of the Cretan *dromeus*. But there are several texts which draw a contrast be-tween two types of hunting: adult hunting, where the spear is used rather than the net, and which takes place by daylight, sometimes in a group, and which is in keeping with the hoplite ethos; opposed to it is hunting by night, a 'black hunt' based on the use of the net. The heroic prototype of the group-hunt is of course the hunt of the famous black Calydonian boar. Now it has been observed that 'the use of nets is not a feature of pictorial representations of the Calydonian boar hunt' – any more than it is of the literary accounts (Chantraine, 1956: 65, quoting La Coste-Messelière, 1936: 130–52 [though Immerwahr, 1885: 52–4 points out that this feature does occur on Roman representations of the hunt on sarcophagi; and see now Koch, 1975. Ed.]). And for this reason: the Calydonian boar hunt is a hunt involving the adult heroes of Greece. Likewise, Hegesandros reports a Macedonian custom whereby no man could dine reclining until he had killed a boar without the aid of net or snare (Athenaeus, *Deipnosophistae* 1.31, 18a). Poor Cassander had to wait until he was thirty-five before he could enjoy this privilege – distinguished hunter though he was. We may put the point slightly differently: unless he had accomplished some signal exploit a young man could not be a full participant in the communal meals which were a feature of so many archaic or marginal societies.

Two Spartan customs neatly illustrate how integral hunting was to the hoplite ethos. According to Plutarch (*Life of Lycurgus* 12.4), anyone who took part in the communal meals had to present the table with the choicest parts of his sacrifice, or if he had been hunting, with part of the bag. One was allowed to dine at home if the sacrifice or hunt had finished late, but the others had to come along too (τοὺς δ᾽ ἄλλους ἔδει παρεῖναι). And Xenophon informs us that hunting dogs and horses were common property; while any food left in the mess after dinner had to be kept in a special place for any hunters who were delayed (*Constitution of the Lacedaemonians* 6.3—4).

By contrast with these heroic and communal exploits, hunting by oneself and with nets seems often to be typical of the adolescent. This is indicated by many texts, though it is true that many are late. According to Oppian, *Cynegetica* 2.25, it was Hippolytus, the prototype of the youth who is unmarried and who refuses to marry, who invented the hunting-net. In the story of young Philios, the first task imposed on him was to kill a lion ἄνευ σιδήρου, 'without an iron weapon'. And he slew it not with a net, but with a typical trick (*apatē*) — he made it drunk (Antoninus Liberalis, *Metamorphoses* 12). And Brelich has emphasized the interest of an odd passage in Xenophon's *Cynegeticus* (2.3), where he defines the hunt as characteristic of the transition from childhood to adolescence and adds: 'the hunter who uses a net must love his art, must be of the Greek tongue and be about twenty years old'. It is in such terms perhaps that one might explain why on the Chigi Vase in the Villa Giulia in Rome there is a line of men creeping through the undergrowth, over against the line of horsemen and the line of hoplites (the Chigi Vase is of course Late-Corinthian). And it is by reference to the same oppositions that we can understand why Nestor has two different initiations into the art of war in the *Iliad*, first as a young man, lightly-armed, taking part in a cattle-raid at night, and then as a heavy-armed adult (*Iliad* 11.670—762, with the decisive discussion of Bravo, 1979).

But I want to argue that the essential evidence for the rôle of the hunt in the various stages of a young Greek male's life is provided by a figure whom it is high time that I dealt with: the Black Hunter, Melanion.

> Let me tell you a little story
> I heard when I was a boy
>   How
> There once was a youth [νεανίσκος] called Melanion, who
> Was so appalled at the prospect of women he flew
> To the mountains rather than marry.[38]
>   And he hunted hares

> And he set his snares
> With his dog there,
> And never came back for anyone!
> (Aristophanes, *Lysistrata* 781—96, tr. Dickinson)

Melanion appears here as an ephebe, but a sort of ephebe manqué — a kind of Hippolytus in fact, as Wilamowitz saw clearly in his commentary (1927: 169—70). If we looked no further than this chorus, we should have here a version of the widespread myth of the gloomy solitary hunter who is either a misogynist or who tries to insult Artemis, and who, in either case, flouts the social rules. It is the well-known type of the hunter Orion — who was indeed, according to Oppian, *Cynegetica* 2.28—9, the inventor of hunting by night.

But look further we must. Putting the story of Melanion back into its mythical context, we can bracket it with the story of a young girl, the Arcadian Atalanta, who was a huntress and who excelled in running.[39] Their legend is set near a frontier mountain, Mount Parthenion, between the Argolid and Arcadia. Pausanias (8.6.4) says that the nearest village was called Melangeia. Like Melanion, Atalanta was brought up in the mountains, suckled by a bear (Artemis's animal). Euripides (frg. 510 Nauck[2]) characterizes her as μίσημα Κυπρίδος, 'hated by Aphrodite' — a social failing parallel to Melanion's. Theognis (1291—4) describes her as 'the blonde Atalanta who strides over the mountain peaks, fleeing from the desire of marriage'. For Hesiod she is the 'light-footed Atalanta' (frg. 73.2, 76.5, 76.20 Merkelbach—West) — the maiden who escapes from the Centaurs' attempts to rape her (Apollodorus, *Bibliotheca* 3.9.2). Aelian knows of her only that she was a virgin (*Variae historiae* 13.1) — just as all that is known of Melanion in Aristophanes's chorus is that he refuses to marry. In Apollodorus's well-known version, she comes home and challenges any comer to a race, stipulating that it shall be an armed race. She thus trespasses on male preserves twice-over. Xenophon says that Melanion won her hand thanks to his skills as a hunter (*Cynegeticus* 1.7); but a widespread mythological tradition (for example, Apollodorus) had it that Melanion beats Atalanta and wins her for his wife by means of an *apatē* of a feminine kind — dropping Aphrodite's three golden apples, one at a time. Both of them were depicted on Cypselus's chest at Olympia (Pausanias 5.19.2). During that period of their lives which was more or less unexceptionable, they both took part in the Calydonian boar hunt: they appear together for example on the 'François vase', Atalanta all light in colour, Melanion all black (in keeping with pictorial convention); and a white hound is about to spring on the black boar. They had a son, whose name, significantly enough, was Parthenopaeus.[40] And once again they violated sexual rules by having intercourse in a

161

shrine sacred to Zeus or Cybele, the Mother of the Gods. And then they were transformed into lions, because, it is said, lions are unable to have sexual intercourse.[41]

The Athenian ephebe is in a sense the true heir of the Black Hunter. The Black Hunter is, as I have observed, an ephebe manqué, an ephebe who may fail at every turn.[42] And many Attic vases depict a young ephebe setting off with his hound: perhaps they do indeed, in their own way, represent the young man on the threshold of adult life.

It is time to draw this paper to a close. In historical terms, the ephebe in Archaic and Classical Greece was a pre-hoplite. By virtue of this, in the symbolic enactments which are the rites of passage, he was an anti-hoplite: sometimes a girl, sometimes a cunning hunter, sometimes black. It is not in the least surprising that a myth like that of Melanthos should have been considered a model for the ephebe.[43] And at the technical level, the ephebe is a light-armed soldier, an anti-hoplite who ensured the perpetuation, often quite unseen, of a mode of fighting which is both pre- and anti-hoplite, and which reappears into the light of day (and of history) during the Peloponnesian War and in the fourth century BC.[44] Creature of the frontier-area, of the *eschatia*, he guarantees in his hoplite-oath[45] to protect the boundary stones of his country, and with them, the cultivated fields, the wheat, barley, olive-trees, vines and figs.

We might extend this study of the *ephebeia* to a consideration of the rôle of the warrior in Greek mythology. Long before the introduction of hoplite warfare into Greece and Rome, the warrior's function in Indo-European society was twofold. On one side was order, which later led to the development of the *phalanx* and the legion; and on the other disorder and the exploits of the individual (cf. Dumézil, 1958: 57–8). As Georges Dumézil has stressed, these personal exploits, through which the young warriors won recognition, derived from their *furor*, *lussa*, *celeritas*, *menos*, from their fighting spirit; but the exploits of the Irish Cúchulainn, which made his return-journey from the frontier-zone so difficult and dangerous, were also tricks.[46] And in just the same way it is by a trick, in Livy's account, that Publius Horatius defeated the three Curiatii (1.25.7–12). There is a striking parallel in Herodotus's story of the battle between 300 young Spartans and 300 young Argives in the frontier area of Thyreatis (1.68) [after which Othryadēs, the sole Spartan survivor, set up a trophy while the two surviving Argives returned to Argos with the news of victory; both sides could thus legitimately claim to have won. Ed.]. Young Horatius may thus be distant cousin to the Black Hunter.

9. Recipes for Greek adolescence

Pierre Vidal-Naquet (1974, 1979)

'I hate travels and explorers.'
Claude Lévi-Strauss

In 1724 there appeared in Paris a book by the Jesuit Joseph François
Lafitau entitled *Moeurs des sauvages amériquains comparées aux moeurs
des premiers temps.*[1] A modest enough title; but the contents constitute a kind of landmark in the historiography of the ancient world.
Lafitau was a missionary, born (1670) in Bordeaux into a family of
rich merchants and bankers. From 1712 to 1717 he lived in Canada
with P. Garnier, who knew the Algonquins, Hurons and Iroquois well.
As an ethnologist who had worked in the field, Lafitau was of course
neither the first missionary nor the first European to favour the con-
quering West with the benefit of the knowledge he had acquired.
Reflection and discovery went hand in hand. In effect ethnology had
established itself since the sixteenth century as a science of barbarian
societies, conceived now as static in relation to a world swept up in the
flux of history. Lafitau's originality lay elsewhere.[2] Arnaldo Momigliano
has put it well: his book 'revealed to the world the simple truth that
also the Greeks had once been savages' (1966: 141). To be sure,
Thucydides had made almost exactly the same point: 'One could point
to a number of . . . instances where the manners of the ancient Hellenic
world are very similar to the manners of barbarians today' (1.6.6). But
Thucydides had been forgotten. Deprecating the results of the conquest
of America, Montaigne — who was yet at moments so close to historical
relativism — wrote: 'Why did not so noble a conquest fall under
Alexander, or the ancient Greeks and Romans: and so great a revolution
and mutation of so many empires and nations, fall into hands that
would have gently levelled, rooted up and made plain and smooth whatever was rough and savage amongst them, and that would have cherished
and propagated the good seeds that nature had there produced; mixing
not only with the culture of land and the ornament of cities, the arts of
this part of the world, in what was necessary, but also the Greek and
Roman virtues, with those that were original of the country?' (*Essays*
III 6 trans. Cotton). Indeed Lafitau went further than Thucydides, by
comparing not only the distant past of the Greeks with the world of
savages, but also Classical Greece itself. In his own way, the Jesuit was

163

drawing a line under the debate between Ancients and Moderns. The Greeks, Romans, even up to a point the Jews (in a sense more decisive still) lost the cultural privilege they had been granted by the scholars of the Renaissance and the seventeenth century. 'I declare', he wrote with extraordinary temerity, 'that if the ancient authors have afforded me illumination to substantiate several happy solutions regarding Savages, the customs of Savages have afforded me illumination the more easily to understand, and to explain, several matters to be found in the ancient authors.' In saying that, Lafitau was taking the opposite line to another founding father of anthropology, the Spanish Jesuit José de Acosta, author of a *Historia natural y moral de las Indias*, published at Seville in 1590 and almost at once translated into French and English [by Edward Grimston, 1604]. De Acosta's epistemological rule, except in matters religious, was that the Graeco-Roman world remained *the* civilization. To be sure Lafitau, learned missionary that he was, found himself, in true classical tradition, an ancient patron: 'The science of the manners and customs of different peoples is so useful and interesting that Homer deemed that he should make it the subject of an entire poem. Its purpose is to celebrate the wisdom of his hero Ulysses who, seeing himself after the siege of Troy carried ever further from his homeland Ithaca by the wrath of Neptune, profits from different mistakes in his voyage to instruct himself in the manners of the nations at which the anger of the winds obliged him to touch, and to derive from each what was in it good and praiseworthy' (1724: 1.3). But these nations are not only the imaginary peoples which Odysseus describes in the palace of Alcinous — they are the Greeks themselves, seen both as the creators and as the objects of a science.

The frontispiece to Lafitau's work (figure 3) is an emblematic engraving. How did he himself interpret it?[3] The writer (apparently a woman) is seated at a writing desk in ancient dress. She is busy 'comparing a number of ancient monuments, pyramids, obelisks, pantheons [statues combining the attributes of several gods], medallions, ancient texts with a number of accounts, maps, voyages and other curiosities of America, among which she is sitting'. In particular one can make out one such idol on the ground, an Artemis of Ephesus lying on its side. Two putti help her in this task. One holds in his left hand the caduceus of Hermes and in his right a Red Indian pipe; the other holds an Iroquois 'turtle' against some sort of rhomb or rattle from a statuette from the Hellenistic East. Higher up, above Adam and Eve, the Risen Christ and the Virgin Mary after the Assumption, surrounded by angels,[4] flank the dazzling Host on an altar. Finally Time takes the writer back 'to the source of all' and makes him 'as it were palpate the connection between all these monuments and the origin of man, between them and the

Figure 3. Frontispiece from J. Lafitau's *Moeurs des sauvages amériquains comparées aux moeurs des premiers temps.* (Redrawn by R.K. Britton)

essence of our Religion'. I do not know whether Lafitau imagined that Time, with his wings and scythe, was a figure from antiquity: we know of course today that it is not (Panofsky, 1962: 69—93). Father Time, descended from ancient Saturn and the mediaeval figure of Death, owes his iconography to the Renaissance: he is contemporary with the men who witnessed the 'Great Expansion'; Lafitau's draughtsman stresses his vitality rather than his destructive aspect (the scythe is not at work). The Jesuit saw no contradiction between the action of Time and comparison, between, as we might say now, the 'diachronic' and the 'synchronic'.

Comparison between the customs of the Indians and the Greeks is legitimate because Indians and Greeks are each descended from Adam and Eve. The scene is given unity by the figures and symbols of Judaeo-Christian myth. Moreover, Lafitau makes his own attempt to historicize the myth by making his Indians the distant cousins both of the Greeks and of their barbarian neighbours (here again he differs from his predecessor de Acosta who thought indeed that the American Indians came from the Old Continent — he had guessed the existence of the Behring Strait — but stressed that these ancestors can hardly have been anything but 'mas hombres salvages y cazadores, que no gente república y pulida' ['savages and hunters rather than a refined and civilized polity'] [5] — 'savages and hunters': the very redundancy of the phrase is characteristic). But Lafitau could hardly ignore (and did not) the fact that even before his own century, and in particular after the Great Expansion, the possibility of another Adam, or of several other Adams, had been raised (Poliakov, 1974: 137—44), sometimes to justify the enslavement of the Indians, but sometimes to assert that they were free of original sin. The death of God, so close to Lafitau's work, while it cut away the top of his picture, in a way left things as they stood. Is that why we now have the right to *compare*, that is, as it were, to annul Father Time?

Nineteenth-century evolutionary theory, in its own way structuralist, injected a dose of secularism into Lafitau's schema. At Stuttgart, in 1861, Johann Jakob Bachofen published his *Das Mutterrecht* (*Matriarchy*). Right from the start the Swiss scholar relied upon a now famous passage of Herodotus (1.173): in Lycia the men took the name not of their father but of their mother — which is what the Iroquois, among others, also did. Now Lafitau knew this text: indeed, he had collected all the texts he could find on what we must after him call 'matriarchy' and 'matrilinearity'. 'Gynaecocracy, the Rule of Women', he observed, 'was practically universal' (1.71). His first reaction on comparing Lycians, Iroquois and Hurons was to suppose that the American Indians were descended from the Lycians (1.64). He was a little doubtful on account of the claimed universality of matriarchy in the ancient world, but having no change of theory at hand, finally concluded that 'the larger part of the inhabitants of America stemmed originally from those barbarians who dwelt on the mainland of Greece and the islands' (1.82—3), before the arrival of the Greeks. Bachofen did not need such a hypothesis. For him, all mankind has passed through a stage of 'matriarchy', a stage of comforting contact with nature which reproduces the mother's breast and which precedes the cultural break brought about by patriarchy. Even earlier than Bachofen and apparently without knowing Lafitau, L.H. Morgan had likened the Lycians to the Iroquois.[6] When the time came for a synthesis in 1877 (*Ancient Society*), God, incessantly on Lafitau's pen, makes an appearance only on the very last page, where Morgan pays homage to these 'savages', these 'barbarians' whose patient toil was 'a part of the plan of the Supreme Intelligence to develop a barbarian out of a savage, and a civilized man out of this barbarian'. A hesitant enough appearance; but all the same necessary. For the parallelism of social evolutions is explained at least partly by the presence in all men, if not of a gleam of original Revelation, then at least of the 'primary germs of thought' which the transition between one stage of social evolution and another allows to develop.[7] Secularized by Engels (*Origin of the Family* was published in 1884), Morgan's schema makes comparison both legitimate and straightforward. To compare two societies, it is necessary and sufficient to determine their co-ordinates on the graph of social evolution. The Iroquois are at the lower margin of the state of barbarism whose upper margin is represented by Homeric Greece. Fine, but what about all the innumerable institutions which Lafitau knew perfectly well could exist in quite different societies? Must we for example forbear to compare the warrior societies of the mediaeval West and Homeric society on the grounds that the one, in Marx's and Engels' terminology, belongs to a social formation founded on slavery, and the other to the 'feudal' period? Even if we do make the sacrifice, the problem refuses to go away. We have to make a choice: either we say, with the Soviet version of Marxism in particular, that all human societies have passed or will pass through the same stages — which is just not true;[8] or we restrict the occurrence of 'feudalism' simply to the mediaeval West and Japan, which involves an extraordinary constriction of the comparative field, one which would disallow a whole series of studies whose very existence proves that you cannot make something true simply by believing it.

Though I have cited Lewis Morgan, it was not — unfortunately — his work, the work of a man who had received a double education, Iroquois and American, and who, in spite of or because of that, insisted upon

167

the unity of the human family, that dominated such interest as anthropologists had in the Greek world. Six years before *Ancient Society*, in 1871, there appeared the first edition of Edward B. Tylor's *Primitive Culture*, and it was through Tylor and his followers, above all Andrew Lang (1844—1912) and J.G. Frazer (1854—1941), that Greek studies were decisively influenced by the work of anthropologists,[9] after the collapse of Max Müller's 'comparative mythology'.[10] Of course there were many points on which Morgan and Tylor were agreed, but their views were at heart different. Right at the beginning of his book Tylor, while allowing for the existence of good savages, sets up an opposition between Savagery and Civilization — that is of course Western imperialist civilization. But comparison is justifiable because of *survivals* (an older notion significantly adapted by Tylor) from the savage world at the heart of the civilized: 'If we choose out in this way things which have altered little in a long course of centuries, we may draw a picture where there shall be scarce a hand's breadth difference between an English ploughman and a negro of Central Africa.'[11] There is a fundamental unity between the lower *classes* of the West and the inferior *races* of the world: in Tylor's day English royalty could not yet be compared with African chiefs. Moreover Tylor made a point which is the origin of many theories of totemism: 'The sense of an absolute psychical distinction between man and beast, so prevalent in the civilized world, is hardly to be found among the lower races.'[12]

What was the place of the Greek world seen through the evolutionary spectacles of the nineteenth century? It is crisply defined by Andrew Lang, a key figure of the age, at once a journalist, a historian on the grand and the small scale, and a foremost anthropologist. It went without saying that, from the age of Homer, the Greek world belonged utterly to Civilization. After all, from then on there were royal houses. But it was equally obvious that the Greeks were conscious of having been savages. Their rituals and their myths are full of odd things, from human sacrifice to cannibalism. Here the notion of survival combined with evolution plays a crucial rôle: the Greeks *had been* savages, they were so no more; their myths are survivals from their past,[13] and mythology *tells* what their ancestors did. Comparison was compatible with hierarchization.

The synthetic systems of the Romantic period and the Age of Positivism are now mere rotted hulks or etiolated to the point of unrecognizability. Let us take a look at a slightly later period; at a time when the kings of anthropology were Frazer on one side and Malinowski on the other, what fresh basis for comparative study could a historian have found? Frazer was a fact-gleaner. Starting from the Graeco-Roman world, which he knew admirably well, he was an indefatigable footnoter

of Pausanias and Ovid without ever explaining what it was that permitted him to compare the Priest-King of Nemi slain by his successor,
Christ dying on the Cross or the God—King of Pharaonic Egypt.
Malinowski dedicated himself to an unprecedented effort of reflection
upon the functioning of a single Melanesian society, over-hastily
equated with the Savage *tout court* (Leach, 1966b: 360—7). For the
historian, the choice might properly appear ruinous. And yet, of the
two, from the time of Salomon Reinach to our own, it was undoubtedly Frazer who was, in France and elsewhere, the more influential. With hardly an exception (but see Finley, 1977), the central
concept which we owe to Malinowski (and refined by his successors,
above all Radcliffe-Brown), 'social function', has hardly been put to use
by historians of the Ancient World. To be sure it was not a clear or a
crisp notion, and it has properly been stressed that the word 'function'
has two senses for Malinowski, an organicist sense — an institution is an
element which has a function, a rôle, in a social aggregate; and a logistic
or symbolic sense — mythology has a symbolic function in the structur-
ing of social relations (Panoff, 1972: 109). But there was here an open
door which almost no one stepped through. One may be allowed to
regret this at a time when anthropology has, once again, rocketed in the
most divergent directions, of which 'structuralism' is just one — though
the one which, even allowing for fashion, attracts many historians most
strongly.

How are we placed now? The latest research, so far from making the
historian's choice easier, simply makes it more painful, because every
historian today knows that what he studies is properly speaking neither
the unique nor the universal — even if the universalism of the 'human
mind' has replaced Frazer's empirical universalism. We all know as historians that the truth of the history of a Breton village is not to be
found in the simple history of a Breton village; but also that the diverse
metahistories which crowd us, from a more or less refurbished Marxism
to psychoanalysis, from the philosophy of the price-curve to that of
universal logic, will never relieve us of the obligation to get back to our
village.

Structural anthropology is one of these metahistories, one of the
Siren-voices — surely one of the most exciting and stimulating, inasmuch as, privileging on the Saussurian model of language the synchronic over the diachronic, it offers the most complete challenge ever
thrown to a discipline which believed that there was no peeping over
the walls of time, unless it was for some rhetorical or pedagogic purpose
to paint what the dissertation-scribblers call a 'picture'. Yet this
challenge does not abolish those offered by earlier generations: it is
simply added to them. For it is not enough to assert, even to prove, as

169

'structuralism' attempts, not unsuccessfully, to do, that the 'human mind' is a universal logical agent, to restore to the historian the security he has lost, and which, one must hope, he will never rediscover. For the 'human mind' is not in itself the object of history, and anyway the ethnologists who postulate, even prove its universality do not claim that it is, if it be that the aim of their undertaking is 'the reintegration of culture in nature and finally of life within the whole of its physico-chemical conditions' (Lévi-Strauss, 1966a: 247). The 'logic of the living', which is also that of things in themselves,[14] is not answerable to historical reason, which is constitutive, not constituted, and which un-endingly makes and remakes its operational fields, its 'scenarios' (Veyne, 1971).

Conversely, though, we cannot appeal to the uniqueness of every event in time and take refuge in the bosom of Singularity. The historian cannot isolate himself in such a view. The individual occurrence is properly unintelligible if it is not set in some relation. The Breton village is in Brittany, France, the West; it is also in the Celtic world: studying its folklore may force one to study Irish or Welsh folklore; and it may not be entirely profitless to take a look at the folklore of the Auvergne or of Provence.[15] At any rate the historian is condemned at every moment to define his contexts, and the contexts of his contexts; his definitions are always provisional — 'Greek culture' is a context, but a potentially illusory one if one isolates the Greek world from the Thracian world or the Illyrian, to say nothing of the Mediterranean con-text; he is doomed to operate simultaneously on the spatial and on the temporal axes; and if he adopts provisionally 'universal' categories like the Raw or the Cooked, it is always to make them dynamic.

In his own way, Lafitau understood and anticipated the dilemma: 'The customs and manners of nations could well guide us to a more refined understanding by comparison of these manners and customs. But some among them were general, instituted upon the earliest ideas which the fathers of the peoples communicated to their children and which were among the majority integrally preserved, or at least without marked alteration notwithstanding their separation in space and their lack of communication. Such are the ideas related to most of the prac-tices of collective life. Assuredly from them one can derive no conclu-sions. In making the comparisons which are proper, therefore, I will not scruple to cite the customs of what peoples soever they be, without claiming to draw any conclusions other than the sole relation of these customs with those of earliest antiquity. It should then only be in the matter of certain distinctive and characteristic features of the peoples newly discovered, in relation to those peoples of antiquity of whom the historians have preserved to us some knowledge, that one could hazard some conjectures, bringing these distinctive features together and comparing them one with another' (1.44–5). Of course 'the general' no less than 'the distinctive' have varied since the Jesuit missionary. All the same, the extraordinary thing is that such a text might serve as a motto as well for the work of Georges Dumézil as for that of Claude Lévi-Strauss.

Among all the many human institutions which Lafitau sought to relate to one another there is one which ethnography was to take up in remarkable fashion – initiation. To adopt a recent definition, initiation is 'a body of rites and oral teachings whose purpose is to produce a radical modification of the religious and social status of the person to be initiated. In philosophical terms, initiation is equivalent to an onto-logical mutation of the existential condition. The novice emerges from his ordeal a totally different being: he has become *another*' (Eliade, 1969: 112). Even before Lafitau the initiations which are, even today, best known and best studied, had been perfectly rehearsed and identi-fied: the means by which the young 'savage' enters upon the adult community. So Robert Beverley, author of *The History and Present State of Virginia*, retailing the rituals undergone by the young Indians:

The Solemnity of Huskanawing is commonly practis'd once every fourteen or six-teen years, or oftener, as their young men happen to grow up. It is an Institution or Discipline which all young men must pass, before they can be admitted to be of the number of the Great men, or Cockarouses of the Nation; whereas by Captain Smith's Relation, they were only set apart to supply the Priesthood. The whole ceremony is performed after the following manner.

The choicest and briskest young men of the Town, and such only as have acquired some Treasure by their Travels and Hunting, are chosen out by the Rulers to be Huskanawed; and whoever refuses to undergo this Process, dare not remain among them. Several of those odd preparatory Fopperies are premis'd in the beginning, which have before been related; but the principal part of the business is to carry them into the Woods, and there keep them under confinement, and destitute of all society, for several months; giving them no other sustenance, but the Infusion, or Decoction of some Poisonous Intoxicating Roots; by virtue of which Physick, and by the severity of the discipline, which they undergo, they become stark, staring Mad: in which raving condition they are kept eighteen or twenty days . . .

(On their return to the village) they must pretend to have forgot the very use of their Tongues, so as not to be able to speak, nor understand anything that is spoken, till they learn it again. Now whether this be real or counterfeit, I don't know; but certain it is, that they will not for some time take notice of any body, nor any thing, with which they were before acquainted, being still under the guard of their Keepers, who constantly wait upon them every where, till they have learnt all things perfectly over again. Thus they unlive their former lives, and commence Men, by forgetting that they have ever been Boys. (1705: 3.8 §32 [pp. 39–41])

But Lafitau improved this initial interpretation in two ways. He allowed into the category of initiations not merely admission into the community but acceptance into smaller groups (secret societies), religious and shamanist initiations and so on. And in the spirit of the

171

general programme of his enquiry, he compared the Indian initiations with those known in classical civilization — the Mysteries of Eleusis as well as Spartan and Cretan education systems — and even mediaeval; for he treated the ritual of admission to knighthood as an initiation — yet another stroke of daring (1.201–56; 2.1–70, 283–8).

It was not indeed until 1909, with the publication of Arnold van Gennep's *Rites de passage*, that this framework was further enlarged and that the first steps were taken towards the elaboration of a formal structure of analysis, the French folklorist demonstrating that the enormous body of rituals such as these could be classified under three headings: rituals of separation, rituals of exclusion, rituals of (re)-incorporation.

This classification obviously presupposes in addition, indeed in first place, an articulation of time and space peculiar to *rites de passage* [*i.e.* rituals of status-transition. Ed.]. Time first. Its rhythm is not that of the continuum, invented by the mathematicians: 'The idea of Time . . . is one of those categories which we find necessary because we are social animals rather than because of anything empirical in our objective experience of the world.'[16] Time in rituals of status-transition is also a human creation: the year is punctuated by the rituals and the ritual itself causes the initiate to pass from the ordinary to the extra-ordinary and back again to the ordinary, now consciously accepted. For the ritual to operate also at the level of conceptions of space, it must itself be broken up: 'human' space in which social life is lived, against 'marginal' space, which may be a symbolic sacred area, 'the bush' whether literal or figurative, forest or mountain[17] — it hardly matters, provided it be perceived as *other*: 'heaven' and 'hell' in children's hop-scotch is a good, if extreme, example. So time and space are 'binary' [that is, each organized into two mutually exclusive — and inverted — categories. Ed.], though the ritual rhythm, as defined by van Gennep, is threefold. Edmund Leach defines three kinds of rôles men find themselves playing in this kind of ritual action: formality, masquerade, rôle reversal (1966a: 135). In the context of initiation of young men into the warrior life, for example, the three terms will be represented by warrior uniform, by disguise, of which countless types are found at the point of marginality, and by the inversion which temporarily turns the man into a woman, which causes him too to behave in exactly the opposite manner from how he is to behave in 'normal' life.

It would be possible to exemplify this rhythm among the Australian aborigines no less than in Africa or among the Amerindians; but as long as we remain on this very general level, we are not actually within the realm of the historical, or the 'sublunary', to use a term Paul Veyne has borrowed from Aristotelianism. Let us see what becomes of these concepts — and they are indeed concepts — in a particular historical society: that of archaic and classical Greece.

Recent excavation at the site of the Greek city of Eretria, on the island of Euboea, by Swiss archaeologists, has revealed among other things a small necropolis surrounding the tomb of a prince or king, datable to the late eighth and early seventh century — precisely the period of the emergence of the archaic city.[18] The tombs excavated form two groups: to the west we find only incineration; to the east, inhumation. It is not a case of change of fashion, since the two groups are contemporary; nor is it a matter of competing funerary customs, such as one finds elsewhere — for example, at the Kerameikos at Athens in the ninth century. We have rather a quite deliberate and significant opposition at the symbolic level: the inhumations are of children, the incinerations of adults. Both sexes are represented in the two groups. Their opposition is signalled in the group of incinerations by the presence of arms in the one case, and of jewellery in the other. Claude Bérard, the excavator, makes the point: 'inhumation was the practice at Eretria until just before adolescence, cremation being reserved for marriageable girls and married women, and for youths and men able to use the lance and to take their place in battle' (C. Bérard, 1970: 50; at Marathon, the adult male Athenians were cremated, but not the Plataeans and the slaves, who fought, but not on the same basis: Kurtz and Boardman, 1971: 246; cf. the conclusions of Loraux, 1978: 810). Trying to determine the age at which the appropriate funerary practice changed, Bérard suggests that at Eretria, and very probably in many other places,[19] it was about the age of sixteen. The mere account of the archaeological finds (is an account ever innocent though?) directs us to the search for a ritual of status-transition which dramatized for the Greek adolescent the transition between Nature and Culture, or, if you wish, between the Raw and the Cooked, in the most concrete sense. This ritual is relatively well known; at Athens in the archaic and classical periods, as Claude Bérard notes, it is identified with admission into the phratry. The distinctive occurrence on the third day of the Ionian festival of the Apatouria (the festival of 'those who have the same father' — that is, of classificatory 'brothers') was an initiation ceremony, the *koureōtis*: the name derives from the shearing (*koura*) of the flocks and of men, and it probably connotes also the young warrior (*kouros*). At Athens, the sacrifice of the *koureion* [probably the offering of the hair itself. Ed.] which marked the admission of the ephebes into the phratry, took place at the age of sixteen.[20]

One point however serves to remind us that we ought not to neglect the 'diachronic' aspect. The opposition between cremation and in-humation employed at Eretria and elsewhere to denote the opposition

between childhood and adulthood obviously cannot predate the introduction of cremation into Greece, which did not happen until after the
collapse of the Mycenaean world.

Nevertheless the discovery, due as we saw to Lafitau, of initiation
rituals in Greece parallel to those of 'primitive' societies, has stimulated, especially in the twentieth century, a very large amount of work
recently synthesized by the Italian historian Angelo Brelich in his
Paides e Parthenoi (1969).[21] Jean-Pierre Vernant, using the evidence of
the mythical tradition especially, has analysed a number of different
religious festivals, summarizing his results as follows: 'If rituals of
status-transition mean for boys entry into the status of warrior, for the
girls associated with them in the same rituals, and frequently themselves subjected to a period of seclusion, the initiation ordeals mean a
preparation for sexual union in marriage. Here again the association,
which is also an opposition, between war and marriage is evident.
Marriage is to the girl what war is to the boy: for each, they mark the
fulfilment of their respective natures, by quitting a state in which each
has still some of the characteristics of the other' (1974: 37—40 cf.
Calame, 1977: 1.239—40; Schmitt, 1977: 1059—73). This is the
explanation, for example, of the fact that the Athenian ephebes wear
the 'black *chlamys*' [a kind of short cloak. Ed.], not always perhaps,
but at least at the solemn occasion of the procession to Eleusis to be
initiated into the mysteries,[22] before they put on, after swearing the
oath, the hoplite panoply (Vidal-Naquet, 1972: 161—2); and it also
explains why the festivals and myths frequently dramatized the young
man's entry into adulthood by having him put on female disguise, and a
girl's into womanhood by means of a male charade.[23] And here of course
we remember Leach's three terms, formality, masquerade, rôle reversal.

The male rituals of the *ephebeia* in particular allow us to define a
twofold structure: on one side the hoplite, who fights by day, in ranks,
face-forward, supporting his fellows, on the level plain; and on the
other the ephebe (or the Spartan *kruptos*), who fights by night, unaided,
resorting to tricks of the kind deplored by hoplite and citizen values,
skulking on the frontiers[24] — all-in-all acting in a manner quite the
reverse of how he must behave when he is integrated into the *polis*.
Surely we have here culture on one side, nature on the other; on one
side savagery — or femininity, on the other civilization. Plato, in common with many other Greek thinkers, defined childhood as the savage
time of human life (*Timaeus* 44a—b; *Laws* 2, 653d—e; 666a—c). The
Greeks made the principle of polarity one of the cornerstones of their
mode of representing the world (Lloyd, 1966). No less than us were
they capable of representing the oppositions which articulated their
world in the form of a table with two columns. Thus the Pythagoreans,

according to Aristotle, 'recognized ten principles, which they list in two parallel columns:

limited	unlimited
equal	unequal
unity	plurality
right	left
male	female
still	moved
straight line	curve
light	dark
good	bad
square	oblong'

(*Metaphysics* 1.5, 986a 22–6)

That list one could easily extend by looking at different aspects of Greek culture: master–slave, Greek–Barbarian, citizen–foreigner – even Apollo–Dionysus perhaps. Here again ancient thought in large measure anticipated modern structural analysis: think for example of how Aristotle asks himself how far the sets adult–child, man–woman, master–slave, employer–craftsman coincide, and the senses in which they do not (*Politics* 1.12, 1259a 37ff.). And do we need to be reminded of the propensity of sophists, tragedians and philosophers to contrast, oppose, compare *phusis* (Nature) and *nomos* (Law, Custom)?

These and other pairs may be considered to constitute the framework of the discourse of the Greeks. But the structural anthropologist and the historian cannot both deal with them in the same manner. For example, if we take the opposition between ephebes and hoplites, fledgling warriors and adult warriors, the comparatist will observe, from the work of Georges Dumézil, that the opposition between the *naked* (i.e. not heavily-armed) warrior, the ephebe, fighting unaided, and the warrior integrated into some group and fully armed, is much earlier than the set ephebe–hoplite, since hoplite warfare makes its appearance in Greece only early in the seventh century; and that the opposition can be traced elsewhere in the Indo-European world. The opposition is the same, but the words used to describe it are not. Thus, in the Indian epic, the 'heavy' warrior is an archer, while in Greece the bow belongs to the Savage (Dumézil, 1968: 63–5; J. Le Goff and Vidal-Naquet, 1978: 273–5).[25] It will be objected that the Indo-Europeans, or at least their conceptions, are nevertheless historical, yet Dumézil, in studying a ritual of warrior-initiation at home, makes use not only of Indo-Iranian and Irish evidence, but also of evidence from Canadian Red-Indians: 'It is British Columbia, the East coast of Canada, which, *by virtue of a coincidence we cannot explain*, best helps us to see the meaning of the Indo-Iranian legends about a three-headed monster'

175

(1942: 128, my stress). The explanation, if indeed it is possible, is here fatally a-historical: no historian can postulate a collocation including Red Indians, Indo-Iranians and Romans, all three. Such a collocation is in fact the human race itself — or better still, the 'human mind'. The Greek historian on the other hand is concerned with a datable reality, the hoplite, and with another datable reality, an institution first evidenced epigraphically in 361/0 BC and whose working is explained some 35 years later by Aristotle, that is the institution called at Athens the *ephebeia*, and its parallels in the rest of the Greek world.

One characteristic of the history of Ancient Greece, from the very beginnings of our knowledge of it, is an extraordinary unevenness of development — an unevenness so marked that for an Athenian of the fifth century some indisputably Greek peoples were thought of as 'savages', almost as the Brazilian Indians were by their sixteenth-century conquerors (see Thucydides 3.94 for example). Following Thucydides, modern historians see the opposition between Sparta and Athens, between the type of conservatism and of rejection of history on the one hand, and the city which by contrast chose, in the fifth century, to identify itself with historical change on the other, as one of the major features of the classical period. In view of that, what of male and female initiations? Put it another way: what differences are there between the two in terms of the sets child—adult and girl—boy (alternatively, male—female)?

The *ephebeia* as described by Aristotle is a form of civic military service.[26] For the philosopher, the two-year period of service is in no sense a period of isolation preparatory to integration into the civic community: he says expressly that the admission of a young man into the deme-lists *precedes* the military service: recognition of citizenship *precedes* the period of probation and is not its consequence. One point only suggests something other than the mere performance of military obligations: 'During these two years of garrison-duty, they wear a *chlamys*, and they are free from all financial impositions; they cannot be involved in a lawsuit, either as plaintiff or as defendant, so that they will have no excuse for absenting themselves. The only exceptions are cases concerned with an inheritance or with an heiress; or when a man has to take up a priesthood hereditary in his family' (*Constitution of the Athenians* 42.5). The *chlamys* is understood not as the dress of ritual seclusion but like the military uniform of our own day. Aristotle also understands the debarment from litigation in purely secular terms; and it is obviously extremely significant that he can take this approach quite naturally. The question of origins is a quite different problem. Long ago it was observed that 'the seclusion of the young, in the period immediately prior to their definite inclusion within the society, is so well attested in all kinds of different societies and, in Greece, in Sparta, that one is inclined to discern a trace of it here' (Roussel, 1921: 459). To be sure, but what exactly do we mean by 'trace'? Is the *function* of an institution in a society to be confused with its *origin*? Is the B.A. degree to be explained by its mediaeval origins? Of course not, any more than Aristophanic comedy is to be explained by a seasonal ritual of fertility as the Cambridge School would have it (for example, Cornford, 1914: 53—69). Of course there are inertias and repeats in society, but it does not live in the past. The past is influential only inasmuch as it is present in the structures of thought, manners, interpretations. To return to the *ephebeia*, it is obvious that in Aristotle's time the ordinary understanding of the ephebes' stay in the frontier forts was not as an exclusion of the young men prior to their entry, or re-entry, into the *polis*; but as garrison-service. And when Thucydides mentions in passing that the *peripoloi* ('those who go round'), that is, the ephebes, went on a *night attack* near Nisaea in 423 together with the new Plataean citizens (4.67), there can be no doubt that the ephebes are not (yet) citizens like other citizens and that they are associated with irregular activities in war; all the same, we must show that such an interpretation was current at the time. In any case it is obvious that it no longer was so in Aristotle's time.

If we look at the historical changes we can obtain some idea of what happened. The earliest *ephebeia* was set in the context of the phratry, an archaic institution, certainly reactivated in the fifth century, but whose rôle was diminished markedly after the Cleisthenic reforms (508 BC) by the demes. One became an ephebe in the civic or military sense of the word at eighteen, but one became an ephebe in the phratry at sixteen. It was within the phratry that there took place the rituals of status-transition which mark entry into adulthood, the most important being the offering of the child's long hair (Vidal-Naquet, 1968: 179—80). But in myths, comedy, in a philosopher such as Plato, and even, as I have tried to show, an entire tragedy of Sophocles, the *Philoctetes*,[27] there is preserved something else — the 'trace' of an initiatory ritual in which the young man, as a guileful 'black' hunter, was sent out to the frontier area until he should perform the 'exploit' symbolically imposed upon the young men in archaic societies. Rituals of this type were real enough in Crete where even in the hellenistic period the official vocabulary of a city like Dreros makes a distinction between city, country and the frontier forts, and where the educational institutions set the 'flocks' (*agelai*) of adolescents over against the sodalities (*hetaireiai*) of the adults (nature against culture) (pp. 155—8 above). These institutions in Athens have been for the most part detached from each other, in a civic world which had been profoundly affected by rationalism — one might almost say secularized. And so Brelich, hardly one to avoid comparison with 'archaic' societies, in his discussion of the Athenian *ephebeia* concluded that 'the original initiatory elements we can discern in it came to be voided of their original functional integrity' (1969: 227). The principle of 'elders first' endured of course. In the Athenian assembly, the old men had first right to speak. In the course of what was perhaps the most crucial debate ever held in the *ekklesia* (Assembly), whether or not to deploy almost all its forces in the expedition to Sicily (415 BC), Nicias appeals to the old men as a group to resist the crazy ideas of Alcibiades and the young men with him, attempting thus to swing the traditional mechanism of age-classes into action; Alcibiades asks the Athenians not to be afraid of his youth: the city is made up of young and old. *Together* they can win (Thucydides 6.13, 17, 18). Alcibiades carried the day, though the Athenians were to regret it; at least his speech suggests that the city is an inclusive *totality* which to a significant degree cancels the opposition between age-classes.

'Old' Nicias thought of a city in which the young held power more or less as an inversion, a topsy-turvy world. The comic poet Aristophanes, imagining a utopian situation in which everything is turned upside down — in *Lysistrata* or *Ecclesiazusae* (*Women in Assembly*) — makes the women of Athens responsible for the decisions of government. In *Lysistrata* (411 BC) the wives of the Athenians have seized the democracy. They decide to go on a sex-strike if peace is not made. In their justification, the chorus of women, using the language of assembly-meetings, declare:

> It's open to anyone to praise
> The city and I to the end of my days,
> Shall love her for giving joy to a gentle child.
>> I was only seven when I
>> Carried the Sacred
>> Vessels; and at ten I
>> Bore the Temple Mill;[28]
> Then in yellow I acted the Little Bear at Brauron,
> And, growing taller,
> And lovelier, took care
> Of the Holy Basket — it was heaven!
>> (638–47, tr. Dickinson)

That looks at first sight like a list of female initiations in which there were several stages, rather like the system for boys at Sparta.[29] But no such thing existed, and we must understand this speech as ideological: Athenian women were not properly speaking citizens, and young girls were not citizens to be, whom the city had to take through the stages of an educative initiation. The Athenian *polis* was founded upon the exclusion of women, just as, in other respects, it was founded upon the exclusion of foreigners (metics) and slaves. The sole civic function of women was to give birth to citizens; the condition imposed upon them by Pericles's law of 451 was to be the daughter of a citizen and of a citizen's daughter. The chorus in *Lysistrata* is arguing *as if* the women of Athens were in fact the citizens. The stages referred to are those of a fictitious cycle. Most of them have nothing whatever, or virtually nothing, to do with rituals of status-transition: there were only two *arrēphoroi* (?'bearers of the secret symbols'), chosen from among girls of noble birth. They were responsible for weaving the *peplos* ('robe') of Athena Polias; and they played a key rôle in the highly secret ritual of the Arrēphoria (or *Arrētophoria*).[30] As for the 'grinders of grain', they prepared the flour and bread for the sacrifices in the cult of Athena; the most important duty of the *kanēphoroi* was to carry baskets in the solemn Panathenaic procession. In short, these are duties undertaken by young girls in the service of the community; even if some of them reveal characteristics of initiation rituals — special dress, seclusion of the *arrēphoroi*, for instance — there is here no question of a regular institution affecting an entire age-class,[31] rather of the city at each festival renewing its contact with divinity. The women of Athens are not altering their status.

The case of the little 'Bears' in the sanctuary of Artemis at Brauron is very different and much more complex. The very name of the animal which the girls represent is that of the divinity, Artemis, goddess of wild nature. The evidence of the scholiasts for the cult and that of other sanctuaries of Artemis in Attica (see Brelich, 1969: 247–9), and archaeological evidence going back to the first half of the fifth century (Kahil, 1965: 20–33; 1976: 126–30), permit no doubt about the general character of the ritual: it involved a seclusion preceding — by a considerable period of time — and preparing for marriage. The girls — so the scholiast Harpokration for example tells us — had to 'become bears before marriage, (in honour of) Artemis of Mounychia or of Artemis of Brauron'. The explanation offered by the aetiological legends for this obligation involve an original killing of a bear by some boys, the retribution for which was at first a human sacrifice, and later this ritual of substitution performed by the girl-bears.[32] Variants or no, the myth is not difficult to explain: in exchange for the very advance of culture implied by the killing of wild animals, an advance for which men are responsible, the girls are obliged before marriage — indeed before puberty — to undergo a period of ritual 'wildness'. Study of the pottery evidence from Brauron reveals that the rituals in honour of the goddess involved (sequentially?) nakedness and the wearing of a special form of clothing (the 'crocus' is a saffron-yellow robe) — perhaps a means of dramatizing the transition between savagery and civilization. But it remains true that it was possible for only a small number of Athenian

179

girls to become 'bears': the very size of the sanctuaries enforces the conclusion. The Aristophanes scholion which gives us our most detailed account (on *Lysistrata* 645; cf. Brelich, 1969: 263—4), says both that the 'bears' were girls who had been 'chosen', and that the goddess had determined — at the original institution of the ritual — that no Athenian girl might marry before she had become a bear in her service. We must then allow that, even if the little bears represent the female community, in the sense in which the Boulē (the Council of 500) represents the city, they constitute an élite of the 'chosen' and that initiation was confined to them. Moreover such a pattern is well known to anthropologists — the pattern of the 'secret society', a small group which fulfils a function for the public weal, the precondition of that being a special degree of initiation.

Let us return to Vernant's parallel which we used as a model: 'Marriage is to the girl what war is to the boy', a formulation which quite evidently can be applied to innumerable societies. We can now see just what happened in Athens. As regards boys, the *ephebeia* as a ritual of entry into adolescence is separated from the *ephebeia* as compulsory military service for all: at this level, there are no longer any groups privileged by birth, wealth or membership of some priestly family. At most, considerations of family-order — establishing one's inheritance, saving an *oikos* [family] from the threat of 'escheat' by marrying an *epiklēros* — could relieve one of the obligation.[33] Depending upon his wealth qualification, a young Athenian would later serve as a rower in the fleet, as a cavalryman or as a hoplite, but in each case he would have served as an ephebe and have sworn an oath based upon the ideology of the hoplite: 'I will not abandon the man who stands next to me in the battle-lines.' Initiatory rituals proper are to an extent separated from the process of entry into the civic community. It is obvious that nothing of the kind existed for girls: certainly marriage involved well-known rituals of status-transition (being carried over the threshold by the husband), and it bestowed the right to take part in specifically female ceremonies for women citizens, the Thesmophoria (Detienne, 1977: 78—81; Detienne and Vernant, 1979: 183—214), which was the only forum which brought women together as citizens of Athens for the one kind of political activity (if one can call it that) allowed them; but age-class initiation properly so called, if it ever had been a collective experience, developed in a direction opposite to that of male initiations: it involved only a minuscule group of initiates who could represent the city only by metonymy.

The image of Sparta transmitted to us by the ancient texts, particularly those deriving from Athens, is that of a society which refused historical change and suspended itself in the changelessness of the 'Constitution of Lycurgus' (Tigerstedt, 1965; Rawson, 1969). Such modern scholars as have not capitulated to the 'Spartan mirage' have directed themselves to 'normalizing' Sparta's oddness — Arnold Toynbee would have it as one of his 'civilizations'. To normalize is the resort both of Henri Jeanmaire in *Couroi et Courètes* (1939), where he discerns 'beneath the mask of Lycurgus' a society exactly comparable with African societies, and of M.I. Finley, in showing that the three fundamental aspects of classical Sparta, the agrarian infrastructure, with the hierarchy of *homoioi* ('the Equals'), *perioikoi* [the free non-Spartiate inhabitants of the towns of Lakonia and probably Messenia. Ed.], and helots; the governmental and the military structure; the system formed by the rituals of status-transition, education (the *agōgē*), age-classes, collective eating etc., were not developed and instituted at a stroke; and that the 'sixth-century revolution' which gave to classical Sparta its characteristic stamp was a complex process of innovation, transformation, and revival of features and institutions apparently transmitted from remote prehistory.[34]

What was true of the Athenian hoplite *at the level of myth* is true of Spartiate *kruptos in practice*: the *kruptos* appears in every respect as an antihoplite. The *kruptoi* were young men who left the city to roam, in secret and in isolation, 'naked' (that is, not heavily-armed), through mountain and countryside, feeding themselves as they might, assassinating helots under cover of night — the helots against whom the Ephors, to ensure that no pollution attached to such killings, each year declared war. According to the scholiast on Plato's *Laws* 3, 633b, the period of seclusion lasted an entire year, though Plato himself expressly remarks that it occurred in winter. We have only to invert this text to find the rules which governed the manner of life and the moral and social behaviour of the hoplite, whose virtues otherwise compose the very fabric of Spartan life: collective living and eating, fighting in the open, by day, on the flat, in summer — a mode of fighting founded upon the face-to-face encounter of two sets of phalanxes. And yet, just as only a tiny number of Athenian girls played the part of 'bears', only a tiny number of Spartiates followed this mode of life which Jeanmaire compared to the 'lycanthropy' known particularly in Africa (Jeanmaire, 1939: 540—69). Plutarch notes that it was 'the most astute' (τοὺς μάλιστα νοῦν ἔχειν δοκοῦντας: *Life of Lycurgus* 28.2) young Spartiates who were chosen for this ritual of status-transition; and it is probable that, once they had become adults and full warriors, it was the *kruptoi* who composed the élite formation of three hundred 'cavalrymen' (*hippeis*: they actually fought on foot), concerned above all with police duties (Jeanmaire, 1939: 542—5). In other words it is impossible to detach the *krupteia* from the practical part which it played in Spartiate

181

society, a rôle which must have been developed for the most part from the eighth century, the date of the conquest of Messenia; that is, to maintain in every way possible a repressive régime faced with the endemic rebellions of the subject population of Messenia and of Lakonia itself. The *kruptos*, like the ephebe of Athenian myth, is a guileful hunter — but he hunts helots (Wachsmuth, 1846: 1.462; 2.304). The temporary 'wildness' of the *krupteia* is an utterly socialized, even political, wildness: it functions directly to maintain the political and social order.

At first glance, the education of the young Spartiate, the *agōgē*, which was the precondition for the entry of a Spartiate into full citizenship, has every appearance of being a system of initiatory rituals of 'primitive' type which remained, in the classical period and even thereafter, fully effective. Indeed Sparta is the only Greek city where we know at any rate the names of the different age-classes which articulated childhood, youth and adolescence (Brelich, 1969: 116–17). According to a Roman historian, 'Lycurgus laid down that the children should be brought up not in the area of the city but in the fields so that they might pass their early years not in luxury but in toil and suffering; and he directed that they should return to the city only when they had become fully-grown men' (Justin 3.3.6). 'Bush' versus city, childhood versus adulthood: the oppositions look transparent. But if we look more closely, things are not so clear. One surprising point first of all, which seems to have escaped notice: it seems difficult, not to say impossible, to fix precisely the point at which a young Spartiate became a full adult.[35] We know of course that around twenty or twenty-one the Spartiate *eirēn* (i.e. ephebe) became a *sphaireus* ('ball-player') (Pausanias 3.14.6). But this moment does not seem to have been made particularly dramatic: nothing at Sparta recalls the oath of the Athenian ephebes when they became hoplites, though such an oath is found in other societies in several respects closer to Sparta than to Athens, for example in Crete. A text of Xenophon has sometimes been used to prove the existence of such a status-transition at this point (Brelich, 1969: 125). But it says nothing of the kind — indeed quite the reverse: 'In respect of those who have passed through the period of adolescence and are now eligible even for the highest public offices, the other Greek states no longer insist that they should keep fit, yet lay upon them nevertheless the obligation to go on campaign; Lycurgus on the other hand laid down that for men of this age hunting was the perfect thing, so long as it did not interfere with any public obligation, so that they too would be able to sustain the physical hardship of campaigning no less than those in the flower of their youth' (Xenophon, *Constitution of the Lacedaemonians* 4.7). It is hard to tell whether

adulthood at Sparta was an extension of childhood; or whether childhood was rather an anticipatory preparation for the life of an adult and
a soldier. At any rate, by contrast with what happened elsewhere, for
example in Crete, marriage is in no sense the point at which adolescence
comes to an end: for several years after his marriage, the husband continued to live in barracks, and saw his wife only in secret (Xenophon,
Const. Laced. 1.5; Plutarch, *Life of Lycurgus* 15). Moreover, whereas
in other Greek cities it was the offering of the child's long hair that
marked the end of adolescence, in Sparta it was customary for the adult
males to wear their hair long (Herodotus 1.82; Plutarch, *Life of
Lysander* 1). The offering of the hair is a ritual of status-transition,
because it involves a 'before' and an 'after'; to keep one's hair is quite
different, because that can hardly be betokened by a ceremony. And
search though one may through the successive ordeals undergone by a
young Spartiate, the most notorious of which is the cheese-stealing
beneath the lash at the altar of Artemis Orthia,[36] for the ghosts of
initiations and even of fictive deaths, not one of these ordeals is in the
least decisive (Brelich, 1969: 136).

By contrast, a patient reading of the well-known texts which describe
the *agōgē*, Xenophon's *Constitution of the Lacedaemonians* and
Plutarch's *Life of Lycurgus*, reveals one striking fact. Childhood at
Sparta has two simultaneous connotations: 'savagery' and hoplite-
culture: the child is at one and the same time a small animal and a pre-
hoplite; and that is the mark of the extent to which properly military
institutions 'consumed' Spartiate education. The vocabulary — so far as
we have any direct knowledge of it — is characteristic. For the groups
of young men, two words were used in antiquity: *agela*, flock; and the
word *ila*, which really means the group of young soldiers.[37] Xenophon's
description is particularly telling: the children are simultaneously introduced, like the *kruptoi*, to guile, to stealing, to activity by night; but
they also mix with the adults at the *sussitia*, the common meals (*Const.
Laced.* 2.5–8; cf. Plutarch, *Lycurgus* 12). One ritual deserves special
emphasis: from time to time two batallions (*moirai* = *morai*, a term
used in the Spartan army) of Spartan 'ephebes' met at Platanistas
['Plane-tree Wood': actually an open space surrounded by plane trees.
Ed.] in Sparta. The fight was simultaneously hoplite and 'wild', since
the combatants were allowed to resort to a number of expedients,
including biting, which were ordinarily forbidden; and it was preceded by the sacrifice to Enyalios, the god of Bloody Fight, of two
dogs, that is of the most domesticated of animals — in fact, to be more
precise, of two puppies (cf. Plutarch, *Quaestiones romanae* 111, 290d).
It was preceded too by a fight between two wild-boars, wild animals if
ever there were, but in this case *ēthades*, which means 'tame'. The vic-

tory of the boar belonging to one or other camp usually ensured the victory of its group of young men.[38] It all looks as if 'the wild' and 'culture' were not enemies whose hostility had to be dramatized, but two opposed principles which it was appropriate as far as possible to bring together.[39] It was the *kruptoi* alone who had the privilege of dramatizing their hostility.

As early as Lafitau it had been noted that the status of women at Sparta was quite different from elsewhere in Greece; and he even used the word 'gynaecocracy' ('rule of women') in this connection (1.73). One might say in general that in the most archaic of archaizing Greek cities the opposition between the sexes was stressed less heavily than in a democratic city such as Athens. In the latter female power is an issue only in comedy and in utopian thinking; at Sparta or Locris and elsewhere it forms part of the historical-legendary tradition, associated moreover with power being seized by the slaves (pp. 189—200 below). In the particular case of Sparta, and of what little we know of its 'female initiations'[40] we know that the Spartiate woman underwent on her marriage rituals of inversion comparable to those known elsewhere in the Greek world: the girl 'was put into the care of a woman called a *numpheutria*, who shaved her hair, dressed her in the clothes and the shoes of a man, and settled her down on a mattress stuffed with leaves, all alone and without light' (Plutarch, *Virtues of Women* 245f; *Lycurgus* 15). But generally speaking what we know of a girl's childhood and adolescence gives less the impression of being a preparation, punctuated by rituals, for marriage, than an imitation of institutions for males — not that the Spartiate woman prepares herself for war, like the female citizens of Plato's *Republic* and *Laws*; but the only specifically female duty which remains is the obligation to produce fine children. The Spartiate family is scarcely an institution of the city, which on the contrary took great pains to restrict family life to the bare minimum.

At any rate, the impression given by the few ancient texts is not so much of a parallelism between the education of girls and that of boys (compare Brelich, 1969: 157), as of a direct reproduction: there were *agelai* of girls as well as of boys (Pindar, frg. 112 Snell); nakedness was obligatory for girls in certain ceremonies as it was for boys (Plutarch, *Lycurgus* 14—15); both sexes had to perform physical exercises and compete (Xenophon, *Const. Laced.* 1.4) — it would be easy to go on. Certainly the reproduction was not complete: little girls and teenagers were not organized into age-classes; in many cults the girls' rôle was different from that of boys; boys alone underwent ordeals to test endurance such as that at the altar of Artemis Orthia; and the *krupteia* was strictly confined to males, just as were all the properly political institutions of ancient Sparta. The Spartiate girl was in a real sense a boy manqué.

It will probably now be clear where the comparison between Athens and Sparta has led us — a comparison which I am not the first, nor the last, to make. In each case the lexical items of the language of initiation are doubtless the same; and it is easy enough to find in them the opposed pairs which modern anthropology has taught us to discover. But their articulation into phrases is radically different — so much so that one would almost want to say that the opposition between Athens and Sparta at the level of practice is nearly as strict as it is in Thucydides's speeches. Yet this opposition is quite evidently the consequence of a historical development which accentuated instead of reducing the differences. No doubt Greek society is a 'historical' society; and we know some have contrasted ' "cold" and "hot" societies; the former seeking, by the institutions they give themselves, to annul the possible effects of historical factors on their equilibrium and continuity in a quasi-automatic fashion, the latter resolutely internalizing the historical process and making it the moving power of their development' (Lévi-Strauss, 1966a: 234). But Sparta is the archetype exactly of a society which refuses to internalize history and which is, for all that, compared with the other Greek states, the consequence of a complex historical evolution. The question now is whether, having borrowed from the anthropologists ideas they themselves took over, with changes, from structural linguistics, we in turn should not require of them the same holism which they have quite properly demanded of us: that they should give the same weight to the diachronic dimension as to synchronic analysis.[41] Unless we make that demand, what significance could the systems of signs possess within which we encapsulate the societies we study — ignoring their scientific import, of course, which is supra-historical, not to say supra-ethnological — but the deposit or the spoor that each of them leaves behind in the form of texts, artworks or ruins? Edgar Morin has a nice comment on the strange world of tourist-guides: 'It is a kind of gigantic Luna-Park. The land is stripped of its sociology [and of its history] for the sake of its ethnology, its archaeology, its folklore and its oddities.'[42] We can admire the work of ethnologists past and present — they have enormously increased the historian's 'proper' field. But without history can ethnology be anything but a kind of day-trip — first-class?

IV: Disorder and deviance

10. Slavery and the Rule of Women in tradition, myth and utopia

Pierre Vidal-Naquet (1970, 1979)

To Simon Pembroke

This paper is an attempt to bring together two different approaches. The first is the straightforward use of social history, of the work done in recent years on the category of unfree persons defined by Pollux as 'between free men and slaves': *metaxu eleutherōn kai doulōn*, such as the helots of Sparta, the *penestai* of Thessaly and the *klarōtai* of Crete. The outcome of this work has been well summarized by M.I. Finley (1963/64: 249; cf. Lotze, 1959): ancient society passed from a state in which personal status was distributed along a continuum with the free man at one end and the non-free at the other; to one, the model or ideal-type being classical Athens, in which the distinction between citizen and slave was clear-cut, crisp and absolute.

Of course, if we look only at the Spartiate *homoioi* (the 'Equals') and at citizens proper, we can maintain, as is often done, that the difference between the democratic city and the type Plato called 'timocratic' is merely one of degree. The two types of city (three if we include property-based oligarchies) are both founded on the principle of equality, differing only in respect of the number of those who possess full rights. But the case is quite different if we consider the social formation as a whole.

Developing this argument, I have tried to show elsewhere (1965: 127–9; 1973a: 29–36; cf. Mossé, 1961: 353–60) that the political nullity of the Athenian slave — whom it is totally impossible to imagine demanding the right to hold political office — contrasts with the genuine political activity of the helots and the *penestai*. One element of Spartan history, right down to the time of Nabis [reigned 207–192 BC] is helot rebellions and demands. Plato took the point in the *Laws* (6, 777d): (If the slaves are to be docile) 'they will not be taken from within the same country (*patriōtas*), nor if possible from the same language-community (*asumphōnous*)'.

I want here to test these conclusions, not with material from political

187

and social history, but from myth, analysed in the manner championed by Claude Lévi-Strauss.[1] Of course the Greek myths, which have come down to us through a scholarly tradition, require subtle treatment. For the sake of simplicity, I shall make a distinction between myths of origin, or about the development of order, and legends. In Greece, the former went through three stages: (1) cosmological-cum-social myths, (2) purely cosmological myths, (3) properly civic myths (Vernant, 1962: 96—113). By this means each city pictured for itself the transition 'in the beginning' from chaos to order and from Nature to Culture. The legendary tradition incorporates mythical elements, but is felt and described as historical. The *utopia* stands on the frontier between the mythical and the social, and it concerns us here inasmuch as what it retains is quite as important as what it rejects: as Lewis Mumford has observed, the Greek utopian writers 'could (not) . . . admit, even as a remote ideal, the possibility of breaking down permanent class divisions or doing away with the institutions of war. It was easier for the Greek utopians to conceive of abolishing marriage or private property than of ridding utopia of slavery, class domination and war' (1965: 277; cf. Finley, 1975a: 178—92).

The justification for examining the place of slaves together with that of women is this. The Greek city in its classical form was marked by a double exclusion: the exclusion of women, which made it a 'men's club'; and the exclusion of slaves, which made it a 'citizen's club'. (One might almost say a threefold exclusion, since foreigners also were kept out; but the treatment of slaves is no doubt merely the extreme case of the treatment of foreigners.) It is of course true that these two exclusions are not of precisely the same order. But Aristotle at least granted a connection between the position of women and that of slaves. In a passage dealing mainly with Sparta, he remarks that women make up 'half the city' (τὸ ἥμισυ τῆς πόλεως) and that the law-giver must therefore bear them in mind; and he goes on to compare the different dangers which stem from over-indulgence (ἄνεσις) towards slaves and towards women (*Politics* 2.9.4—5, 1269b7ff. Ross). In each case the threat is political in a direct and immediate sense: indulgence towards helots leads them to revolt and to demand equality; and if women rule the rulers, they therefore rule the city (καίτοι τί διαφέρει γυναῖκας ἄρχειν ἢ τοὺς ἄρχοντας ὑπὸ τῶν γυναικῶν ἄρχεσθαι; 2.9.9, 1269b 33—4).[2] He returns to this question in a discussion of tyranny and democracy (5.11.11, 1313b32—9). Here the danger is the same but it is less directly and immediately political: laxity towards slaves (*doulōn anesis*) or women's rule in the home (*gunaikokratia . . . peri tas oikias*) leads the democratic city into tyranny — which means neither the rule of slaves nor the rule of women, strictly speaking: Aristotle simply explains that under tyrants women and slaves do not conspire because, as under the previous democracy, they are treated with laxity.[3]

It may also be remarked that for Aristotle the distinction between master and slave, as well as that between male and female, are of the same order as the distinction between body and soul, between that which commands and that which obeys (*Politics* 1.5.4–7, 1254a34–b16). And elsewhere he comments, 'Both a woman and a slave can also be good; but a woman is perhaps an inferior being – and a slave utterly worthless' (καὶ γὰρ γυνή ἐστιν χρηστὴ καὶ δοῦλος, καίτοι γε ἴσως τούτων τὸ μὲν χεῖρον, τὸ δὲ ὅλως φαῦλόν ἐστιν: *Poetics* 15, 1454a20–2 Kassel). The nuance is worth remembering.

Were there traditions in Greece about the rule of slaves or the rule of women? If so, is there any connection between them? On the first point, if we set aside such famous but obscure episodes of Hellenistic history as the 'City of the Sun' founded by Aristonicus (Eumenes III) of Pergamum (Robert, 1962: 264–71; Dumont, 1966: 189–96; Finley, 1975a: 183–4), or the anecdote about Chios reported by Nymphodorus of Syracuse (ap. Athenaeus, *Deipnosophistae* 6, 265c–266e),[4] evidence in myth for the city of the slaves (*Doulopolis* or *doulōn polis*) is thin. To a Greek, the very expression was of course contradictory. A character in the *Anchises* of Anaxandrides (a writer of Middle Comedies, mid-fourth century BC) puts the point succinctly: 'Slaves have no city, old man' – οὐκ ἔστι δούλων, ὦγάθ', οὐδαμοῦ πόλις (frg. 4 [*CAF* 2, p. 137] = Athenaeus, *Deipnosophistae* 6, 263b). There are references in historians, comedians (quoted, unfortunately, only by lexicographers) and paroemiographers to a 'city of slaves',[5] a place where all one had to do to become free was to bring a stone (Hecataeus of Miletus, *FGrH* 1 F 345, from Stephanus of Byzantium). This city is barely distinguished in the tradition from the City of Crooks (*Ponēropolis*: Pliny, *HN* 4.41; Plutarch, *De curiositate* 10, 520b),[6] or from the one in which there is only one free man, the priest (Hecataeus, *FGrH* 1 F 345).

The one interesting feature of these texts is the location ascribed to this 'city of slaves'. Sometimes it is placed in barbarian territory (Egypt, Libya, Syria, Caria, Arabia); sometimes in Crete.[7] And what interested Sosicrates and Dosiadas, who both wrote *Histories of Crete* (*FGrH* 461 F 4 and 458 F 2, 3, from Athenaeus, *Deipnosophistae* 6, 263f–264a), was precisely the different terms used for 'slaves' – or rather the statuses 'between slave and free' – on the island, the place par excellence in antiquity where technical terms of this kind were developed (cf. Vidal-Naquet, 1965: 128 n. 46). Not one text locates a 'city of slaves' in any part of Greece where slavery in the strict sense existed – that is, chattel-slavery based on slave-trading.[8]

That implies that when the Greeks wanted to describe a 'city of slaves' they could choose only between complete marginalization (barbarian countries) and locating it in a country where a 'slave' was not quite a slave. There is a sense in which Naupactus (founded in the midfifth century by helots who had fled from Messenia), and other cities established by the Messenians, and Messene itself (refounded after Epaminondas's expedition, 369 BC), might be added to Cretan *Doulopolis*. Yet even when they had become helots, the Messenians continued to be thought of as Greeks and Dorians, just like the Spartans themselves. Pausanias claimed not only that they had not lost their Dorian dialect even after three centuries of exile for many of them; but that, in the Empire, it was the purest Doric in the Peloponnese (4.27. 11). The right of these really peculiar 'slaves' to a political existence or revival, a right which they repeatedly asserted, could be legitimated by means such as these.

And what of women? Research in this area has been greatly stimulated by the work of Simon Pembroke on Greek traditions about 'matriarchy'.[9] In the last century Bachofen, followed by Engels and many others, saw matriarchy as a universal stage in the history of man. Its 'survivals' — such as the institutions of Lycia described by Herodotus (1.173) — were seen as evidence for an earlier period. Pembroke has shown that the ancient sources do not stand up to critical examination, and that the Lycian inscriptions, for example, show no trace whatever of a matriarchal system. But he has also explained the logical structure of the concept of matriarchy itself: whether we are talking about the Amazons or the Lycians, it is the Greek *polis*, that male club, which is being defined by its historians and its 'ethnographers' in terms of its opposite (cf. now Rosellini and Saïd, 1978: 949—1005). There is a splendid example of this technique of inversion, or reversal, in Herodotus's statement that the institutions of Egypt are exactly the opposite of those of the Greeks (2.35). The imaginary polity of the Amazons is the inverse, set in a precise location, of the Greek city. Lemnos, the island notorious for its 'atrocities', is also characterized as 'ruled by women'.[10] The chorus in Aeschylus's *Libation-bearers*, referring to Clytemnestra,[11] picks up expressions from the first play, the *Agamemnon*: the man—woman (*Agamemnon* 10—11; 350 cf. 259—60) and the 'female that kills the male' (θῆλυς ἄρσενος φονεύς: *Ag.* 1231) — human monsters who have failed to pass the barrier separating savagery from civilization:

> The female force, the desperate
> love crams its resisted way
> on marriage and the dark embrace
> of brute beasts, of mortal men.
> (599—601, tr. Lattimore)

The word rendered here as 'the female force' is *thēlukratēs*, an adjective which can mean both 'which conquers women' and 'where the female has power'; and the first example then given is that of the Lemnian women (631–4), whose 'power' took the form of the murder of their husbands.

Now the tradition does know of female power exercised honourably. But the relevant texts speak not of Athens (see p. 198 below) but of Sparta, which was of course the male city par excellence – but also the city Aristotle believed to be threatened politically by a takeover by women, as we have seen (p. 188 above). Plutarch records a famous witticism by Gorgo, wife of Leonidas and, according to Herodotus (5.51), the woman who prevented Cleomenes from doing as Aristagoras of Miletus wished [i.e. to support the Ionian revolt against the Persians in 499/98]: to a woman who observed, 'You Spartan women are the only women who give men orders', she was supposed to have replied, 'Yes, because we are the only women who give men birth' (*Life of Lycurgus* 14.8; cf. *Apophthegmata Lacedaemoniarum* [Gorgo] 6, 240e; *Apophthegmata Lacedaemoniorum* [Lycurgus] 13, 227e). And it was Sparta, not Athens, which provided Plato's model when he gave women their place in his *Republic*.

In view of all this, it is perhaps worth enquiring whether there was an ancient tradition in any way linking the exercise of power by women and by slaves. I argue that such a tradition did indeed exist, and in at least four forms.

The first is connected with a well-known historical event, the defeat of Argos by the Spartans at the battle of Sepeia, which has been dated variously between 520 and 490 BC.[12] Our earliest source is Herodotus (6.77, 83), who prefaces his account with a Delphic oracle in verse predicting a drama in which 'the female will prevail over the male and win glory among the Argives':

ἀλλ'ὅταν ἡ θήλεια τὸν ἄρσενα νικήσασα
ἐξελάσῃ καὶ κῦδος ἐν Ἀργείοισιν ἄρηται.

Argos is defeated, and loses all its men. The affairs of state are run by the slaves (ἐχηρώθη οὕτω ὥστε οἱ δοῦλοι αὐτῶν ἔσχον πάντα τὰ πρήγματα ἄρχοντες) until the young Argive citizens reach manhood. The 'slaves' thereupon flee to Tiryns, whence they are ultimately driven out by the Argives. In this account the two elements, rule of women and rule of slaves, are present but are kept separate: the first occurs in the oracle while the second appears in the historical account. This scheme disappears in the later versions, which no doubt involves an alteration of the original material; but this hardly matters, since my task is not to reconstruct the 'facts' but to understand the logic of the myths. What is important is that even in Herodotus Argos is an

191

upside-down world: the female has overcome the male and the slaves are in power.[13]

Plutarch (*De mulierum virtutibus* 4, 245f) gives his own gloss to Herodotus in quoting him as saying that when the city lost its men the 'slaves' married the Argive women; and introduces, from the historian Socrates of Argos, a new character, Telesilla, a poetess. She organizes the women of Argos to defend the city, dressing them in men's clothes — which later gave them the right of putting up a commemorative monument to Enyalios, the god of warriors (245c—e). Most important of all, he says that this episode was the origin of a festival still celebrated in Argos, the *hybristika*, which commemorates the women's courage, and in the course of which men and women wear each other's dress (245e—f).

Pausanias's version is different again (2.20.8—9). According to him, Telesilla called upon all those who could take part in the defence of the city — women, the old men, the young boys, the slaves (*oiketai*): in other words, all those normally excluded from fighting for the *polis*. [He also quotes Herodotus's oracle, however: 2.20.10. Ed.]

But who exactly were these slaves? Aristotle's own mention of this 'servile interregnum' (*Politics* 5.3.7, 1303a6—8) says nothing of women at all: he observes simply that the Argives 'had been forced to admit into the city a certain number of *perioikoi*': ἠναγκάσθησαν παραδέξασθαι τῶν περιοίκων τινάς. It has been shown that Aristotle generally uses the word *perioikoi* to mean rural dependants or bondsmen rather like the helots of Laconia (Willetts, 1959: 496). And in fact there can be no doubt but that our sources' Argive 'slaves' are to be identified with the occupants of the servile status-category known in Argos as the *gumnētai*: those who were 'naked' by contrast with those who wore the hoplite panoply. Equally important, when Aristotle wants to give a comparable example from Athens, he speaks not of the recruitment of slaves but of hoplites from *outside the register* — that is, the *thētes*, the citizens of the lowest category in terms of property.

A tradition known from much later texts offers a parallel so precise with the Argive episode as to be suspicious. This time we are at Cumae, in Magna Graecia, where in 505/4 BC Aristodemus made himself tyrant, put to death or exiled the aristocrats and bestowed their property, their wives and their daughters, upon the slaves who had murdered their masters.[14] That left, according to our principal source, Dionysius of Halicarnassus, only the fate of the male children to be determined. At first, Aristodemus thought of putting them all to death; but after appeals from their mothers, and the latters' new lovers, decided to send them off to the fields to lead servile lives of agricultural or pastoral labour. The world is turned upside-down: the young aristocrats take the place of the 'slaves' whom they now serve. So far, we can interpret the story in common-sense terms: but what follows is rather odd. These young slaves in the fields are brought up as girls: long curly tresses, kept in a net; embroidered dresses; living in the shade of parasols, with endless baths and perfume (Dionysius of Halicarnassus, *Ant. Rom.* 7.9.4 Jacoby). It is hard not to suppose a ritual comparable to the Argive *hybristika* or the *Oschophoria* in Athens (see pp. 156–8 above). There comes a time when the 'sons' — who seem, as in Argos, to be all of an age — rise in revolt and with the help of the exiles suppress the tyrant (*Ant. Rom.* 7.9.6). It is Plutarch who supplies the dimension of the episode relevant to the theme of the rule of women (*De mulierum virtutibus* 26, 262c–d): Xenocrite, the daughter of an exile, became Aristodemus's mistress; and it was she who persuaded the young men to suppress the tyrant (c. 491/90), together with an unnamed woman of Cumae who remarked to them that Aristodemus was the sole man (*anēr*) in the city (262b).

Here again servile power and female power are linked, the women assuring the continuity of legitimacy. But it is less easy to say what precisely the 'slaves' were, though the 'helot-type', given that these men seemingly lived in the fields and made an effort to act politically or collectively, is more likely than the 'Athenian' type.

My third example comes from the well-known tradition about the origins of Epizephyrian Locris in Southern Italy, a colony founded by mainland Locrians, whether Opuntian or Ozolian is unclear.[15] The foundation of the city was the subject of an acrimonious debate, reported by Polybius, between Aristotle (or more probably the author of the Peripatetic *Constitution of Locris*) and the Sicilian historian Timaeus of Tauromenium; Polybius reports the debate as part of his own polemic against Timaeus.[16] Aristotle said that Locris had been founded by riffraff, runaway slaves and slave-dealers; in reply, Timaeus argued that in the very early period 'it was not the national custom of the Greeks to use slaves bought with money'.[17] No doubt repeating Aristotle, Polybius then tells the story of how, when the Locrians were the allies of Sparta in the Messenian War (presumably the first war), they were prevented — perhaps by an oath, as in the legend of the foundation of Tarentum (see p. 195 below), but certainly effectively — from having intercourse with their wives. The wives then turned to substitute husbands, the slaves; and it was these women and slaves who later became the first colonists of Italian Locris. Consequently hereditary nobility in the colony was derived originally not from the men but from the women: πάντα τὰ διὰ προγόνων ἔνδοξα παρ' αὐτοῖς ἀπὸ τῶν γυναικῶν οὐκ ἀπὸ τῶν ἀνδρῶν ἐστιν (Polybius 12.5.6). We also know that some of the female founders of Locris belonged to the hundred noble families who had the 'privilege' of sending two girls each year to serve Athena of Ilion.[18]

Irenically-minded readers will doubtless observe that it is not impossible to reconcile Aristotle and Timaeus, at least in terms of the coherence of the tradition. Certainly a famous inscription, the bronze plaque from Galaxidi [Ozolian (Western) Locris], seems to prove the existence of helotage in Locrian territory at an early date (early fifth century BC).[19] The inscription gives the regulations for the colony established by the Eastern Locrians at Naupactus, and prescribes as the penalty for a magistrate who refuses justice to a plaintiff the confiscation of his property, the land itself together with its 'slaves' (woikiatai): καὶ χρέματα παματοφαγεῖσθαι, τὸ μέρος μετὰ Ϝοικιατᾶν (lines 43–5). Notwithstanding that Hesychius identifies the oikiētēs (which occurs only here) with the chattel-slave (οἰκιήτης: ὠνητὸς δοῦλος), there can be little doubt but that the Locrian woikiatas, whose position is linked closely with the citizen's land-allotment, is more like that of the Cretan woikeus (Ϝοικεύς): he is in effect a helot. So there is no reason not to accept that in the tradition followed by Aristotle and Polybius the Locrian 'slaves' who married their mistresses were in a category similar to that of the Argive gumnētai.

The women's rôle is no less important, though Polybius does not say, as has been claimed, that at Epizephyrian Locris nobility descended through the female line: he says simply that originally in the Locrian 'nobility' there was a group of women; they were citizens, and many of them of good families; and their husbands were slaves.[20] And he explains by reference to the same tradition the fact that a procession, which he says was taken over from the Siculi, was led by a girl and not by a boy (12.5.10–11).

This connection between female citizens and 'slaves' recurs in a legendary tradition whose variants are far more complex, that of the Foundation of Tarentum.[21] Although all the sources agree in describing the founders of Tarentum as a minority felt to be undesirable in their country of origin, Sparta, and who were called the Partheniai, there were at least three versions. The oldest is represented by Antiochus of Syracuse, a contemporary of Thucydides (FGrH 555 F 13, from Strabo 6.3.2 [278–279C] cf. Vidal-Naquet, 1973b: 23–42). He says that during the first Messenian War the Spartiates disfranchised those of their number who had not taken part in the fighting: they were declared slaves (ἐκρίθησαν δοῦλοι) and thereafter termed 'helots', as were their descendants, the Partheniai. The latter plotted together, but were discovered by the ephors [the annual magistrates of Sparta]; they were expelled from the city and sent to Italy. This version contains two myths: one about the foundation of Tarentum, the other about the origin of Spartan 'slavery': the original helots are supposed to have been *tresantes*, those Spartiates who had failed in war and so been disfranchized (Herodotus 7.231; Plutarch, *Life of Agesilaus* 30; *Life of Lycurgus* 21.2; cf. now Loraux, 1977: 105—20).

Strabo rejects this version in favour of one followed by the fourth-century historian Ephorus and consequently by many others, whether directly or indirectly (*FGrH* 70 F 216, from Strabo 6.3.3 [279—80C]).²² The Spartans were at war with Messenia and had sworn not to return home until they were victorious. But the war dragged on, and the next generation could not be born. It was decided that the young men, who had not taken the oath, should return home to Sparta and all of them should have intercourse with all the young women (*parthenoi*) so far as possible: συγγίνεσθαι ταῖς παρθένοις ἀπάσαις ἅπαντας.²³ It was the offspring of these promiscuous unions, *who knew their mothers but not their fathers*, who received the name *Partheniai*. In other words, the *Partheniai* were the result not of normal marriage but of a sort of original scramble (Rosellini and Saïd, 1978: 955—66, 995—1003).

The third and simplest version is analogous to that of the foundation of Epizephyrian Locri: while the Spartiates were away fighting, their wives slept with their slaves, and the *Partheniai* were the resulting bastards.²⁴

There are some further texts which are not quite parallel to any of these versions. A rather elliptical passage of Aristotle (*Politics* 5.7.2, 1306b27—31) seems to suggest that the *Partheniai* suffered from some kind of political discrimination without there being any question about their birth.²⁵ To make things even more complicated, a fragment of Diodorus Siculus published in 1827 (8.21) gives a composite account of a rebellion which occurred in Sparta after the First Messenian War.²⁶ The most important group of rebels were the *epeunaktai*, who are defined by Hesychius as συγκοιμῆται, 'bed-fellows'; they were responsible for the plot, and later got in touch with Delphi in order to found a colony. The other group was the *Partheniai*, who came to terms with Sparta as soon as the conspiracy was discovered. It is tempting, but unprovable, to suppose that the second are the sons of the first.²⁷ They are often confused, all the more easily in view of Hesychius's equivalent for the very similar word *epeunaktoi*: *Partheniai*. But Theopompus does explain the identity of the *epeunaktai* (though he calls them *epeunaktoi*): they were helots who during the Messenian War — he does not say which one — took the place of the dead Spartiates, not in their marital beds but 'on their beds in camp': ἐπὶ τὰς στιβάδας (*FGrH* 115 F 3, from Athenaeus, *Deipnosophistae* 6, 272a; cf. Pembroke, 1970: 1245—7). It is important to understand that in the myths relating to

Sparta a 'slave' could substitute for a citizen in his basic duty, that of fighting.

Although these versions are all so different, there is one constant: it is the women who ensure the continuation of the population. In short, the *Partheniai* are the sons of young *women* before they are the sons of *men*. The versions disagree only about the identity of their fathers. And yet as a whole they are quite coherent. In the first case (Antiochus) they are cowards, in the second (Ephorus) *young* men, in the third (Heracleides) 'slaves'; and perhaps for Aristotle political inferiors. In the first case they are made distinctive by a moral judgement; in the second by their place in the system of age-classes; in the third by a social judgement; and in the fourth by their place in the political hierarchy. The variants have a common theme: the fathers of the *Partheniai* both are and are not of the city — they are *marginal*. Exactly the same was true of the Argive 'slaves' and of the husbands of the women who founded Locris; the normal hierarchy is inverted.

Other texts on the foundation of Tarentum make this inversion quite explicit, though it is unfortunate that they are often contaminated by traditions about the foundation of Rhegium (Vallet, 1958: 68–76; Ducat, 1974: 93–114; Valenza Mele, 1977: 512–17). An oracle is said to have advised the founders of Tarentum to settle where they saw a she-goat mounting a buck,[28] or where they saw rain falling out of a clear sky (Pausanias 10.10.6).[29] Both are ways of suggesting an inverted world. The parallel texts about Rhegium quite explicitly direct the founder, Antimedes of Chalcis, to a place where he saw 'the male mounted by the female': τὸν ἄρρενα ὑπὸ τῆς θηλείας ὀπυόμενον (Diodorus Siculus 8.23.2; Heracleides Ponticus, *Peri Politeiōn* 25 = *FHG* 2, 220) — which takes us right back to the oracle Herodotus says was given to the Argives (p. 191 above).

All the same, this topsy-turvy world which gives extraordinary prominence to women and to 'slaves' is an imaginable one. Whereas at Athens the exceptional use of slaves in war was logically followed by their emancipation,[30] in Sparta there was nothing unusual about helots as such fighting — as in the case of Theopompus's *epeunaktoi* (cf. Herodotus 9.29; Thucydides 4.80 etc.). Likewise, the Gortyn Law Code provides for the possibility of a marriage between a male slave and a free woman: 'If the slave (*dōlos*) goes to the free woman and marries her, their children will be free; but if the free woman goes to the slave and marries him, their children will be slaves': [αἰ κ' ὁ δῶλος] Ι ἐπὶ τὰν ἐλευθέραν ἐλθὸν ὀπυίει, Ι ἐλεύθερ' ἔμ Ι ἐν τὰ τέκνα, αἰ δέ κ' Ι ἀ ἐλευθέρα ἐπὶ τὸν δῶλον, δῶλ' ἔμ Ι ἐν τὰ τέκνα (*IC* 4, no. 72, col. 6, 56; 7, 1–5).[31] Moreover, although in the classical period Spartiate marriage-rules did not permit such liaisons, they at least gave both husband and wife the right to take a substitute partner (Xenophon, *Constitution of the Lacedaemonians* 1.7—8). And there was at Rome, in a religious context, an association between slaves and women: at the *Saturnalia* masters (*domini*) served their slaves (*servi*), while at the *Matronalia*, wives were honoured by their husbands and prepared a feast for their *male* slaves:[32] yet another detail that makes archaic Rome look more like Sparta than Athens.

It was inconceivable in Athens that an Athenian woman might marry a slave. And in general the Athenian attitude towards marriage was much stricter (Vernant, 1974: 52—81). With the exception of the special case of heiresses (see p. 261, n. 33 below), marriage at Athens involved the transfer of a young woman from one *oikos* [household] to another; in Sparta, on the other hand, well-known texts indicate that a Spartiate woman could belong simultaneously to two *oikoi* (Xenophon, *Constitution of the Lacedaemonians* 1.7—8; Plutarch, *Life of Lycurgus* 15). Even crisis-measures were different: a tradition that may go back to Aristotle says that when there was a scarcity of men, the law permitted male citizens to get children by a *citizen* woman other than their wife.[33] It was naturally only a matter for citizens — there was no question of the law allowing the recruitment of substitute wives from among the metics (resident foreigners) or the slaves, even though the metics regularly served in the army.

A good illustration of the contrast here between Spartiate and Athenian practice is provided by Herodotus's parallel accounts concerning the island of Lemnos, one of which relates to the Spartans, the other to the Athenians (4.145, 6.137—8). In the first, some descendants of the Argonauts and the women of Lemnos come to Sparta, saying that they are indigenous Minyans (that is, from prior to the Pelasgians); the Spartiates welcome them and exchange wives with them. But the strangers turn arrogant, and it is determined to put them to death. The 'Minyans' are then saved by their wives, who change clothes with them, and they escape to the mountains dressed as women.[34] Eventually, they become the colonists of Thera. In the other story, the Pelasgians have been expelled from Athens for insulting the daughters of the Athenians. They move to Lemnos, and in revenge take with them some Athenian women whom they use as concubines. The women bring their children up according to Athenian ways and speaking Attic Greek and in the end are massacred with their children.[35] This story is plainly an inversion of the Spartan one: at Sparta marriage with foreigners leads to colonization, while at Athens concubinage with foreigners leads to destruction — to one of the versions of the 'crime of the women of Lemnos'. And the value-judgements in the two societies are symmetrically inverse.

At least after the law of 451 BC, marriage at Athens stands midway between two equally repellent extremes. One extreme is of course incest: 'Can a bird that eats bird's-flesh be pure?' asks Danaus in Aeschylus's *Suppliant Women* (226). The other is revealed by Theseus's outrage at an Argive who on the advice of an oracle from Apollo had married his daughters to a boar and a lion, two wild animals, to Tydeus and Polyneices, foreigners both:

> Theseus: To strangers, then, you wedded Argive girls?
> Adrastus: Yes: Tydeus and Polynices, of Theban stock.
> Theseus: How did you come to want them for your kin?
> Adrastus: Puzzling riddles of Phoebus lured me on . . .
> That I gave my daughters to a boar and a lion . . .
> Theseus: They were beasts? You gave your girls to them? . . .
> Theseus: First, bowing to Phoebus' words, like one who thinks
> The gods exist, you gave your girls to strangers:
> A mating of fair with foul, to hurt your house!
> Wrongdoers' bodies should not be joined to the just . . .
> (Euripides, *Suppliant Women* 135–45, 219–24, tr. F.W. Jones)

As a traditional place of refuge — even if only for the Neleids of Pylos supposed to have fled there before going on to settle in Ionia (Sakellariou, 1958) — Athens did of course have some myths very similar to those of Sparta. But in the classical period there is not a word about marriage with a foreign male; and the democracy put an end, at least in principle, to the inverse process, marriage between an Athenian citizen and a foreign woman (which had been very common among the aristocrats), by the law of 451.

Although it is found only in late sources, we can reconstruct one myth to tell us about two matters, the origin of male democracy and the origin of Athenian marriage (see Pembroke, 1967: 26–7, 29–32). According to Varro (quoted by St Augustine, *De civitate dei* 18.9), in the time of Cecrops there occurred a dispute between Athena and Poseidon as to which of them should be patron of Athens. An oracle told the king to put the choice of patron divinity to the vote by all the inhabitants including women, 'for at that time it was customary in those parts for even women to have their say in public votes' (*mos enim tunc in eisdem locis erat ut etiam feminae publicis consultationibus interessent*); and because there were more women than men, the choice fell on Athena. The men took their revenge by deciding that 'from henceforth the women of Athens shall not vote; that children shall no longer be known by their mother's name; that the women shall not be called "women of Athens" '. Thus in the classical city there are no 'women of Athens' — only the wives and daughters of the 'men of Athens'. That remains the case even in the comedy which reverses their rôles: in the *Thesmophoriazusae*, Aristophanes speaks of the *demos* (People) of Women, and of the Council of Women, but never of the *demos* of the Women of Athens (335–6, 372–3; cf. Loraux, 1980b). The second decision is explained by those texts which make Cecrops the inventor of marriage.[36] Cecrops's usual epithet 'double-natured' (διφυής) was normally explained by saying that he was part man, part animal; but these texts account for it by saying that, as the inventor of marriage, he taught that each man had both a father and a mother. According to Clearchus, before that sexual unions took place at random and no one knew who his father was; which implies that individuals were known by their mother's name only. So Cecrops's role here is that of a culture-hero — and indeed the scholiast on Aristophanes's *Plutus* 773 says as much: 'he brought the Athenians out of savagery to civilization' (ἀπὸ ἀγριότητος εἰς ἡμερότητα ἤγαγεν). The rule of women in Varro's report (the women not only vote, they are in the majority) thus corresponds to the state of nature, to the original scramble. We have already seen that the same features recur in the accounts of the Foundation of Tarentum; but what is 'in the beginning' for Tarentum is at Sparta part of 'history' and is used to legitimate a number of actual practices in society.

The passages just discussed do indeed tell us about the Athenian account of the origin of marriage and the exclusion of women from the body politic; but they have nothing to say about the connection — or inversely, the distinction — between the status of women and that of slaves. And it is on this point that Athens can be seen to be the exact opposite of Sparta or Locris.

It will be clear from what I have already said that in a topsy-turvy world like that of the legends about the First Messenian War, 'slaves' getting above themselves might occur with a temporary tracing of descent through the female line. Now in the late fifth century BC classical Athens also had its topsy-turvy worlds, above all in Aristophanes's utopian comedies. The hoopoe in the *Birds* has a bird-slave and when Euelpides expresses surprise at this, the slave tells him, 'I think he likes to be reminded he was a man' (70–5). In *Lysistrata* the women take over the Acropolis (345ff.) and at once the theme of topsy-turvydom makes its appearance in an oracle (which recalls Herodotus's Argive oracle):

> When all the Swallows gather into one place, eschewing the
> Hoopoe-birds and their amorous pursuits, then is come the end of
> all Evils, and it is ordained by Zeus the Thunderer that the low shall
> be exalted over the high.
>
> (770–3, tr. Dickinson)[37]

All the same, Lysistrata at one point calls for a Scythian archer, and slaves appear on a number of occasions (18, 184, 241).

But of course my best evidence here comes from *The Assembly of Women* (*Ecclesiazusae*). The play is based upon a double transvestism, first that associated with the festival of Athena Skiras (the *Skiraphoria*) when women dressed up in beards (18, 25, 38, cf. p. 156 above), but also the comedy's own: the Athenian women disguise themselves as men in order to vote themselves into power in the Assembly. The communist system they start is presented as the fulfilment of democracy and involves the sharing of all wealth visible and invisible, including slaves. It is forbidden that some should have much and others nothing at all. But of course the land itself will be worked by slaves — while their masters relax and wait for their dinners (593, 602, 631, 651–3, cf. *Plutus* 510). Now all this is reasonably familiar; perhaps less so are the sexual implications of this femino-communist democracy. For the women propose to equalize sexual opportunity (944–5) — for the young citizens naturally: of male slaves, not a word. By contrast, the female slaves are expressly excluded from citizen-amours: they have to make arrangements with male slaves (725–7).

Aristotle's point remains true then: there is some difference between women and slaves. An Aristophanic utopia can put women on top, just as Plato later can set them almost on the same level as men. But chattel-slaves are simply not part of the city at all. And I would say that myth, legendary tradition and utopias as well, respected this state of affairs even though it was of recent date.[38] A myth accounts for the reduction of the status of women at Athens as one brick in the wall between savagery and disorder on the one hand, and civic order on the other. But the distinction between free men and slaves simply was not a 'problem' of this kind. In archaic societies on the other hand (of which Sparta is the best known), the situation is quite different. Slavery was understood there as having an origin in history (I have discussed one of the traditions in this connection, but there are many others), and on a number of occasions the status of women and the status of slaves are seen as linked. Each occupies a variable position on the continuum between the free and the non-free.

I began by observing that Athens and Sparta can be seen as logical opposites; I hope that this study serves to reinforce the point.

11. Athens and Atlantis: structure and meaning of a Platonic myth

Pierre Vidal-Naquet (1964, 1979)

Harold Cherniss once observed of the problem of Atlantis, the subject of so much debate since classical times, that 'it is easier to conjure the djinn out of the bottle than to get him back in again' (1977: 200). Very true; but what exactly is the problem?[1] At the beginning of the *Timaeus* and in the unfinished dialogue *Critias*, Plato describes, in the form of a tradition learned by Solon from the priests of the goddess Neïth at Saïs in Egypt and passed on by him to his relative Critias the elder, through whom it came to the younger Critias, one of the 'Thirty Tyrants' and Plato's uncle,[2] the institutions, the political geography and the history of two cities which disappeared almost nine thousand years earlier — prior to the last of those catastrophes (universal conflagration or general flood) which recur periodically on this planet (*Timaeus* 22d ff. and 23e) — proto-Athens and Atlantis.

What is the point of this description? Socrates and his friends have just been through the fundamental characteristics of the Platonic city as put forward in books 2 to 5 of the *Republic*: the group of Guardians, both male and female, separate from the rest of the population; community of women and children; the rational and secret ordering of sexual relations (*Tim.* 17b—19b). Socrates then says that he would wish to see a real city of such a kind in existence; in a word, to place it in the actual world, the world of war and international relations. Does that mean place it in history, in our sense of the word? No indeed: it means constructing one of those mechanical models which Plato so loved to work out and which allowed him to dramatize an abstract discussion (cf. Schuhl, 1968a: 71—105).

But the conflict between proto-Athens and Atlantis is a model in a second sense besides. For in Plato, any paradigm presupposes that there is a structural homology between pattern and product, between reality and myth (cf. especially Goldschmidt, 1947: 81ff.). Thus, in the *Politicus*, the ruler is defined in terms of the image of the weaver, because the ruler of a state is a weaver, a craftsman who works with his eye fixed on the divine model. The problems involved in the accounts of the *Timaeus* and the *Critias* are endlessly more complex: the City whose fundamental institutions are described in the *Republic* provides the paradigm for the constitution of proto-Athens, so that the description of Atlantis, of its empire and the final catastrophe which engulfs it, is determined by its relation to the fixed point provided by the just city. But this 'Tale of Two Cities' is itself intimately linked to the physics of the *Timaeus*, as Plato expressly says. One cannot enterprise, as the *Critias* does, a detailed account of this human history without first defining man's place in nature — in that nature laid bare for us by the physiologue of Locris (*Tim.* 27a, b). Physics itself, because its object belongs to the world of becoming, can only ground a 'probable myth' (*Tim.* 29d). But the narrator has known through contemplation that 'Being which is eternal, and which has no share in the world of becoming' (τὸ ὂν ἀεί, γένεσιν δὲ οὐκ ἔχον), just as the demiurge has, who understands not through 'opinion linked to sense-impressions' (δόξα μετ᾽ αἰσθήσεως) but through 'intelligence combined with reasoning' (νόησις μετὰ λόγου) (*Tim.* 28a) — in short, what is in the truest sense 'the same'. And for that reason, his account is no less founded in truth, worthy of the goddess whose festival is being celebrated (i.e. Athena). Socrates could even characterize it as 'a true account, not merely an imaginative fiction' (μὴ πλασθέντα μῦθον ἀλλ᾽ ἀληθινὸν λόγον) (*Tim.* 26e).

There are then three rules for the historian who wishes to understand the myth of Atlantis. He must not sunder the two cities which Plato has linked so closely together. He must refer himself constantly to the physics of the *Timaeus*. And consequently, he must relate the historical myth whose structure he is trying to explain to Plato's 'idealism'. The success of a properly historical interpretation depends entirely upon the extent to which this preliminary task is performed.[3]

Although for Plato it is proto-Athens which is the paradigm, Atlantis has attracted enormously greater attention thanks to the simultaneously circumstantial and imaginative character of the myth.[4] In antiquity his account was taken in various ways: sometimes as a story which might agreeably bear imitation, as did Theopompus in the fourth century, substituting for Solon's meeting with the priests of Saïs a dialogue between Silenus and King Midas, and for Atlantis a warlike city (*Machimos*), for Athens a reverent one (*Eusebēs*).[5] Alternatively, it could be made the occasion for a lesson in geography, a speculative mode — more nicely discriminate of language than of reality — encouraged by Hellenistic philology; Strabo at any rate was amply justified in his criticism of Poseidonius's credulity, and in his comment — recalling Aristotle's on Homer — that the continent had been done away with by its own maker.[6] We know much less about philosophical interpretations, which we hear of almost exclusively through Proclus's *Commentary on the Timaeus*; he observed, intelligently enough, that the beginning of the *Timaeus* was a presentation in the form of images of the theory of the Universe (τὴν τοῦ κόσμου θεωρίαν) (*in Tim.* 1.4.12f. Diehl). His own interpretation, and those of his predecessors, are sometimes lunatic, but at least did not divorce Athens from Atlantis and related the myth systematically to the *Timaeus*'s physics, for all their failure to eschew realist hypotheses (*in Tim.* 1.75.30ff.). But these philosophers, soaked in a social and religious world completely different from Plato's, simply did not comprehend at all the political aspects of his thought. Later still, a Christian geographer turned Solon into Solomon and accused Plato of distorting an account he had got from the Chaldaean Oracles . . . [7]

If a 'realist' reading made little headway in the ancient world, the case since the Renaissance has entirely altered. In the late seventeenth, and in the eighteenth, century Atlantis became the focus of great debate: was Plato's continent the New World, America? Was it the land whence civilization for Christians had developed — was it Jewish Palestine? Or was it rather an Anti-Palestine, watershed of the Arts and Sciences, that could be located in Siberia or in the Caucasus? The first stirrings of modern nationalisms played their part too. A Swede, Olaf Rudbeck, marshalled a learning of almost inconceivable weight in order to prove that Atlantis could lie nowhere but in Scandinavia.[8] And of course the quest passed from the hands of scholars to those of would-be scholars,[9] and so to mythomaniacs and charlatans, those who, even to this day, 'discover' or peddle Atlantis anyplace between Heligoland and the Sahara, between Siberia and Lake Titicaca.[10] The 'realist' reading has been exterminated in science. But has it really disappeared? Failing a submerged continent, Plato might have known, we are often assured, a tradition which more or less faithfully reproduced a memory of an actual historical event or a local saga.

As early as 1841, Thomas-Henri Martin, in his justly famous *Études sur le Timée de Platon*, in spite of placing Atlantis in the region of the 'Island of Utopia' (1841: 332), wondered whether Plato had not been thinking of an Egyptian tradition (323). Since Evans's discoveries, it is of course Crete that has provided most ammunition: it was practically inevitable that the bull-sacrifice in the oath of the kings of Atlantis should point someone to the land of the Minotaur; and the destruction of the fabulous kingdom has been assimilated into the fall of Knossos.[11] It is unfortunate simply that such claims remain completely undemonstrable; but one is compelled to wonder whether any progress has been made in the interpretation of the text since Olaf Rudbeck when one finds an archaeologist declaring that the site of Atlantis is amazingly similar to that of Lake Copais — with just one problem: 'The greatest discrepancy is the fact that Atlantis according to Plato lays far to the West, while the Copais basin is in the midst of Greece'[12] (Scranton, 1949: 159—62).

At the heart of these lucubrations, a weird image of the philosopher is to be found: Plato the historian, whose 'sources' have to be looked into, as one might in the case of Herodotus or of Diodorus Siculus. But Plato did not think in terms of 'sources', of what Herodotus called *opsis* and *akōe* [using one's eyes and ears], but precisely in terms of models.[13] And the enquiry into these 'models' has been a good deal less enthusiastic than the search for 'sources'. And where there has been enquiry, one could hardly call the method employed empirical; which compels me now to turn to these arguments and comment upon them.

Many scholars have compared the island of Atlantis with the Phaeacians' Scheria.[14] And the parallelism cannot be doubted. After all, the kingdom of Alcinous, with its idealized patriarchal monarchy and its palace filled with marvels, is the first utopian city in Greek literature (Finley, 1977: 100—2, 156). At least, that might have been the impression of a fourth-century Greek. Again, it is important that we have a utopia connected with the sea. Scheria, like Atlantis, is a city of sailors:

> They, confident in the speed of their running ships, cross over
> the great open water, since this is the gift of the Earthshaker
> to them . . . (*Odyssey* 7.34—5, tr. Lattimore)

The kings of Atlantis were descended from the union of Poseidon and a mortal woman, Kleito, while Alcinous and Arete were the descendants of the union of Poseidon and the nymph Periboia (*Critias* 113de; *Od.* 7.56f.). The one temple on Scheria is consecrated to the god of the sea, as is the one temple described by Plato (*Od.* 6.266; *Critias* 116d—117a). Homer speaks of two springs, as does Plato (*Od.* 7.129; *Critias* 117a). And so on.

The local colour then is epic; and Plato actually notes at the very beginning of the *Timaeus* that Solon, had he so wished, could have equalled Homer and Hesiod (*Tim.* 21c). The names of some of the kings of the great island are borrowed from Homer. But here Homer's world is inverted: the land that bids welcome has become an empire from which will set sail the armies determined upon the destruction of Greece; the parallelism does not explain everything — even if it ought certainly to figure in any discussion of Plato's relation to Homer.

Then again, Paul Friedländer, and Joseph Bidez after him, have stressed the many reasons for supposing Atlantis, which Plato sets at the western edge of the world, to be an idealized transposition of the East and of the world of Persia (Friedländer, 1958: 273—7; Bidez, 1945: Appendix II, 32—4). It is certainly plausible that Plato's description of the walls of the capital city and the city itself may have been inspired by Herodotus's description of Ecbatana and Babylon (*Hdt.* 1.98, 178; and *Critias* 116a ff.). The Greeks thought of an oriental king as a lord of the waters. Herodotus describes the legendary heart of Asia, a plain, encircled by mountains, which gives rise to an imaginary mighty river which flowed through the mountains in five branches until the Great King built five sluice-gates that he alone could open (3.117).[15] I need hardly recall what he says about the Nile, about Egypt and the Pharaohs. The massive irrigation works undertaken by the kings of Atlantis (*Critias* 117cd) and the scale of the kingdom itself are sufficient indication that Plato is thinking here primarily not of the tiny world of the Greek city-states but of the universe of oriental despotism. Such an interpretation might obviously lead one, as it has many (so Rivaud, 1925: 252), to view the struggle between Athens and Atlantis as a mythical transposition of the struggle between Greeks and Barbarians, and the Persian Wars in particular. One can even show, as I do not think it has been, that Plato was directly influenced by Herodotus. For in the *Timaeus* he says (20e):

And he told my grandfather Critias (according to the story the old man used to repeat to us) that there were great and admirable exploits performed by our own city long ago, which have been forgotten through lapse of time and the destruction of human life. (Tr. Cornford)

This is how Herodotus begins his history (1.1):

These are the researches of Herodotus of Thurii which he publishes in the hope of thereby preserving from decay the remembrance of what men have done, and of preventing the great and wonderful actions of the Greeks and the Barbarians from losing their due meed of glory . . . (Tr. Rawlinson)

For his part, the historian tried to be fair to each of the warring sides.[16]

But if the model is really the Persian Wars, then Plataea here comes before Marathon. Athens starts out as leader of the Hellenes, but she wins the victory alone, and she alone sets up the trophy and liberates the Greeks and the subjects of Atlantis's empire (*Tim.* 25bc) — those very cities and peoples over which the Athens of history had extended her sway after the war. Should we find that surprising? The second Persian war was for Plato marred by the naval engagements at Artemision and Salamis (*Laws* 4, 707bc). When he discusses the matter, it is certainly not to praise Themistocles's daring and the decisive role of the fleet. While Xerxes made his preparations to invade Attica,

(The Athenians) considering that there was no salvation for them either by land or by sea . . . One chance of safety remained, slight indeed and desperate, but their only one. They saw that on the former occasion they had gained a seemingly impossible victory, and borne up by this hope, they found that their only refuge was in themselves and in the Gods. (*Laws* 3, 699ac, tr. Jowett)[17]

But Plato's remodelled Athenians do not get on board their ships: his Athenians defeat the seafaring men of Atlantis not on the sea but on land. An odd Athens; and an odd 'Orient'. But a closer look at the texts leads us, without rejecting what we have learned, to a more complex interpretation of the struggle between the two cities. Plato's Athens meets and vanquishes Atlantis; in so doing, she in reality overcomes herself.

That may sound strange;[18] but let us look once more at the facts and at the texts.

On the west face of the pediment of Pheidias's and Iktinos's Parthenon was represented the mythical dispute between Athena and Poseidon. I think it no exaggeration to say that this dispute was one of the mythical foundations of Athenian history. The ironical funeral speech in the *Menexenus* declares (237c):

Our country is worthy to be praised, not only by us but by all mankind; first, and above all, as being dear to the gods. This is proved by the strife and contention of the gods respecting her.[19] (Tr. Jowett)

This passage is directly contradicted by one from the *Critias* (109b):

In the days of old, the gods had the whole earth distributed among them by allotment. There was no quarrelling; for you cannot rightly suppose that the gods did not know what was proper for each of them to have, or, knowing this, that they would seek to procure for themselves by contention that which more properly belonged to others. (Tr. Jowett)

According to this, it was Dikē who shared out the allocations. Athens was assigned to Athena and Hephaestus, and Atlantis became the realm of Poseidon (*Critias* 109c and 113c). The two divinities worshipped together in the Erechtheum are thus separated; and Plato separates and opposes likewise the two Greek forms of power: the Athenians, stemming from the seed of Hephaestus and Gaia (*Tim.* 23e), inherited power on the land; the kings of Atlantis, children of Poseidon, power by sea. But that very fact reveals to us that Plato is presenting his native city from two different points of view: the city of Athena and the olive-tree is identified with proto-Athens; and the city of Poseidon, Lord of horses and of the sea, is realized in Atlantis.

Let us take a closer look at the topography and the institutions of this idealized Athens. It is essentially an enormous acropolis, which includes, besides the classical Acropolis, the Pnyx and Lycabettos, and thus extends as far as the Eridanus and the Lycabettos rivers; and it is covered in earth. It is thus quite different from the harsh rock which Plato knew (*Critias* 111e–112a). Its summit forms a level area enclosed by a *single* wall (ἐνὶ περιβόλῳ προσπεριβεβλημένοι: 112b),[20] and is where the second class of the population, the warriors, live. The craftsmen and the farmers live outside and work the fields beyond. Plato describes the class of warriors (τὸ μάχιμον γένος) characteristically by means of an expression denoting what never changes: it is *auto kath' hauto.*[21] Civic space is organized in a manner quite unlike that of the classical city. There is no Agora to be the *meson* (centre) of political life; no temple which might be the prototype of those built in the fifth century. To the north, there are common barracks, refectories suitable against bad weather, and temples. To the south, gardens, gymnasia and summer refectories (112bd). In the middle is the sanctuary of Athena and Hephaestus, an evident transposition from the Hephaesteion which still dominates the Agora today, and in front of which Pausanias records that there stood a statue of Athena (which we know, like that of Hephaestus, to have been the work of Alkamenes) — a conjunction he found quite unsurprising in view of the myths of Erichthonius (1.14.6; cf. Broneer, 1949: 52; Thompson and Wycherley, 1972: 140—9).

What does this divine pair signify here? The Homeric Hymn to Hephaestus sang of the God: 'With Athena of the glittering eyes he taught men on earth wondrous crafts' (20.2—3). But this is not the only *technē* which may be relevant.

Hephaestus and Athena, who were brother and sister, and sprang from the same father (ἅμα μὲν ἀδελφὴν ἐκ ταὐτοῦ πατρός), having a common nature (κοινὴν φύσιν ἔχοντες), and being united also in the love of philosophy and art (*technē*), both obtained as their common portion this land, which was naturally adapted for wisdom and virtue.[22] (*Critias* 109c, tr. Jowett)

Hephaestus and Athena thus guarantee the close relationship between the two classes, guardians and producers, of proto-Athens.

I have already observed that this Athens is land-based. The term really applies to Attica as a whole, more extensive than Plato's city, since it reached down to the Isthmus of Corinth (*Critias* 110e).[23] It is a land wonderfully fertile, covered with fields and forests, 'able in those days to support a vast army, exempt from the labours of the soil' (*Critias* 110d—111e), and thus permitted soldiers to be soldiers only, Plato hoped, proof of the development of military *technē* and professionalism; while he was also eager to reconcile this evolution with the ideal of the citizen-soldier, as even Sparta had failed to do (cf. esp. *Republic* 2, 373a ff.). To the very end of its history, the city of the *Timaeus* and the *Critias* is a republic of the land. When the terrible cataclysm comes, its army is swallowed by the earth (τὸ μάχιμον πᾶν ἀθρόον ἔδυ κατὰ γῆς), whereas Atlantis is engulfed by the sea (κατὰ τῆς θαλάττης δῦσα ἠφανίσθη) (*Tim.* 25d). It is hardly necessary to remark that in his account of prehistoric Athens Plato devoted no space to the life of the sea. The country is surrounded by sea, but there are no harbours. A republic of the land: a republic united and unchanging. Unity is the foundation of all Plato's 'constitutions';[24] and here it is assured by the divine pair and by community of women and offspring. He stresses this unity and the lack of change even in tiny details: there

207

is only one spring, and its water is of a temperature equally convenient in summer and in winter.[25] Changlessness appears in the number of warriors, which so far as possible shall not alter; and in the way in which the constitution and the organization of their land has been ordained once and for all.[26] And, more jokingly, in the art of house-building, which the inhabitants pass down 'to others like themselves, always the same' (*Critias* 112c).[27]

One might ask whether there is any further connection between this structure based on the land, this unity and this changelessness, beyond those that are obvious? In the cosmology of the *Timaeus*, of the four elements, it is precisely earth that cannot be transformed: οὐ γὰρ εἰς ἄλλο γε εἶδος ἔλθοι ποτ'ἄν (*Tim.* 56d). Movement in this cosmology consists in the commingling, at every level, of the principle of change-lessness, 'of the indivisible Existence that is ever in the same state' (τῆς [γὰρ] ἀμερίστου καὶ ἀεὶ κατὰ ταὐτὰ ἐχούσης οὐσίας), the Same (τὸ αὐτό), with 'the divisible Existence that exists in bodies' (τῆς αὖ περὶ τὰ σώματα γιγνομένης μεριστῆς), the Different (τὸ ἕτερον) (*Tim.* 35a ff.). One might see prehistoric Athens as the political manifestation of the Same. The tenor of the myth is no less evident at a political level. It is not a matter of chance that Plato takes Solon as the intermediary for his knowledge of this Athens: by the mid-fourth century the Archon of 594 had become the grand old man of the moderates, the supporters of the *patrios politeia*.[28] The great cataclysm deprived Athens of the larger part of her land. The small remainder, of first-rate quality, is a token of what once was (*Critias* 110e), just as among the Athenians of Solon's day, 'a little of the seed' of the Athenians of for-mer days was preserved (*Tim.* 23c). Athens is not then 'lost', if the word means anything in Plato's philosophy; but the city Plato describes is the antithesis of the real city of the fifth and fourth centuries — in a word, an Anti-Athens.

Plato presents in the *Politicus*, in the form of a myth, two cycles in the universe.[29] At times, 'God in person accompanies the movement of the universe, putting his own hand to the wheeling of its circles' (tr. Taylor). The world then comes to know what the poets have called the Age of Cronus, men under the sway of divine shepherds. 'Sons of the earth', men lead a life exactly the reverse of ours: they are born greybeards and die babies. Then the cycle goes into reverse and God abandons the helm. At first men succeed reasonably well in organizing things; 'but in process of time, as forgetfulness comes over (the world), the old discord prevails ever more and more'. The threat is then that the world will be swallowed up 'in the boundless place of unlikeness' (εἰς τὸν τῆς ἀνομοιότητος ἄπειρον ὄντα τόπον) (*Pol.* 273d).[30] God takes a hand, and the world reverses itself once again. In books 8 and 9 of the *Republic* Plato outlines an analogous shift, from timocracy to oligarchy, from oligarchy to democracy, from democracy to tyranny: the ideal model is progressively distorted, yet each type preserves elements of the preceding constitution. Equally, each stage is a little further removed from the ideal of unity: democracy is like 'an emporium of constitutions where one can choose the model he likes best' (Cornford) (ὥσπερ εἰς παντοπώλιον ἀφικομένῳ πολιτειῶν, καὶ ἐκλεξαμένῳ οὕτω κατοικίζειν: *Rep.* 8, 557d). And Plato is especially fond of the adjective *poikilos* to describe democracy and its logical consequence, tyranny (*Rep.* 8, 557c, 558c, 561e, 568d). These two forms of constitution push 'diversity', 'chiaroscuro', to the very limit.

In order to characterize this 'chiaroscuro' quality — or, in a different image, this *apeiron*, this lack of limits — Plato uses oppositions, big and little, hot and cold, pitched and unpitched, etc.:

> Wherever they are present they exclude any definite quantity. They always imbue activities with greater strength over against greater mildness and conversely, rendering them more or less whatever it may be (τὸ πλέον καὶ τὸ ἔλαττον ἀπεργάζεσθον), and ruling out definite quantity ... If they do not obliterate definite quantity, but allow degree and measure to appear in the midst of more or less, or strongly and mildly, they in fact abandon the territory they occupied. For in admitting of definite quantity they would no longer strictly be hotter or colder. For the hotter goes on without pause, and the colder in the same way, while a definite quantity comes to a particular point and goes no further. So on the present argument the hotter and at the same time its opposite would come out as indeterminate.[31] (*Philebus* 23cd, tr. Gosling)

It is easy to recognize in this passage the well-known 'indeterminate dyad' (δυὰς ἀόριστος) of great and small, by which Aristotle defined the material principle in Plato; and of course, the 'Other' of the *Timaeus*.[32]

It is in this last dialogue that we find, in close mutual relationship, the two cycles which in the *Politicus* are sundered. The circle of the Same corresponds to the movement of the stars, and moves from left to right, while the Other, divided into seven unequal circles (the planets), moves from right to left. But the turning of the Other is brought about by the turning of the Same which it imitates (*Tim.* 36c ff.).[33] The harmony of the universe can thus be accounted for, but also the unforeseen eventualities to which it is subject.

If proto-Athens is the political expression of the triumph of the Same, what of Atlantis? I do not say that it *is* the political expression of the Other, because the Other does not exist in itself. What is subject to coming into being and is visible (γένεσιν ἔχον καὶ ὁρατόν) is an imitation of the model (μίμημα δὲ παραδείγματος), which is itself alone intelligible and eternal (νοητὸν καὶ ἀεὶ κατὰ ταὐτὰ ὄν) (*Tim.* 48e–49a).[34]

To grasp what Atlantis is, it would be sensible first of all to look once again at the fate of Athens. The prehistoric city lost what gave it permanence: 'For the fact is that a single night of excessive rain washed away the earth and laid bare the rock' (*Critias*, 112a); 'in comparison with what then was, there remain only the bones of the wasted body . . . the mere skeleton of the land being left' (111b). It became the rock that Plato describes thus: 'The whole country is only a long promontory extending far into the sea away from the rest of the continent' (πᾶσα ἀπὸ τῆς ἄλλης ἠπείρου μακρὰ προτείνουσα εἰς τὸ πέλαγος οἷον ἄκρα κεῖται: *Critias* 111a).[35] Athens is therefore condemned to seafaring and all that that involves — political change, commerce, imperialism. But is not that the fate of Atlantis? Is this extraordinary world, this island 'larger than Libya and Asia together' (*Tim.* 23d),[36] and whose Homeric and oriental characteristics we have explored, *Athenian*?[37] Early on in his account, Plato has recourse to a very odd expedient to explain why the names he is going to use are Greek: 'You must not be surprised if you should perhaps hear Hellenic names given to foreigners' (οἷα καὶ τῇδε ὀνόματα) (*Critias* 113b): the story told to Solon came to him from the Egyptian tongue and was then turned into Greek. An entirely pointless thing to say; unless the point is precisely to intimate that 'Hellenic names given to foreigners' might reveal realities no less similar. The structure of Athens is fixed once and for all; that of Atlantis, by contrast, is a continuous creation. First of all, it is on an island, and it has a fertile plain, like that of Athens, which is close to the sea. Above this plain, a mountain inhabited by a couple, Euenor and Leucippe, 'born from the earth' (*Critias* 113cd).[38] In the beginning, then, Atlantis was of the earth; and Poseidon, Lord of the island, before he became God of the sea, was a divinity of the soil. To keep his affair with Kleito secret, however, he fashioned round the mountain two circular enclosures of earth, and three of sea; but Plato remarks: 'no man could get to the island, for ships and voyages were not yet thought of' (*Critias* 113de). The opposition between earth and water nonetheless became from that moment a fundamental aspect of the structure of Atlantis. A spring rises in the island's centre, no longer as a *single* source which could be used at any time of year as at Athens, but as two fountains, one hot, the other cold, which the God himself caused to flow, just as he caused the famous 'sea' of Erechtheus to exist at Athens (*Critias* 113e, 117a, cf. Herodotus 8.55).[39] Indeed, water appears on Atlantis in a rather less likely way, too: its soil is rich in every conceivable metal, and especially in gold and the mysterious orichalcum (114e); and in the *Timaeus* Plato tells us that metals, and the purest metal, gold, in particular, are merely varieties of water (*Tim.* 58b ff.).[40]

This temporal relationship between earth and water, which is in itself significant, is only the most striking aspect of a dualism which Plato stresses constantly and which proves that the structure of Atlantis is constituted by the play of the *apeiron*, of non-identity.

The island refuge in the centre is five stades across; then there comes a stretch of water one stade wide, and then two groups of enclosures of earth and water, two and three stades across respectively (*Critias* 115d–116a).[41] Thus we have a sequence which is more or less that of an inverted fugue: 5(3+2),1,2,2,3,3; anyone who leaves the island's centre rapidly enters the world of doubleness.

Closely corresponding to the five enclosures which protect the island are the five pairs of twins which Kleito bears to Poseidon. In giving us the tally of these twins (one of which bears both a barbarian and a Greek name: Gadeiros-Eumēlos), Plato carefully distinguishes elder from younger (*Critias* 113e–114d). Again, he records that some of the buildings were simple (ἁπλᾶ) and others of different stones (ποικίλα); some of the cisterns were open to the sky and others covered over; 'twice in the year they gathered the fruits of the earth', making use of rain during the winter, and in the summer water from the canals. The kings held their meetings 'every fifth and every six year alternately, thus giving equal honour to the odd and to the even number' (τῷ τε ἀρτίῳ καὶ τῷ περιττῷ μέρος ἴσον ἀπονέμοντες) (*Critias* 116b, 117b, 118e, 119d).[42] When he describes in the *Timaeus* the formation of the natural world, from the World-Soul to man, and from man to fish, Plato is also describing the advances of non-homogeneity, which is supreme in nature (*phusis*). Nature appears in Atlantis in all its limitlessness: trees, different sorts of plants, fruit, animals, and in particular the elephant, 'the largest and greediest of the animals' (*Critias* 115a). This structure has a history: the ten sons of Poseidon give rise to ten royal dynasties, and these dynasties perform construction-works which link the centre of the island to the sea beyond (*Critias* 115b–116a);[43] the kings build bridges and open the land to seafaring (117e). They improve the plain by means of a grandiose system of canals (118ae).[44] They provide themselves with a large army (119ab).[45] And, finally, they lay out in the centre of the island a monumental area complete with a palace, a sanctuary of Poseidon, and even a horse-racing circuit, as one might expect on an island consecrated to that god (*Critias* 116c–117a). Plato gives us figures for most of these undertakings: the temple, for example, was 'a stade in length, and half a stade in width, and of a proportionate height (συμμετρόν) (116d). If we convert that into *plethra*, we get 6:3:2 — a simple example, one of many, of a play on the ten primary numbers, and above all, on the number 10, of which Atlantis provides many instances.[46]

The descendants of Poseidon established a political system of singularly mixed character (*Critias* 119b—120d). Within his own domain, each king is sovereign, with power over life and death, which might correspond as well, in the case of a philosopher, to the ideal situation in the *Politicus* (292d—297b), as to tyranny, in the opposite case. As a group, the ten kings constitute an oligarchy or aristocracy, which governs collectively in accordance with the precepts engraved by the first kings on a column of orichalcum at Poseidon's behest.[47] When justice has to be done, these rules are assured by the legendary oath, which consists essentially in the pouring of the consecrated blood of a bull, the characteristic means by which non-philosophers are able to maintain a constitutional ordinance.[48] And when a member of the royal family is to be put to death, it must be decided by a majority verdict. From its institutions, Atlantis might then appear to be one of those successful mixed constitutions described in the *Politicus*, the *Timaeus*, the *Philebus* and the *Laws*; and indeed, for many generations, 'the kings were obedient to the laws, and well-affectioned towards the god, whose seed they were' — they even thought 'lightly of the possession of gold and other property, which seemed only a burden to them' (*Critias* 120e—121a).[49] But the divine element withered, and the kings were filled 'with unrighteous ambition and power' (πλεονεξίας ἀδίκου καὶ δυνάμεως) (121ab).[50] And it was then that, to punish them, Zeus called together the company of the gods to the centre of the universe, to a place 'which ... beholds all created things' (ἣ ... καθορᾷ πάντα ὅσα γενέσεως μετείληφεν) and that ... The dialogue breaks off (121bc). The history of Atlantis thus reveals the selfsame advance towards disunity that we have seen in its physical structure.

At this point, it is appropriate to stress, more than I have done so far, the Athenian aspects of the mighty island. Kleisthenes's reforms divided Athens into ten tribes; and it is into ten parts that Poseidon divides his own domain (δέκα μέρη κατανείμας) (*Critias* 113e).[51] When Plato speaks of orichalcum, the metal which played so large a part in the prosperity of the kings of Atlantis, he mentions that it was 'more precious in those days than anything except gold' (114e).[52] The description of the harbours and their fortifications is greatly indebted, as has often been noted, to the complex Kantharos, Zea, Mounychia, the naval yards (*Skeuothēkē*) and the Arsenal. The naval dockyards of Atlantis had triremes lying in them; and Plato observes of the ports: 'they were full of vessels and merchants coming from all parts, who, from their numbers, kept up a multitudinous sound of human voices, and din and clatter of all sorts night and day (φωνὴν καὶ θόρυβον παντοδαπόν) (117e).[53] In other words, just like the Piraeus.

Unlike the royal palace, the temple of Poseidon is described at length. And in spite of its exotic decoration, it reminds one astonishingly of the Parthenon. In the sanctuary stands the statue of Poseidon, mounted in a chariot and surrounded by a hundred Sea-nymphs on dolphins; he is 'of such a size that he touched the roof of the building with his head', just like Pheidias's statue of Athena Parthenos (116d; cf. Picard, 1939: 374). All these statues were of gold. We are reminded of what Pericles says in Thucydides: 'The gold with which the image of the goddess was overlaid ... weighed forty talents pure' (2.13.5). All around the temple are statues, and in particular those of the wives of the ten kings (the ten eponymous heroes of Kleisthenes's city?); and Plato remarks, curiously enough, that there were 'many other great offerings of kings and of private persons, coming both from the city itself and from the foreign cities over which they held sway' (*Critias* 116e–117a) – as though he were thinking of Pheidias's two Athenas on the Acropolis, Athena Promachos, set up by command of Pericles, and Athena Lemnia, which took its name from the Athenian cleruchs of Lemnos who dedicated it.[54]

Finally, and most important, Atlantis became an imperial power:

Now in this island of Atlantis there was a great and wonderful empire which had rule over the whole island and several others, and over parts of the continent. (*Timaeus* 25a; cf. *Critias* 114c)

Not satisfied with all this, its leaders embarked on an overseas expedition. Their clash with prehistoric Athens brought upon them a catastrophe comparable to that suffered by the Athens of history in Sicily, or recently experienced by her at the time when Plato was writing the *Timaeus* and the *Critias*, at the hands of her rebellious allies.

But we have still to explain, if we are able to conclude the demonstration, why Plato should so oddly have mixed Athenian with 'oriental' features in this historical myth. In the *Laws*, he analyses briefly the two constitutions which 'are two mother forms of state from which the rest may be truly said to be derived' (3, 693d): the despotism of Persia, and Athenian democracy. The account is quite unhistorical, but Plato's description of their development (*Laws* 3, 694a–701b) establishes a strict parallel between the two of them, strikingly reminiscent of the history of Atlantis: the same just, if precarious, equilibrium in the beginning, the same disastrous evolution, which leads in the first case, under the impulse of gold and imperialism, to the despotism of an absolute ruler; and in the second, after the Persian Wars, and then the abandonment of the old *mousikē* ['moral education'] to 'theatrocracy'. I need hardly add that the Persian king had by the fourth century become enormously influential in the Greek world, whether directly or through the use of satellites.

We can now understand the true significance of the praise of Athens in the *Timaeus* and in the *Critias*. The technique is common in Plato (see Schaerer, 1948). In the *Phaedrus*, he praises the young Isocrates (278e–279ab),[55] who at the time was actually an old man and Plato's opponent. In doing so, he calls attention away from the real Isocrates to a possible Isocrates, the philosopher-orator that he was not. The Athenian Stranger in the *Laws* raises a protest when his Spartan and Cretan interlocutors account for the institutions of their countries by appealing to military necessity; and Plato then gives us a philosophical Sparta and a philosophical Crete out of his imagination: 'the order of them is discovered to his eyes, who has experience in laws gained either by study or by habit, although they are far from being self-evident to the rest of mankind like ourselves' (*Laws* 1, 632d; cf. the philosophical Sparta in *Protagoras* 342b).

Nevertheless, the moral of our story is complicated. Athens is triumphant. The city of Unity defeats the city which has allowed itself to be taken over by disunity and by heterogeneity. The waters close over Atlantis. Their absolute victory halts the advance of non-identity. But Athens loses her foundation in the earth and becomes Atlantis.[56] Is this 'serious'? 'I say that about serious matters a man should be serious, and about a matter which is not serious he should not be serious . . . only God is the natural and worthy object of our most serious . . . endeavours' (σπουδῆς ἄξιον) (*Laws* 7, 803c). But Plato has just said that if 'human affairs are hardly worth considering in earnest . . . yet we must be in earnest about them, – a sad necessity constrains us' (803b). Man is nothing but a puppet in the hands of God, a plaything made by God for his own pleasure (θεοῦ τι παίγνιον μεμηχανημένον) (1,644d ff., 7, 803c). And so man pays God homage by 'playing the most beautiful games he can' (παίζοντα ὅτι καλλίστας παιδιάς) (7,803c). Myth and history, like all things that come from imitation, are among these games. As the *Timaeus* has it (59cd):

A man may sometimes set aside meditations about eternal things, and for recreation turn to consider the truths of generation which are probable only; he will thus gain a pleasure not to be repented of, and secure for himself while he lives a wise and moderate pastime (μέτριον . . . παιδιὰν καὶ φρόνιμον).

All the same, the game is worth it: at the beginning of the dialogue, Critias craves his hearers' indulgence by saying that he is going 'to speak of high matters' (ὡς περὶ μεγάλων μέλλων λέγειν) (*Critias* 106c). It is more difficult, he says, to speak of men than of the gods, because a man is always demanding when a painter undertakes to paint his portrait (107d). Pointless — if Plato were not saying to his contemporaries what the seventeenth-century philosopher was saying to his: *de te fabula narratur.*[57]

12. Between Beasts and Gods

Marcel Detienne (1972; 1977)

Strong feelings were aroused at the end of the last century when the English anthropological school claimed to have discovered 'survivals of a savage state' in the thought, and in the society, which western civilization had confidently deemed the tap-root of its own values and principles. Could the Greeks — the Greeks, who had miraculously divined Reason to be incarnate in man, and had thus been the first to recognize the privileged status of human beings in the world, possibly have tasted human flesh, have been cannibals, like the Iroquois or the savages of Melanesia? Tylor and his followers claimed that myths contained evidence for previous states of a society. If so, the banquet of Thyestes, Lykaon's sacrifice, the myth of Cronus, were now become so many irrefutable proofs that Plato's forefathers bore an uncomfortable resemblance to the American Indians (Lang, 1885).

Though modern classicists may have insomnia, however, it is not because they fret that Plato's great-grandpapa might have been a cannibal; and the problem is nowadays discussed in different terms.[1] With the exception of a quite unusual ritual such as that of the wolf-man, during which initiates partook of human flesh mixed with pieces of an animal victim, cannibalism in ancient Greece is now seen in symbolic terms, whether in myth, religious thought or political ideology. Consequently, its explanation can be in one of two forms. First, some kind of thematic reading covering all the myths and stories in which the motif occurs, however incidentally: Dionysus eaten by the Titans, Tereus and Thyestes feasting on their children, the Theban Sphinx who ate the young men with whom she copulated, the offering by Tantalus and Lykaon of human flesh to the gods, Cronus swallowing down the offspring borne him by Rhea . . . The motif of cannibalism is obvious enough in each of these myths, but the very act of collecting them for study is enough to reveal fundamental differences. In each case the meaning of what seems to be an act of cannibalism depends on the context: only the context can make clear its true significance. Two examples will serve to show that this first method offers ultimately no solutions. Take the story of Cronus. A naïve reading of Hesiod may leave the impression that Cronus is a cannibalistic father in that he devours each new-born child as Rhea presents it to him (*Theogony* 459–60). But the account takes on quite a different meaning when

215

placed in its proper context, the myths of sovereignty (cf. Detienne and Vernant, 1978: 64—7). Like Zeus, who has an identical function in Hesiod's myth, Cronus is a sovereign god fated to be dethroned by his son, a child more powerful than his father. To prevent this, Cronus and Zeus alike devour (*katapinein*) their offspring. Cronus does not eat the children Rhea bears him limb by limb: he gulps them down entire and alive, and so is able later to disgorge them under the influence of the drug administered him by Zeus's accomplice Metis — the selfsame Metis whom Zeus, in his own turn threatened with dethronement by a more powerful son, decides to swallow after their marriage so as to possess himself of all that swift cunning without which his reign would be as brief as Cronus's. Neither Cronus nor Zeus is a real cannibal. They are both sovereign gods who swallow their enemies so as to defend or to establish their power.

Our second example is provided by the myths of Tereus and Polytechnos (Mihailov, 1955: 77—208), two versions of a story about a man who unwittingly eats the flesh of his own child served him by his own wife. Taken out of context, this horrifying supper is open to any number of misinterpretations — it might, for example, be a Dionysiac banquet or a cannibalistic meal.[2] But if we look at the mythological context, we find that the stories belong to a complex of myths about honey, and this allows us to define more closely the cannibalism of Tereus and Polytechnos.[3] The two myths are in fact parallel versions of a story which begins with an *excessive honeymoon* and ends with the *decomposition* of honey or its transformation into *excrement*. In the Tereus version, the husband who abuses the honeymoon is condemned first to seduce and violate his sister-in-law, then to eat the flesh of his son, and finally to change into a hoopoe, a bird which feeds on human excrement. In the Polytechnos version (where Polytechnos is the wood-pecker, the master of bees and honey), another excessive honeymoon leads the guilty husband by the same path — rape and cannibalism — to death by honey: he is rolled in it and left to be bitten and stung. The punishment fits the crime perfectly, for he 'wallowed too long' or 'ate too much' honey — both images used by the Greeks to refer to honeymoons and the pleasure given each other by a newly-married couple. The myths of Tereus and Polytechnos tell how an improper use of honey transforms something eatable into the opposite, excrement or rot. This transformation is mediated by a cannibalistic phase, defined in other myths of the same group as the state prior to the discovery of honey: in these myths, men ate each other until the Bee-Women taught them how to feed off honey gathered in the forest.[4]

A structural analysis, then, allows us to understand the cannibalism of these myths in two ways, as at once the sign of a reversion to the period before honey and as the first stage of a breakdown of the honey-diet, before it turns into dung (in the case of the hoopoe) or rottenness (in the case of the woodpecker).

An alternative to a systematic reading of the different groups of myths to which the stories concerning cannibalism belong is this: cannibalism can be defined within the structure of Greek thinking — located within the cluster of images which the Greeks constructed, about themselves and about outsiders, at the level of eating habits. For them, the eating of human flesh was one of a number of forms of cannibalism. As such, it was an essential term in a dietary code which, in their religious and social thought, constitutes a grid capable of representing the structure of relations between man, nature and the supernatural.[5] So we have to make use of the system as a whole if we are to rescue cannibalism from the sliding into which it was explicitly shunted by the Greeks. For although Greek society rejected cannibalism utterly, yet, by virtue of what it did have to say about it, it compelled dissident individuals and groups to express their rejection of society in terms of this very form of illicit consumption.

We cannot, in other words, define cannibalism in Greece simply within the system of politico-religious ideas. We must also define it from 'outside', by looking at different ways in which Greeks expressed their rejection of the city and its values. These rejections were of different kinds. Sometimes it was simply a matter of more or less isolated individuals, such as the Orphics or the Cynics. But protest could be expressed in more or less organized sects or groups — the Pythagoreans, or the worshippers of Dionysus. It is impossible to say whether they actually thought of themselves as alternative *systems* or were simply protests against the city. Nevertheless, these four movements, Pythagoreanism, Orphism, the Dionysiac sects and the Cynics, can be seen as a set of four terms each of which projects a mirror-image of the politico-religious system of the Greeks, in which cannibalism is given a particular stress, either positive or negative.

We may begin by describing the politico-religious system which was dominant in ancient Greece. It was based on a ritual of sacrifice which lies at the heart of Greek political life and which codified Greek rules about eating. In Greece, the consumption of meat was intimately related to the sacrifice, to the gods, of a domestic animal. The flesh of this animal men kept for themselves, granting the gods the smoke from the burning bones combined with the scent of the aromatics burned with them. Such a practice marks a sharp division between men and gods at the level of rules about food. Men receive the meat because to live they have to eat flesh, perishable flesh, such as they themselves are made of. The gods alone receive the aromas, perfumes, the incorruptible substances which constitute the superior foods reserved for the immortals.

All this defines the human condition in one direction. But there is another definition implied in sacrifice — against animals. But here, for a number of reasons, the boundary is less sharp. Men and animals both need to eat, and both suffer from hunger, which is a 'sign' of death. Some animal species, like man, are carnivorous. Moreover, whereas men and gods are so far separated that it is necessary to burn incense to attract the gods to men's sacrifices, men and animals are close neighbours — sometimes so close that it may be difficult for a group to draw a clear distinction between its own members and, say, the plough-ox.

Within the framework of the city, the dominant set of ideas about the relationship between man and the animal world in ancient Greece is to be found in the writings of Aristotle and the Stoics. It is agreed that animals exist for man's benefit. They are there to provide him with food, to supply him with clothing and help him in his work. According to Aristotle, it is a just law of nature that man should use animals for these purposes.[6] This view is echoed by the opponents of vegetarianism: to give up using animals, they said, would risk man's 'leading a bestial life' (Porphyry, *De abstinentia* 1.4). Man is free in sovereign manner to divide the animal world into two groups: the animals he protects for the services he expects from them; and those he hunts for fear of the harm they may do him. But domestic or wild, animals are invariably regarded as creatures lacking reason, with whom men can establish no relation of law. For animals are incapable of 'making agreements among themselves that they should neither inflict nor suffer harm'.[7] The animal world knows neither justice nor injustice; and it is this fundamental ignorance which the Greeks regarded as the essential distinction between animals and mankind. Separated from men, who live under the rule of *dikē*, within legally-defined relations, animals are condemned to eat each other. The kingdom of cannibalism begins at the frontier where justice ends. 'This is the law which the Son of Cronus has decreed for men: fish and wild beasts and the birds of the air may eat each other, for there is no justice among them. But to men he has given justice, which is by far the best.'[8] Consequently, just as between men and gods, so the true distinction between men and animals is to be found at the level of rules about eating — except that here there is a double distinction, two levels. The most basic of these is the issue of cooking: 'Man is not an animal that eats raw flesh' (Porphyry, *De abstinentia* 1.13). In all Greek thinking, human food is inextricably linked with the fire of sacrifice; while even the least wild of domestic animals, the herbivores, are still condemned to eat food that is not cooked (Detienne, 1977: 13). In effect, the notion of 'bestiality' begins with the consumption of uncooked food — and finishes up in cannibalism.

Man's median position between beasts and gods is entrenched, buttressed by the entire politico-religious system, by way of the daily practice of sacrifice of animals whose flesh is then eaten. But in so rigid a form, this three-term model is neither adequate nor correct. It becomes so only when we accept that it has a dynamic dimension: the human condition is defined not simply by what it is not, but by what it *no longer is*. In the Greek city, where a proper history of culture usurped the function of mythical discourse about how things began, there developed a twofold tradition, according to which the Golden Age can substitute for barbarism, and vice versa. Sometimes, as in Hesiod, men become eaters of meat where once they had shared the food of the gods; and sometimes, as in the myth of the Bee-Women, men developed their present eating-habits only after living for a long while like animals, eating things raw and eating each other. We may put it thus: the model contains two symmetrical starting-points, one at the 'top', the other at the 'bottom'. They represent inverse orientations within the same conceptual area, and their symmetry is emphasized by the presence at each point, 'top' and 'bottom', of the same mediator, Prometheus. In the one case, through the invention of sacrifice, he brings about the transition from the Golden-Age fellowship with the gods to a diet of meat (Vernant, *Introduction* to Detienne, 1977: xxvii–xxviii, and see pp. 59–62 above). In the other, he extricates mankind from savagery, directs it away from an animal existence, by his gift of fire and by inventing the different technical skills (Cole, 1967: 6, 20–1, 150). The city does not feel compelled to make a choice between these two ways of putting it: it gives equal status to both versions. In its sacrificial practice it implicitly assumes the process sketched by Hesiod's myth; but in the various systems centred on its own history it tends to stress the shift from cannibalism to a food-code characterized by the eating of bread and meat.

The politico-religious system of thought, then, clearly proclaims cannibalism to be a form of bestiality which the city unambiguously rejects. It sets it on the very margin of its history, in a previous age of human existence, or on the fringes of its geographical extension, among the tribes which make up the Barbarian world. The geographical distribution of 'savages' is organized on the principle that the consumption of raw food is a form of bestiality though it falls short of cannibalism (cf. Festugière, 1972: 145–9). Eaters of raw meat are accordingly found in remote areas of Greece itself, such as northern Aetolia, the home of the Eurytanes, 'who, it is said, speak a completely unintelligible language and eat raw meat' (Thucydides 3.94). Genuine cannibals live in far-off lands. One example is the Scythians, who eat human flesh and, like others of their kind, drink mare's milk (Ephorus, in *FGrH* 70 F 42 [= Strabo 7.3.9 (302C)]). Herodotus calls one tribe the Man-eaters (Androphagoi), and says, 'their customs are utterly bestial; they do not observe justice nor do they have any law. They are nomads . . . and alone of these peoples, eat human flesh' (4.106). Aristotle speaks quite clinically about 'bestial dispositions', and finds them likewise among the peoples of the Pontus area, who show 'a tendency to murder and cannibalism', sometimes institutionalized among certain tribes said to provide each other with children for banquets (*Nicomachean Ethics* 7.5, 1148b19–25; *Politics* 8, 4, 1338b19–22). All of these are examples of cannibalism on the margins of the civilized world which the Greeks can simultaneously characterize, with Plato, as survivals of a primitive human condition or cite, like Aristotle's contemporaries, as the origin of the Lamia, the bogeyman who comes at night to devour foetuses and disembowels pregnant women to reach them (*Laws* 6, 782b6–c2; Anon. Scholiast on *Nicom. Eth.* 7.6 = *CAG* 20, p. 427.37–40).

This sociological perception of cannibalism must be supplemented by another, which confirms the city's radical rejection of all cannibalistic behaviour. In Greek thought of the fifth and fourth centuries, the tyrant (*turannos*) is a type explicitly defined in terms of the three-fold model which underpins the city's sacrificial practice and eating rules. Because his power derives from himself, without his either having had it granted him or being obliged to return it to the 'centre' (*es meson*), the tyrant sets himself above other men and above the laws. He is all-powerful, which puts him on a level with the gods. However, by the same token, he is excluded from the community, is banished to an area within which political theory ceases to distinguish supermen from sub-men — where it obliterates the chasm between god and beast (Vernant and Vidal-Naquet, 1972: 116–17, 128–30). In Plato's *Republic*, the tyrant's behaviour is seen as the naked irruption into the world of primitive lusts which ordinarily are aroused in us only in sleep, when, under the influence of alcohol, the animal part of the soul (*to thēriōdes*) dreams that it commits incest with the mother, rapes god, man or beast, murders the father or devours its own children (9,571c–d; cf. 10,619b–c). Outside the frame of the city and the hierarchical structure with which it is linked, man, god and beast are merely inter-changeable objects of the tyrant's desires, which compel him to incest and parricide and finally to auto-cannibalism. In eating his own flesh and blood, the tyrant proclaims that he is outside the rules, a social outcast — just as the scapegoat was expelled from the city in the course of certain spring festivals in various parts of Greece.

To eat human flesh is to enter a non-human world from which there is usually no return. When, in his madness, Cambyses determined to conquer the 'Long-lived' Ethiopians, who were supposed to share the banquet of the Sun and live in bliss at the ends of the earth, his armies, as they advanced further and further and ran out of food, were by degrees reduced first to eating their pack-animals, then to feeding on grass and plants, and finally to eating every tenth man, selected by lot. Mad though he was, says Herodotus, Cambyses at once abandoned the expedition, so much did he fear that his men would eat one another and become as wild beasts;[9] like those Phoenician mercenaries and Libyan dissidents who were reduced by hunger to eating each other and whom Hannibal Barca, who conquered them, had trampled by his elephants on the grounds that cannibals 'could not, without sacrilege, continue to live with other men' (Porphyry, *De abstinentia* 2.5.7). The same model has proved its effectiveness as a means of exclusion in countless polemics against groups whom it was desirable to denounce as enemies of humanity. That they slept with their mothers or their sisters; that they cut the throats of new-born babes to devour their flesh, dipped bread in the blood and drank it — these were the crimes of which the first Christians were accused. The slanders were said by the Greek Christian apologists Origen and Justin to have been started by the Hellenized Jews in the second century AD; which did not prevent their being used against the Jews in their turn more than once in centuries to come.[10]

However that may be, inversion is a basic mechanism in a whole area of thought whose true significance lies in the dynamic relationship between four kinds of anti-system, each of which converts the terms of the basic model for its own purposes. By taking one of the two directions available in the original — up or down — the politico-religious system can be transcended, in a movement either towards the gods, or towards the beasts. The Pythagoreans and Orphics explored the first possibility, Dionysiac movements and, later, Cynicism, the second. But whatever the form taken by rejection of the politico-religious system, or protest, in the city, those involved were invariably compelled to adopt a certain view of cannibalism and to define themselves in relation to it.

In Greek religion Orphism and Pythagoreanism are of course the best known forms of deviance. Speaking generally, they were in origin religious movements which rejected the city's system of values, and challenged its assumption of a fundamental relation between men and gods founded on the division established by Prometheus at the moment when, by reserving the meat for mankind, he deprived them for ever of their former fellowship with the gods. The main thrust of Pythagoreanism is directed towards dietary rules; it insists, with varying degrees of strictness, on a diet which does not contain meat (Detienne, 1977: 40—57). In practice, Pythagoreanism adopted two different attitudes towards blood-sacrifice and the city. On the one hand, there is the intransigent rejection on the part of a sect which set itself up as an anti-city. On the other, a milder form of rejection practised by a group which was political rather than religious, and which tried to reform the city from within. The first group rejected any form of meat; the second compromised by determining that some sacrificial victims — pigs and goats — were not 'meat' in the strict sense. True meat is the flesh of the plough-ox, and its slaughter they strictly forbade.

Of these two approaches, only the first deserves to be described as 'renunciation' (which is the basis of its claim to be an anti-system). The strict vegetarians regarded all blood sacrifice as murder, and in the extreme case, cannibalism. It was this that they attacked in their myths about the bean. The mythical food of the gods and of the Golden Age was spices. The bean, a leguminous plant, is the polar opposite of spices: because it has no nodes on the stem, the bean is in direct contact with the world of the dead, to which it anyway belongs because of its associations with rottenness. Inversely, spices, which belong to the world of the gods by virtue of their solar nature and their dryness, effect direct communication with the divine. For the Pythagoreans, however, the bean is even more: it is a creature of flesh and blood, the double of the man by whose side it grows, on the same dungheap, feeding on the same decomposition. Consequently, it is for them as grave a crime to eat beans as to 'gnaw the heads of one's parents'. They proved this by a series of experiments described in the Pythagorean tradition. A bean was placed in a pot or in a closed vessel and covered in dung or buried in the earth: this in some mysterious way 'cooked' it. After a gestation period of indeterminate length, the bean was transformed either into a woman's vulva with a partly-formed child's head attached to it, or into a human head with already recognizable features.

In these experiments the pot is a matrix designed to reveal the bean's true nature; the same end could be achieved by biting or squeezing the bean and then leaving it for a few moments in the sun. It then gave off, by all accounts, a smell either of sperm or of blood shed in murder. To the vegetarians those who ate the sacrificial victims, the city-carnivores, are to be classified with one of the two extreme forms of bestiality: with the Lamia, who eats the foetuses she tears from the wombs of pregnant women, or with the cannibal son who devours the heads of those who are nearest and most precious to him. The 'pure' Pythagoreans reversed the model which subtends the *polis*, and so made their sect into an anti-system, a counter-*polis*. They first reduced that model from three terms to two (meat : not-meat); and then said that cannibalism is not relegated to distant savages but is to be found in the *polis* itself, among the men who sacrifice on the altars in honour of the gods. And that is the meaning of the tradition which says that Pythagoras invented vegetarianism in order to wean his contemporaries from their previous custom of eating each other.[11]

The Orphics were no less radical; their rejection of the world involved them in the same sharp inversion as the extreme Pythagoreans. There is a paradox in Orphic thinking: the most important teaching that Orpheus left to mankind was the instruction to 'abstain from murder' (*phonoi*) — a sect *symbolon* for the rejection of the practice of blood-sacrifice and the eating of meat. On the other hand, the Orphics' central myth is an account of a sacrifice involving cooking and eating. The young Dionysus is the victim; the Titans his sacrificers. The victim is eaten after being cooked in two ways: first by boiling, and then by roasting on the spit. Now this must remain paradoxical so long as we regard the myth as an account of some sort of communal meal. But what if we see the Titans' sacrifice in relation to that of Prometheus? It becomes at once apparent that both are primordial sacrifices: Prometheus's sacrifice established the relationship between men and gods; but the Orphic story presents the Titans' sacrifice as a cannibal meal whose sacrificial character is underlined by the methods of cooking employed. The Titans' sacrifice has two consequences: immediately, their punishment — they are destroyed by a thunderbolt; but from their ashes is born the human race which, every time it offers sacrifice to the gods, unwittingly repeats the murder and cannibal banquet performed by its remote forebears.[12]

The Orphics' distinction coincides exactly with the Pythagoreans': 'cannibals' are those who eat meat and do not follow the *bios orphikos*, the Orphic way, that is, who do not attempt to purify the divine element imprisoned in man by the greed of the Titans, or to overcome the rift cut by blood-sacrifice between mankind and god. In effect, then, cannibalism has for these two sectarian movements the same negative connotations that it has for the *polis* itself, in spite of their being inversions of the dominant politico-religious system in Greece.

It is quite otherwise with the other two protest movements which constitute this group of four anti-systems in the history of the Greek *polis* between the sixth and the fourth centuries BC. Both in Dionysiac cult and in Cynicism cannibalism is seen as an extension of 'eating raw' and becomes a means of achieving that subversion of the order of the *polis* which is their shared aim, a subversion from within, the one at a religious level, the other at a socio-political one.

In relation to the *polis*, the position of Dionysiac cult is plain: it effects from 'below' the rejection of sacrifice which Orphics and

223

Pythagoreans effected from 'above'. In Dionysiac cult, in utter contempt of the rules for *polis*-sacrifice, an animal is hunted in the mountains, torn to pieces while still alive and consumed raw. By this means the boundaries between animals and men are effaced, human and animal interpenetrate, become indistinguishable. The Maenads and Bacchantes suckle young wild beasts at their breasts. At the same time, they tear panthers and deer limb from limb. It is as if, in an attempt to become more utterly 'wild', the worshippers of Dionysus had first to soften the creatures of the wild, make friends with them even to the point of self-identification. But Dionysus the wild hunter is not simply an 'eater of raw flesh' (*ōmadios*, *ōmēstēs*). The practice of eating raw flesh which he demands of his followers leads them to imitate wild animals in performing the cruellest acts of cannibalism (Schmidt, 1939: 380–2; Jeanmaire, 1951: 256). A number of ritual details confirm the better-known literary accounts of the myth. On Chios, Tenedos and Lesbos, Dionysus hungers for human flesh; the victim torn apart in his honour is a man. In Euripides's *Bacchae*, Agave is possessed by the god whom her son Pentheus has scorned; and when Pentheus comes to the mountains to mock the maddened women, she hunts him down — seeing him as a lion-cub or young bull, 'shaggy like a wild animal' (1185–9), a victim which she tears apart with her own hands and starts to devour. The same frenzy attacks the daughters of Minyas. They are weaving, more interested in getting married than in going off to bacchic orgies in the bush. Dionysus makes them join the Maenads; in their madness they conceive 'a desire for human flesh', and choose by lot one of their own children, tearing him limb from limb as though he were a young animal.[13]

In all these traditions, cannibalism appears within the context of 'eating raw flesh'. It clearly constitutes the ultimate form of the state of 'savagery' to which Dionysiac cult claims to restore us. To eat human flesh, to engage in cannibalism, seems to be part of a pattern of behaviour designed to make men 'savage', to put them in closer contact with the supernatural (represented here by Dionysus Eater of Men) through possession.

But we should enquire whether the cult of Dionysus invariably attributed to cannibalism the same positive value it attached to the raw consumption of a wild animal caught by hunting. In one version of the story of the daughters of Minyas, the killing of the child provokes an angry reaction from other Bacchantes: they abandon their wild dance through the mountains and turn on the unnatural mothers (Aelian, *Varia historia* 3.42). Likewise, at the end of Euripides's play, the death of Pentheus is presented as a murder incurring pollution: Agave is sent into exile (1674). On this occasion, it is Dionysus himself who pronounces the sentence, thus condemning the behaviour which he himself had apparently commanded. It is of course true that in each case 'the eater of raw flesh' only turns those into cannibals who resist him and refuse to have anything to do with his 'savagery'. This does not however mean that the practice of cannibalism is foreign to Dionysiac worship: it is rather an essential element within it, but an ambiguous one. This is clear particularly in the story of the Bassarai, the worshippers of Dionysus in Thrace. 'Not content with offering sacrifices of bulls, the Bassarai of old engaged in the madness of human sacrifice — even to the point of eating the victims' (Porphyry, *De abstinentia* 2.8). Porphyry goes on to note that the Bassarai 'did in this respect exactly as we do with animals, since we too offer the first portion to the gods, and eat the rest in the feast'. But the parallel stops there. For, as he continues, 'everyone knows the story of how they were stricken with madness, attacked and killed one another, actually eating the bleeding flesh, not resting till they had wiped out the family which had first practised such sacrifice'.

At this point cannibalism reveals its inner contradictions. In the cult of Dionysus it appears as the extreme form of 'savagery' which Dionysus offers as a path for his worshippers. But here Dionysus does not intervene to condemn the eaters of human flesh: they destroy themselves. Possessed by a manic hunger, the Bassarai are not able to restrain themselves from attacking each other. Furiously they tear each other apart and eat the flesh, a cannibal-crescendo. But, and this is my point, cannibalism cannot reach its crescendo without destroying itself. The choice is simple. Either the Bassarai destroy themselves to the last woman, or the cannibalism at the heart of Dionysiac religion must be severely restricted. To end the epidemic of cannibalism, which threatens to wipe the worshippers of Dionysus out, the Bassarai must kill those of the group who are known to have begun these dreadful rites. In its pure form, cannibalism is impossible. Dionysiac worship, which nurses it and integrates it into some of its rituals, can use it only under severe controls ... And the extent to which it does tolerate cannibalism corresponds exactly to the degree to which the Dionysiac movement, while maintaining 'transcendence through savagery' as an ideal, remained an essential part of the religion of the *polis*. It was always opposed, but always *inside*. It never took the form of an anti-system totally alien to the official religion.

It was this 'impossible' cannibalism which was taken up by the Cynics as part of their programme. At first sight, this programme looks as if it were parallel to the Dionysiac one, in that it too involves a return to primitive 'savagery' (Haussleiter, 1935: 167—84). But where the Dionysiac movement operates mainly at the level of religion,

Cynicism is a system of ideas which attacks society at every level. In theory and in daily life, the Cynics developed a critique, not merely of the *polis*, but also of social order and civilization. Their protest was a general assault upon civilized life.[14] It developed in the fourth century BC with the general crisis of the *polis*, and one of its main themes was a return to a state of 'savagery'.[15] Negatively, it decried the life of the city and rejected the material comforts of civilization. Positively, it tried to get back to the simple life of the first men, who drank spring-water and fed on acorns gathered on the ground or on plants which they collected.[16] Cynics proposed two models for the process of re-education so that men might be able to consume raw plants: the savages who had preserved this way of life intact; and animals, who had never been corrupted by Promethean fire. In effect, Cynicism was permeated by an anti-Promethean current, directed against the invention of manu-facturing, civilizing, fire.[17] To become 'savage' it was not enough to eat raw like Diogenes (who paid with his life when he fought with some dogs over a piece of raw octopus: Dio Chrysostom 6.25; Plutarch, *Aqua an ignis util.* 2, 956b). It was also necessary to dismantle the system of values on which society was based. The journey back to 'savagery' began with a critique of Prometheus — not here the first sacrificer responsible for the separation of gods and men, but the civilizing Titan of cultural anthropology, the mediator responsible, by his Greek gift of fire, for educating man out of his primitive state.

The cult of Dionysus sprinted into the state of savagery, in pursuit of possession and contact with the supernatural; it was quite otherwise among the Cynics. Among them, we find a *retreat* into 'savagery', a gradual descent in several stages. First, raw food and the condemnation of fire. Then two basic demands, for the abolition of the incest taboos; and for toleration of auto-cannibalism. Both can be found in Diogenes of Sinope. The first occurs ironically: 'Why did Oedipus complain so violently of being both brother and father to his children, at once husband and son of the same woman? Cocks, dogs and donkeys don't make such a fuss, nor do the Persians' (Dio Chrysostom 10.29–30). As for the second demand, not content with observing that at least one society has no taboo on eating human flesh, Diogenes was supposed to have actually 'taught children that they should herd their mothers and fathers to the sacrificial altars and eat them to the last scrap' (Theophilus, *Ad Autolycum* 3.5 = *SVF* 3 F 750). Incest, parricide, cannibalism: the basic interdictions are overthrown. The dismantling of society reaches down to virgin soil, to where Cynicism could find nothing but the pure individual, prior to society, prior to any collective life. It is only in this context of the radical questioning of civilized life that cannibalism could acquire an utterly positive value — a value it could never either so openly or so easily be given by the cult of Dionysus, a collective movement that was unalterably Greek. For it is obviously only 'intellectuals' like the Cynics who can afford the luxury of making the cannibal son an *ideal* so as to assert the rights of the individual against the collectivity, against any form of civilization.

These four solutions, all based on the dominant model of the *polis*, differ in relation to their judgement upon cannibalism, and can be classified in two groups. The first, Pythagoreanism and Orphism, by their own account anti-systems, merely reverses the *polis*-model and condemns within the *polis* the cannibalistic activity the *polis* condemns in the world 'beyond'. The other, starting from within the politico-religious system of the *polis*, tries to use cannibalism against the *polis* so as to destroy it or to introduce into it what Plato would call the Other. At the same time, the four schemas do not exhaust the solutions theoretically available by combining the elements offered by the model from which we began. We are offered in effect two solutions only, each of which appears in two different forms between the sixth and fourth centuries BC. All the same, I am inclined for a number of reasons to speak of a *system* of ideas. There is first the constant substitution, in the mythical and legendary tradition concerning the aboriginal state of man, between Golden Age and a state of 'savagery'. And there is the character of Prometheus, which shifts according to whether he effects the mediation once men lost fellowship with the gods; or whether he becomes the mediator by bringing about the end of the state of 'savagery' which men once shared with the animals.

To these two arguments history adds a third, which confirms the coherence of the system and the relation between its symmetrical starting-points. This is the transformation of one solution into its opposite, which can be seen taking place in the second third of the fourth century BC when, after political and religious failure, some Pythagoreans turn into Cynics almost before our eyes.

By the end of the fifth century, Pythagoreanism had finally failed in its political aim of reforming the city. Persecuted and harried, the disciples of Pythagoras scattered. A small group managed to survive at Phlius. Archytas went to make a career at Tarentum. The majority abandoned Magna Graecia (von Fritz, 1963: 214–19). As a group the Pythagoreans were finished: neither sect nor brotherhood remained. A few survivors gathered in Athens, and some details of their character and way of life are preserved in fragments of the Athenian comic poets, Antiphanes, Aristophon and Alexis (Méautis, 1922: 10–18; Burkert, 1972a: 198–201). Extraordinarily, the Pythagorean has become a character in comedy. Not a trace of the grave, white-robed figure, dedicated to asceticism, who strove after holiness within the sect's narrow rules. The new Pythagorean is a tramp. Barefoot and filthy, he drinks from streams and goes down into ravines to feed on wild herbs such as sea-purslane.[18] A beggar-bag on his back, a shabby short cloak slung over his shoulders, he wears his hair long and sleeps rough summer and winter. People couldn't get over it. Could these shabby unshaven hoboes still be called Pythagoreans? There was nothing whatever in their behaviour to distinguish them from Cynics; they even borrowed the Cynic's characteristic labels, the beggar-bag and the short cloak.[19]

This very question was asked already by ancient historians of philosophy; and their perplexity is often shared by modern scholars.[20] There lived in Athens in the first half of the fourth century BC a strange philosopher named Diodorus of Aspendus, who claimed to be a disciple of Pythagoras but who dressed and behaved like a Cynic. According to a contemporary, he 'was a follower of Pythagoras, but gathered a large following by his pachydermous fatuity and repertoire of insults' (Stratonikos *ap.* Athenaeus, *Deipnosophistae* 4.56, 163e–f). But do we really have to follow the author of the little-known *Philosophers in Sequence* in accusing Diodorus of affectation in wearing long hair and a short cloak, 'where in former times the Pythagoreans dressed neatly, practised massage, cut their hair and trimmed their beards in the usual way' (Sosicrates, *ap.* Athenaeus, *Deipnosophistae* 4.56, 163e–f)? Is it not more likely that Diodorus's ambiguity is to be seen as an example of a shift evidenced at the same period in the Comic writers, whose most successful skit on it is the scene in which strict vegetarians fight greedily over bits of dog's flesh (Alexis, *Tarentines* frg. 219 [*CAF* 2, pp. 377–8])?

It looks very much as if, with the failure of the solution from 'above', the last Pythagoreans had to make a choice between two, and only two, possibilities. They could either go back into the *polis* and be absorbed; or they could attempt from the 'bottom', taking the individualist tack, that transcendence of the *polis* which they had failed to achieve from 'above'. And there can be little doubt but that the model *gods : men : beasts* allows us to account most satisfactorily for the fact that the image of the child eating its parents should have been evaluated, over a time-span of two centuries, first negatively and then positively by the same dissident movement of the ancient world.

Abbreviations used

AIPH	Annuaire de l'Institut de Philologie et d'Histoire Orientales de l'Université libre de Bruxelles (Bruxelles)
AJA	American Journal of Archaeology (Princeton)
AJPh	American Journal of Philology (Baltimore)
ArchClass	Archeologia Classica. Rivista dell'Istituto di Archeologia dell' Università di Roma (Roma)
ARW	Archiv für Religionswissenschaft (Leipzig; Leipzig–Berlin)
ASNP	Annali della Scuola Normale Superiore di Pisa, Classe di Lettere e Filosofia (Pisa)
ASSPh	Annuaire de la Société Suisse de Philosophie (Studia Philosophica) (Basel)
BARB	Bulletin de la Classe des Lettres de l'Académie Royale de Belgique (Bruxelles)
BCH	Bulletin de Correspondance Hellénique (Paris)
BEFAR	Bibliothèque des Écoles Françaises d'Athènes et de Rome
BJ	Bonner Jahrbücher des Rheinischen Landesmuseums in Bonn und des Vereins von Altertumsfreunden im Rheinlande (Kevelaer)
CAF	Th. Kock, Comicorum Atticorum Fragmenta, 3 vols., 1880–8, Leipzig
CAG	Commentaria in Aristotelem graeca, 24 vols., 1883–1909, Berlin
CAIEF	Cahiers de l'Association internationale des Études Françaises (Paris)
CHM	Cahiers d'Histoire mondiale (Neuchâtel)
CPh	Classical Philology (Chicago)
CQ	The Classical Quarterly (Oxford)
CR	The Classical Review (Oxford)
CRAI	Comptes Rendus de l'Académie des Inscriptions (Paris)
CSSH	Comparative Studies in Society and History (Cambridge)
Daremberg-Saglio	Ch. Daremberg, Edm. Saglio (ed.), Dictionnaire des Antiquités grecques et romaines d'après les textes et les monuments, 5 vols. in 10, 1877–1919, Paris
DELG	Pierre Chantraine, Dictionnaire étymologique de la langue grecque: histoire des mots, 1968– , Paris
FGrH	Felix Jacoby, Die Fragmente der Griechischen Historiker, 3 vols. in 14, 1923–58, Berlin and Leiden
FHG	K. and Th. Müller (eds.), Fragmenta Historicorum Graecorum, 5 vols., 1878–85, Paris
FVS	H. Diels and W. Kranz (eds.), Die Fragmente der Vorsokratiker, 6 ed., 3 vols., 1951–2, Berlin–Grunewald
GGA	Göttingische Gelehrte Anzeigen (Göttingen)
GGrM	K. Müller (ed.), Geographi Graeci Minores, 2 vols., 1882, Paris
HThR	Harvard Theological Review (Cambridge, Mass.)
IC	Margherita Guarducci (ed.), Inscriptiones Creticae opera et consilio Friderici Halbherr collectae, 4 vols. Istituto di Archeologia e Storia dell'Arte. 1935–50, Roma

Abbreviations

IEG	M.L. West (ed.), *Iambi et Elegi Graeci ante Alexandrum cantati*, 2 vols., 1971–2, Oxford
IG	*Inscriptiones Graecae*, 1873– , Berlin
IJG	R. Dareste, B. Haussoullier, Th. Reinach (eds.), *Recueil des inscriptions juridiques grecques*, 2 vols., 1891–8, Paris
JdAI	*Jahrbuch des deutschen Archäologischen Instituts* (Berlin)
JESHO	*Journal of the Economic and Social History of the Orient* (Leiden)
JHI	*Journal of the History of Ideas* (Ephrata, Pa)
JHS	*Journal of Hellenic Studies* (London)
JÖAI	*Jahreshefte des Österreichischen Archäologischen Instituts* (Wien)
JWCI	*Journal of the Warburg and Courtauld Institutes* (London)
LGRM	W.H. Roscher (ed.), *Ausführliches Lexicon der Griechischen und Römischen Mythologie*, 8 vols., 1884–1937, Leipzig
MEFR	*Mélanges d'Archéologie et d'Histoire de l'École Française de Rome* (Paris)
OF	Otto Kern (ed.), *Orphicorum fragmenta*, 1922, Berlin (repr. 1963)
PCPhS	*Proceedings of the Cambridge Philological Society* (Cambridge)
PG	J.-P. Migne (ed.), *Patrologia – series graeca*, Paris
PMG	D.L. Page (ed.), *Poetae Melici Graeci*, 1972, Oxford
POxy	*The Oxyrhynchus Papyri*, 1898– , London
PP	*La Parola del Passato: Rivista di Studi antichi* (Napoli)
QUCC	*Quaderni Urbinati di Cultura Classica* (Roma)
RA	*Revue Archéologique* (Paris)
RBPH	*Revue Belge de Philologie et d'Histoire* (Bruxelles)
RE	Wissowa, G., Kroll, E., etc. (eds.), *Paulys Real-Encyclopädie der classischen Altertumswissenschaft*, 1893– , Stuttgart
REA	*Revue des Études Anciennes* (Bordeaux)
REG	*Revue des Études Grecques* (Paris)
RGVV	Religionsgeschichtliche Versuche und Vorarbeiten (Giessen, later Berlin)
RHDFE	*Revue Historique de Droit Français et Étranger* (Paris)
RhM	*Rheinisches Museum* (Frankfurt)
RHR	*Revue de l'Histoire des Religions* (Paris)
RIDA	*Revue Internationale des Droits de l'Antiquité* (Bruxelles)
RPhFE	*Revue Philosophique de la France et de l'étranger* (Paris)
SMSR	*Studi et Materiali di Storia delle Religioni* (Roma)
SVF	J. von Arnim (ed.), *Stoicorum Veterum Fragmenta*, 3 vols. with Index, 1905–24, Leipzig
TAPhA	*Transactions and Proceedings of the American Philological Association* (Cleveland)
YCS	*Yale Classical Studies* (New Haven)
ZPE	*Zeitschrift für Papyrologie und Epigraphik* (Bonn)

Notes

1. The union with Metis and the sovereignty of heaven

1 Hesiod, *Theogony* 886: Πρώτην . . . Μῆτιν ('First, Metis . . . '); 901: Δεύτερον . . . Θέμιν ('Second, Themis . . . '). Attention has often been drawn to the regular triadic structure of Hesiod's listing of Zeus's wives from *Theogony* 907 (marriage to Eurynomē following that to Themis) to 929, the end of the catalogue. I except lines 910–11, excised by Mazon (Budé edition) and Solmsen (OCT). From this point of view, Zeus's first two wives are separate from the rest of the series, both falling outside the triadic pattern of the catalogue of later marriages. The fact that they share this exceptional position is emphasized by the occurrence of the same formula to round off the passage devoted to each: ἀγαθόν τε κακόν τε ('good and evil'), 900 (Metis) and 906 (Themis).

2 If we think of this pair of female divinities from the human standpoint rather than that of the gods, they may be said to relate, in the same way, to opposite aspects of oracular activity. The oracular utterance of Themis reproduces the necessity and intransigence of the gods' decrees, which mortals cannot gainsay. Metis corresponds to that feature of the use of oracles which involves a tussle between gods and men, that discreet and dangerous game in which nothing is firmly settled beforehand, and in which the players have to know precisely the right moment to ask their question, to know whether to accept or reject the oracle, and even how to turn to their own advantage a response given by the god in favour of their opponent.

My understanding of the pair Themis–Metis may be of some help in making sense of Alcman's association between *Aisa* and *Poros* in his *Partheneion*, where he presents them as primal divinities, the 'oldest of the gods': γεραίτατοι [θιῶν] (= θεῶν) (or, in another reconstruction, [δαιμόνων] γεραίτατοι) [see Page's apparatus to lines 13–14; also p. 34]. Fränkel, 1975: 163–4, cf. 253, regards *Aisa* as the principle of destiny understood as absolute constraint, and *Poros* as a name for the scope for individual initiative which the future grants anyone intelligent enough to turn it to advantage. The relation between *Aisa* and *Themis* is obvious; and that between *Poros* and Metis would be apparent even without the evidence provided by Plato. The link between *Aisa* and *Poros*, taken as a compound and contrastive pair of forces, is exactly that between Themis and Metis. Let me add that although the passages in the *Theogony* concerning Metis and Themis both end with the same expression ἀγαθόν τε κακόν τε (see n. 1), the formula means precisely the opposite in each case. In the case of Metis, it refers to the good and the evil against which Metis warns Zeus in advance, so that the king of the gods will always be in a position to find a way of ensuring the first and escaping the second. But with Themis, it refers to the good and the evil assigned once and for all time to wretched mortals by the three *Moirai* [sometimes hereafter called 'Fates']. The names of the Moirai make it quite clear that there is no earthly way in which men can annul or deflect the destiny (*Aisa*) they serve out by virtue of the privilege granted them by Zeus 'possessed of *mētis*' (τιμὴν πόρε μητίετα Ζεύς, 904).

3 Μητίετα: *Th.* 56, 520, 904, 914; *Works and Days* [*WD*] 104; μητιόεις: *Th.* 286, 457; *WD* 51, 769.

4 The manuscript has πικράν, for which F.A. Paley and Goettling read μικράν. The question is whether we should follow Cook, 1914—40: 3.744 n. 4, and read πικράν, in the sense 'antidote' (the Greeks knew of one which they called 'sacred antidote', ἱερὰ πικρά). If so, Zeus would have persuaded Metis to turn herself into a few drops of liquid which he could easily take. That would be the inverse of the swallowing we find in the case of Cronus: Metis gets him to drink a *pharmakon* (philtre, charm, drug) which compels him to disgorge the gods he had intended to keep inside for ever. Zeus succeeds in changing Metis into a *pharmakon* so that he can swallow her, and keep her inside the pit of his belly for ever. [See also n. 22 below. Ed.]

5 See Schwartz, 1960: 343—56; and Cook, 1914—40: 3.734—5.

6 This is an ancient tradition, with connections with the version in Hesiod's *Theogony*: see Cook, 1914—40: 3.743 n. 9 and especially Kauer, 1959.

7 In this version, Hera in revenge goes off and produces Hephaestus partheno-genetically. Hephaestus is supreme among the gods in knowledge and skill of a practical-technical order, while Athena, to whom Zeus gives birth unaided, is supreme in all forms of pragmatic intelligence. [On this theme of Hera's 'spontaneous' parturition, see now Detienne, 1976: 75—81. Ed.]

8 The text has πολὺ διρεύουσαν 'for all her turning', for which Bergk reads πολυδηνή ἐοῦσαν 'clever though she was'. If we retain πολὺ διρεύουσαν, the 'turning' must be understood to mean Metis's metamorphoses, her constant shifting from one shape to another.

9 The scholiast says, 'Metis had the power of changing into any shape she wished' [on line 886, p. 110 di Gregorio].

10 Thetis and Peleus: see Apollodorus, *Bibliotheca* 3.13.5; cf. Pindar, *Nemean* 4.62 Snell; scholiast on Lycophron, *Alexandra* 175, 178 (1, pp. 85 and 88 Scheer); scholia on Apollonius of Rhodes, *Argonautika* 1.582 (p. 50. 19—20 Wendel); Quintus Smyrnaeus, *The Fall of Troy* (the '*Continuation of Homer*') 3.618—24; Ovid, *Metamorphoses* 11.229—65.
   Proteus and Menelaus: *Odyssey* 4.383—570.
   Nereus and Herakles: Apollodorus, *Bibliotheca* 2.5.11; scholiast on Apollonius of Rhodes, *Argonautika* 4.1396 (p. 315.22—3 Wendel).

11 See *Odyssey* 4.437, 453 (*dolos*, 'trick'); 441, 463 (*lochos*, 'ambush', 'trap'). The *dolos* which Idothea suggests is to disguise Menelaus and his friends by putting on seal-skins. Maybe, when the humans slip into the pelts of freshly-skinned sea-creatures, they don something of their adversary's slipperiness and share in his devious *mētis*.

12 Apollodorus, *Bibl.* 2.5.11: συλλαβὼν δὲ αὐτὸν κοιμώμενον, 'getting a grip on him as he slept'.

13 *Iliad* 385—91: Ares is shut up for thirteen months in a bronze jar, hog-tied by Ōtos and Ephialtes the sons of Alōeus, and would have perished (ἀπόλοιτο), insatiable god of war though he be, had Hermes not found a way of releasing him; and when he does escape, he is shrivelled and faded (ἤδη τειρόμενος).

14 Note the expressions φαγὼν δολόεσσαν ἐδωδήν, 'after eating the food of deception' (*OF* frg. 148) and τὸν διὰ μέλιτος δόλον, 'the trick with the honey' (Porphyry), for example; cf. Waszink, 1950: 639—53.

15 The first passage has δεσμὸν γὰρ αὐτῷ τὸν ὕπνον μεμηχανῆσθαι; the second τὸν γὰρ ὕπνον αὐτῷ μεμηχανῆσθαι δεσμὸν ὑπὸ τοῦ Διός.

16 Vian, 1960: 34 rightly observes that 'Ullikumi is a stone mass, blind and deaf, formidable only because he is so huge. Strictly speaking, he is, like Indian Vṛta, a symbol of passive resistance, a force of inertia, the Obstacle ... Typhoeus is something very different.'

17 Cf. *Theogony* 829—30, φωναὶ ... παντοίην ὄπ' ἱεῖσαι, 'noises of every conceivable kind ... ', and Antoninus Liberalis, *Metamorphoses* 28 [Typhon].1, φωνὰς δὲ παντοίας ἡφίει.

18 Nonnus of Panopolis, *Dionysiaka* 1.157—62; 2.250—7, 367—70; scholiast on
. Aeschylus, *Prometheus Bound* 351 (p. 123.12 Herington); see also West, 1966:
386.

19 Hesiod's text heavily stresses the affinity between the chaotic pit of Tartarus,
the disorderly nature of Typhoeus and the whirlwinds' confusion: compare
Theogony 742 (Tartarus), 832—5 (Typhoeus) and 875—6 (whirlwinds).

20 In the technical sense in which the word is used by historians of religion.

21 See on this point Rudhardt, 1971: 94—7, who makes 'the correlation between
the myths about Styx and those concerning ambrosia' quite plain.

22 My whole argument provides, I think, good reasons for accepting Cook's
retention of πικράν, 'antidote', in the scholion to *Theogony* 886, in keeping
with the manuscript reading (see n. 4 above).

2. The 'Sea-Crow'

1 See for example Keller, 1909—13: 2.243; Steier, 1932: 2412—18; Thompson,
1936: 27—9, and 1938: 335—9.

2 A similar confusion is characteristic of the Latin term *mergus*, gull: André,
1967: 101—3.

3 Scholiast on the *Odyssey* 5.66 [p. 248 Dindorf] (cf. on 1.441 too) and
Hesychius, s.v. αἴθυιαι 1, no. 1893 Latte. We should perhaps identify this 'sea
crow' with a subspecies of the Manx Shearwater, *Puffinus puffinus yelkouan*,
with Thompson, 1938 and André, 1967: 61. [This bird is local to islands and
coasts of the Adriatic, Aegean and Black Seas, and is certainly compatible in
behaviour and density of population with ancient accounts of the *aithuia*: see
most recently Cramp, 1977: 145—50. Ed.]

4 Such an account is given by Dionysius Periegetes, *Ixeuticon* 2.5 (p. 26, 15 ff.
Garzya), of the *laros*; but the terms *laros* and *aithuia* are so closely associated,
and even confused, that the shift from one to the other is easy: see Steier,
. 1932: 2414—16. [Such a confusion seems to me more likely in learned tradition, among scholars for whom all sea-birds are more or less indistinguishable,
than among actual sea-farers in the Archaic period: we have only to remember
Lévi-Strauss's observation that traditional societies tend to be extremely
observant of natural distinctions (1966a). Ed.]

5 Theophrastus, *On weather-signs* 2.28; Aratus, *Phaenomena* 950 Martin;
Scholiast on Aratus, *Phaenomena* 918 (p. 511. 10 ff. Maass).

6 Two studies have been devoted to Athena *aithuia*; one of them (Kiock, 1915:
127—33) collected a number of relevant passages, and the other (Anti, 1920:
270—318) drew attention to a number of monuments which could be representations of a marine Athena either clad in a cloak covered in stars (cf.
phôsphoros) or accompanied by a sea-bird. Neither of them paid any attention
to the rôle of *mētis* in Greek thinking about Athena of the sea.

7 In this context, the *erōidios* is doubtless some species of heron, perhaps the
Night Heron (*Nycticorax nycticorax*) [or the Squacco Heron (*Ardeola
ralloides*). Ed.].

8 Cf. *Iliad* 10.242—7 (Diomedes speaking):
'If indeed you tell me myself to pick my companion,
how then could I forget Odysseus the godlike, he whose
heart and whose proud spirit are beyond all others forward
in all hard endeavours, and Pallas Athene loves him.
Were he go to with me, both of us could come back from the blazing
of fire itself, since his mind is best at devices' (ἐπεὶ περίοιδε νοῆσαι).
(tr. Lattimore)

9 There is a definite parallelism between Jason 'with one sandal' (*monokrēpis*)
and the *Argo* that loses part of its stern: just as Jason loses one of his sandals

233

while crossing a ford (a *poros*) and thus becomes fit to undertake the expedition to fetch the Golden Fleece, so the *Argo* (and the bird which precedes it through the Symplegades, a *poros* at sea) is marked in a very similar way in a very similar location. Roux, 1949: 92—3, has rightly pointed out the initiatory character of this incident.

10 See Usener, 1899: 254; Krappe, 1936: 245—6; Hornell, 1946: 142—9; Barnett, 1958: 228—30; David, 1960: 153—60; Wachsmuth, 1967: 189—92.

11 Note especially Pliny, *Historia naturalis* 6.83 (on a custom reported from Taprobanes = Ceylon); Charon of Lampsacus in *FGrH* 262 F 3; Asclepiades of Tragilus in *FGrH* 12 F 2b; Scholiast on Apollonius of Rhodes, *Argonautika* 2.328A etc.

12 For example, Sophocles, *Antigone* 590; Pindar, *Pythian* 4.209 Snell; *Isthmian* 3/4.18a Snell. [Also Alcaeus frg. 37 Edmonds = frg. Z2 (326) Lobel—Page. Ed.]

13 For 'left, right' see *Odyssey* 5.327; in *Iliad* 23.320 it is used metaphorically, for the path of the charioteer who drives without *mētis* — 'all over the place'. For 'up, down', see Verdenius, 1964: 387.

14 For example, Pindar, *Pythian* 3.104—5 Snell; *Isthmian* 3/4.23—4 Snell; *Olympian* 7.94—5.

15 For example, Euripides, *Ion* 1506; Aristophanes, *Peace* 945 Hall—Geldart; Plato, *Republic* 6, 508d. The most recent treatment of the sea in Greek thought is Wachsmuth, 1967: 202ff.

16 See Hesiod, *Theogony* 360. According to [Plato], *Axiochus* 368b, when man (who is defined as one who ought to live on the land) launched himself on to the deep as though he were amphibian, he became entirely the plaything of *Tyche*.

17 Aeschylus, *Suppliant Women* 523: πειθὼ δ' ἔποιτο καὶ τύχη πρακτήριος, 'may Persuasion and Fortune attend me!' (tr. Benardete). *Praktērios* here means 'achieving the goal'.

18 A passage in Plato's *Laws* shows this admirably (4, 709b—c). The Athenian observes that one might be tempted to say that human history is nearly all a matter of chance (τύχας δ' εἶναι σχεδὸν ἅπαντα τὰ ἀνθρώπινα πράγματα). 'Still, the same may be said of the arts of the sailor, and the pilot, and the physician, and the general, and may seem to be well said; and yet one can say something else about them no less plausibly ... That God governs all things, and that chance (*Tyche*) and opportunity (*Kairos*) co-operate with him in the government of human affairs. There is, however, a third and less extreme view, that art (*technē*) should be there also; for I should say that in a storm there must surely be a great advantage if the pilot's art can use the opportunity which it affords' (tr. Jowett, slightly altered).

19 The inscriptions have been studied by Guarducci, 1966: 279—94, though she misunderstands the significance of this new *Kairos*. First of all, she does not take the inscription to Poseidon *asphaleios* ('the securer') (no. 1) separately from the other three (which date from the fifth century and were all found in the same small sacred enclosure), even though she herself dates it to the first half of the fourth century BC. Secondly, she translates *Kairos*'s epithet *Olumpios* as 'of/from Olympia' instead of 'Olympian'. Kairos of course is the 'youngest child of Zeus' (Ion of Chios, quoted by Pausanias 5.14.9). My own interpretation follows Pugliese-Carratelli, 1970: 248—9 and 1971: 347—53, the latter of which answers Guarducci, 1971: 124—41.

20 See Arrian, *Periplus Ponti Euxini* 37 (in *GGrM* 1.401); Marcianus of Heraclea, *Epitome peripli maris interni Menippi* 7 (in *GGrM* 1.568—9), both cited by Cook, 1914—40: 3.142 nn. 10—11 (and cf. p. 148).

21 *Pontos Axeinos* is the oldest form of the Greek name for the Black Sea, and represents a version of Scytho-Iranian *axsaena*, 'dark'. *Axeinos* means 'un-

friendly to strangers' and was changed euphemistically into *Euxinos*: see Danoff, 1962: 951—2.

22 Note a lyric passage in Sophocles, *Philoctetes* 855, where the context twice stresses the significance of *kairos* (837—8 and 862—3). [The image of 'fair wind' here is clearly motivated by what Neoptolemus has said a few lines earlier, 779—81. Ed.] See also Aeschylus, *Choephori* 812—14 and Homeric *Hymn* 7 (to Dionysus) 26 (οὖρον ὄρα).

23 Aeschylus, *Suppliant Women* 592—4 (lyric):
<αὐτὸς ὁ> πατὴρ φυτουργὸς αὐτόχειρ ἄναξ,
γένους παλαιόφρων μέγας
τέκτων, τὸ πᾶν
μῆχαρ οὔριος Ζεύς.
'The father I urge of my green life I Whose own hand has sown me I Lord I Ancient in wisdom I Who crafted my people I Allhelp I Whose fair breath has sped me' (tr. Lembke, lines 794—801). *Mēchar* in 594 is connected with the word *mēchanē*, 'contrivance'.

24 Alcaeus, frg. 249 Lobel—Page (= *POxy* 2298, fr. 1, l. 6ff.), with Barner's excellent commentary (1967: 113—26).

25 Note Pindar, *Nemean* 7.17—18 (Snell):
σοφοὶ δὲ μέλλοντα τριταῖον ἄνεμον
ἔμαθον, οὐδ᾿ ὑπὸ κέρδει βλάβεν.
'Wise men know when the third wind is coming, and avarice does not distort their judgement' (tr. Lloyd-Jones. [By ignoring the context, D. misinterprets these lines, which have nothing to do with 'winds that will blow in two days' time' as he suggests (p. 213 n. 56 of the original). 'The third wind is the wind that will stir up the third and most formidable of three successive waves ... "Wise men" in Pindar often means "poets", but the wise men here are clearly not poets; they are men who have done noble deeds, and are not prevented by avarice from spending money to ensure that the memory of these deeds will live in poetry' (Lloyd-Jones, 1973: 130). Ed.] But according to Pausanias, when the wind which would enable the Greeks to leave Aulis for Troy suddenly (ἐξαίφνης) started to blow, everyone was taken by surprise and consequently sacrificed to Artemis the first animal to come to hand, whether male or female (9.19.7). Cf. Callimachus, fr. 200b Pfeiffer [on Artemis Colaenis, worshipped at Amarynthus in Euboea].

26 Lines 335—7 Jebb: τοῦτο καὶ πολιοῦ πέραν
πόντου χειμερίῳ νότῳ
χωρεῖ, περιβρυχίοισιν
περῶν ὑπ᾿ οἴδμασιν ...   (= 334—7 Pearson)
'[Man is] the power that crosses the white sea, driven by the stormy south-wind, making a path under surges that threaten to engulf him' (tr. Jebb).

27 Pindar, *Olympian* 7.94—5 Snell; cf. *Pythian* 3.104—5; *Isthmian* 3/4.23—4 Snell.

28 Note Aratus, *Phaenomena* 761—2 Martin:
μόχθος μέν τ᾿ ὀλίγος, τὸ δὲ μυρίον αὐτίκ᾿ ὄνειαρ
γίνετ᾿ ἐπιφροσύνης αἰεὶ πεφυλαγμένῳ ἀνδρί
'Small is the trouble, and thousandfold the reward of his heedfulness who ever takes care' (tr. Mair).

29 Just like 'wily' (*polumētis*) Odysseus, in fact, who expertly steers his ship from his seat by the steering-oar (*Odyssey* 5.269—77, and see p. 32 below). Note also Aeschylus, *Seven against Thebes* 2—3:
ὅστις φυλάσσει πρᾶγος ἐν πρύμνῃ πόλεως
οἴακα νωμῶν, βλέφαρα μὴ κοιμῶν ὕπνῳ
'[he] that in the city's prow watches the event I and guides the rudder, his

eye not dropped in sleep' (tr. Grene, slightly changed), with Van Nes, 1963: 122–8.

30 Ἄστροις τεκμαίρεσθαι or σημειοῦσθαι, 'to calculate from the stars', is a proverbial expression for those who undertake long solitary voyages: Hesychius, s.v. ἄστροις σημειοῦσθαι (1, no. 7911 Latte); Suda, s.v. ἀστρονομία (1, no. 4257 Adler); Diogenianus paroemiographus, s.v. ἄστροις σημαίνεσθαι [2.66] (*Corpus paroemiog. graec.*, edd. Leutsch and Schneidewin, 1: 206, with Leutsch's notes); Eustathius, *Comment in Hom. Od. 5.276* (p. 1535.58–1536.3).

31 *Tekmōr/tekmar* means both a reference-point or land-mark and the design of an intelligent creature capable of making sense of such a topographical 'sign' (see Detienne and Vernant, 1978: 148–53 and 288–9). Texts relevant to *ithunein* in a nautical sense are to be found from the Homeric epics to the end of antiquity: for example, *Iliad* 23.316–17; Aratus, *Phaenomena* 44 Martin; Apollonius of Rhodes, *Argonautika* 1.562 (ἐξιθύνειν).

32 Indeed, the pilot's intelligence can be said to be stochastic in nature: Maximus of Tyre, *Dialexeis* 30.2 (p. 352.13 ff. Hobein).

33 Like Hermes ὁδαῖος ('of the road/roadside') or πομπαῖος ('conductor', 'guide'), [or ἡγεμόνιος ('guide')] ; or Artemis ἡγεμόνη ('guide'). Wide, 1893: 61, translated *keleutheia* as 'protector of the path', while Farnell related the name of the place where Athena *Keleutheia* was worshipped to her name, and saw her as 'the divine *starter* of the race' (1896–1909: 1.311). See also Gruppe, 1906: 1216 n. 3.

34 Frisk, 1954–72: 1.815 (s.v. κέλευθος) reviews various etymologies unfavourably. Pisani, 1929: 9–10 and 1943–4: 552–4, has offered two different etymologies, neither of them convincing [1929: *κε [particle in κεῖνος/ἐκεῖ etc.] + *λευθ-/λουθ- [root of ἐλεύσομαι] ; 1943–4: *κελο-/λευθος. Ed.].

35 Callimachus, *Bath of Pallas* 13–32 mentions Athena running in the *diaulos* [once up and down the stadium, about 400 yards: Gardiner, 1910: 51, 280, 382], which enables him to link her with the Dioscuri, one of whom, Castor, was supposed to have won the very first foot-race at Olympia (Pausanias 5.8.4): see Cahen's commentary, 1930: 225.

36 Kaibel 795, quoting Pausanias 5.15.4. Kaibel also compares this dedication of Roman date to an epigram by Philoxenos (*Anthol. Palat.* 9.319 = Gow–Page, *Hellenistic Epigrams* p. 165; ? second half of third century), lines 3–4 of which read: ἀλλὰ πονεῖτε/μαλθακὸν ἐκ γονάτων ὄκνον ἀπωσάμενοι, 'strive then, driving soft reluctance from your knees!' [see also the remarks of Gow–Page, II p. 479–80. Ed.].

37 In the Gulf of Magnesia there was a place called *Aphetai*. Herodotus 7.193, says that the Argonauts intended to take on water there and 'launch out' into the open sea (εἰς τὸ πέλαγος ἀφήσειν).

38 Close by there were two altars of gods with the epithet *Amboulios* ('counsellor'), one of Zeus and Athena jointly, the other of the Dioscuri.

39 'Good starts' would also imply 'good finishes' too; inasmuch as both are points of change, they are both dangerous: note for example Greek rituals connected with embarking and disembarking, or the practice of making sacrifices before one started off (Popp, 1959: 63ff.).

40 The word *terma* is used (in the plural) in *Odyssey* 8.193 to mean the marker indicating the point at which a discus hits the ground: Odysseus threw the discus far beyond everyone else, and Athena, in the guise of a man, 'marked the throw' (ἔθηκε δὲ τέρματ' Ἀθήνη). In the games described in *Iliad* 23, *terma* means the turning-post (e.g. 358: 'Achilles pointed out the turning-post', σήμηνε δὲ τέρματ' Ἀχιλλεύς, to the competing charioteers as they line up at the start).

41 There were some exceptions. For example de Ridder, 1912: 523–8, saw her as

the Athena who preserves the laws, 'the august guardian of the city' (Athena βουλαῖα ['with a statue in the council-chamber'/'giving good counsel'] or πολιοῦχος ['protector of the city.']). He supposed her to be gazing at an inscription on the stela.

42 Fairbanks, 1902: 410–16 had earlier advocated the thesis that this was an Athena who presided over the games in the Palaestra.

43 To the extent that he recognizes that the notion of *kairos* is important, Chamoux does allow *mētis* its proper place in explaining Athena's relation to the palaestra (1972: 266).

44 See Rayet and Collignon, 1888: 143–52, and the fuller description in Furtwängler, 1885: 1, nos. 347–473 (Poseidon alone); 474–537 (Poseidon with Amphitrite) + 3920, 3921; 646–61 + 3924 (ships); 787–845 (double-sided *pinakes* with the same subjects).

45 As Aelius Aristeides points out, Athena has a double relation to Poseidon, inasmuch as he is god 'of horses' (ἵππιος) and 'of the sea' (πόντιος): *Oration* 37.20 Keil.

46 Ships can be said to be the 'horses of the sea': *Odyssey* 4.707–9; Artemidorus, *Interpretation of Dreams* 1.56 (p. 64.17 Pack); cf. the direct comparison between chariot-horses and ship in *Odyssey* 13.81–5. The horse is 'yoke-bearing', or 'enduring' φερέζυγος (Ibycus frg. 287.6 *PMG*), just as the ship is (Alcaeus frg. 249.3 Lobel—Page). Herodotus uses the word *kelēs* to mean 'riding horse' (7.86) as well as a fast, light galley (8.94) [– a usage commonplace in the fifth century. I have omitted the rest of this note which is misleading. Ed.].

47 The anchor is sometimes called χαλινός, 'bit and bridle', as in *IG* II² 1610.2.14; Euripides, *Hecuba* 539 (χαλινωτήρια); Pindar, *Pythian* 4.24–5; Oppian, *Halieutikon* 1.229. In a densely metaphorical passage, Aeschylus calls horses' bits 'steering-oars in horses' mouths':

> ἱππικοί τ' ἄπυον πηδαλίων διὰ στόμια
> πυριγενετᾶν χαλινοί
> (*Seven against Thebes* 206–7: lyric)

an image picked up by Euripides in an extended comparison of Hippolytus trying to stop his chariot-horses from bolting with a man hauling at the oar (*Hippolytus* 1221–6). A fragment of Sophocles, twice quoted by Plutarch, uses οἴαξ 'steering oar' and χαλινός 'bit/bridle' as virtual synonyms (frg. 869 Radt), a usage Plutarch appropriates to himself (*De Iside et Osiride* 45, 369c). [I have made some alterations to this note. Ed.]

48 Apollodorus, *Bibliotheca* 2.1.4; Hyginus, *Fabulae* 277 (end); Eustathius, *Comment. in Hom. Iliadem* 1.42 (p. 37, 22–8); cf. Waser, 1901: 2095, and 2096–7.

49 Compare Hesiod, *Works and Days* 430–1 ('servants of Athena' making ploughs); Diodorus Siculus 5. 73.8 (Athena as the teacher of all kinds of *epistēmai*, 'knowhow'); *Anthologia Palatina* 6.204, 205 (= Gow—Page, *Hellenistic Epigrams*, Leonidas VII, VIII [p. 109]).

50 Αἴθυια δέ, ὅτι καὶ πλοῖα ἡ φρόνησις κατεσκεύασε καὶ δίκην αἰθυίας ἐδίδαξε τοὺς ἀνθρώπους ναυτίλλεσθαι ἐπ' αὐτῶν διαπεραινομένους τὴν θάλασσαν (Schol. in *Lycophr. Alexandran* 359, p. 139.27–30 Scheer).

51 For the meaning of ξέω as 'scrape', 'plane', 'polish', see Chapot, 1887–1919: 333–4, and Orlandos, 1966–8: 1.42–3.

52 For the methods Odysseus uses, and the type of ship, see Casson, 1964: 61–4, and 1971: 217–19. [Note his earlier remark, p. 202: 'a form of ship-building . . . so refined that it more resembles cabinet-work than carpentry'. Ed.]

53 *Odyssey* 17.341; 21.44; 23.197; Sophocles, frg. 474.5 (p. 384 Radt).

54 The image is used in a moral sense by Theogonis, *Elegies* 945–6:

> εἴμι παρὰ στάθμην ὀρθὴν ὀδόν, οὐδετέρωσε
> κλινόμεονς · χρὴ γάρ μ' ἄρτια πάντα νοεῖν,

'I'll walk a path straight as a line, inclining to neither side: for all my thoughts must be right-formed.' For the sense, see Van Groningen, 1966: 325 on line 856. The line as an image of straight-thinking is to be found elsewhere in Theogonis, for example 534—4 and 805—10 Bergk (with Van Groningen, 1966: 215, 309).

55 Note *Iliad* 8.109—10; 11.527—8; 24.149—50 = 178—9, 362 [though in none of these cases is there any question of *mētis*: the first two emphasize only determination to enter battle, while in the citations from Book 24 *ithunein* means scarcely more than 'drive'. Ed.] ; [Hesiod] , *Shield of Heracles* 323—34 [again, *ithunein* simply means 'drive' — a goal is not even mentioned. Ed.] .

56 [Translated by W.H.D. Rouse. Victor Bérard's French is much wittier: 'Dugaillard, Vitenmer, Laviron, Lenocher, Delaproue, Dubord, Delamare, Dularge . . . '.]

57 As held by Dümmler, 1896: 1944; Gruppe, 1906: 1215 n. 7 and Nilsson, 1967: 439 for example.

58 Pausanias 4.35.8 mentions an Athena ἀνεμῶτις ('stiller of winds'), who at Diomedes's entreaty stilled forever the violence of the winds in the area of Mothone (on the SW coast of Messenia).

59 The word used here is ἐλαύνειν ('drive') not ἰθύνειν ('guide [straight] '), the ship being propelled by the oarsmen's arms (cf. *Odyssey* 13.76—8).

60 As happens to the ship which has taken Odysseus back to Ithaca, on the return journey: *Odyssey* 13.162—4.

61 The quadrennial festival at Sounion, involving a theoric ship (Herodotus 6.87) and a trireme race (Lysias, *Oration* 21.5), was probably in honour of Poseidon (so Deubner, 1932: 215 [following Schoemann]).

62 The name *Phrontis* is as expressive as that of the boatman *Noëmōn* son of *Phronios* ('Knowing, son of Clever') from whom Athena obtains a ship for Telemachus's voyage (*Odyssey* 2.386).

63 φράζομαι ('consider', 'ponder') belongs to the language of *mētis*: note *Odyssey* 3.126—9; 11.510—11.

64 See Scholiast on Aratus, *Phaenomena* 351 (p. 411.19 ff. Maass); Geminus, *Eisagoge* 2; Eustathius, *Commentarius in Dionysium Periegeten* 11, in *GGrM* 2, p. 219; and Rehm, 1919: 1882; Röder, 1919: 1873.

65 See Blinkenberg and Kinch, 1931—60: 2.1 Chronique du temple (no. 2) B § XII = lines 73—4 (cols. 165—6). [In keeping with Blinkenberg's rather odd convention, I have not added accents or breathings. Ed.]

66 Soon after the ship has entered the Black Sea. The opposition between the two helmsmen was noted, with some sarcasm, by La Ville de Mirmont, 1895: 280—2.

67 [It should be noted that Euphemus, as well as Tiphys, plays an important part in this episode; not only does he release the rock-dove, but he encourages the Argonauts to row immediately after Tiphys has avoided the giant wave (588—90). Tiphys does not seem to me to be given as impressive a part in the passage of the Symplegades in Apollonius's version as D. implies. Ed.]

68 [This account too is rather misleading, when placed in context. Everyone is very relieved after the passage of the Symplegades (607: ἀνέπνεον), feeling they have been saved from death; relieved rather than despondent. Tiphys's speech is mainly about Athena's miraculous intervention, and relies for its hope entirely upon Phineus's prediction (615—18). Finally, Jason's speech immediately afterwards (622—37), though 'despondent', is deliberately intended to test the heroes (recalling Odysseus's comment on Agamemnon's parallel speech in *Iliad* 2.190—7). They duly shout back confidently (638—9). Ed.]

69 [The beam had spoken before, even when Tiphys was alive — right at the beginning of the expedition (1.524—7). More generally, it must be understood that the misfortunes the Argonauts suffer on the return journey are a direct result

of the murder of Apsyrtus and Zeus's subsequent anger (4.557—61 etc.). In this situation merely human skill, assisted or not by Athena, can be of little use. Ed.]

70 [It should be noted that 'all those who knew about ships' agree with Ankaios's point here (4.1277—8) — as well they might, since the Argonauts end up by having to carry the *Argo* bodily to Lake Tritonis (4.1566—9). Ed.]

71 [This is misleading: the prophetic beam says that Polydeukes and Castor (who are of course members of the expedition) are to pray the gods to open 'paths [through the sea] of Ausonia', where they will find Circe. They do so, and the ship finds its way to the river Rhodanus without difficulty (4.627). While the ship is in the 'charge of the Dioscuri', it is constantly aided by Hera — including one of the passages D. has already quoted to show how useless Ankaios is (4.640—4). I see no reason to suppose that it is anything but the special relationship between the Dioscuri and Zeus that makes it appropriate for Apollonius to introduce them here; and they are certainly not heard of again. There is an obvious 'aetiological' point too: Apollonius can explain the origin of the cult of the Dioscuri on the Stoichades (651—5). Ed.]

72 [In fact it was the prophetic beam which told the Argonauts to do this. Ed.]

73 It is in terms of the same contrast, of black against white, that another marine divinity, Thetis, is presented in Book Four of the *Argonautika*, where she plays a role in the passage of the *Planktai*, the Wandering Rocks, analogous to that of Athena in Book 2. Like Metis, she is a marine deity; and she figures in Alcman's cosmology as a great primordial goddess whose emergence at the heart of a chaotic world wrapped in darkness gives birth to daylight and the brilliant shimmer of the stars. As a divinity of the primordial waters, her power, older still than that of Poseidon, partially doubles his in some parts of the Greek world. For example, when a terrible storm pounced on the Persian fleet off Cape Sepias (in Magnesia, to the north of Euboea), the Magi tried to stop it by sacrificing to Thetis and the Nereids, besides making offerings and chanting prayers at the top of their voices to the howling winds (Herodotus 7.191). But in the passage of the *Argonautika*, Thetis acts just like Athena — with the help of the Nereids (who are explicitly likened to *aithuiai*: 4.966—7), she takes hold of the *Argo* by the stern and shoves it forward; just like Athena earlier, she opens up a path for the Argonauts' ship and guides it through the crooked rocks (Θέτις δ᾽ ἴθυνε κέλευθον: 4.938). [Immediately afterwards, however, the Nereids are imagined as girls playing ball on the beach — they pass the *Argo* from hand to hand over the rocks and water, for the length of a spring day: 4.948—63. Ed.]

But though the resemblance is close, the comparison cannot be pursued, at least on the level at which I am working — a structural analysis of the Olympian deities. For though, like Athena, Thetis is a goddess who employs *mētis*, she does not belong to the same generation — unlike Poseidon or the Dioscuri. As a primordial power possessed of *mētis*, she transcends, like Metis herself, the different modes and particular forms of the *mētis* of the Olympian gods, as revealed by the specific categories of action of Athena, Hermes, Aphrodite, Hephaestus and Zeus. That being so, Thetis *may* intervene in the same way as Athena does — she might equally have appeared as a ship-wright; but her *mētis* is fundamentally non-specific (see further, Vernant in Detienne and Vernant, 1978: 141—2).

4. Sacrificial and alimentary codes in Hesiod's myth of Prometheus

1 In his rôle as the organizer of the first sacrifice, Prometheus does not appear as the actual slaughterer of the animal. Rather, he it is who brings it to the spot, and who divides it up before lighting the fire on the altar. A quasi-

technical language is used of what he does: ὀστέα λευκὰ βοὸς . . . εὐθετίσας
κατέθηκε καλύψας ἀργέτι δημῷ (540—1). Above all, his function is to distribute, to divide among the onlookers, the parts of the sacrificial victim:
δασσάμενος in 537, διεδάσσαο μοίρας in 544. This function, which is essential,
if hardly highlighted, in the ritual of sacrifice, is heavily stressed in the context
of the *Theogony* itself.

2 I say Zeus 'appears' to be tricked, because in Hesiod's *Theogony* all that comes
to pass in the universe does so in the final analysis because of the god's sovereign will, because he has planned it so, because of his *boulē*. Prometheus's trick
is thus, in a sense, part of Zeus's plan, since he already intended to give men
the miserable lot which is theirs. Besides, at the very moment at which the
Titan presents him with the choice between the deceptive portions, that he
may take that which is to belong to the gods, the text immediately makes clear
that 'Zeus, whose wisdom is everlasting, perceived the trick and did not mistake it. But he indited in his heart evil against mortal men, that was indeed to
come to pass' (551—2). Does that mean that everything is ordained in advance,
and that in this struggle whose issue is in a sense foreordained there is no place
either for a genuine confrontation or for any initiative, let alone success, even
of a temporary kind, for Prometheus? To think so would be to misunderstand
the logic of the text. Although it affirms, as a truth in principle, the infallibility
of Zeus, it takes great pains to stress, as the action unfolds, Prometheus's
achievements, the successes he scores, Zeus's disconcertion and wrath at seeing
himself first countered and then duped by the Titan (cf. *Th.* 533: χωόμενος;
554: χώσατο, χόλος; 568: ἐχόλωσε; *WD* 53: χολωσάμενος). *Works and Days*
says that the cause of his anger was Prometheus's theft of fire λαθὼν Δία (52),
'unbeknown to Zeus'. The latter addresses the Titan in the following words:
'It gives you joy to have stolen fire and to have cozened my wits (ἐμὰς φρένας
ἠπεροπεύσας: 55).' If we should accept that Zeus has foreseen all, we must at
once add that this foresight involved Prometheus's taking the initiative in entering into competition with him, succeeding in deceiving him, the king of the
gods being furious, and bringing to pass evil for men, not directly, but by
means of the very advantages that their protector had wrung from him. If one
feels tempted to find such an interpretation too 'sophisticated', one may
remember that Christian theology affirms simultaneously the omnipotence and
omniscience of God and a freedom of choice for man, which implies that his
decisions are not predestined. To go back to Hesiod, let me just point out that
if, in the *Theogony*, Cronus devours his first children, he does so because he
has discovered from Gaia and Ouranos that his destiny is fixed: his doom is one
day to fall to his own son 'by the plan of mighty Zeus' (465). Yet Zeus has not
yet been born. Things are then going to happen according to the plans of Zeus,
Διὸς . . . διὰ βουλάς, even before Zeus enters the world of the gods, and before
he could possibly make plans.

3 The episode as a whole is characterized by this seesaw effect: it is only at the
end of the struggle, when the game is played and over, that the assertion that
everything that happens is at every moment the consequence of the will of
Zeus becomes true. This does not mean that Prometheus has not scored points
during his confrontation, any more than that, in the war between Olympians
and Titans, the fact that the issue is decided in advance (Cronus's destiny to be
overcome by his son) means that the battle cannot remain uncertain for ten
whole years (637—8). The narrative technique is to propose from the outset a
Zeus who sees everything in advance, only to show him later twice surprised
and tricked before his victorious counterattack. Its purpose is to reveal progressively to the reader, by the use of a narrative in dramatic form, the
deceptive nature of Prometheus's gifts, whose doubtful blessings always in the
end recoil on their recipients.

4   *Th.* 535, 552, 564, 588, 592, 600; *WD* 92, 103.
5   ἐπὶ χθονί: *Th.* 556, 564; *WD* 90; cf. also 101.
6   κακόν, κακά: *Th.* 512, 551–2, 595, 600, 602, 609, 612. κήδεα λυγρά: *WD* 49, 95, 100; πῆμα: 56; κακόν, κακά: *WD* 58, 88, 91, 101.
7   ἀλφηστής, one who eats barley: *Th.* 512 and *WD* 82. These are the only passages in the two poems in which the word is used of men (elsewhere, cf. Hesiod fr. 73, line 5, Merkelbach—West, Atalanta hoping to escape marriage with ἀνδρῶν ἀλφηστάων, and the *Shield of Heracles* 29, where the epithet serves to register a distinction between gods and the human followers of Alcmene's husband). In each case, the word is applied to men in the context of the appearance of Pandora, first woman and wife. The link between marriage and the production of corn is already obvious here. As Pierre Vidal-Naquet observes, following Chantraine (p. 245 n. 8 below), *alphēstēs*, eater of bread, is formed from the root *ed-od*, eat. It is therefore a parallel, if inverse, formation to *ōmēstēs*, one who devours meat raw.
8   *Th.* 513–14, 592, 600–1, 603–12; *WD* 80–2, 94 ff.
9   Cf. frg. 1, Merkelbach—West = 82 Rzach: 'For in those days Immortals and mortals shared together their meals and their places.'
10 Cf. *Odyssey* 3.44, 336; *Iliad* 24.69. The expression *dais theou* or *theōn* stresses the aspect of division in the sacrificial meal, between men on one hand, and between men and gods on the other. On the idea of a gift, cf. Plato, *Euthyphro* 14c8–9: 'Does not to sacrifice mean to offer gifts to the gods?'
11 *WD* 112 ff. In the reign of Cronus, the men of the Age of Gold lived ὡς θεοί, like gods: permanently youthful, sheltered from pain, troubles, work and old age; far from all evil, κακῶν ἔκτοσθεν ἁπάντων, they enjoyed every good thing, ἐσθλὰ δὲ πάντα τοῖσιν ἔην; and they spent their time making merry at the feasts which the furrows of a generous and fertile earth of their own accord made ready for them, without any need for toil: ζείδωρος ἄρουρα αὐτομάτη.
12 Hesiod's text makes no mention of the *splankhna*, the internal organs. Given the religious significance of the viscera and their ritual consumption, this cannot be merely the consequence of forgetfulness. The poet's omission is intentional: he wishes only to take into consideration the two portions of the victim whose different allocation and treatment unequivocally point up the contrast between the tribe of the gods 'who live forever', and the tribe of mortal men who, in order to live, must submit to the necessity of eating a certain kind of food. As organs filled with blood, and roasted directly on the altar-flames, the *splankhna*, while constituting a human food, also belonged to the gods. Such a classification muddles the sharp cleavage between the two different kinds of ontological status (cf. Detienne, 1979a: 84–7). That is why Hesiod uses the word *enkata*, entrails, to refer to the animal's innards along with the flesh in which they are enclosed (*sarkai*). The *enkata* include the *entera*, the intestines, as well as the viscera proper — that is, the digestive organs and the organs filled with blood (cf. Berthiaume, 1976). By taking flesh and entrails together (σάρκας τε καὶ ἔγκατα πίονα δημῷ, 538) as parts of the victim which are equally available for eating by men, by contrast to the *ostea leuka* (540), reserved for the gods, Hesiod succeeds up to a point in obscuring the problem of the *splankhna*, which men eat but whose sacrificial status will not allow to be fully equated with the *krea* or *sarkai* [= what we would mean by 'red meat', viz., striated muscle and the surrounding fat. Ed.]. The ambiguity of the word *enkata*, which can mean intestines (*Odyssey* 9.293) or viscera (*Od.* 12.363–3) indifferently, allows him, without actually compromising himself, to lump together everything which cannot be classified as *ostea leuka*, white bones. [Cf. now J.-L. Durand in Detienne and Vernant, 1979: 139–50.]
13 *Th.* 74, 112: ὥς τ' ἄφενος δάσσαντο καί ὡς τιμὰς διέλοντο; 885: ὁ δὲ τοῖσιν ἐὰς διεδάσσατο τιμάς.

14 *Th.* 535–6: '(It was) when gods and mortal men separated themselves, ἐκρίνοντο, at Mēkōnē.'

15 Compare *Th.* 535: ἐκρίνοντο; 537 and 544: διεδάσσαο (Prometheus, in the quarrel between men and gods), with *Th.* 882: κρίναντο and 885: διεδάσσατο (Zeus, in the quarrel between Titans and Olympians).

16 Prometheus to Zeus: Ζεῦ κύδιστε μέγιστε θεῶν (*Th.* 548); Zeus to Prometheus: πάντων ἀριδείκετ' ἀνάκτων (*Th.* 543). Note especially Zeus's employment of the word *pepōn* (544 and 560), which, denoting 'well-cooked', 'mild', 'kindly', contains an element of humour under the circumstances. Throughout this passage of the *Theogony* Zeus is given by Hesiod the epithet ἄφθιτα μήδεα εἰδώς, 'whose wisdom is everlasting' (545, 550, 561); and at the height of his anger, the god calls Prometheus πάντων πέρι μήδεα εἰδώς, 'clever beyond all creatures' (559), according his rival his own proper epithet. During their confrontation, the two antagonists never cease to be courteous to one another; indeed, they play the gentleman by concealing their enmity beneath smiles, and cloaking aggression with raillery. If in *Works and Days* Zeus, furiously angry (χολωσάμενος, 53), laughs out loud (ἐγέλασσε, 59), in the *Theogony* the Titan's small smile (ἐπιμειδήσας, 547) is his response to Zeus's taunts (κερτομέων, 545), while he plans his treacherous move (δολίη τέχνη), makes ready his deception (ἐξαπάτησεν, 565). The *eris* between the two gods thus employs the softly seductive treachery of language, the enticement of sweet reason, not physical violence; an *eris* in the country ordinarily of Aphrodite, Eros and Himeros. For the sphere of that goddess, besides softness and sweet delight, is the thoughts of young women, secret smiles, μειδήματα, little deceptions, ἐξαπάτας (*Th.* 205–6).

One ought to add however that, in relation to his division of the sacrifice, Prometheus caricatures the manner of a good king who renders justice in the name of Zeus in 'straight sentences': διακρίνοντα θέμιστας ἰθείῃσι δίκῃσιν (85–6). In adjudicating a quarrel, the king who is inspired by the Muses turns, not to force of arms, but to sweet reason, soft courtesy, the soothing honey of silken words. The music of his just utterance has the power of aimiable resolutions; it gives the plaintiff redress, restores a proper equilibrium, but mildly, without violence, without oppression: μετάτροπα ἔργα τελεῦσι ῥηιδίως (89–90). So far from restoring equilibrium, however, Prometheus confounds it by his partial adjudication (cf. 544: ἑτεροζήλως διεδάσσαο μοίρας).

17 Cf. *Th.* 392–6 and 423–8, which describe the object and the forms of Zeus's *dasmos* with regard to the gods (cf. 885).

18 One may compare *Th.* 657: Cottus praises Zeus for having 'spared' (ἀλκτήρ) the Immortals from chill doom; and 614: 'kindly Prometheus' (in relation to men), ἀκάκητα Προμηθεύς.

19 Cf. *Th.* 386 ff. In the divine world ordered by Zeus, *Zēlos* (Emulation, Rivalry) no longer has his old place, no longer stirs up confrontations and dissension. Like his brother and sister, *Kratos* (Might) and *Bia* (Force), who are Zeus's shadows and accompany him wherever he goes, *Zēlos* now appears as the guarantor of the supremacy of the new King of the Gods. He is closely associated with *Nikē* (indeed, they form a pair), and his job is to bring to nought any attempt by a rival of Zeus to dispute his sovereignty.

20 *Th.* 782–806. If we compare this passage with *Works and Days* 190–200, we can see clearly the difference in the status of *eris* between the divine and the human worlds. When some *eris* arises among the gods, the Oath-ceremony automatically reveals the guilty party, who is forced to perjure himself (ἐπίορκος, 793). The sinner is at once 'hidden' in an evil, dead sleep (798) and expelled from the divine company (801–4). Among men, when the time shall come that a wicked *eris* shall find its way everywhere and become the inseparable companion of poor mankind, there will be no value, no delight, in an oath (*WD*

190); the wicked will pile lies on perjury, ἐπὶ δ᾽ ὅρκον ὀμεῖται (194) — but this time it will not be the sinner who will be hidden away and expelled. On the contrary. It will be *Aidōs* [Respect for the Rules] and *Nemesis* [Appropriate Anger], the two deities still present on earth as the last link yet connecting the world of men to that of the gods, who will themselves hide (198), and abandon men devoted to *eris*, in order to regain the company of heaven (199—200).

21 *Eris* comes into being among the gods with Cronus's attack upon his father Ouranos. Ouranos chides his children (νεικείων: 208), and tells them that in return for this crime there will one day be a *tisis*, vengeance. And the *tisis* is the conflict between the Titans and the Olympians, this *eris* and *neikos* ('quarrel', 'feud'). For when Rhea is about to give birth to Zeus, she asks Gaia and Ouranos to devise with her a plan to save Zeus and to repay the debt to the *erinys* of her father (τείσατο δ᾽ ἐρινῦς πατρὸς ἑοῖο: 472). A struggle for power then ensues between Cronus the king and mighty Zeus (476), until the latter is victorious. With that victory, the *tisis* is paid and order re-established.

22 *WD* 113—18: in the Age of Gold men lived ἄτερ πόνων, without toil that wearies; happy with what they had, ἐθελημοί; and at peace, ἥσυχοι, that is, without envy or rancour, without *eris*.

23 Benedetto Bravo has pointed out to me that the words *erga*, *ergazomenoi* are twice in the *Works and Days* used of navigation and sea-trade, at lines 45 and 641. It remains true that within the poem these words are basically connected with agricultural labour: there are about 50 passages in which this is so.

24 Cf. *Iliad* 5.339—43:   '. . . that immortal fluid,
             ichor . . . the blood of blissful gods
          who eat no food, who drink no tawny wine,
          and thereby being bloodless have the name
          of being immortal.'   (tr. Fitzgerald)

  Plutarch, in *Conviv. Septem Sap.* 160b2—3, comments on this passage: 'He means by this that food is a precondition not only of life, but also of death': ὡς μὴ μόνον τοῦ ζῆν ἀλλὰ καὶ τοῦ ἀποθνῄσκειν τὴν τροφὴν ἐφόδιον οὖσαν.

25 After noting that agriculture cooks the nutriment of plants and activates it, Aristotle states (*Problemata* 20.12, 964a19—21): 'the products of this tillage are called 'cultivated', *hēmera*, because they have gained advantage from being tilled, as though they had been educated by it (ὥσπερ παιδευόμενα).'

26 Cf. *Odyssey* 5.488—90:
          As when a man buries a burning log in a black ash heap,
          in a remote place in the country, where none live near as neighbours,
          and saves the seed of fire, having no other place to get a light
          from . . .   (tr. Lattimore)

  Also *Hom. Hymn to Hermes* 237—8; Pindar, *Pyth.* 3.66; and above all, *Olympian* 7.86—7 (Snell): when they instituted the first sacrifice to Athena, the people of Rhodes 'went up, having not the bright seed of flame (σπέρμα φλογός)' (tr. Lattimore). They were thus responsible for the introduction of sacrifice without fire; and Pindar comments on this forgetting the seed of fire, 'Respect for Prometheus/forethought puts on man goodliness and delight also' (79—81). [Snell's text prints προμαθέος, 'forethought'; but the context, with its clear reference to Prometheus earlier, suggests at least an ambiguity. Ed.]

27 See Herodotus 3.16: The Egyptians 'believe fire to be a live animal, which eats whatever it can seize, and then, glutted with the food, dies with the matter which it feeds upon' (tr. Rawlinson). The Greek attitude is to be found in Aristotle (*Parva nat.*: *De iuvent. et senect.* 5, 469b21—6): 'When there is no more food/fuel (*trophē*), and the heat can no longer feed itself, the fire dies.'

28 For the use of θεσπιδαής as an epithet for fire, see Graz, 1965: 104—8.

29 Just as no one eats any of the animals slaughtered on the pyre, whether edible (sheep and cattle) or not (horses and dogs) — let alone the Trojans.

30 See *Iliad* 23.76: ἐπήν με πυρός λελάχητε. For the use of πῦρ in the genitive with λαγχάνω, see Graz, 1965: 212—18.

31 These are exactly those parts which Hesiod, *Th.* 538, classifies as 'flesh and entrails' (σάρκας τε καὶ ἔγκατα) over against the white bones. The cannibalistic meal of the Cyclops in the *Odyssey* (9.293), who eats like a wild animal, mixes indiscriminately flesh, entrails and bones: ἔγκατά τε σάρκας τε καὶ ὀστέα μυελόεντα. [Cf. p. 86 below.]

32 *Iliad* 23.238—40:   . . . αὐτὰρ ἔπειτα
      ὀστεα Πατρόκλοιο Μενοιτιάδαο λέγωμεν
      εὖ διαγινώσκοντες· ἀριφραδέα δὲ τέτυκται.
      Then come,
      we'll comb the ashes for Patróklos' bones!
      They will be easy to pick out . . .   (tr. Fitzgerald)

33 Because Zeus concealed corn in the earth, to get corn, men must hide the seed, the *sperma*, in the earth. See *WD* 470—1: As the farmer ploughs, 'let a slave, with a mattock, give *ponos* to the birds σπέρμα κατακρύπτων, by hiding deep the seed'.

34 A point Plutarch makes in an exceptionally interesting passage which has not, I think, received the attention it deserves. In *Quaest. rom.* 109, 289e—f, Plutarch says that flour is an incomplete and uncooked food, and he continues:
      For neither has it remained what it was, wheat (ὁ πυρός), nor has it become what it must become, bread (ὁ ἄρτος), but it has both lost the germinative power of the seed and at the same time it has not attained the usefulness of cereal food (τὴν σιτίου χρείαν).   (tr. Babbitt, slightly altered)
He goes on then to meat (*Quaest. rom.* 110, 289f—209a), and wonders whether the same is not true of *to kreas* as of *to aleuron* (flour). And he then says:
      For neither is it a living creature nor has it yet become cooked food. Now boiling or roasting, being a sort of alteration and mutation, eliminates the previous form; but fresh raw meat does not have a clean and unsullied appearance, but one that is repulsive, like a fresh wound.   (tr. Babbitt)
One could hardly state more clearly that what bread is to the raw plant (the wheat while still living and growing) and to flour (dead but still uncooked), cooked meat is to the beast on the hoof (the animal while living) and to a cut of bloody meat (dead but still uncooked). In each case, for food, whether animal or vegetable, to be eatable by men, it must undergo a kind of transformation which causes it to pass from one state to another. Its original condition is that of a living creature in the natural state. From that, it must enter a new classification, as a cultural object appropriate for human consumption. This transformation involves an intermediate stage in which that which was once alive becomes dead. And this transition-stage between nature and culture (flour, raw meat) involves 'impurity' for what has been deprived of life, which has been killed without having yet been granted full status as food fit for consumption: it becomes untouchable. It is only cooking and cookery that complete the transformation and expunge all traces of impurity, integrating food, animal and vegetable, fully into the sphere of civilized human life, the life given men by Prometheus.

5. Land and sacrifice in the Odyssey: a study of religious and mythical meanings

1 On the Hesiodic 'myth of the races', see Vernant, 1971: 1.31—41 and 42—79.

2 Strictly, the contrast is between the 'race of iron' and all the earlier ones. Even the men of bronze, who 'work with bronze' (χαλκῷ δ' εἰργάζοντο: 151), do not 'work' in the strict sense: they perform a military rite (see Vernant, 1971: 1.28). Only the 'race of gold' is described explicitly as not working.

3 *WD* 167–73, restoring 169 (on the rule of Cronus) to its position in the manuscripts [= 173a Solmsen, whose *apparatus* should be consulted. Ed.].

4 Vernant, 1971: 1.32–3 and esp. 51–4, has demonstrated the close connection between this myth and that of the races.

5 Line 93, which I have restored here, is a quotation from *Od.* 19.360.

6 Commentators have perhaps been too quick to reject *WD* 108 as an interpolation (Lehrs, followed notably by Mazon, 1944 [and Solmsen, 1970]). For the line introduces the myth of the races by connecting it with the myth of Pandora: ὡς ὁμόθεν γεγάασι θεοὶ θνητοί τ᾽ ἄνθρωποι: 'for gods and mortals have the same origin'.

7 It is well known that these formulae appear frequently in the texts of oaths: see in particular the oath of the Amphictyons in Aeschines, *Against Ctesiphon* 111, and the oath of the people of Dreros in *IC* 1.9 (Dreros).1: 85–9. And when *hubris* is triumphant, as at the end of the myth of the races, we are told: 'the father will no longer resemble his sons, nor the sons their father' (*WD* 182).

8 Vernant, 1971: 1.33, remarks that Pandora's double, Anesidora, is depicted in painting and sculpture as rising out of the ground. Pandora herself is given to bring 'unhappiness to bread-eating men' (πῆμ᾽ ἀνδράσιν ἀλφηστῇσιν: *WD* 82). It may be relevant that *alphēstēs*, 'bread-eating', which is a Homeric adjective, is formed from the root *ed/*od, 'to eat'; and is a formation parallel (and in sense opposite) to *ōmēstēs*, 'raw-eating' = 'carnivorous': see Chantraine, 1933: 315.

9 The parallelism is emphasized by the repeated use of ἔπειτα in *Th.* 536 and 562. The whole affair takes place in the same period of time: 'It was in the time when the quarrel between gods and mortal men was being settled' (ὅτ᾽ ἐκρίνοντο ... [535]). I am grateful to Jean Bollack for drawing my attention to this point.

10 Note that the Hesiodic accounts leave no space for a nomadic period in the history of man: man is either a cultivator, or no man at all.

11 A typical example is Havelock, 1957, the second chapter of which, 'History as Regress' (pp. 36–51), analyses the 'myth of the races' side-by-side with the myths in Plato's *Politicus* and *Laws*. It should scarcely be necessary to observe that neither the idea of 'progress' nor that of 'regress' was thinkable in Hesiod's time: for there was no idea of 'history' in our sense. This objection does not however apply to a very useful book by a follower of Havelock, Thomas Cole (1967), which concentrates on a precise period and deals with genuine ideological disputes.

12 The most useful collection of material for such a study is certainly Lovejoy & Boas, 1935.

13 One example (there are many others) is Empedocles, *Purifications* frg. 128 Diels–Kranz: 'In the reign of Kypris (Aphrodite), all sacrifices consisted of myrrh, incense and honey.' Blood-sacrifices, and indeed all eating of meat, were considered abominations. Plato's myth in the *Politicus* (272a–b) says much the same; and vegetarianism is implicit in what Hesiod says. For a general survey, see Haussleiter, 1935.

14 For example, Euhemerus ap. Lactantius, *Institutiones Divinae* 1.13.2: 'Saturn and his wife and the other men of this time used to eat human flesh. Jupiter was the first to prohibit the practice' (Euhemerus as translated by Ennius); Dionysius of Halicarnassus, *Antiquitates Romanae* 1.38.2: 'It is said that the ancients sacrificed to Cronus according to the mode used in Carthage while that city existed'; Sextus Empiricus, *Outlines of Pyrrhonism* (p. 190 Mutschmann): 'some people sacrificed a man to Cronus in the same way that the Scythians sacrificed strangers to Artemis.' See Lovejoy & Boas, 1935: 53–79, for further references.

15 Cf. Diogenes Laertius, *Lives of the Philosophers* 6.34, 72—3; Dio Chrysostom 10.29—30; Julian, *Orationes* 6.191—3. See further, Haussleiter, 1935: 167—84 [and Detienne, pp. 225—7 below].

16 On the subject of cannibalism and *allēlophagia* in Greek literature, see, in addition to Lovejoy & Boas, 1935 and Haussleiter, 1935, Festugière, 1972: 138—64.

17 See *Politicus* 272d—e: οὔτ' ἄγριον ἦν οὐδὲν οὔτε ἀλλήλων ἐδωδαί, πόλεμός τε οὐκ ἐνῆν οὐδὲ στάσις τὸ παράπαν: 'there were no wild tribes among them (the animals), nor cannibals; and war and political strife were completely absent'. The passage concerns animals, but the language employed is deliberately 'human'.

18 See the vase described and illustrated by Robertson, 1931: 152—60.

19 The formula κύσε δὲ ζείδωρον ἄρουφαν ('he kissed the grain-giving earth') occurs earlier, in the description of Odysseus's arrival on Scheria (5.463), but the first part of the line is naturally different. The connection turns out not to be accidental.

20 The two separate worlds of the *Odyssey* are clearly delineated by Germain, 1954a: 511—82.

21 To be exact, a nine-day storm; on the tenth day, they reach the Lotus-Eaters (9.82—4). See Germain, 1954b: 13: 'The number nine is used essentially to symbolize a period of time at the end of which, on the tenth day or year, a decisive event happens.'

22 'Der Sturm verschlägt dem Helden ins Fabelland': Mühll, 1940: 720.

23 Menelaus has just returned, as Nestor puts it (3.319—20), from a region whence men rarely return.

24 There is one other place from which communication is feasible, but fails: Aeolus's floating island (10.3).

25 The second account to Penelope (19.262—307) contains a serious difficulty: Odysseus introduces the Phaeacians where they are clearly out of place, since Penelope does not yet know anything of Odysseus's adventures or his identity. Lines 273—86, of the 'interpolations' discovered by nineteenth-century critics, are one of the few passages which almost certainly deserve to be rejected. In his first account, Odysseus heads for Crete after rounding Cape Malea (19.187), which is perfectly reasonable and restores 'geographical' truth precisely at the point at which it was abandoned. Elements of 'truth' slipped in among the 'lies' — and contrasted with the 'lies' which constitute the 'true' tales — are fundamental to the Homeric story; see Todorov, 1967: 47—55.

26 I need hardly add that I do not expect to discourage enthusiasts for Homeric 'geography' and the 'identification' of sites, though the sport has been aptly likened by J.-P. Darmon to the search for the rabbit-hole through which Alice enters Wonderland. Of course this is not to deny that Homeric wonders, like all wonders, bear some relation to the realities of their time, which means essentially the western Mediterranean (and perhaps, in an earlier period, the eastern Mediterranean, if one believes Meuli, 1921). After all, there is presumably more resemblance between the wonders seen by Alice and Victorian England, than between that Wonderland and Manchu China.

27 'The movement of the *Odyssey* is essentially inwards, homewards, towards normality' (Stanford, 1963: 50); and see above all Segal, 1962.

28 Similarly, Polyphemus 'did not resemble a man who eats bread' (9.190—1).

29 A point not noticed by Richter, 1968.

30 I cannot understand why Haussleiter thought that the Cicones were cannibals (1935: 23): the text does not mention it.

31 I owe this reference to Yvon Garlan.

32 The use of the phrase *zeidōros aroura*, 'grain-giving earth', is not very satisfactory as a criterion, because Hesiod uses it of the golden age. For what it is

worth, of nine occurrences in the *Odyssey*, only three refer to a precise place (Ithaca: 13.354; Phaeacia: 5.463; Egypt: 4.229). The rest have a more general referent, roughly = 'here below'.

33 There is also smoke coming from Circe's house (10.196—7); and when Odysseus approaches Ithaca after leaving the island of Aeolus, he can see men around a fire (πυρπολέοντας: 10.30).

34 The identification of the figures encountered by Odysseus with savage tribes is explicitly raised as a possibility in 1.198—9, where Athena, in the guise of Mentes, wonders whether he is the prisoner of men who are χαλεποί, ἄγριοι ('harsh', 'brutish'); and when Odysseus himself asks what class of men the inhabitants of Cyclopia belong to: ὑβρισταί τε καὶ ἄγριοι or δίκαιοι, ἦε φιλόξεινοι, 'violent and brutish' or 'righteous men who welcome strangers' (9.175—6). The same question recurs at 13.201—2, on Ithaca, before Odysseus recognizes that he is in fact back home; and earlier, when he lands on Phaeacia (6.120—1). Compare the excellent chapter on the Cyclopes in Kirk, 1970: 162—71.

35 It is scarcely sufficient to say, with Haussleiter, 1935: 23 n. 2: 'the cannibalism of the Cyclops Polyphemus seems on the whole to be an isolated case.' The incident deserves more than a mere footnote.

36 These and other details have been well stressed by Page, 1955: 1—20, who compares Homer's Cyclops with the Cyclopes of folklore.

37 On the *Abioi*, *Gabioi* or *Hippēmolgoi*, see also Nicolaus of Damascus, *FGrH* 70 F 104.

38 The main texts are collected by Lovejoy and Boas, 1935: 304, 358, 411. The most curious of them is doubtless the speech Plutarch puts into the mouth of one of Odysseus's companions who was turned into a pig on Circe's island. Taster of both human and animal existence, he praises the 'life of the Cyclopes', comparing Polyphemus's rich earth with the thin soil of Ithaca (*Gryllus* 986f—987a).

39 Note also the Androphagoi ('Man-Eaters') in Herodotus 4.18, who live on the edge of the desert, and are themselves at the limits of the human. [On these Scythians and the Androphagoi, see now Rosellini and Saïd, 1978: 955—74.]

40 See p. 82 above; in the *Iliad*, when Achilles and Hecuba reach extremes of grief and anger, they fantasize about eating their enemies: 22.347; 24.212.

41 There is no reason to alter the σίτῳ of the manuscripts in line 235.

42 In line 287, Hermes simply says to Odysseus that if he 'carries this excellent remedy', τόδε φάρμακον ἐσθλὸν ἔχων, he will be safe. It is then not a charm to be used but a talismanic object.

43 It is Hermes, the god closest to humankind, who gives Odysseus the *moly*; and it is to Hermes that Eumaeus sacrifices a pig (14.435).

44 See Eustathius's comment on 12.359: καὶ τὰ ἐξῆς τῆς πολλαχοῦ δηλωθείσης θυτικῆς διασκευῆς, 'and throughout the following description of the sacrificial preparations'; and on 357. On the role of the *oulai-oulochutai* in Homeric sacrifice, see Rudhardt, 1958: 253.

45 The most curious feature of this episode is that whereas water is normally in Homeric sacrifice used to prepare for the actual killing (it is contained in the χερνίβες, bronze vessels) (Rudhardt, 1958: 254), Homer here does not mention water. Instead, he concentrates on the libation of wine which follows the killing. This passage was noticed by Samson Eitrem, 1915: 278—80, who believed that it presented evidence for a rite more ancient than blood sacrifice, as did the scattering of leaves attested in some funeral rituals: 'They (Odysseus's companions) knew that in a previous period or in other places, this form had been used.' Of course, when explained (!) in this way, the text loses all significance. Ziehen, by contrast, saw it as 'an idea of the poet's, influenced by the situation' (1939: 582).

46 In Herodotus, the legendary Ethiopians, who in the *Odyssey* feast with Poseidon, enjoy food which is the exact opposite of Odysseus's companions' sacrilegious feast. On a plain outside their city, the earth itself supplies them directly with the 'Table of the Sun' — the boiled flesh of domestic animals (3.18). With their scented fountain of youth (3.23), the 'long-lived Ethiopians' are scarcely mortal — even their corpses do not smell unpleasant (3.24); in relation to the sun, they are guests, not utter strangers as are Odysseus's companions [see also Vernant, p. 78 above, and 1972: xiv—xvii; and Rosellini and Saïd, 1978: 962—4].

47 The same applies to other countries which receive simply a bare mention. One of them, Syros, from which Eumaeus comes, presents a particular problem. It certainly produces corn and wine (15.406), but there is no illness or hunger there, and death comes without pain (407—11). It lies 'where the sun sets' (404), and cannot therefore be the Aegean island of the same name (I am grateful to F. Hartog for bringing this point to my notice). I cannot here discuss the problem of the mysterious 'Taphians'.

48 13.244—6; for corn, see also 13.354; 20.106—10 (mills); for cows, 17.181. Odysseus also owns cows on Cephallenia (20.209—10).

49 On this text, which suggests a conception of kingship very archaic even in Homer's day, see Finley, 1977: 97—8.

50 Note the details: barley and lustral water, 3.440—7; the ritual cry of the women, 450—2; cf. also 15.222—3.

51 By contrast, Odysseus says 'I am not a god' (16.187).

52 Despite the nineteenth-century arguments recently revived by Hirvonen, 1968: 135—62, there is nothing in the treatment of Penelope to justify a reference to matriarchy — or even 'traces' of it. Penelope's 'special position' is to be explained simply by the absence of Odysseus.

53 See 2.56; 14.74; 16.454; 17.181; 17.600 [ἱερήϊα]; 20.3; 20.250—3.

54 See 18.414—28. Amphinomus is killed at 22.89—94; the hecatomb of 20.276—83 is anonymously offered, but clearly not by the suitors.

55 Liodes, the suitors' *thuoskoös*, is killed by Odysseus at 22.310—29, making it clear that the sacrifices performed in the past on the suitors' behalf have not been accepted. A *thuoskoös* is a seer: see Casabona, 1966: 118—19.

56 See also 2.423—33 (Telemachus); 4.761—7 (Penelope); 14.445—8 (Eumaeus); 18.151 (Odysseus); 19.198 (Odysseus's 'false' story); 1.60—2; 4.762—4; 17.241—3 (Odysseus's past sacrifices); 19.397—8 (list of sacrifices offered by Autolycus, the grandfather of Odysseus). And we should remember the sacrifices promised by Odysseus, as well (p. 85 above).

57 Casabona observes (1966: 23): 'the idea of "banquet" becomes predominant' — an excessive litotes. [Cf. Vernant, p. 61 above.]

58 See also 1962: 27: 'The Phaeacians ... while the instrument of Odysseus's return to the world of reality, are also the last afterglow of the phantasy realm he is leaving.' I believe that the whole of Segal's case should be accepted, but without the 'symbolist' and psychological language he sometimes employs. See also Segal, 1967: 321—42; Clarke, 1967: 52—6 and Hartog, 1970.

59 Though he was helped by Ino-Leucothea and the river-god of Phaeacia (5.333—53, 445—53). [Cf. Detienne, p. 18 above.]

60 The two trees share the same trunk. The ancient world unanimously understood *phuliē* as 'wild olive' (see Richter, 1968: 135); it is only in the modern world that a few critics have thought that myrtle was intended (Pease, 1937: 2006).

61 Much has been made of this line by historians of colonization; see Asheri, 1966: 5, for example.

62 It must be clear that we cannot excise this famous description from the *Odyssey* on the staggeringly inadequate grounds that the 'solid but narrow

precincts' of the Mycenaean cities could never have had 'room within their walls for the four acres of this orchard, double vineyard and kitchen-garden' (J. Bérard, 1961: 1.186). It is instructive to note that the passage's utopian and mythical character was clearly recognized in antiquity — Iamboulus's hellenistic Utopia quotes lines 7.120—1, for example (Diodorus Siculus 2.56).

63 There is here a difficulty which I feel incapable of resolving. All the comparisons made in this article tend, it seems to me, to support those who accept at least an overall 'architect' — what Kirk calls a 'monumental composer', who gave the Homeric poems their present structure (1962: 159—270; to be supplemented by Parry, 1967: 175—215). This is also my position. But it must be admitted that there are many anomalies, especially in the language, of Book 24, and that it presents special problems (see Page, 1955: 101—36 — an extreme view — and Kirk, 1962: 248—51). We also know that the hellenistic critics Aristarchus of Samos and Aristophanes of Byzantium regarded the *Odyssey* as ending at line 286 of Book 23. If, for the sake of argument, we accept these criticisms as valid, does it follow necessarily that the parallel drawn between Book 7 and Book 24 is nonsense? For those who practise structural analysis on the basis of linguistic criteria alone, the question has little meaning; and indeed it is difficult to see why they should not 'structure' a complex composed of the *Iliad*, the *Mahabharata* and *Paradise Lost* . . . At this point, the historian must make a graceful exit. But a quite different approach is possible. The work of Propp and his immediate, and later, followers (see Propp, 1968; Bremond, 1964: 4—32 and 1968: 147—64; and the whole of *Communications* 8 [1962]) suggests that, within a common cultural area, a complex of stories may be reduced to a small number of simple elements which may occupy a variety of different structural positions. It seems clear to me that, in the *Odyssey*, the motif of the golden-age garden is parallel to that of the garden cultivated by men; just as the motif of the hospitable girl is parallel to that of the girl who prepares visitors for death. I also believe that thematic analysis of epic narrative of the kind practised by the followers of Milman Parry leads in the end in the same direction (Lord, 1960: 68—98), by showing that an ancient theme — and it is hard to imagine the long-awaited meeting between Odysseus and Laërtes could be anything but an ancient theme — may have acquired a fixed form only relatively late. These two approaches would benefit from mutual acquaintance.

   For these reasons, I do not believe that an *Odyssey* which is partly composite, historically speaking, cannot also be, from a structuralist point of view, homogeneous; though I admit that a strict proof has yet to be offered.

64 More accurately, these are the equivalents of those states to which Hesiod and his successors give the names 'age of Cronus' and 'age of Zeus'; for of course the land of the Cyclopes is also tended by Zeus (9.111, 358). Homer's Cronus is the father of Zeus and is imprisoned in Tartarus (*Iliad* 8.478—81).

65 Eumaeus, too, has dogs which are quite real and bark: 14.21—2.

66 That is, the Phaeacians have the same privileges as the legendary Ethiopians (1.23—6); see also 6.203—5: 'We are very dear to the immortals; we live in seclusion in the midst of the swelling sea, at the edge of the world (*eschatoi*), and no mortals visit us' (see Eitrem, 1938: 1523). That familiarity with the gods which is symbolized by shared feasts is correlated with isolation from mortal men.

   When Athena takes part in the first sacrifice offered by Nestor and his sons (3.41—44), she does so in disguise [as Mentor], whereas Alcinous stresses the fact that among the Phaeacians the gods do not assume disguise: οὔ τι κατακρύπτουσιν (7.205); they eat the sacrificial meal in common (7.203). Similarly, Poseidon is present at the Ethiopians' feast (δαιτὶ παρήμενος: 1.26). It might seem as though Athena does the same in Nestor's palace (ἦλθε . . . ἐς δαῖτα, 'she came to the feast': 3.420); but after she has revealed herself by turning into a bird (3.371—2), she takes her share as an invisible divinity (3.435—6). Nestor and Telemachus do not therefore enjoy the same privilege as the Phaeacians.

67 The hospitality, though, is fairly ambiguous, for Athena, in disguise, warns Odysseus: 'The people here do not welcome strangers or give a friendly reception to visitors from abroad' (7.32—3). Nothing in what follows justifies the warning, of course, but Nausicaä has just said (6.205) that few mortals visit them (n. 66 above); and Athena covers Odysseus with a mist 'in case one of the proud Phaeacians should cross his path, and insult him, and demand to know his name' (7.14—17). Peeping through the motif of the Phaeacians' hospitality is the image of a Phaeacia comparable with the land of the Cyclopes.

68 A scholiast notes that 'Hesiod' regarded Alcinous and Arete as brother and sister (see Schol. Odyss. η (7), 54, [1, p. 325 Dindorf] = Hesiod, frg. 222 Merkelbach—West [repr. Solmsen, 1970: 185]; see also Eustathius on η (7), 64 [p. 1567]). This leaves two possible solutions: to agree with what the scholiast says, τοῦτο μάχεται τοῖς ἑξῆς, 'this conflicts with what follows', and then, as has been done since the time of Kirchoff, 1869: 54—6, regard as interpolated lines 56—68 and 146 (where Arete is called the daughter of Rhexenor); or to accept that the poet gave the royal couple an appearance of incest, which was later corrected, so as to draw a parallel between Aeolus and Alcinous (see Germain, 1954a: 293).

69 Most obviously, of course, the king and queen: the same formulas are used to describe the royal couples' retirement for the night at Pylos, Sparta and on Scheria: 3.402—3; 4.304—5; 7.346—7.

70 For example, there is a housekeeper on Scheria (7.166, 175; 8.449), as on Ithaca (17.94) and at Pylos (3.392); a nurse (7.7—12) as on Ithaca (19.353—6, 482—3); a bard (8.261 ff.), also as on Ithaca (22.330—1). The Phaeacian episode and the scenes on Ithaca have often been compared: note, for example, the arguments, so curiously similar despite the time-lapse of 65 years and the difference in the explanations offered (a mass of 'interpolations' against oral composition), of Eitrem, 1904 and Lang, 1969: 159—68.

71 As will be seen by reading 7.146 ff. free of the kind of preconceptions about matriarchy to be found in Lang, 1969: 163.

72 Compare Echeneus's speech with that of old Aegyptius, 2.25—34.

73 A point made to me by M.I. Finley.

74 I fully accept the general tenor of Finley's remarks here; but it should be remembered that by the time of the later hellenistic period utopias used a complex mixture of archaic and millennarian myths and political images (Gernet, 1968a: 139—53). The situation was different in the fifth century BC: a utopia like that of Hippodamus of Miletus (Aristotle, *Politics* 2.5, 1267b30 ff.) cannot be explained by appeal to mythical thinking.

75 I would like to thank Richard Seaford for reading through this version of the article with me.

6. The myth of 'Honeyed Orpheus'

1 This approach was used by Gruppe, 1906, for example.

2 As suggested by Wilamowitz-Moellendorff, 1955: 244 n. 2; see also Wilkinson, 1969: 325—6.

3 The analysis presented here in summary form, without full documentation, will be developed in detail in a general study of honey myths in Greece, which will also contain a discussion of purely literary approaches, such as Segal, 1966: 307—25.

4 Aristotle, *Historia animalium* 9.40, 626a26 ff.; Theophrastus, *De causis plant-arum* 6.5.1 etc.
5 According to Aristophanes of Byzantium (*Anecdota graeca*, ed. Rose, 2, p. 23, 2—8), this was the practice in Egypt.
6 Aelian, *Historia animalium* 5.11; Cassianus Bassus, *Geoponica* 15.2.19.
7 Plutarch, *Quaestiones naturales* 36 (ed. Sandbach, Loeb ed., vol. 11, pp. 218—20).
8 Servius, *in Verg. Georg.* 4.317; Scholion Bern. *in Verg. Georg.* 4.493 (ed. Hagen).
9 Claude Lévi-Strauss, 1977: 60—7, has described some aspects of this method of analysis.
10   De ses desirs impetueux
                l'amant habile est toujours maître.
See Bellas, 1970: 234.
11 See further, Detienne, 1979: 1—19.

7. 'Value' in Greek myth

1 This cannot be done in such a way as to render the distinction universally valid; see Meyerson, 1948: 75—115.
2 On strictly private property and its characteristic social presentation, see Bruck, 1926: 39—74.
3 Laum, 1924: 10—13; in the Roman context, Lévy-Bruhl, 1947: 98—100.
4 In relation to a perceptibly aesthetic and 'abstract' attitude towards the statue, which contrasts with another, originally Aegean, which sees the cult-statue as the locus of 'mystical' qualities; not but what this notion of something mysterious occurs occasionally in the word *agalma*: note the curious, essentially metaphorical, development of the idea in Plato, *Laws* 11, 930e—931e.
5 1904: 72—6, 95—6, 109—16. Bücher shows that these objects, which we too easily tend to think of in terms taken from other historical periods, were made in fact for a small group of aristocrats; he also demonstrates that it was the games above all which made particular items famous.
6 The institution of *anathēmata* ('offerings') appears only at a relatively late stage of religious development (Laum, 1924: 86—93). Laum relates it to the belief that gods have a personality which is constant, which contrasts with the conception of *Augenblicksgötter* ('here and now gods'), to which it is appropriate to offer things which can be eaten (p. 88). I wonder whether the relationship is not the exact opposite: whether there is not a process of continuous objectification on both levels — ritual and the conception of divinity — at the same time.
7 Aristotle, *Nicomachean Ethics* 4.2, 1123a4—5; Plato, by contrast, sharply limits wealth in the city sketched in the *Laws* and also restricts the magnificence of both private and public offerings.
8 The notion of *objective offence* persists in this connection to some degree into fourth-century Athens (to judge from the two pseudo-Demosthenic speeches *Against Aristogeiton*).
9 Let us not quibble over the word to be used. Even if one believes that 'myth' properly denotes a special kind of story, different from those with which I am here concerned, the same kind of social conception is at work, involving motifs sometimes identical at different stages of the imaginative process, which we designate by the formulaic terms myth, legend and folktale. And from the psychological point of view, that is all that matters, at least here.
10 [Note especially 4.2 Ziegler: ἡ τοῦ τρίποδος περίοδος καὶ διὰ πάντων ἀνακύκλησις καὶ ἀνθύπειξις μετ᾽ εὐμενείας φιλοτίμου γενομένη, and cf. 4.5—6:

ὑπ᾽ ἐκείνου (Thales) δ᾽αὖθις ἀπεστάλη πρὸς ἄλλον ὡς σοφώτερον. εἶτα περιιὼν καὶ ἀναπεμπόμενος ... The same words recur in section 7. Ed.]

11 This group of social customs and its ideology has been discussed in relation to a neighbouring culture, the Thracians, but on the basis of a highly interesting Greek text [Xenophon, *Anabasis* 7.3.10—39], by Mauss, 1921: 388—97.

12 Oddly characterized here as a traditional 'sage', and in particular as a prophet inspired by god [ἐς δόμον ἀνδρὸς ἵκηται, | ὃς σοφὸς ἢ τά τ᾽ ἐόντα τά τ᾽ ἐσσόμενα πρό τ᾽ ἐόντα. There is a very similar form of words in the version given by Diodorus Siculus 9.3.2. Ed.]

13 Pausanias 3.24.3 (the chest in which Dionysus and Semele were cast adrift) is a typical instance: see Usener, 1899: 138—80, and Pfister, 1909: 215.

14 They are picked up by a fisherman whose name, Diktys, has been connected with the word for a fisherman's net; note too the goddess *Diktunna*, who was also saved in a fishing-net. See Robert, 1920—6: 1.232—3 [and Glotz, 1904: 51—2. Ed.].

15 That is, Plutarch's version in *Life of Solon* 4.3—4 Ziegler; this is parallel to that in Diogenes Laertius, *Lives* 1.32—3: we have here two variants of the same version which seems to have enjoyed special currency.

16 The intermediary here is one of the king's 'friends' — an oriental feature. [Note that Diogenes here also quotes Euanthes of Miletus (or possibly Samos). Ed.]

17 Even in the early fourth century BC, we find a gold cup, a '*symbolon* obtained from the Persian king', used as a letter of credit (Lysias, *Oration* 19.24—6).

18 We are reminded of the goddess who escorts a king — which is a feature of the triumphal procession, as we know from other evidence.

19 An identical mode of self-consecration is made use of in the ritual of the 'Great Oath' at Syracuse [Plutarch, *Life of Dion* 56.5]: cf. Glotz, 1877—1919: 752.

20 See Carl Robert, 1920—6: 3.915—22; and cf. 1915: 205—10.

21 This cup had a special shape and name, *karkhēsion*: see Pherecydes (*FGrH* 3 F 13a) and Herodorus of Herakleia (*FGrH* 31 F 16) quoted by Athenaeus, *Deipnosophistae* 11.49, 474d—f (cf. Macrobius, *Saturnalia* 5.21.3 Willis, who quotes Pherecydes); see also the remarks of Charon of Lampsacus (*FGrH* 262 F 2) on the *skyphos* in Athenaeus, *Deipn.* 475b—c. Macrobius uses the expression *pretium concubitus* here: such cups were given by a male, whether god or aristocrat, to a woman not his wife in return for sexual favours. Crowns are also attested in this connection (Herodotus 6.69.1), as are rings, whose mythical significance I take the opportunity here to stress: they are found as talismans guaranteeing legitimacy in historical legends as well as in legend more generally; see Justin 15.4.2—6 Seel.

22 For example, on the late-Corinthian *krater* (sixth century BC) [*Berlin* 1655; now lost], which illustrates the same subject (the departure of Amphiaraus) as Cypselus's chest, described by Pausanias 5.17.7—8 [see Payne, 1931: 329, cat. no. 1471, and the photograph easily accessible in Henle, 1973: 14, fig. 7. Ed.].

23 A ritual similar to that described at the end of Euripides's *Helen* [1238—71, 1554—88 Kannicht]; its occasion is certainly different but not its frame. Compare too a sailors' ritual at Syracuse which involves throwing an earthenware *kylix* into the sea from a boat (Polemon of Ilium in *FHG* 3, 136 frg. 75 = Athenaeus, *Deipnosophistae* 11.5, 462b—c).

24 The most circumstantial account is to be found in Bacchylides's third dithyramb (17, lines 57—66, 74—80 Snell). It should be remembered that the legend of Theseus, in the form in which it is known to us, must have been invented in the sixth century BC.

25 This has been discussed in relation to funerary ritual and the magical power of the horse by Schuhl, 1968a: 67—8.

26 On the pre-monetary rôle of the ring, see Ure, 1922: 148—9, following Babelon and Ridgeway.

27 See Ure, 1922: 149—52 (the story of Gyges is discussed on p. 151); on seals, Laum, 1924: 139—43.
28 Let me mention an interesting parallel from a quite different culture, China; see Mestre, 1937: 33—61.
29 The form of the ceremony is the same as that in the story of Polycrates (p. 123 above) [ἐς τὸ πέλαγος ἀνεπλεῖ *Anabasis* 6.19.5 ~ μετὰ δὲ ἀναγαγεῖν ἐκέλευε ἐς τὸ πέλαγος Herodotus 3.41.2. Ed.]
30 The scimitar is here conceived as something precious: Xerxes makes a gift of one elsewhere, and it is clearly a very lavish one (Herodotus 8.120). [Note that this latter scimitar is expressly said to be made of gold; the other gift which accompanies it is a 'tiara' made of gold-thread. Ed.]
31 [I am not sure that the text allows one to make this inference: Arrian says (He threw the bulls into the sea after sacrificing them) καὶ σπείσας ἐπὶ τῇ θυσίᾳ τὴν φιάλην . . . ἀνέβαλεν ἐς τὸ πόντον . . . Ed.]
32 For example, Pausanias 3.20.9 (a sacrifice north of Sparta by Tyndareus); *Iliad* 23.171—2 (at Patroclus's funeral pyre). The sumptuous ritual offering of chariots and chariot-horses corresponds to their status in myth.
33 For the Homeric world, see Bruck, 1926: 28—32, 75—100; cf. Weiss, 1923: 146—9; Westrup, 1934: 167—72.
34 The act has a number of resonances: bulls were sacrificed by throwing them into a river-head near Syracuse where Hades went back into the underworld after the rape of Persephone (Diodorus Siculus 4.23.4); horses were sacrificed to Poseidon by being thrown into the sea off the coast of the Argolid near a *genethlion*, a 'place where births take place' — perhaps where souls are re-incarnated? (Pausanias 8.7.2 [κατὰ τὸ Γενέθλιον]): in Pindar, *Pythian* 4.42—3 Snell, the *bōlos* is called 'the immortal seed of wide Libya': ἄφθιτον . . . Λιβύας εὐρυχόρου σπέρμα.
35 Here, as often elsewhere, horses are connected with Poseidon, particularly in his capacity as god of the sea; but horses are also related to Hades, god of the underworld: cf. Stengel, 1905: 203—13.
36 In the story connected with the house of Pelops, the sources usually speak of the animal itself (the 'golden lamb'), but in one or two places its fleece is thought of as something quite independent; the reverse is true in the story we know as that of the 'golden fleece'.
37 Note also the lyric passages in Euripides's *Orestes*, 812—18, 995—1012 di Benedetto.
38 Some memory of a festival of royal investiture, with sacrifices and choir-singing, persisted into fifth-century Sparta [Gernet here refers to Thucydides 5.13.6, which has nothing to do with his point here, and I cannot think which Thucydidean passage he meant; but compare Xenophon, *Constitution of the Lacedaemonians* 15.9. Ed.].
39 The legendary plot here once again allows us to see a royal drama connected with investiture as king, with an identical 'opposition' between brothers which is entirely typical of the theme.
40 To this end he has seduced (as in Euripides's version) Atreus's wife. I simply note here the significance of the theme of the woman's rôle in the transfer of a talisman or precious object from one person to another.
41 On the mythical notion of sterility [a situation caused by offence against divine rules, and marked specifically by the inability of crops, flocks and men alike to reproduce successfully], which is the opposite of wealth/well-being — and so structurally homologous — see Delcourt, 1938: 9—28 (an important study).
42 There is a dramatic symbolic substitution in Herodotus 9.197.2—3, which concerns practices (allegedly human sacrifice) which were current in a part of Thessaly where the legend is sometimes set. The story seems to be a kind of homologue of these practices.

43 The link was made long ago by Seeliger, 1884—6: 674; cf. Nilsson, 1906: 11—12. [For a discussion of the cult, see Cook, 1914—40: 1.420—8; 2.2.871 ff. Ed.]

44 See most clearly the dedication preserved as *Anthologia Palatina* 3.10 [reprinted by Bond, 1963: 148—9 with a better text than Dübner, 1 pp. 42—3. Hypsipyle's sons seem to have been recognized by means of the golden vine (see Bond, 1963: 19, with frg. 765 Nauck² [= p. 51 Bond] and *POxy* 7.852 frg. 64 line 111 [= p. 49 Bond]; see too Bond's notes to frg. 57 line 10 and frg. 64 lines 58—62). Ed.]

45 [This citation refers in fact to Apollo Hyperboreos, who gave the arrow to Abaris, who gave it in turn to Pythagoras. Ed.]

46 On mythology as a form of thinking, see Usener, 1907: 37—65.

47 [Osthoff's etymology is still favoured by both Frisk, 1954—72: 2.878 s.v. and by Chantraine, *DELG* 4.1.1105—6 s.v. Ed.]

48 This is just a glance towards the enormous importance in 'primitive' (Greek) religion of weaving — a craft-skill that belongs exclusively to women.

49 Let me here call attention to a relevant item of late evidence, concerning a feast held by a religious confraternity, to be found in a curious passage of the *Hypomnemata* ('Memoirs') of Ptolemy VIII Euergetes II [= *FGrH* 234 F 9] recorded by Athenaeus, *Deipnosophistae* 12.73, 549e—550a; note also the Macedonian marriage-feast described by Hippolochos of Macedon in Athenaeus, *Deipn.* 4.1, 128a—130e; and a fragment of Poseidonius, *FGrH* 87 F 13 = Athenaeus, *Deipn.* 11.15, 466b—c.

50 On classical practices in relation to the offering; on 'symbolic offerings'; and on the fact that in most cases vessels which were consecrated to the gods 'differ from those in domestic use only by their inscribed dedication and find-spots', see Homolle, 1887—1919: 368—78, especially 372—3 on furniture, tripods and vases.

51 It is also worth noting that the hero Meleager's 'life-surety', the log taken from the fire, was kept in a *larnax* according to Bacchylides 5.140—2 Snell [cf. Robert, 1920—6: 1.88, 91—6. Ed.].

52 Cf. Reisch, 1905: 1687—8; Schwendemann, 1921: 161—81; Guillon, 1943: 90—1.

53 On the tripod as Apollo's winged vehicle, see Cook, 1914—40: 1.334—5 [esp. 335 n. 5], picked up by 2.1.204—5 with fig. 144.

54 The change of sense of the word *thalamos* in *Iliad* 4.141—5 is worthy of note: it means here 'work-room' [so Cunliffe]; moreover, in Homer, an *agalma* is reserved exclusively for a 'king' [that, at any rate, is the burden of this passage. Ed.]: an instructive antinomy.

55 Diogenes Laertius, *Lives of the philosophers* 1.31 [quoting a well-known tag by Alcaeus (frg. 360 line 2 Lobel—Page) about the Spartan Aristodamus: χρήματ' ἀνηρ, πένιχρος δ' οὐδ' εἷς πέλετ' ἔσθλος οὐδὲ τίμιος, 'Wealth is the man; no poor man is a true man, no poor man has *timē* ('honour')' — surely an unexceptionably aristocratic sentiment of a traditional kind. Ed.].

8. The Black Hunter and the origin of the Athenian 'ephebeia'

1 This is a considerably revised version of the original article. I have taken account of several points which have been made to me, especially by O. Picard, and of the criticisms of Maxwell-Stuart, 1970: 113—16.

2 For the controversy, see Wilamowitz-Moellendorff, 1893: 1.193—4; Robert, 1938: 297—307; Jeanmaire, 1939; Pélékidis, 1962 (with full bibliography); Marrou, 1956: 36—45, 105—12, 186—9. Reinmuth, 1971: 123—38 has shown from the inscriptions that the *ephebeia* existed in 361 BC, considerably before the period of Lycurgus's domination of Athenian political life. To be sure, the

date of the inscription which Reinmuth relies on has been questioned by Mitchell, 1975: 233–43; but the scholar who found the stone, M. Mitsos, was in a position to defend Reinmuth (cf. J. and L. Robert, 1976: no. 194). And most important of all, Philippe Gauthier has shown decisively in his discussion of Xenophon, *Ways and Means* 4.51–2 (which had not hitherto been adduced in the debate) both that the *ephebeia* antedates Lycurgus — the *Ways and Means* was written in 355 BC — and that, prior to Lycurgus, it was not a duty imposed upon all young male citizens (1976: 190–5).

3 On *peripoloi* generally in the Greek world, see Robert, 1955: 283–92; we may add two recent items from Acarnania and Epirus: cf. J. and L. Robert, 1973: nos. 229 and 260.

4 Xenophon, *Ways and Means* 4.52 thus uses the verb *peltazein* rather than *hopliteuein*, the *peltē* being a light shield [and *hopliteuein* referring to the performance of military service equipped with heavy hoplite armour, especially the shield, *hoplon*. Ed.] : cf. Gauthier, 1976: 192–3.

5 Young men were only used to fight under exceptional circumstances, and so are normally specifically mentioned: note the episode in the first Peloponnesian War, a battle against Megara involving the *neōtatoi* (the young men not normally called up) and the *presbutatoi* (the older men no longer normally called up): cf. Thucydides 1.105.4 and Lysias, *Oration* 2.50–3, with Loraux, 1980a.

6 I am not here concerned with the mutual inconsistencies of these passages.

7 See *IC* 1.9 (Dreros), 1.126–7; and for *oureuō* = 'be a young soldier in the frontier forts', van Effenterre, 1948b: 1033–4. Thucydides 5.41.2 reproduced in Bengtson, 1962: 124–5, no. 192) offers a clear-cut, official distinction between the frontier areas and the territory proper of Argos and Sparta.

8 The text sets formal combat against stratagem, an opposition whose significance is discussed below.

9 Here is a list — assuredly incomplete — of the 'sources' (a quite inadequate term, as will at once be realized, for most of these texts): Hellanicus, *FGrH* 4 F 125 = 323a F 23 (= Scholiast T on Plato, *Symposium* 208d) with Jacoby's commentary; Ephorus, *FGrH* 70 F 22 (= Harpokration, s.v. ἀπατούρια [1, pp. 42–3 Dindorf]); Konon, *Diēgēseis* in *FGrH* 26 F 1, 39 (Μέλανθος); Strabo 9.1.7 (393C); Frontinus, *Strategemata* 2.5.41; Frontinus, *Strategemata* 1.19; Justin 2.6.16–21; Pausanias 2.18.8–9; 9.5.16; Eusebius, *Chronicon* p. 56 (ed. Schoene); John of Antioch, in *FHG* 4, p. 539 § 19; Proclus, *in Timaeum* 21b (1.88.11–90.12 Diehl); Nonnus of Panopolis, *Dionysiaka* 27.301–7; Michael Apostolius, s.v. ἀπιὼν ἐς Ἀπατούρια in *Corp. paroemiogr. gr.*, edd. Leutsch and Schneidewin, 2, p. 294; Michael Psellus, *De Actionum nominibus* 40 (= Migne, *PG* 122, cols. 1017d–20a); Joh. Tztetzes, *Commentarium in Aristophanis Ranas* 798a (4.3, pp. 907–9 Koster); Lycophron, *Alexandra* 767 with scholia (ed. Scheer); *Etymologicon Magnum* s.v. ἀπατούρια (cols. 336–7 Gaisford), and s.v. κουρεῶτις (1522–3 Gaisford); *Lexica Segueriana* s.v. ἀπατούρια (in Bekker, *Anecdota graeca* 1, pp. 416–17); Scholiast on Aelius Aristeides, 1 (*Panathenaikos*) 118.20 (3, pp. 111–12 Dindorf); Scholiast on Aristophanes, *Acharnians* 146 (p. 7 Dübner), and *Peace* 890 (p. 315 Dübner); Suda, s.v. ἀπατούρια (1, no. 2940 Adler); s.v. Μέλανθος (3, no. 458 Adler); s.v. μέλαν (3, no. 451 Adler); s.v. Ξάνθος (3, no. 8 Adler); George Syncellus in *FHG* 4, p. 539. These sources have recently been assembled and discussed by Fernandez Nieto, 1975: 2.15–20 (no. 3).

10 [This is not quite accurate: Plutarch, who is here discussing wine and its uses, makes one of his characters say: σὺ δ' (i.e. his interlocutor, Niger) ἀξιοῖς τοῦ νυκτερινοῦ καὶ μελαναίγιδος ἐμφορεῖσθαι, 'But you want us to fill up on [wine] "dark as night and sable-skinned" ', which seems to be a cult-title of Dionysus;

but V.-N.'s general point remains valid, cf. Suda s.v. Μέλαν (3, p. 350 no. 451 Adler); Konon in *FGrH* 26 F 1 § 39 lines 27—30. Ed.]

11 There is here more than a mere etymological play on words. As Pauline Schmitt informs me, there was according to Pausanias 2.33.7, on the island of Sphaeria near Troezen, a temple of Athena Apatouria, which played an important part in the initiation of young girls. The 'original' *apatē* (deception) is the union of Poseidon and Aethra, mother of Theseus; see Schmitt, 1977: 1059—73.

12 Usener, 1912—13a: 4.292—7, following a suggestion by Maass, 1889: 805 n. 13; see also Usener, 1912—13b: 4.437—47.

13 Farnell's theory was very like Nilsson's (1951—60a: 1.61—110, 111—16), which of course he did not know.

14 Marie Delcourt's remarks in 1965: 18 are completely unfounded, being based upon mistaken facts.

15 Dolios himself is a sympathetic figure: *Odyssey* 24.222—5, 387—90, 397—411 [and at least some of his sons, apparently. Ed.]. Annie Schnapp has discussed this theme of *dolos*—Dolon in a forthcoming article.

16 This point has been challenged by Maxwell-Stuart, 1970: 113—16. He tries to minimize the significance of Philostratus, *Lives of the Sophists* 2.550, according to which the ephebes wore in assembly and in public processions a black *chlamys*. His criticism does not carry conviction because, although he is familiar with Roussel's article (1941: 163—5) — which to my mind is decisive — he persists in thinking that *IG* II^2 1132 (honorific inscription for Herodes Atticus) refers to Herodes's father, Claudius Atticus, whose vow Herodes was fulfilling. But Roussel showed that the text in fact refers to Theseus: it says 'the son of Aegeus much to his dismay forgetting his father . . . ' (λήθην πατρὸς ἀκεώμενος | Αἰγείδεω: 20). Moreover, there is no way of showing that this inscription refers to the mysteries of Eleusis. On the other hand, I have taken account of two important points by Maxwell-Stuart, and removed a reference to Xenophon, *Hellenica* 1.7.8 (which I interpreted wrongly) and the evidence of the vases (which I misrepresented).

17 See Plato's *Laws* 1, 633b and the relevant, and very important, scholia on it; Heracleides of Pontus in *FHG* 2, p. 210; Plutarch, *Life of Lycurgus* 28; note too Plutarch, *Life of Cleomenes* 28, which mentions one Damoteles, who was in Cleomenes's army the head of the *krypteia* (that is, in charge of ambushes) [cf. Köchly, 1881—2: 1.586—7. Ed.].

18 It would be diverting to compare these 'military' interpretations in the nineteenth century with the liberal, not to say Louis-Philippian, one of Henri Wallon, the 'father of the Republic', for whom the *krypteia* was essentially a police-operation.

19 Plutarch, *Life of Lycurgus* 28.4 (quoting Aristotle). For a defence of the seriousness of this tradition, see Finley, 1975b: 165 with n. 9; 176—7.

20 At the level of ideology, of course; the actual social organization of the Spartiate hoplite-body is more complicated than this, as Nicole Loraux reminds me (see Loraux, 1977: 105—20).

21 See Lévi-Strauss, 1966b: 19—30, and, more generally, 1970, with Yalman, 1967: 71—89; also Jaulin, 1967: 40—119, 141—71 (the astonishing account of the author's 'initiation' by a tribe in Chad), and Dumézil, 1968: 63—5 (on another type of opposition between the 'naked' and the 'heavily-armed' warrior).

22 Rational decision (*gnōmē*) is for Thucydides the opposite of fortune (*tychē*); discourse the opposite of action, just as the hot is the opposite of the cold or the dry of the wet in Milesian cosmological thinking.

23 On the concept of inversion, one could quote the whole of Lévi-Strauss's work; see also Pembroke's important paper, 1967: 1—35.

24 On the Oschophoria, see Mommsen, 1898: 36, 278—82; Rutgers van der Loeff, 1915: 404—15; Deubner, 1932: 142—6; Severyns, 1938: 2.243—54; Jeanmaire, 1939: 346—7, 524, 588; Jacoby, *FGrH* 3 b 1: 285—304; 3 b 2: 193—223; Faure, 1964: 170—2.

25 The entire literary tradition on the Oschophoria and Skira is printed in Jacoby, *FGrH* 3 b 1 (Supplement): 286—9 in his commentary upon some of the most important passages (Philochorus, 328 F 14—16). The only significant inscription relevant to the Oschophoria is that belonging to 363 BC which gives us the record of an agreement between the two segments of the Salaminian *genos* which had been in dispute (first published, with a full commentary, by W.S. Ferguson, 1938: 1—74; conveniently reprinted in Sokolowski, 1962: 49—54, no. 19).

26 See Sokolowski, 1962: 50, line 49. The same *genos* provided two female *deipnophoroi* ('food-carriers') who brought food to the young people 'shut away' during the seclusion ceremonies in Phaleron; cf. Nilsson, 1951—60e: 2.731—41.

27 Jacoby, *FGrH* 3 b 2 (Supplement): 200—3. The sanctuary of Athena Skiras is said to be 'outside the city' (ἐξ τῆς πόλεως): *Etymologicon Magnum* p. 717. 28 [= Jacoby, *FGrH* 3 b 1 (Supplement): 287 no. 7. Ed.].

28 *Amphithalēs* has two meanings: 'a child with both parents alive'; and 'one who cuts and handles green branches or twigs in rituals or processions': see Robert, 1940: 509—19.

29 See Plutarch, *Life of Theseus* 23.3—4, quoting the Atthidographer Demon [*c.* 300 BC]; Proclus, *Chrestomathia* 88—91 (pp. 56—7 Severyns) [= Photius, *Bibliotheca* 239].

30 These points seem to have gone unnoticed.

31 Proclus, *Chrestomathia* 91—2 (p. 57 Severyns): εἴπετο δὲ τοῖς νεανίαις ὁ χορὸς καὶ ᾖδε τὰ μέλη. ἐξ ἑκάστης δὲ φυλῆς ἔφηβοι διημιλλῶντο πρὸς ἀλλήλους δρόμῳ ('the chorus followed the young men [the procession with the two boys dressed as girls V.-N.] and sang the songs; ephebes from each tribe competed against each other in a running race'); see also the scholiast on Nicander of Colophon, *Alexipharmaka* 109 [p. 36 Ábel and Vári: ὠσχοφόροι δὲ λέγονται Ἀθήνησι παῖδες ἀμφιθαλεῖς ἁμιλλώμενοι κατὰ φυλάς, οἱ λαμβάνοντες κλήματα ἀμπέλου ἐκ τοῦ ἱεροῦ τοῦ Διονύσου ἔτρεχον εἰς τὸ τῆς Σκιράδος Ἀθηνᾶς ἱερόν: 'Oschophoroi means at Athens boys who carried sacred branches and who competed by tribes; they ran with vine-branches from the temple of Dionysus to the temple of Athena Skiras.' Ed.]. The inscription of the Salaminioi, quoted above, apparently alludes to this competition (*hamillos*) in lines 61—2 (Sokolowski, 1962: 51): τὸ δὲ πρόθυμα τοῦ ἁμίλλου ἐν μέρlει ἑκατέρους κατάρχεσθαι: 'Each party (i.e. the two segments of the Salaminian *genos* whose dispute is here resolved) shall perform in turn the sacrifice which precedes the contest' [cf. Ferguson, 1938: 37. Ed.].

The literary tradition is hopelessly confused, since the sources seem to mix up at least four festivals, the Oschophoria, the Skira, the Skiraphoria and the Thesmophoria. The first and last of these took place in the month Pyanepsion (September—October) and the Thesmophoria was confined to married women. But what about the Skira? Aristodemus of Thebes, a late hellenistic Boeotian writer, assigned the ephebic race, which I have assigned to the Oschophoria on the authority of Proclus, to the festival of the Skira, which was connected with Athena Skiras, just as the Oschophoria was (*FGrH* 383 F 9, from Athenaeus, *Deipnosophistae* 11, 495e). The scholiast to Aristophanes, *Ecclesiazusae* 18 (p. 315 Dübner) says that the Skira was a June festival (12 Skirophorion). If so, it is impossible to suppose that the youths carried *ōschoi*, bunches of *ripe* grapes. I cannot therefore agree with Jacoby when he writes: 'Our tradition is perfectly clear: the procession is attested for the Oschophoria, the race for the Skiraphoria' (or the Skira, perhaps); and then clarifies this 'tradition' by arguing that part of Proclus's text is interpolated (*FGrH* 3 b 1 (Supplement), commentary on 328 F 14—16). Additional support for my interpretation is provided by the existence at Sparta of a ritual race very close to that described by our sources, linked to a festival of the phratries (the Carneia), and in which the runners carry bunches of grapes in just the same way (see p. 157 below).

On the Skira, see Dow and Healey, 1965: 16—17, 33, 39—41, 44, revising and commenting upon *IG* II² 1363 (though the book must be used with caution: cf. J. and L. Robert, 1967: 481—2 [no. 217] and the authors they cite, especially Jean Pouilloux and Georges Roux).

[V.-N.'s comments on Jacoby here are surely justified; but I do not think we can be certain that the parallel between the Oschophoria and the Staphulodromia in Sparta was quite as exact as he argues. The only source which states categorically that the ephebes who ran in the race carried *oschoi* is the Scholiast on Nicander of Colophon in the passage I have translated above. Proclus himself says only that it was the two young men dressed as girls who carried vine-branches and grapes: τοῦ χοροῦ δὲ δύο νεανίαι κατὰ γυναῖκας ἐστολισμένοι κλῆμα τ' ἀμπέλου κομίζοντες μεστὸν εὐθαλῶν βοτρύων: 'two young men from the chorus, dressed as women and carrying a vine-branch covered with fat grapes ... '. In view of the much greater circumstantiality of this passage, and section 92, it seems easier to suppose that it is the scholiast on Nicander which has compressed a fuller account to the point of confusion, or muddled a procession in the Oschophoria involving (1) two young men carrying vine-branches and (2) a race between *ephebes* with a similar one in the Skiraphoria, when the grapes were just starting to set. In this connection, it is instructive that this scholiast thought that *ōschē* meant simply 'a vine branch', and by extension the branch of any tree, thus missing the point stressed, for example, by Proclus, and by the *Etymologicon Magnum* 619.32 Gaisford, that the branch carried ripe bunches of grapes. Ed.]

32 See also Aristodemus of Thebes, *FGrH* 383 F 9 and Proclus, *Chrestomathia* 91—2 (p. 57 Severyns).

33 '(They call the ephebes) *apodromoi* in Crete because they do not yet take part in the running races': ἐν ... Κρήτῃ, ἀποδρόμους, διὰ τὸ μηδέπω τῶν κοινῶν δρόμων μετέχειν: Eustathius, *Commentarius in Hom. Odyss.* 8.247 [p. 1592. 58], quoted by Willetts, 1955: 11 n. 8.

34 It will be recalled that there were festivals, such as the *Pannychis* during the Athenian Panathenaia, from which all but the young were excluded, and which were held at night (cf. Euripides, *Heracleidae* 780—3); note too the ritual mentioned by Herodotus 3.48, discussed by Schmitt, 1979: 226—7.

35 See *IC* 1,9 (Dreros), 1.11—12; 98—100 (p. 85); 1,19 (Mallos), 1.17—18, with Guarducci's commentary on pp. 87, 232; cf. Schwyzer, 1928: 237—48 and van Effenterre, 1937: 330—2.

36 The main work on hunting in classical Greece remains Otto Manns, 1888: 7—38; 1889: 3—20; 1890: 3—21. There is some information to be gleaned from Aymard, 1951 (mostly about Roman hunting), and cf. Brelich, 1958: index, s.v. Caccia. When this article was first published, I did not know Kerényi, 1952: 131—42, which raises a number of the problems discussed here. See now also Schnapp, 1973 (still unpublished); Brelich, 1969: 198—9; and Pleket, 1969: 281—98, which is thought-provoking.

37 In the well-known opposition between hoplite and archer in Euripides's *Herakles*, the archer is rejected, since he hunts wild animals (153—8).

38 ['To the mountains' translates ἀφίκετ' ἐς ἐρεμίαν, | κἀν τοῖς ὄρεσιν ᾤκει: 'he went to the wild land, and dwelt in the mountains' (lines 786—7). Ed.]

39 The literary texts concerning Atalanta are given, for example, by Immerwahr,

1885: 1—28. Bowra, 1950: 52—69, though devoted to Swinburne's poem *Atalanta*, is suggestive; but the fundamental discussion is now Arrigoni, 1977; cf. Detienne, 1979a: 27—34, 40—2, 44—51. On the episode of the apples, see Trumpf, 1960: 20.

40 'A half-child man' (ἀνδρόπαις ἀνήρ), says Aeschylus, *Seven against Thebes* 533; the very name, Parthenopaeus, means 'with a face like a girl's'.

41 Apollodorus, *Bibliotheca* 3.9.2; Ovid, *Metamorphoses* 10.560—607; *Vatican Mythographer* 1.39 (ed. Mai); Hyginus, *Fabulae* 185; Servius *in* Vergil. *Aeneid*. 3.113. The sources differ concerning the name of Atalanta's husband.

42 This type of figure in myth should be compared with the whole range of those who refuse transition. That is a subject which has not yet been explored.

43 Starting from here, I have tried to show that one can interpret Sophocles's *Philoctetes* in terms of the *ephebeia* (1972: 161—84) (see n. 27, p. 261 below).

44 Xenophon's work on war and hunting reveals this modification of the hoplite tradition extraordinarily well. Many sentences — for instance those which advise the training of youths and older men for war by the practice of hunting — have a polemical significance which has hardly been noticed.

45 This is as far as I go along with the remarks of Pleket, 1969: 294 on the ephebe as a hoplite-in-the-making. On the ephebic oath as a hoplite oath, see Siewert, 1977: 102—11.

46 See Dumézil, 1942: 37; 1956: 23; and more generally, Vian, 1968: 53—68. In the properly Roman context, several studies by J.-P. Morel have thrown new light on the rôle of the *iuventus* (the age-class of young men) in the age-class structure: cf. 1969: 526—35; 1976: 663—83.

9. Recipes for Greek adolescence

1 [*Customs of the American Savages compared with the Customs of Earliest Times*], cited in the second edition, 4 vols., *duodecimo*. [The book was translated into Dutch in 1751 and into German in 1752, but never into English. Ed.]

2 See especially Kälin, 1943, and the authors he cites, especially Arnold van Gennep, 1913; some additional information may be found in Duchet, 1971: 14, 15, 72, 99, 101, 105, and especially the chapter 'Discours ethnologique'; cf. Lemay, 1976: 1313—28.

3 Lafitau, 1724: 1, 'Explanation of the engravings and figures in the First Volume'.

4 It is hard to say whether the bearded figure below Mary is a prophet, or whether, more probably, it is the Eternal Father addressing himself to Adam and Eve. Lafitau makes no comment. [The Iroquois 'turtle' was the emblem of one of the three common Iroquois clans, the Turtle, the others being the Wolf and the Bear; so, at least, Morgan, 1877: 136. Ed.]

5 de Acosta, 1954: 34. The translation of 1598: 50 is a mollification of the original. [On de Acosta and Lafitau, see briefly in English Meek, 1976: 42—9, 57—64. Ed.]

6 Morgan, 1857: 145; cf. Pembroke, 1967: 3. [By 1877 he is himself quoting Bachofen (359, 464 n. 1) within the context of his own argument. On Lewis Morgan in English, see Resek, 1960; Eggan, 1960: 179—201; Harris, 1968: 180—9. Ed.]

7 Morgan, 1877: 4 ['As we re-ascend along the several lines of progress toward the primitive ages of mankind, and eliminate one after the other, in the order in which they appeared, inventions and discoveries on the one hand, and institutions on the other, we are enabled to perceive that the former stand to each other in progressive, and the latter in unfolding relations. While the former class have had a connection, more or less direct, the latter have been developed

from a few primary germs of thought. Modern institutions plant their roots in the period of barbarism, into which their germs were transmitted from the previous period of savagery. They have had a lineal descent through the ages, with the streams of blood, as well as a logical development.' Ed.].

8 See, for example, the discussions in Garaudy, 1969, and Godelier, 1970; also Vidal-Naquet, 1964, and Sofri, 1969. [In English, note Anderson, 1974: 397— 431, 462—549; and Hobsbawm, Introduction to Marx, 1964: 9—65. Ed.]

9 Note the sort of 'manifesto' edited by R.R. Marett, 1908, involving five classicists [Arthur Evans, Gilbert Murray, F.B. Jevons, J.L. Myers, W. Warde-Fowler] and an anthropologist-historian, Andrew Lang. The manifesto summarized the work of a generation.

10 See Gaidoz, 1884/85: cols. 97—9. [For an account in English, see Sharpe, 1975: 35—46 and 47—71, *passim*. Ed.] On this, and several other changes, see Detienne, 1979b: 72—7.

11 Tylor, 1903: 1.7; chapters 3 and 4 are devoted to 'Survival in Culture' (1903: 1.70—159). On Tylor and his contemporaries, see Mercier, 1971: 50—79; there is some information on the notion of 'survival' in Tylor to be found in Hodgen, 1936: 36—66, and especially Burrow, 1970: 228—59.

12 Tylor, 1903: 1.469. [The passage continues: 'Men to whom the cries of beasts and birds seem like human language, and their actions guided as it were by human thought, logically enough allow the existence of souls to beasts, birds, and reptiles, as to men. The lower psychology cannot but recognize in beasts the very characteristics which it attributes to the human soul, namely, the phenomena of life and death, will and judgement, and the phantom seen in vision or in dream.' Ed.]

13 Lang, 1887: 2.255—88. Note the respect accorded to Lafitau: '[He] was perhaps the first writer who ever explained certain features in Greek and other ancient myths and practices as survivals from totemism. The Chimera, a composite creature, lion, goat and serpent, might represent, Lafitau thought, a league of three totem tribes, just as wolf, bear and turtle represented the Iroquois league' (1.73). For a critical modern view, see Detienne, pp. 215—17 below. [On Lang's anthropological work, see in English, Rose, 1951; de Cocq, 1968. Ed.]

14 See Lévi-Strauss's finale, in 1971: 559—621, which argues the point in striking fashion.

15 For an example which is not Breton but from Poitou, see Le Goff and Le Roy Ladurie, 1971: 587—622.

16 Leach, 1966a: 125; on van Gennep and *rites de passage* see Belmont, 1974: 69—81.

17 It has been demonstrated by Margarido, 1971, that in initiation rituals the selfsame area can 'be' sometimes the world of the wild, and sometimes the humanized world; indeed, the function of rituals of initiation is to humanize both the age-classes and the 'wild'.

18 See C. Bérard, 1970; also Rolley, 1974: 307—11; and Auberson, 1975 (especially the remarks of Auberson, Mele, Martin and Lepore), although I think that Bérard has answered these objections. More generally, note Snodgrass, 1977.

19 Archaeologists have habitually ignored burials of children and adolescents because the bodies were laid just beneath the surface — though they have carefully recovered the remains of babies (which were placed in amphorae) and of adults (which were placed in cinerary urns). But *somebody* must have died between the ages of two and eighteen: see C. Bérard, 1970: 52.

20 See Labarbe, 1953: 358—94; Vidal-Naquet, 1968: 161—81, and pp. 149—50 above; Vernant, 1974: 31—56.

21 Of special importance are Jeanmaire, 1913: 121—50 and 1939; Nilsson, 1951—

60b: 2.826—69; Roussel, 1941: 163—5; 1951: 123—228; Thomson, 1941; Brelich, 1961 and 1965: 222—31. On *Paides e Parthenoi* (1969), as well as on earlier work by Nilsson, Jane Harrison, Jeanmaire etc., see Calame, 1971: 7—47; C. Sourvinou-Inwood, 1971a: 172—7; Vidal-Naquet, 1968: 161—81 and pp. 147—62 above; Vernant, 1974: 31—56.

22 See Roussel, 1941: 163—5; Vidal-Naquet, pp. 153—6 above; Maxwell-Stuart, 1970: 113—16.

23 There is an extensive literature, but note Gernet and Boulanger, 1932: 39—40; Jeanmaire, 1939: 442; Delcourt, 1961; Vernant, 1974: 34—40 and Vidal-Naquet, pp. 155—8 above.

24 See Brelich, 1961 and Ellinger, 1978: 7—35 (a study of a particularly radical form of myth about warrior-ruses or stratagems).

25 In the Greek world, as in the mediaeval, there were bows and bows; the bow drawn by Odysseus at the end of the *Odyssey* is the type-case of the bow classified 'positively'.

26 See the very detailed commentary on *Constitution of the Athenians*: 42 by Pélékidis, 1962: 83—6 cf. 87—152; also Brelich, 1969: 216—27. For the date, see p. 147 n. 2 above.

27 See Vidal-Naquet, 1972: 161—84, whose fundamental conclusions I stand by, despite the arguments of di Benedetto, 1978: 191—207.

28 Literally, 'I ground the grain for our *Archēgetis*', which refers to Athena, despite Souvinou-Inwood, 1971b: 341, who argues for Artemis; only Athena could be Archēgetis at Athens.

29 See Brelich, 1969: 229—30, who properly criticizes the assumption; I continue to agree with Brelich, despite Calame, 1977: 1.67—9.

30 The fundamental text is Pausanias 1.27.3; the evidence is collected in Cook, 1914—40: 3.165—91 (with an extraordinary commentary) and especially in Burkert, 1966: 1—25, who indeed emphasizes the initiatory aspects of the cult, but fails, I think, to relate it to the transition between one age-class and another. On the number of *arrephoroi*, see Brelich, 1969: 233, 282.

31 Even though Aristophanes chooses to present the situation as though it were, for dramatic and comic reasons that have not really been understood; see Loraux, 1980b.

32 The two periods are sometimes telescoped into one.

33 ['Escheat' is a feudal, not an ancient legal term, and is technically inappropriate here because of course the land did not revert to the crown in classical Athens in default of direct heirs. Nevertheless the word conveys a sense of the danger of a family's land being dispersed beyond its control in such a case. The French is 'tomber en déshérence' (p. 156). An *epiklēros* was a woman who, on the death of her father, found herself the sole surviving direct heir, and who in Athenian law was compelled to marry her nearest agnatic kin. See further, Harrison, 1968: 10—11, 132—38. Ed.]

34 Finley, 1975b: 161—77. ['Beneath the mask of Lycurgus' is the title of Chapter 8 of Jeanmaire's *Couroi et Courètes*, pp. 463—588. Ed.]

35 Pericles, in Thucydides 2.39.1, plays on the doubt at Sparta for the benefit of the Athenians when he declares that the Spartiates 'by dint of harsh training pursue the state of manhood [or manly things] while still youths', ἐπιπόνῳ ἀσκήσει εὐθὺς νέοι ὄντες τὸ ἀνδρεῖον μετέρχονται; cf. Loraux, 1975: 6.

36 Xenophon, *Const. Laced.* 2.9. This custom is not to be confused with what it became in the Roman period — a mere spectacular.

37 Plutarch, *Life of Lycurgus* 16.4—5; Xenophon, *Const. Laced.* 2.11. Nilsson, 1951—60b: 2.831, is of the opinion that Plutarch's *agela* is a translation of *ila*. The official title, attested epigraphically, of the group-leader was *Bouagos*, 'Herdsman' [cf. Hesychius, s.v. βουαγόρ· ἀγελάρχης, ὁ τῆς ἀγέλης ἄρχων παῖς. Λάκωνες 1, no. 867 Latte. Ed.]

38 Pausanias 3.14.8, 20.8. One of the competitions between the young men which we know from the dedications to Artemis Orthia was called by a name which indisputably means 'hunt'; the others seem to have been musical competitions: Brelich, 1969: 175.

39 We might pursue the play of these institutionalized metaphors: thus, as Nicole Loraux has noted (1977: 116), in the last stages of the battle at Thermopylae (480 BC), the three hundred Spartiates — that is the former *kryptoi* now serving as *Hippeis* — fought 'with their hands and with their teeth', or 'like boars sharpening their tusks': Herodotus 7.225.3; Aristophanes, *Lysistrata* 1254—6.

40 See Brelich, 1969: 157—66, and Calame, 1977: 1.251—357.

41 I would note among the best efforts in this sense, Wachtel, 1971: 793—840 and Zuidema, 1971 (with a preface by Wachtel).

42 Morin, 1965: 223. [See also the similar point made by Roland Barthes, 'The Blue Guide' in 1972: 74—7. Ed.]

10. Slavery and the Rule of Women in tradition, myth and utopia

1 For a preliminary attempt, see my earlier article on the Black Hunter (pp. 147—62 above).

2 [The drift of this seems to me rather misleading. Aristotle begins his discussion of Sparta and Crete by considering helotage (2.9, 1269a—29 ff.) and says that, because of the difficulty in knowing how to treat such helots, states which suffer from revolts or from insolence on the helots' part cannot be said to have found 'the best way' (1269b11—12). He then at once proceeds to consider a correlative disadvantage at Sparta, the licence granted women: there is no direct comparison between slaves and women, although the one matter evidently caused Aristotle to turn to the other immediately afterwards. But there may be a veiled reference to miscegenation between free women and helots at 2.9.11, 1270a1—3. Ed.]

3 [Again, this seems to me slightly inaccurate. Aristotle is here talking specifically of the maintenance of tyranny (5.11.4—34, 1313a34—1315b10), and makes no mention (here) of the historical/moral filiation between democracy and tyranny: laxity towards slaves and use of female spies are means by which tyrants rule ('over true men'), just as under democracy . . . because democracy is a sort of tyranny (1313b38—9). Ed.]

4 See Vidal-Naquet, 1973a: 35—6, and, for an attempt at an historical interpretation, Fuks, 1968: 102—11.

5 See Cratinus frg. 208 (*CAF* 1, p. 76, quoted by Stephanus of Byzantium); Eupolis frg. 197 (*CAF* 1, p. 312, quoted by Hesychius); Ephorus, *FGrH* 70 F 50 (quoted in the Suda); Mnaseas of Patrae, quoted in the *Appendix proverbiorum*, 3.91 s.v. μὴ ἐνὶ δούλων πόλις (*Corpus paroem. gr.*, ed. Leutsch and Schneidewin, 1, pp. 433—4 = *FHG* 3, p. 155, frg. 38); Sosicrates, *FGrH* 461 F 2 (quoted by the Suda); Pliny, *HN* 5.44; Olympianus, quoted by Stephanus of Byzantium, s.v. δούλων πόλις (p. 237 Meinecke); Apostolius 6.35 (*Corpus paroem. gr.*, edd. Leutsch and Schneidewin, 2, p. 371 s.v. δούλων πόλις). Most of these references are to be found conveniently in three lexica, s.v. δούλων πόλις: Hesychius, p. 437 Schmidt; Stephanus of Byzantium, p. 237 Meinecke; the Suda, no. 1423, 2, p. 133 Adler.

6 A fabulous city supposed to have been founded by Philip of Macedon in Thrace.

7 Our source, Ephorus (*FGrH* 70 F 29, from Athenaeus, *Deipnosophistae* 6.263f) says that around the town of Kydon there were festivals in which no free man could enter the city and 'οἱ δοῦλοι παντῶν κρατοῦσι', 'the slaves are in control of everything'. We also have the information from Stephanus of Byzantium.

8 Possible counter-examples are the slave-camp on Chios mentioned by Nymphodorus (see Fuks in n. 4 above), or the slave-kingdom set up in the second century BC round Etna in Sicily; but these were institutions created by slaves, not 'cities' described as servile.

9 See Pembroke, 1965: 217—47; 1967: 1—35; 1970: 1240—70 (which deals with the traditions concerning Epizephyrian Locris and Tarentum). His arguments are not affected by the dissertation of Kaarle Hirvonen, 1968, which anyway ignores them.

10 See the texts assembled by Dumézil, 1924; at least one text uses the term γυναικοκρατουμένη ('ruled by women') in connection with Lemnos: Apollodorus, *Bibliotheca* 1.9.17.

11 On Clytemnestra in Greek tragedy as the usurper of male powers, see Vernant, 1971: 1.134—5, and Zeitlin, 1978: 149—89.

12 There is a vast, though often quite worthless, literature on this topic. There are however two useful articles I may mention, Luria, 1933: 210—28 and Willetts, 1959: 495—506; and a summary of the problem in Crahay, 1956: 172—5. This text of Herodotus, and many other parallel ones including a number of those discussed here, have now been dealt with by my friend David Asheri, 1977: 21—48. His commonsense perspective is very different from my own, but his full collection of evidence may allow a re-examination of the problem. Let me also mention the criticisms made of my article by Van Compernolle, 1975: 355—64.

13 Cf. Willetts, 1959: 502: 'It is well to bear in mind that ἡ θήλεια τὸν ἄρσενα νικήσασα ('the female victorious over the male') represents a proverbial idea for topsy-turvy conditions.'

14 The major sources are Dionysius of Halicarnassus, *Antiq. Rom.*, 7.2—12 esp. 7.9.1—11.4 Jacoby, and Plutarch, *De mulierum virtutibus* 26, 261e—262d. [Further references are to be found in Berve, 1967: 2.611, though his discussion (1.160—3) is not illuminating] ; see now Asheri, 1977: 22—3.

15 See the discussion by Lerat, 1952: 2.22—5: he favours the western (Ozolian) Locrians.

16 Polybius 12.5—11; the passage of Timaeus appears as *FGrH* 566 F 12. An account similar to Polybius's (i.e. Aristotle's) is given by the scholiast to the second-century AD geographer Dionysius Periegetes, 366 (= *GGrM*, 2, p. 495 line 30). See Walbank, 1967: 2.333—41; Pembroke, 1970: 1240—70 (especially important) and Sourvinou-Inwood, 1974: 188—94.

17 More or less the same expression occurs in Athenaeus, *Deipnosophistae* 6, 264c; 272a (= *FGrH* 566 F 11).

18 The essential document is the inscription 'of the Locrian maidens' (reprinted in Schmitt, 1969: no. 472 [pp. 118—26]), brilliantly elucidated by Wilhelm, 1911: 163—256. Further references to the relevant literary texts, and some idea of the enormous modern bibliography, can be found in Schmitt, 1969: 123, 125—56 and in Vidal-Naquet, 1975b: 496—507.

19 Reprinted in Meiggs and Lewis, 1969: no. 20 (pp. 35—40), who strangely omit the important commentary in *IJG* 1.180—92 (no. 11).

20 This point is firmly established by Pembroke, 1970: 1253—4; he also shows that no support for matrilineal descent in Locris can be derived from the epigram in *Anthologia Palatina* 6.265 (= 2801—2 Gow and Page). Lerat also came to the same conclusion about the Locrians (1952: 139—40).

21 Sources and bibliography are to be found in Wuilleumier, 1939: 39—47; Jean Bérard, 1957: 162—75. I have relied heavily upon Pembroke's discussion, 1970: 1241—9.

22 Imitators of Ephorus, whether direct or indirect: Polybius 12.6b.9; Dionysius of Halicarnassus 19.2—4; Justin 3.4.3—11 are the most important.

23 Similar expressions occur in Justin: *promiscuos omnium feminarum concubitus*

263

('indiscriminate couplings with [or by] all the women'), and Dionysius of Halicarnassus: ἐκ τούτων γίνονται τῶν ἀδιακρίτων ἐπιμιξίων παῖδες ('sons were born from these indiscriminate couplings'). Note also Servius, *ad Vergilii Aeneidem* 3.551: *sine ullo discrimine nuptiarum* ('there were no rules at all in these sexual encounters') — but he makes the fathers slaves.

24 Scholia ([Acron] and Porphyrion) on Horace's *Odes* 2.6.12; Servius, *ad. Vergil. Aeneid.* 3.551; *ad Vergil. Eclog.* 10.57; Heracleides Ponticus, *Peri politeiōn* 26 (in *FHG* 2, p. 209) = Aristotle, frg. 611.57 Rose.

25 Aristotle has just been emphasizing the dangers facing aristocracies 'when the mass is composed of men who are ambitious to be equal [to their superiors] in valour': ὅταν ᾖ τὸ πλῆθος τῶν περφρονηματισμένων ὡς ὁμοίων κατ' ἀρετήν. 'For example, in Sparta, the group called the *Partheniai* (descendants of the *Homoioi* ['The Equals']), whom the Spartans sent to found Tarentum after catching them in a conspiracy': οἷον ἐν Λακεδαίμονι οἱ λεγόμενοι Παρθενίαι (ἐκ τῶν Ὁμοίων γὰρ ἦσαν), οὓς φωράσαντες ἐπιβουλεύσαντας ἀπέστειλαν Τάραντος οἰκιστάς. The sense of the expression *ek tōn homoiōn* here is unclear. As well as 'descendants of the *Homoioi*' it could mean 'who belonged to the *Homoioi*', but that would make the passage meaningless. On my interpretation, it may be regarded as just compatible with Ephorus's account; and even with that of Antiochus of Syracuse.

26 Another passage in Diodorus Siculus, 15.66, more or less follows Ephorus. Justin 3.5, which is parallel to Diodorus Siculus 8.21, refers explicitly to the Second Messenian War.

27 Commentators on this passage usually confuse them; credit for distinguishing them must go to Simon Pembroke, 1970: 1245–7.

28 Cf. Dionysius of Halicarnassus 19.1.3–2.1 (Jacoby): the buck-goat motif is gradually bowdlerized to a (male) wild fig-tree enveloped by a (female) vine.

29 The 'clear sky' is Aithra, the wife of the founder of Tarentum, Phalanthos. She weeps while holding her husband's head in her lap (Pausanias 10.10.7).

30 Aristophanes, *Frogs* 694–5 with the scholiasts; Lycurgus, *Against Leocrates* 41; cf. Robert, 1938: 118–26; Garlan, 1972: 29–67 and Welwei, 1974.

31 *Opuiēn*, which in the language of the Athenian comedy-writers means something like 'to fuck', is in the Gortyn Code the technical term for the marital union. The exact status of the *dōlos* has been the subject of endless discussion, since the laws of Gortyn mention another slave, the *woikeus*, who is, everyone agrees, similar to the Spartan helot. Effenterre, 1948a: 92, concludes that *dōlos* indicates the juridical aspect and *woikeus* the social aspect of the same individual, while Finley, 1960: 168–72 argues for the simple equivalence of the terms, developing a point of Lipsius's. The latest editor of the Gortyn Code, Willetts (1967), is more hesitant: 'the word *dōlos* is sometimes synonymous with *woikeus* and sometimes denotes a chattel-slave' (p. 14); a *dōlos* could, for example, be purchased in the agora (col. VII, 10). My own conclusion is that by the time the Gortyn Code was written down, social reality had altered (in particular because of chattel-slavery), but the vocabulary had not followed suit exactly.

32 See Dumézil, 1970: 2.618. The texts are: Macrobius, *Saturnalia* 1.12.7; Johannes Lydus, *De mensibus* 3.22 (Wünsch); Justin 43.1.3–5 (for the Saturnalia); and Macrobius and Johannes Lydus *ibidem* (for the *Matronalia*).

33 Diogenes Laertius, *Lives of the Philosophers* 2.26; Athenaeus, *Deipnosophistae* 13, 556a–b, quoting the περὶ εὐγενείας ('On Good Birth') attributed to Aristotle; Aulus Gellius, *Noctes Atticae* 15.20.6. On this matter, see Jean Pépin in Schuhl, 1968b: 123–5; and on the authenticity of the 'decree' quoted by Hieronymus of Rhodes, Harrison, 1968: 17. Athenaeus and Aulus Gellius, but not Diogenes Laertius, speak of a second *marriage*. [The reference is to Athens.]

34 Dumézil, 1924: 51–3 regarded this myth as the aetiology of a Spartiate ritual with a procession and disguise; see also Pembroke, 1970: 1266.

35 Dumézil, 1924: 11–12 sees here an aetiology for a ritual of separation and initiation. My own interpretation is not intended to be exclusive: I am simply trying to stress why this account is Athenian.

36 Clearchus, quoted by Athenaeus, *Deipnosophistae* 13, 555d (= *FHG* 2, p. 319, frg. 49); Justin 2.6; Charax of Pergamum (*FGrH* 103 F 38); John of Antioch in *FHG* 4, p. 547, frg. 13.5; Nonnus of Panopolis, *Dionysiaka* 41.383; scholiasts on Aristophanes, *Plutus* 773.

37 See Willetts, 1959: 496. ['The low shall be exalted over the high' translates τὰ δ' ὑπέρτερα νέρτερα. Ed.]

38 It is not possible to say exactly when. It was a process which ended only with Pericles's law of 451 BC. Clearly, if we could credit all 'laws of Solon' quoted by Plutarch, one could point to an implicit contrast between two passages in the *Life of Solon* (21.4 and 1.6), between the provision of the Law on wills which disqualifies the testator who acts 'under the influence of a woman' (γυναικὶ πειθόμενος), and the law which forbids slaves to oil themselves for exercise in the gymnasium or to practise pederasty with citizen minors. This second restriction is twice repeated by Plutarch (*Convivium* 7, 152d and *Amatorius* 4, 751b). There is an epigraphic parallel, for in the inscription concerning the 'Mysteries of Andania' (*Sylloge*³ 736 line 109 [= Sokolowski, 1969: no. 65, pp. 120–34]), there occurs the expression δοῦλος δὲ μηθεὶς ἀλειφέσθω: 'no slave may oil himself'.

These 'laws of Solon' are not to be trusted, but they do provide a good illustration of the text of Aristotle cited earlier. It is quite true that Plutarch says immediately afterwards in the *Amatorius* that Solon 'did not forbid sexual relations between slaves and (free) women': χρῆσθαι δὲ συνουσίαις γυναικῶν οὐκ ἐκώλυσε; but this negative affirmation, if I may call it that, is not to the point here, because the context shows quite clearly that for Plutarch himself it is merely a matter of an inference drawn by Protogenes in the dialogue, not of a tradition believed to be ancient.

11. Athens and Atlantis: structure and meaning of a Platonic myth

1 A preliminary sketch of my argument here is to be found in Lévêque and Vidal-Naquet, 1964: 134–9. I am most grateful to P. Lévêque for allowing me here to make use of work that was done together. A version of the paper was read to the Association pour l'encouragement des études grecques on 2 December 1963. I was fortunate enough there to receive both encouragement and help from Jean Bollack and H. Wisman, both of them masterly students of the *Timaeus* and the *Critias*; and would also like to thank those who disagreed with me, especially H. van Effenterre and R. Weil.

2 The undoubted chronological difficulties of this filiation are discussed by Davies, 1971: 325–6. For my part, I am inclined to think that Plato took a perverse delight in its implausibilities. Note that one of the other speakers in the dialogue, Hermocrates, was also a well-known political figure at the end of the fifth century (leader of the Syracusan opposition in Thucydides), and it is natural that he should be talking with an Athenian politician of his own generation.

3 The task has but rarely been either sketched or attempted. I find it quite extraordinary, for example, that these problems are scarcely even mentioned in the great commentaries by Taylor (1928) and Cornford (1937). But note Gegenschatz (1943), who at least sees that there is a problem.

4 There was for long astonishingly little written on Proto-Athens — one excep-

tion was Broneer, 1949: 47—59, although he was mainly interested in archaeology and the history of religions; but see now Herter, 1969: 108—34. By contrast, recent work on the *Critias* (see Cherniss, 1959: 79—83) reveals a spate of studies of Atlantis.

5 See *FGrH* 115 F 75 (a fragment of Theopompus's *Meropia*, his account of the human condition — a sort of narrative fiction: the basic source is Aelian, *VH* 3.18).

6 Strabo 2.3.6 (102C); 13.1.36 (598C). Couissin, 1927: 29—71 contains many references to ancient opinions about Atlantis; cf. also Ramage, 1978: 3—45.

7 Cosmas Indicopleustes, *Christian Topography* 452a11 ff. Winstedt. Wolska, 1962: 270, rightly points out that Cosmas's Platonic references are by no means completely ignorant; and this Byzantine monk is at least strongly sceptical of the historicity of Plato's account. It would in fact be interesting to examine the traces of the myth of Atlantis in patristic thought.

8 Rudbeck, 1689—98: especially 1.144—302. Rudbeck energetically attacks those who simply assumed that Atlantis was America. [The first edition of this book appeared in 1675, in Swedish. V.-N. quotes from the enlarged second edition, in three volumes with a volume of plates, which has a Latin text by Andreas Norcopensis. The Swedish text is most conveniently available in the edition by Axel Nilson (Lychnos-Bibliothek: Studies and sources published by the Swedish History of Science Society: 2.1—2: Uppsala-Stockholm, 1937), 1.91—190. Ed.] On Rudbeck, see Simon, 1960: 267—307 (a reference I owe to H.-I. Marrou). I am at the moment working on a study of seventeenth- and eighteenth-century interpretations of Atlantis.

9 Having had occasion to read Pierre Benoît's monstrous fiction, I confess that at first I took the geographer Berlioux to whom he often refers to be the spontaneous product of Benoît's imagination. That was simply ignorance. I am now able to refer the reader to Berlioux, 1884: 1—70, which is one of Benoît's sources. And one might recall that this piece was written at about the same time as the French colonization of the Sahara [see Julien, 1964. Ed.].

10 Couissin (1928) provides an amusing account of this literature. Since then, the spate shows no sign of diminishing. The reader will forgive me for not citing the authors of this stuff, in spite of their sociological interest, and notwithstanding that among them are to be found eminent men — a Lutheran pastor, a colonel and a lieutenant-colonel.

11 So far as I know, the first scholar to produce this argument was Frost, 1913: 189—206. A more complex form of the same hypothesis (legend replacing an historical tradition) appears in Brandenstein (1951). Finally, according to Marinatos, 1950: 195—213, Atlantis is indeed Cretan, but only after a detour through Egypt — which makes the legend labyrinthine. Perhaps these authors should have thought a little more about Proclus's observation: τὴν γὰρ Κρήτην ἀντὶ τοῦ νοητοῦ τάττειν εἰώθασιν οἱ θεολόγοι, 'the theologians often put Crete when they mean the Intelligible' (*in Timaeum* 1.118.25 Diehl).

Marinatos's article has now been revised and filled out to become a book (Marinatos, 1971) — but neither expansion nor translation has altered its fundamental silliness; the same applies to J.V. Lucas's article in Ramage, 1978: 49—78 — note the comments of J.R. Fears, pp. 103—34.

12 Needless to say, the article is called 'Lost Atlantis found again?'. Since A. Schulten, people have also looked for Atlantis in Tartessus; cf., for example, the wonderfully imaginative book by Gaudio, 1962: 141—6.

13 I need hardly say that in making this point I am not criticizing those studies which attempt to relate Plato's 'information' to the real institutions of his own day, of which Gernet, 1951: xciv—ccvi, is an admirable example. A. Vincent, 1940: 81—96, has in fact shown what can be done by comparative means in relation to the oath of the kings of Atlantis; cf. also, Gernet, 1968c:

207—17. It is also necessary however to show how this 'information' relates to Plato's thought, and I would criticize R. Weil, 1959: esp. 31, for only half performing that task.

14 See Pallottino, 1952: 228—40, who, however, unfortunately combined sensible observations with much more problematic theses concerning Atlantis and Crete. One of the crackpots, J. Spanuth, 1953: 163, has no perceptible hesitation in writing: 'The analogies, even in detail, are so striking, that one wonders whether Homer did not make use of the original account of the history and disappearance of the island of Atlantis when he was telling the story of Odysseus's journey to the land of the Phaeacians.'

15 On the 'hydraulic' aspects of oriental despotism, see Vidal-Naquet (1964).

16 I am pretty sure that Plato even borrowed the name Atlantis from Herodotus. The latter places his Atlantes at the western edge of what he knew of the bulge of the Sahara; of which he says that it extends still further west, beyond the Pillars of Hercules (4.184—5). These Atlantes lived on a mountain in the shape of a column. It was enough for Plato to push the geographical myth a little farther by transferring his island 'in front of the straits which are by you called the pillars of Hercules' (*Tim.* 24e).

17 There is no need to stress the disdain which the aristocratic Plato felt for the sea and everything connected with it: see Luccioni, 1959: 15—47 and Weil, 1959: 159—64.

18 The thesis is not entirely new. The Athenian aspects of the account of Atlantis have often been noted, particularly its Hippodamian geometrism: cf. for example, Kluge, 1910: 286; Friedländer, 1958: 1.273—7; Rivaud, 1925: 249—50, and, more perceptively, Herter, 1928: 28—47. In our comparison between the imperialism of the Atlantans and that of classical Athens, Lévêque and I (1964: 138) are in accord with C.H. Kahn, 1963: 224. Though he argues on the same lines, G. Bartoli, 1779: 34 ff., combines deft intuitions with a cloud of errors.

19 Note that according to tradition the arbitrator of the dispute was Cecrops — whom Plato makes one of the military leaders of his proto-Athens (*Critias* 110a).

20 The expression suggests a circular enclosure.

21 Rivaud unaccountably translates 'separate from the rest'; if the expression is indeed translatable, it means rather 'always identical to itself'.

22 Plato does not mean to suggest that Athena is a pure philosopher. On the contrary, statues of Athena as warrior prove to him that in those days women fought just as men did (*Critias* 110b).

23 Northwards, the frontier reaches as far as the peaks of Cithaeron and Parnes, and includes the territory of Oropus.

24 Cf. Aristotle, *Politics* 2.2, 1261a15 f.: λέγω δὲ τὸ μίαν εἶναι τὴν πόλιν ὡς ἄριστον ὂν ὅτι μάλιστα πᾶσαν · λαμβάνει γὰρ ταύτην ὑπόθεσιν ὁ Σωκράτης, 'I am speaking of the premiss from which the argument of Socrates proceeds, "that the greater the unity of the state, the better".' There are many Platonic passages; see above all *Republic* 4, 462ab. Of course no tribal organization like that of classical Athens impairs the unity of the city of the *Critias* and the *Timaeus*. On the tribes in the city of the *Laws*, see Lévêque and Vidal-Naquet, 1964: 141—2.

25 This is how I understand the phrase εὐκρὰς οὖσα πρὸς χειμῶνά τε καὶ θέρος (112d) (with J. Moreau, in his Pléiade translation); unlike Rivaud, who translates 'equally healthy in summer and winter', thus simply omitting the idea of blending — which occurs in relation to the seasons (ὥρας μετριώτατα κεκραμένας 111e; cf. also *Timaeus* 24c: τὴν εὐκρασίαν τῶν ὡρῶν).

26 *Critias* 112d: 'And they took care to preserve the same number of men and women as could already perform, or could still perform, military service —

that is to say, about twenty thousand.' A moment earlier, we learn that the Athenians were 'the leaders of the Hellenes, who were their willing followers' (τῶν δὲ ἄλλων Ἑλλήνων ἡγεμόνες ἑκόντων).

27 All this is well understood by Proclus, *in Timaeum* 1.132 ff. (Diehl).

28 Cf. Lévêque and Vidal-Naquet, 1964: 118—19, and the authors cited there. E. Ruschenbusch, 1958: 400, has noted that all the allusions to Solon in the Attic orators are, with three exceptions, later than 356 BC, the date of Athens' defeat in the Social War and the break-up of the Second Athenian Empire. The *Timaeus* and the *Critias* can be dated precisely to this period.

29 *Politicus* 269c—274e; cf. on the relation between the structure of this myth and Empedocles's thought, Bollack, 1965: 133—6, and Vidal-Naquet, 1978: 137—9.

30 I cite the text of the manuscripts. The indirect tradition (Proclus, Simplicius) usually cites the passage with the substitution of πόντον for τόπον, which has been accepted by many editors, for example A. Diès, who translates: 'in the bottomless Ocean of dissimilarity'. The passage has been much debated; cf. in particular, J. Pépin, 1954: 257—9. My preference for τόπον is merely ascetic, since πόντον is too suitable for my own thesis for me not to be conservative. There is no doubt that the earlier images, of the pilot and the helm, and of storm, might naturally evoke the image of Ocean (as Diès says); no less naturally, however, might they have inspired a correction.

31 Note that Plato here uses the dual number throughout.

32 On the rôle of the *apeiros* in Platonic teaching, see the very clear discussion of Gaiser, 1963: 190—2. The second hypothesis of the *Parmenides* is a study of the dilution of the One in the world of the Dyad; cf. also *Theaetetus* 155bc.

33 The same characteristic divisions of the World Soul are reproduced at each level of the hierarchy of souls. Each of the two circles is formed, according to fixed proportions, from the substance of the Same, of the Other, and of that which results from their blending. It is its position in the universe which determines the primacy of the circle of the Same.

34 I omit here any discussion of the *chōra*, the material receptacle which makes it possible for differentiation to proceed: *Timaeus* 50b ff.

35 Plato at once goes on to make a comparison with islands.

36 There is nothing unusual in a comparison between imperial Athens and an island: Pericles tells the Athenians at the beginning of the Peloponnesian War to behave as if they were islanders (*Thucydides* 1.92.5); the same image is used by the 'Old Oligarch' (pseudo-Xenophon, *Const. Athen.* 2.14) and by Xenophon (*Poroi* 1).

37 Others have seen here, perhaps rightly, reminiscences of Plato's visit to Syracuse: see Rudberg, 1956: 51—72.

38 The earliest inhabitants of Atlantis were thus autochthonous, just as the inhabitants of Attica were (*Critias* 109d). Plato underlines the point by giving one of the kings of Atlantis the name Autochthonos (113c). Deliberate play on the etymology of proper names is characteristic of the entire account of Atlantis: Euenor is 'the good man', Leucippe 'the white horse' (of Poseidon), their daughter Kleito 'renown', and so on.

39 I have already mentioned (p. 204 above) this Homeric reminiscence: a good example of the many-layered significance of Platonic texts.

40 Stones, of which there are so many in Atlantis, are similarly the result of passing earth through water (60b ff.). These scientific ideas about the origin of metals surely have a mythical background. One is reminded of the first lines of Pindar's First Olympian ode:

Ἄριστον μὲν ὕδωρ, ὁ δὲ χρυσὸς αἰθόμενον πῦρ
ἅτε διαπρέπει νυκτὶ μεγάνορος ἔξοχα πλούτου ·

Best of all things is water; but gold, like a gleaming fire
by night, outshines all, pride of wealth beside. (tr. Lattimore)
There are of course no metals in proto-Athens, and they are anyway forbidden
by the laws (*Critias* 112c).

41 See the diagram in Lévêque and Vidal-Naquet, 1964: 137. Note also the role
played by double and triple intervals in the structure of the World Soul
(*Timaeus* 36d); the double interval corresponds to the octave, the relation 3:2
to the fifth.

42 Equal and unequal, like hot and cold, dry and wet, were part of the famous
table of opposites (*sustoichia*) which Aristotle attributes to the Pythagoreans
(*Metaphysics* 1.5, 986a15). I think that the interpretation of Plato's many
numbers in his account of Atlantis in Brumbaugh's stimulating book (1957:
17–59) is highly debatable. I do not think that Plato intended to provide us
with a world badly constructed in terms of an archaic mathematics. But
Brumbaugh is right to stress the rôle of the numbers 6 and 5 in Plato's
description: there are five pairs of twins, and five enclosures; the centre of
the island is five stades across; the relation between the total area of the rings
of water and that of the rings of earth is 6:5; the statue of Poseidon shows him
driving six horses (116d); the central level area measures 6,000 stades square
(118); it is rectangular, not square, which puts it on the 'bad' side of the table
of opposites'. The number six and its multiples play a fundamental rôle in the
military organization (119ab). I have no desire to interpret these points in
detail here; but simply note that Plato himself stresses that the opposition between 5 and 6 is a form of the opposition between the equal and the unequal;
which is to say, according to the Pythagorean table of opposites, between good
and evil. [For the table, see p. 176 above.]

43 The kings build both the canals and the bridges at the same time, thus ending
the earlier isolation of Kleito's island. This is yet another step in the progress
of disunity.

44 Note that in the *Laws* 3, 681d f., the constitution under which men colonize
the plains after the cataclysms is 'one in which all other forms and conditions
of polities and cities are kingled together' (quoting *Iliad* 20.216–18): ἐν
ᾧ δὴ πάντα εἴδη καὶ παθήματα πολιτειῶν καὶ ἅμα πόλεων συμπίπτει
γίγνεσθαι.

45 This army has both Greek and barbarian characteristics: hoplites and chariot-
fighters exist side-by-side. It is wrong to claim, as does E. des Places *ad loc.*
(cf. Gernet et al. [1951]), that slings were also a barbarian weapon: note the
Rhodian slingers mentioned by Thucydides 6.93.

46 The number 10 is the sum of the first four primary numbers, and corresponds
to *tetraktys*, on whose rôle in Pythagoreanism and in Plato, see Lévêque and
Vidal-Naquet, 1964: 100 and the works by P. Boyancé, A. Delatte and P.
Kucharski cited there; also Gaiser, 1963: 118–23 and the Aristotelian texts
cited on p. 542. See also Brunschwig, 1956: 149–52 (using some unpublished
work of mine). For Plato, the *tetraktys* is a form of *genesis*: cf. esp. *Timaeus*
53e; to say nothing of the construction of the World Soul, in the form of a
double *tetraktys* (*Timaeus* 32b–35bc). It seems to me, in the case of the
Critias, that the genesis of numbers corresponds closely to the play of *phusis*.

47 One is reminded of the *kurbeis* on which were engraved the laws of Solon.

48 The rôle of the oath in the constitution of Atlantis is analogous to that of
incantations and myths in the *Laws*. To echo an expression from E.R. Dodds,
1951: 207, the object is to stabilize the Inherited Conglomerate.

49 There is probably nothing in the typology of social disharmony in *Republic*
8–9 quite so surprising as the analysis of the rôle of gold. Gold did not exist
in the timocratic city of Spartan type (8, 547b–548b), but it makes its

appearance in the oligarchic city, where it provides the basis of the right to rule (8, 550de) and becomes the object of envy on the part of those who have lost their position and who found democracy (8, 555b f.); but it is not enough to level righ and poor, and a lust for gain drives the latter into the arms of the tyrant (8, 556 ff.).

50 Note that this is the language commonly used to describe imperialism.

51 On the significance of this division, see Lévêque and Vidal-Naquet, 1964: 96—8, 110—11, 135—6 and 141—2, which offer analyses of the texts particularly from the *Laws* which allow us to define Plato's reactions to the institutional innovations of Kleisthenes.

52 There is an evident reference to the silver of Laureion.

53 θόρυβος is a word regularly employed by Plato to describe what goes on in democratic assemblies: see *Republic* 6, 492bc, for example. In the *Timaeus*, 42c, the union of the soul with the body also involves a *thorubos*. In contrast, true and eternal reason (λόγος ὁ κατὰ ταὐτὸν ἀληθής) occurs silently, without a sound (ἄνευ φθόγγου καὶ ἠχῆς: 37b). The discussion in the *Republic* takes place in the Piraeus, after a procession in honour of a foreign goddess, in the house of the arms-manufacturer Cephalus, in the midst of a boisterous gathering of young people: philosophy is the last thing they care about. That being so, should we not see the very first words of the dialogue: Κατέβην χθὲς εἰς Πειραιᾶ, 'I walked down to the Piraeus yesterday', as an image of the philosopher's descent back into the cave, as Henri Margueritte has suggested (during his seminars in the École pratique in 1952—3)?

54 See Pausanias 1.28.2. I am indebted for most of these remarks on the archaeology to Pierre Lévêque; see also Lévêque and Vidal-Naquet, 1964: 138.

55 There is little point in referring here to the many discussions of this text; cf. the remarks of Bollack, 1963: 152—3.

56 The eschatological myth of *Laws* 10, 903e—904e, depends upon an analogous reversal.

57 The problems discussed in this article have since been taken up elsewhere and developed, sometimes in a slightly different direction; see Brisson, 1970: 402—38; Gill, 1976: 1—11 and 1977: 287—304.

12. Between Beasts and Gods

1 A great deal of material has been collected, and divergently analysed, by Delcourt, 1966: 139—88; Piccaluga, 1968, and Burkert, 1972b.

2 So Welcker, Hiller von Gaertringen, Cazzaniga and others.

3 They would thus find their place in a Lévi-Straussian reading of Greek myths connected with honey.

4 See my 'The myth of Honeyed Orpheus', pp. 95—109 above.

5 See Detienne, 1977: 37—58 with J.-P. Vernant's introduction, pp. v—vi; xxix—xxxi; and the work of P. Vidal-Naquet, in Vernant and Vidal-Naquet, 1972: 135—58; 1975a: 129—42; and pp. 80—94 above.

6 Porphyry, *De abstinentia* 1.6; Aristotle, *Politics* 1.8, 1256b7—26; see also Moraux, 1957: 100—7; Laffranque, 1964: 468, 478 together with the remarks of Voelke, 1966: 287.

7 Epicurus, *Sententiae selectae* 32 (= Usener, 1887: 78.10—14) with the analysis by Moraux, 1957; cf. Mélèze-Modrzejewski, 1975: 75—102.

8 Hesiod, *Works and Days* 276—9; Plato, *Politicus* 271d; *Protagoras* 321a. The Hesiodic and Aristotelian orthodoxy is however to be contrasted with the tradition of the fable about an animal kingdom in which the eagle's *hybris* shatters the fairness, the *dikē*, which the fox expected when he joined the bird that soars in heaven (Archilochus 168—76 [eds. Lasserre-Bonnard = Traditi]). For the Christian tradition, see Passmore, 1975: 195—218.

9 Herodotus 3.25; cf. Vernant, 1972; xiv–xvii = Detienne and Vernant, 1979: 239–49.
10 Waltzing, 1925: 205–39 [and, in English, Cohn, 1974: 1–59. Ed.].
11 Cf. Detienne, 1977: 149 n. 98.
12 This argument is further elaborated in Detienne, 1979a: 68–94.
13 Plutarch, *Quaestiones graecae* 38, 299e; Antoninus Liberalis, *Metamorphoses* 10 [Minyades]. For the evidence as a whole, see Kambitsis, 1975.
14 On a number of issues, it is doubtless appropriate to see similarities between Cynics and the hippies of the sixties: see Shmueli, 1970: 490–514.
15 'Back to the jungle' is the expression used by Plutarch, *De esu carnium* 995c–d, referring to Diogenes. [The literal meaning of the Greek, *ton bion apothēriōsai*, is 'to put civilized life back among the wild beasts'. Ed.]
16 Diogenes Laertius, *Lives of the Philosophers* 6.56, 105; Julian, *Orationes* 7, 214c; Dio Chrysostom, *Orationes* 6.62; 21–2.
17 Dio Chrysostom, *Or.* 6.25; Plutarch, *Aqua an ignis utilior* 2, 956b; cf. Cole, 1967: 150–1.
18 Tramp: Aristophon frg. 9 (*CAF* 2, p. 279); Alexis frgs. 196, 197 (*CAF* 2, p. 370); cf. Aristophon frg. 10 (*CAF* 2, p. 280). Sea-purslane: Antiphanes frg. 160 (*CAF* 2, p. 76).
19 *Pēra* (Antiphanes in his *Mnemata* uses the synonym *kōrukos*) and *tribōn*: Aristophon frgs. 12, 13 (*CAF* 2, pp. 280–1).
20 See Tannery, 1925: 201–10. Although Burkert, 1972a: 198–208 perceives the links between these comic Pythagoreans and a figure such as Diodorus of Aspendus, he is more concerned with their continuity in relation to the 'Acusmatics' than in their break with tradition. The new type of Pythagorean Cynic was a marginal figure, outcast now by the *polis* and radically cut off from the old Pythagorean community and its members.

Works cited

Acosta, José de. 1954. *Obras del P. José de Acosta* (ed. Francisco Mateos). Madrid. This includes de Acosta's *Historia natural y moral de las Indias* (1590), translated into French by Robert Regnault Cauxois: *Histoire naturelle et moralle des Indes tant Orientalles qu'Occidentalles* (Paris, 1598). [Repr. Paris, 1979.]

Anderson, Perry. 1974. *Lineages of the Absolutist State*. London.

André, Jacques. 1967. *Les Noms d'oiseaux en Latin*. Études et commentaires 66. Paris.

Anti, Carlo. 1920. 'Athena marina e aleata', *Monumenti antichi della Reale Accademia dei Lincei* 26.270–318.

Arrigoni, G. 1977. 'Atalanta e il cinghiale bianco', *Scr. Phil.* 1. 9–47.

Asheri, David. 1966. *Distribuzione di terre nell'Antica Grecia*. Memorie dell' Accademia delle Scienze di Torino: Classe di scienze morali, storiche e filologiche, Ser. 4a, no. 10. Torino.

Asheri, David. 1977. 'Tyrannie et mariage forcé: essai d'histoire sociale grecque', *Annales ESC* 32.1. 21–48.

Auberson, P. (et al.) 1975. *Contribution à l'étude de la société et de la colonisation eubéennes*. Cahiers du Centre Jean Bérard 2. Naples.

Aymard, Jacques. 1951. *Essai sur les chasses romaines des origines à la fin du siècle des Antonins – Cynegetica*. BEFAR 161. Paris.

Bachofen, Johann Jakob. 1861. *Das Mutterrecht. Eine Untersuchung über die Gynaikokratie der alten Welt nach ihrer religiösen und rechtlichen Natur*. Stuttgart. [Re-edited by Karl Meuli, 2 vols., Basel, 1948 (= J.J. Bachofen's *Gesammelte Werke*, vols. 2–3).]

Barner, Wilfried. 1967. *Neuere Alkaios-Papyri aus Oxyrhynchos*. [Dissertation.] Collection Spudasmata 14. Hildesheim.

Barnett, Richard D. 1957. 'Early shipping in the Near East', *Antiquity* 32.220–30.

Barthes, Roland. 1972. *Mythologies*. London [ET, abbreviated, of *Mythologies*, Paris, 1957.]

Bartoli, Giuseppe. 1779–80. *Essai sur l'explication historique que Platon a donnée de sa République et de son Atlantide et qu'on n'a pas considerée jusqu'à maintenant* (1799). Bound with *Discours par lequel Sa Majesté le roi de Suède a fait l'ouverture de la diète, en suédois, traduit en françois et en vers italiens*. 2 parts in 1 vol. Stockholm and Paris. [For full details, see *Catalogue général de la Bibliothèque Nationale* (1901), vol. 8, p. 334. Ed.]

Bellas, Jacqueline. 1970. ' "Orphée" au XIXe et au XXe siècle: interférences littéraires et musicales', *CAIEF* 22.229–46.

Bellessort, André. 1920. *Virgile, son oeuvre et son temps*. Paris.

Belmont, Nicole. 1974. *Arnold van Gennep, créateur de l'ethnographie française*. Collection science de l'homme. Paris.

di Benedetto, V. 1978. 'Il Filottete e l'efebia secondo Pierre Vidal-Naquet', *Belfagor* 33. 191–207.

Bengtson, Hermann. 1962. *Die Staatsverträge des Altertums*, vol. 2: *Die Verträge der griechisch-römischen Welt von 700 bis 338 vor Christ*. Kommission für alte Geschichte und Epigraphik, München. München–Berlin.

Benveniste, Émile. 1966. *Problèmes de linguistique générale*. Paris.

Bérard, Claude. 1970. *L'Hérôon à la porte de l'Ouest*. Eretria, Fouilles et Recherches 3 (ed. Karl Schefold). Berne.

272

Bérard, Jean. 1957. *La Colonisation grecque de l'Italie méridionale et de la Sicile dans l'antiquité. L'histoire et la légende.* 2 ed. Publications de la Faculté de Lettres de Paris, Série Études et méthodes 3. Paris.

Bérard, Jean. 1961. *Homère: Odyssée* (trans. V. Bérard; introduction and notes by J. Bérard). Bibliothèque de la Pléiade 115. Paris.

Berlioux, F. 1884. *Les Atlantes: Histoire de l'Atlantis et de l'Atlas primitif ou Introduction à l'histoire de l'Europe.* Annuaire de la Faculté de Lettres de Lyon 1.1–70. Lyon.

Berthiaume, G. 1976. 'Viandes grecques: le statut social et religieux du cuisinier-sacrificateur (mageiros) en Grèce ancienne.' Thèse 3e cycle, Université de Paris VIII. (To be published as *Boucherie, cuisine et sacrifice dans la Grèce ancienne.*)

Berve, Helmut. 1967. *Die Tyrannis bei der Griechen.* 2 vols. München.

Bettelheim, Bruno. 1962. *Symbolic wounds: puberty rites and the envious male.* 2 ed. (Collier Books) New York.

Beverley, Robert. 1705. *The History and Present State of Virginia, in four parts . . . By a native and inhabitant of the place.* 4 parts, separately paginated. London. (2 ed., anonymous, Amsterdam, 1772.)

Bidez, Joseph. 1945. *Eos ou Platon et l'Orient.* (Gifford Lectures, 1939) Appendix II, additional pages 19–40: *L'Atlantide.* Bruxelles.

Blinkenberg, Christian S. and Kinch, K.F. 1931–60. *Lindos. Fouilles et recherches, 1902–14 and 1952.* Copenhagen Carlsbergfondet. 3 vols. in 6. Copenhagen and Berlin.

Blümner, Hugo. 1875–87. *Technologie und Terminologie der Gewerbe und Künste bei Griechen und Römern.* 4 vols. Leipzig. [Repr. Hildesheim, 1969.]

Bollack, Jean. 1963. Commentary to Plato's *Phaedrus* (translated into German by E. Salin). Exempla classica 85. Frankfurt a/M.

Bollack, Jean. 1965. *Empédocle,* I: *Introduction à l'ancienne physique.* Paris.

Bond, G.W. (ed.) 1963. *Euripides' Hypsipyle.* Oxford.

Bowra, C. Maurice. 1950. 'Atalanta in Calydon.' *Essays by Divers Hands,* no. 25 (ed. Sir Edward Marsh) = *Transactions of the Royal Society of Literature of the United Kingdom* N.S. 25, pp. 52–69. Oxford.

Brandenstein, W. 1951. *Atlantis. Grosse und Untergang eines geheimnisvollen Inselreiches.* Arbeiten aus dem Institut für allgemeine und vergleichende Sprachwissenschaft, Heft 3. Wien.

Bravo, Benedetto. 1979. *Sulân. Représeilles et justice privée contre les étrangers dans les cités grecques.* Paris.

Brelich, Angelo. 1958. *Gli eroi grechi: un problema storico-religioso.* Nuovi Saggi 21. Roma.

Brelich, Angelo. 1961. *Guerre, agoni e culti nella Grecia arcaica.* Antiquitas, Reihe 1, Bd 7. Bonn.

Brelich, Angelo. 1965. 'Initiation et histoire', in *Initiation*: Contributions to the theme of the Study-Conference held at Strasburg, Sept. 1964 (ed. C.J. Bleeker), pp. 222–31. Studies in the history of religions 10. Leiden.

Brelich, Angelo. 1969. *Paides e parthenoi.* Incunabula graeca 36. Roma.

Bremond, Claude. 1964. 'Le message narratif', *Communications* 4.4–32.

Bremond, Claude. 1968. 'Postérité americaine de Propp', *Communications* 11. 147–64.

Brisson, Jean-Paul. 1966. *Virgile. Son temps et le nôtre.* Textes à l'appui 17, Paris.

Brisson, Luc. 1970. 'De la philosophie politique à l'épopée: le *Critias* de Platon', *Revue de Métaphysique et de Morale* 75.402–38.

Broneer, Oscar. 1949. 'Plato's description of Early Athens and the origin of Metageitnia', *Hesperia*, Supplement 8 (*Commemorative studies in honour of T.L. Shear*) pp. 47–59.

Bruck, Eberhard F. 1926. *Totenteil und Seelgerät im griechischen Recht. Eine* entwicklungsgeschichtliche Untersuchung zum Verhältnis von Recht und Religion, mit Beiträge zur Geschichte des Eigentums und des Erbrechts. Münchener Beiträge zur Papyrusforschung und Antiken Rechtsgeschichte, Heft 9. München.

Brumbaugh, Robert S. 1957. *Plato's mathematical imagination*. Bloomington, Indiana.

Brunschwig, Jacques. 1956. Review of Paul Kucharski, *Étude sur la doctrine pythagoricienne de la tétrade* (Paris, 1952). *RPhFE* 146.149—52.

Bücher, Karl. 1904. *Die Entstehung der Volkswirtschaft. Vorträge und Versuche.* Ed. 4. Tübingen.

Buffière, Félix. 1956. *Les Mythes d'Homère et la pensée grecque*. Paris.

Burguière, André. 1971. Introduction to 'Histoire et structure', *Annales ESC* 26.3, i—vii.

Burkert, Walter. 1966. 'Kekropidensage und Arrhephoria', *Hermes* 94.1—25.

Burkert, Walter. 1972a. *Lore and Science in Ancient Pythagoreanism*. Cambridge, Mass. [ET of *Weisheit und Wissenschaft. Studien zu Pythagoras, Philolaus und Platon*, Nürnberg, 1962.]

Burkert, Walter. 1972b. *Homo necans. Interpretationen altgriechischer Opferriten und Mythen*. RGVV 32. Berlin—New York.

Burrow, John W. 1970. *Evolution and Society: a study in Victorian social theory*. 2 ed. Cambridge. (1 ed., 1966.)

Cahen, Émile. 1930. *Les Hymnes de Callimaque. Commentaire explicatif et critique*. BEFAR 134bis (published 1931). Paris.

Calame, Claude. 1971. 'Philologie et anthropologie structurale: à propos d'un livre récent d'Angelo Brelich', *QUCC* 11.7—47.

Calame, Claude. 1977. *Les choeurs de jeunes filles en Grèce archaïque*. 2 vols. Filologia e Critica 20—1. Roma.

Casabona, Jean. 1966. *Recherches sur le vocabulaire du sacrifice en grec, des origines à la fin de l'époque classique*. Publications des Annales de la Faculté des Lettres, Aix-en-Provence, n.s. 56. Aix—Gap.

Cassin, Elena. 1960. 'Le sceau: un fait de civilisation dans la Mésopotamie ancienne', *Annales ESC* 15.4, 742—50.

Casson, Lionel. 1964. 'Odysseus's boat: *Odyssey* 5,244—57', *AJPh* 85.61—4.

Casson, Lionel. 1971. *Ships and Seamanship in the Ancient World*. Princeton.

Chamoux, François. 1957. 'L'Athéna mélancholique', *BCH* 81.141—59.

Chamoux, François. 1972. 'L'Athéna au terma', *RA* n.s. 263—6.

Chantraine, Pierre. 1933. *La Formation des noms en grec ancien*. Collection linguistique, vol. 38. Paris.

Chantraine, Pierre. 1956. 'Quelques termes du vocabulaire pastoral et du vocabulaire de la chasse', in *Études sur le vocabulaire grec*, pp. 31—96. Études et Commentaires 24. Paris.

Chantraine, Pierre. 1962. 'Hesychius: δυοχοῖ ου δρυοχοῖ?', *Revue de Philologie*, sér. 3.36.258—9.

Chapot, Victor. 1887—1919. Art. 'Tignarius'. Daremberg—Saglio 5.332—6.

Cherniss, Harold. 1959. 'Plato, 1950—1957', *Lustrum* 4.5—308, continued in 5.321—618.

Cherniss, Harold. 1977. 'Some war-time publications concerning Plato, 2', in *Selected Papers* (ed. Leonardo Tarán), pp. 176—216. Leiden. [Repr. from *AJPh* 68 (1947), 225—65.]

Clarke, Howard W. 1967. *The Art of the Odyssey*. Englewood Cliffs.

Cocq, Antonius P.L. de. 1968. *Andrew Lang, a nineteenth-century anthropologist*. Tilburg (Netherlands).

Cohn, Norman. 1974. *Europe's Inner Demons*. Columbus Centre Series. London.

Cole, Thomas. 1967. *Democritus and the sources of Greek anthropology*. Philological Monographs no. 25. Cleveland.

Cook, Arthur Bernard. 1914—40. *Zeus. A study in ancient religion.* 3 vols. in 5. Cambridge.

Cornford, Francis M. 1914. *The origin of Attic comedy.* London. [Repr. Cambridge, 1934; Gloucester, Mass., 1968.]

Cornford, Francis M. 1937. *Plato's Cosmology.* London.

Couissin, P. 1927. 'Le mythe de L'Atlantide.' *Mercure de France* 15 February, 29—71.

Couissin, P. 1928. *L'Atlantide de Platon et les origines de la civilisation.* Aix-en-Provence.

Crahay, Roland. 1956. *La Littérature oraculaire chez Hérodote.* Bibliothèque de la Faculté de Philosophie et Lettres de l'Université de Liège 138. Liège—Paris.

Cramp, Stanley (ed.). 1977. *Handbook of the Birds of Europe, the Middle East and Africa: The birds of the Western Palaeoarctic, 1: Ostrich to Ducks.* Oxford—London—New York.

Danoff, Chr. M. 1962. Art. 'Pontos Euxeinos'. *RE Suppl.* 9, cols. 866—1175.

Daux, Georges. 1965. 'Deux stèles d'acharnes.' *Charisterion dédié à Anast. K. Orlandos,* 4 vols. (1965—68), 1.78—90. Société archéologique d'Athènes. Athens.

David, Madeleine. 1960. 'Le récit du Déluge et l'épopée de Gilgameš', in *Gilgameš et sa legende* (edited by P. Garelli), pp. 153—60. Proceedings of 7me Rencontre Assyriologique Internationale, Paris, 1958. Paris.

Davies, J.K. 1971. *Athenian propertied families, 600—300BC.* Oxford.

Delcourt, Marie. 1938. *Stérilités mystérieuses et naissances maléfiques dans l'antiquité classique.* Bibliothèque de la Faculté de Philosophie et Lettres de l'Université de Liège 59. Liège and Paris.

Delcourt, Marie. 1961. *Hermaphrodite. Myths and rites of the bisexual figure in Classical antiquity.* London. [ET of *Hermaphrodite,* Paris—Gembloux, 1957.]

Delcourt, Marie. 1965. *Pyrrhos et Pyrrha. Recherches sur les valeurs du feu dans les légendes helléniques.* Bibliothèque de la Faculté de Philosophie et Lettres de l'Université de Liège 174. Paris.

Delcourt, Marie. 1966. 'Tydée et Mélanippe.' *SMSR* 37.139—88.

Delorme, Jean. 1960. *Gymnasion. Étude sur les monuments consacrés à l'éducation en Grèce des origines à l'Empire romain.* BEFAR 196. Paris.

Desport, Marie. 1952. *L'Incantation virgilienne. Virgile et Orphée.* Bordeaux.

Detienne, Marcel. 1963. *Crise agraire et attitude religieuse chez Hesiode.* Collection Latomus 68 (1964). Bruxelles.

Detienne, Marcel. 1967. *Les maîtres de vérité dans la Grèce ancienne.* Paris.

Detienne, Marcel. 1976. 'Potagerie des femmes ou comment engendrer seule.' *Traverses* 5/6.75—81.

Detienne, Marcel. 1977. *The Gardens of Adonis: spices in Greek mythology.* Hassocks, Sussex. [ET of *Les Jardins d'Adonis: la mythologie des aromates en Grèce,* Paris, 1972.]

Detienne, Marcel. 1979a. *Dionysos slain.* Baltimore. [ET of *Dionysos mis à mort,* Paris, 1977.]

Detienne, Marcel. 1979b. 'Repenser la mythologie', in *La fonction symbolique. Essais d'anthropologie* (edited by M. Izard and P. Smith), pp. 71—82. Paris.

Detienne, Marcel, and Vernant, Jean-Pierre. 1978. *Cunning intelligence in Greek culture and society.* Hassocks, Sussex. [ET of *Les ruses de l'intelligence: la mètis des grecs,* Paris, 1974.]

Detienne, Marcel, and Vernant, Jean-Pierre. 1979. *La cuisine du sacrifice en pays grec.* Paris.

Deubner, Ludwig, 1932. *Attische Feste.* Berlin. [Repr. New York—Hildesheim, 1969.]

Deubner, Ludwig. 1933. 'Die Bedeutung des Kranzes im klassischen Altertum', *ARW* 30.70—104.

Works cited

Dodds, E.R. 1951. *The Greeks and the Irrational*. 1st ed., with several printings. Berkeley.

Dow, Sterling, and Healey, Robert F. 1965. *A sacred calendar of Eleusis*. Harvard Theological Studies 21. Cambridge, Mass., and London.

Ducat, Jean. 1974. 'Les thèmes des récits de la fondation de Rhégion', *Mélanges helléniques offerts à Georges Daux*, pp. 93—114. Paris.

Duchet, Michèle. 1971. *Anthropologie et histoire au siècle des lumières. Buffon, Voltaire, Rousseau, Helvétius, Diderot*. Bibliothèque d'anthropologie. Paris.

Dumézil, Georges. 1924. *Le Crime des Lemniennes. Rites et légendes du monde égéen*. Paris.

Dumézil, Georges. 1942. *Horace et les Curiaces*. (Les mythes romains.) Paris.

Dumézil, Georges. 1956. *Aspects de la fonction guerrière chez les Indo-Européens*. Paris.

Dumézil, Georges. 1958. *L'idéologie tripartite des Indo-Européens*. Collection Latomus 31. Bruxelles.

Dumézil, Georges. 1968. *Mythe et épopée, I: L'idéologie des trois fonctions dans l'épopée des peuples indo-européens*. Paris.

Dumézil, Georges. 1970. *Archaic Roman Religion*. 2. vols. Chicago. [ET of *La Religion romaine archaïque*, Paris, 1966.]

Dümmler, Georg F. 1896. Art. 'Athena'. *RE*, cols. 1941—2020.

Dumont, J.-C. 1966. 'À propos d'Aristonicus', *Eirene* 5.189—96.

Effenterre, Henri van. 1937. 'À propos du serment des Dreriens', *BCH* 61.327—32.

Effenterre, Henri van. 1948a. *La Crète et le monde grec de Platon à Polybe*. BEFAR 163. Paris.

Effenterre, Henri van. 1948b. 'Fortins crétois', *Mélanges d'archéologie et d'histoire offerts à Charles P. Picard*, 2 vols. [= *RA*, sér. 6, nos. 29—32], 2.1033—46. Paris.

Eggan, Fred. 1960. 'Lewis H. Morgan in kinship perspective', in *Essays in the Science of Culture in honor of Lewis White* (eds. G.E. Dole and R.L. Carneiro), pp. 179—201. New York.

Ehrenberg, Victor L. 1965. 'Eunomia', in *Polis und Imperium: Kleine Schriften* (edited by K.F. Stroheker and A.J. Graham), pp. 139—58. [Repr. from Charisteria Alois Rzach, Reichenberg 1930, pp. 16—29 with additions.]

Eitrem, Samson. 1904. *Die Phaiakenepisode in der Odyssee*. Videnskabs-Selskabet i Christiania, Skrifter: Historisk-filosofisk klasse, no. 2. Christiania (Oslo).

Eitrem, Samson. 1915. *Opferritus und Voropfer der Griechen und Römer*. Videnskaps-Selskapet i Kristiania, Skrifter: Historisk-filosofisk klasse (1914), no. 1. Kristiania (Oslo). [Repr. Hildesheim—New York, 1977.]

Eitrem, Samson. 1938. Art. 'Phaiaken.' *RE*, cols. 1518—33.

Eliade, Mircea. 1969. *The Quest: history and meaning in religion*. Chicago.

Ellinger, P. 1978. 'Le gypse et la boue, I. Sur les mythes de la guerre d'anéantissement', *QUCC* 29.7—35.

Fairbanks, Arthur. 1902. 'On the Mourning Athena relief', *AJA* 6.410—16.

Farnell, Lewis, R. 1896—1909. *The Cults of the Greek States*. 5 vols. Oxford.

Farnell, Lewis, R. 1909. 'The Megala Dionysia and the origin of tragedy' [résumé], *JHS* 29.xlvii.

Faure, Paul. 1964. *Fonctions des cavernes crétoises*. École française d'Athènes. Travaux et mémoires, fasc. 14. Paris.

Fears, J. Rufus. 1978. 'Atlantis and the Minoan thalassocracy: a study in modern mythopoeism', in Ramage, E.S. (1978): 103—34.

Ferguson, William S. 1938. 'The Salaminioi of Heptaphylai and Sounion', *Hesperia* 7,1.1—74.

Fernandez Nieto, F.J. 1975. *Los acuerdos belicos en la antigua Grecia (epoca arcaica y clasica)*. 2 vols. Monografias de la Universidad de Santiago de Compostela 30—1. Santiago de Compostela.

Festugière, A.-J. 1972. 'À propos des arétalogies d'Isis', in *Études de religion grecque et hellénistique*, pp. 138—64. Paris. [Repr. from *HThR* 42 (1949), 209—34.]

Finley, Moses I. 1960. 'The servile statuses of Ancient Greece', *RIDA*, Ser. 3,7. 165—89.

Finley, Moses I. 1963/64. 'Between Slavery and Freedom', *CSSH* 6.233—49.

Finley, Moses I. 1975a. 'Utopianism Ancient and Modern', in *Use and Abuse of History*, pp. 178—92. London and New York. [Repr. from *The Critical Spirit. Essays in honor of Herbert Marcuse*, edited by K. Wolff and Barrington Moore jr, Boston, 1967, pp. 3—20.]

Finley, Moses I. 1975b. 'Sparta', in *The Use and Abuse of History*, pp. 161—77. London and New York. [Repr. from Vernant, Jean-Pierre (ed.), 1968, 143—60.]

Finley, Moses I. 1977. *The World of Odysseus*. 3 ed. London and New York. (1 ed., 1953).

Fränkel, Hermann F. 1975. *Early Greek poetry and philosophy: a history of Greek epic, lyric and prose to the middle of the fifth century BC*. Oxford; [ET of *Dichtung und Philosophie des früheren Griechentums*, ed. 3, München, 1969.]

Frazer, James George. 1898. *Pausanias's Description of Greece (trans. and comm.)*. 6 vols. London.

Friedländer, Paul. 1958. *Plato: an introduction*. I. [ET of *Platon: Seinswahrheit und Lebenswirklichkeit*, 2 ed., 1954.] London.

Frisk, Jöns Ivan Hjalmar. 1954—72. *Griechisches Etymologisches Wörterbuch*. Indogermanische Bibliothek, Abt. 1, Reihe 2. 3 vols. Heidelberg.

Fritz, Kurt von. 1963. Art. 'Pythagoreer.' *RE*, cols. 209—68.

Frost, K.T. 1913. 'The Critias and Minoan Crete', *JHS* 33.189—206.

Fuks, Alexander. 1968. 'Slave war and slave troubles in Chios in the third century BC', *Athenaeum* 46.102—11.

Furtwängler, Adolf. 1885. *Beschreibung der Vasensammlung im Antiquarium*. Königliche Museen zu Berlin. 2 vols. Berlin.

Gaidoz, Henri. 1884—85. 'La Mythologie comparée: un mot d'explication', *Mélusine* 2, cols. 97—9.

Gaiser, Konrad. 1963. *Platons ungeschriebene Lehre: Studien zur systematischen und geschichtlichen Begründung der Wissenschaft in der platonischen Schule*. Stuttgart.

Garaudy, Roger (ed.). 1969. *Sur le 'mode de production asiatique'*. Centre d'Études et de Recherches Marxistes. Paris.

Gardiner, Edward Norman. 1910. *Greek Athletic Sports and Festivals*. Handbooks of Archaeology. London.

Garlan, Yvon. 1972. 'Les esclaves grecs en temps de guerre', in *Actes du Colloque d'Histoire sociale* (Besançon, 1970), pp. 29—67. Besançon—Paris.

Garlan, Yvon. 1975. *War in the Ancient World: a social history*. London and New York. [ET of *La Guerre dans l'Antiquité*, Paris, 1972.]

Gaudio, A. 1962. *Les Empires de la mer*. Paris.

Gauthier, Philippe. 1976. *Un commentaire historique des 'Poroi' de Xenophon*. Centre de Recherches d'Histoire et de Philologie de la IVe section de l'École Pratique des Hautes Études, 3: Hautes Études du monde greco-romain 8. Genève—Paris.

Gegenschatz, Ernst. 1943. *Platons Atlantis*. Zürich.

Gennep, Arnold van. 1913. 'Contributions à l'histoire en France de la méthode ethnographique', *RIIR* 67.321—38.

Gennep, Arnold van. 1960. *The rites of passage*. London. [ET by M.B. Vizedoni and G.L. Caffee of *Les Rites de passage. Étude systématique des rites*, Paris, 1909.]

Works cited

Germain, Gabriel. 1954a. *Genèse de l'Odyssée: le fantastique et le sacré*. Paris.
Germain, Gabriel. 1954b. *Homère et la mystique des nombres*. Paris.
Gernet, Louis. 1948. 'Jeux et droit (Remarques sur le XXIIIe chant de l'Iliade)', *RHDFE*, sér. 4, 26.177—88. [Repr. in Gernet, 1955, 9—18.]
Gernet, Louis. 1955. *Droit et société dans la Grèce ancienne*. Publications de l'institut de Droit romain de l'Université de Paris 13. Paris. [Repr. 1964.]
Gernet, Louis. 1968a. 'La cité future et le pays des morts', in *Anthropologie de la Grèce antique*, pp. 139—52. Paris. [Repr. from *REG* 46 (1933), 293—310.]
Gernet, Louis. 1968b. 'Dolon le loup (à propos d'Homère et du *Rhesus* d'Euripide)', in *Anthropologie de la Grèce antique*, pp. 154—71. Paris. [Repr. from *AIPH* 4 (1936), 189—208.]
Gernet, Louis. 1968c. 'Droit et predroit en Grèce ancienne', in *Anthropologie . . .*, pp. 175—260. Paris. [Repr. from *L'Année Sociologique*, sér. 3 [1951], 21—119.]
Gernet, Louis, and Boulanger, André. 1932. *Le génie dans la religion*. Paris. [Repr. Paris, 1970.]
Gernet, Louis (with E. des Places and A. Diès). 1951. *Les Lois de Platon*. Platon: Collection des Universités de France (Budé), vol. 11, 1. Introduction, Part 2: 'Les *Lois* et le droit positif', pp. xciv—ccvi.
Gill, Christopher. 1976. 'The origin of the Atlantis myth', *Trivium* 77.1—11.
Gill, Christopher. 1977. 'The genre of the Atlantis story', *CPh* 72.287—304.
Glotz, Gustave. 1877—1919. Art. 'Iusiurandum', in Daremberg—Saglio, 3.1. 748—69.
Glotz, Gustave. 1904. *L'ordalie dans la Grèce primitive. Étude de droit et de mythologie*. Paris.
Godelier, Maurice (préf.). 1970. *Sociétés Précapitalistes. Textes choisis de Marx, Engels, Lénine*. Centre d'Études et de Recherches Marxistes. Paris.
Goldschmidt, Victor. 1947. *Le paradigme dans la dialectique platonicienne*. Paris.
Graz, Louis. 1965. *Le Feu dans l'Iliade et l'Odyssée:* πῦρ, *Champ d'emploi et signification*. Études et commentaires 40. Paris.
Gruppe, P. Otto. 1906. *Griechische Mythologie und Religionsgeschichte*. Ivan Müllers Handbuch der Altertumswissenschaft 5.2. München.
Guarducci, Margherita. 1966. 'Divinità fauste nell'antica Velia', *PP* 21.279—94.
Guarducci, Margherita. 1971. 'Da Olympios Kairòs al Principe degli Apostoli', *Arch. Class.* 23. 124—41.
Guillon, Pierre. 1943. *Les trépieds du Ptoion*. 2 vols in 1 BEFAR 153, 153bis. Paris.
Halliday, W.R. 1926. 'Xanthos-Melanthos and the origins of tragedy', *CR* 40. 179—81.
Harris, Marvin. 1968. *The rise of anthropological theory: a history of theories of culture, 1750—1965*. London and New York.
Harrison, A.R.W. 1968. *The Law of Athens. The Family and Property*. Oxford.
Harrison, Jane E. 1927. *Themis: a study of the social origins of Greek religion*. 2 ed. Cambridge. [1 ed. 1912; repr. London, 1963.]
Hartog, F. 1970. 'Les Phéaciens dans l'Odyssée: un peuple à la croisée des mondes.' Diplôme de Maîtrise, Nanterre: Faculté des Lettres (unpublished).
Haussleiter, Johannes. 1935. *Der Vegetarismus in der Antike*. RGVV 24. Berlin.
Havelock, Eric A. 1957. *The Liberal Temper in Greek politics*. London and New Haven. [Repr. 1964.]
Henle, Jane. 1973. *Greek myths: a vase painter's notebook*. Bloomington, Indiana and London.
Herter, Hans. 1928. 'Platons Atlantis', *BJ* 133.28—47.
Herter, Hans. 1969. 'Urathen, der Idealstaat', *Politeia und Res publica. Beiträge zum Verständnis von Politik, Recht und Staat in der Antike (Denkschrift Rudolf Stark)* (ed. P. Steinmetz), pp. 108—34. Palingenesia, Monographien und Texte zur klassischen Altertumswissenschaft 4. Wiesbaden.

Hirvonen, Kaarle. 1968. *Matriarchal survivals and certain trends in Homer's female characters*. Annales Academiae Scientiarum Fennicae [Suomalaisen tiedeakatemian toimituksia], Sarja-ser. B, nide-tom. 152. Helsinki.

Hodgen, Margaret Trabue. 1936. *The doctrine of survivals: a chapter in the history of scientific method in the study of man*. London.

Homolle, Th. 1882. 'Comptes des Hiéropes du Temple d'Apollon délien', *BCH* 6.1–167.

Homolle, Th. 1887–1919. Art. 'Donarium' in Daremberg-Saglio, 2,1.363–82.

Hornell, James. 1947. 'The role of birds in early navigation', *Antiquity* 20.142–9.

Humphreys, S.C. 1978. *Anthropology and the Greeks*. London.

Immerwahr, Walther. 1885. *De Atalanta*. Diss., Berlin.

Janni, Pietro. 1965. 'Σώτειρα e σωτήρ in Pindaro', *Studi Urbinati*, n.s. 39.104–9.

Jaulin, Robert. 1967. *La Mort sara. L'ordre de la vie ou la pensée de la mort au Tchad*. Paris.

Jeanmaire, Henri. 1913. 'La cryptie lacédémonienne', *REG* 26.121–50.

Jeanmaire, Henri. 1939. *Couroi et Courètes. Essai sur l'éducation spartiate et sur les rites d'adolescence dans l'antiquité hellénique*. Lille–Paris. [Repr. New York, 1978.]

Jeanmaire, Henri. 1951. *Dionysos*. Paris. [Repr. Paris, 1970.]

Juden, Brian et al. 1970. 'Le Mythe d'Orphée au XIXe et au XXe siècle.' (Proceedings of 21st Congress of the Association internationale des Études françaises, 23–25 July 1969.) *CAIEF* 22.137–246.

Julien, Charles-André. 1964. *Histoire de l'Algérie contemporaine. La conquête et les débuts de la colonisation (1827–71)*. Paris. [Ed. 2, Paris, 1979.]

Kahil, Lilly G.- 1965. 'Autour de l'Artémis attique', *Antike Kunst* 8.20–33.

Kahil, Lilly G.- 1976. 'Artémis attique', *CRAI* 126–30.

Kahn, C.H. 1963. 'Plato's funeral oration: the motive of the Menexenus', *CPh* 58.220–34.

Kälin, Kaspar. 1943. *Indianer und Urvölker nach Jos. Fr. Lafitau (1681–1746)*. Freiburg, Switzerland.

Kambitsis, I. 1975. Minyades kai Proitides. Ioannina.

Kauer, Sigrid. 1959. *Die Geburt der Athena im altgriechischen Epos*. Würzburg.

Keller, Otto. 1909–13. *Die Antike Tierwelt*. 2 vols. Leipzig. [Repr. Hildesheim, 1963.]

Kerényi, Karl. 1952. 'Il dio cacchiatore.' *Dionisio* 5.131–42.

Kiock, A. 1915. 'Athena Aithyia', *ARW* 18.127–33.

Kirchoff, Adolf. 1869. *Die Composition der Odyssee. Gesammelte Aufsätze*. Berlin.

Kirk, Geoffrey S. 1962. *The Songs of Homer*. Cambridge.

Kirk, Geoffrey S. 1970. *Myth: its meaning and function in ancient and other cultures*. Sather Classical Lectures 40. Cambridge, Berkeley and Los Angeles.

Kirsten, Ernst, and Kraiker, Wilhelm. 1967. *Griechenlandkunde: ein Führer zu klassischen Stätten*. 5 ed. Heidelberg.

Kluge, Friedrich. 1910. *De Platonis critica*. Dissertationes philologicae Halenses 19, 3. Halle.

Koch, G. 1975. *Die mythologischen Sarkophage*, 6: *Meleager*. Berlin.

Köchly, Hermann A.T. 1881–82. 'De Lacedaemoniorum cryptia commentatio', in *Opuscula philologica*, 2 vols., edited by G. Kinkel and E. Böckel, 1.580–91. Leipzig. [Repr. from *Festschrift B.G. Weiske*, Leipzig, 1836, 7–24.]

Krappe, Alexander Haggerty. 1936. 'Les dieux au corbeau chez les Celtes', *RHR* 124.236–46.

Kucharsky, Paul. 1963. 'Sur la notion pythagoricienne du καιρός', *Revue philosophique* 153.141–69.

Kuiper, K. 1916. 'Le récit de la coupe de Bathyclès dans les Iambes de Callimaque', *REG* 29.404–29.

Kurtz, D.C., and Boardman, John. 1971. *Greek burial customs*. London.

Works cited

Labarbe, Jules. 1953. 'L'âge correspondant au sacrifice du κούρειον et les données historiques du sixième discours d'Isée', *BARB*, 5 sér. 39.358—94.
Labarbe, Jules. 1957. *La Loi navale de Thémistocle*. Bibliothèque de la Faculté de Philosophie et Lettres de l'Université de Liège, fasc. 143. Paris—Gembloux.
La Coste-Messellière, P. Frotier de. 1936. *Au Musée de Delphes. Recherches sur quelques monuments archaïques et leur décor sculpté*. BEFAR 138. Paris.
Lafitau, Joseph-François. 1724. *Moeurs des Sauvages Ameriquains comparées aux moeurs des premiers temps*. (2 vols. in 4°; later 4 vols. in 12°.)
Laffranque, Marie. 1964. *Poseidonius d'Apamée. Essai de mise au point*. Publications de la Faculté des Lettres et Sciences humaines de Paris, Sér. 'Recherches', vol. 13. Paris.
Lang, Andrew. 1885. *Custom and Myth*. 2 ed. London. (1 ed. 1884; then 1893; 1898; 1904.)
Lang, Andrew. 1887. *Myth, Ritual and Religion*. 2 vols. London. (2 ed. 1899).
Lang, Mabel. 1969. 'Homer and oral technique', *Hesperia* 38.159—68.
Laum, Bernhard. 1924. *Heiliges Geld. Eine historische Untersuchung über den sakralen Ursprung des Geldes*. Tübingen.
La Ville de Mirmont, H. de. 1895. 'Le navire Argo et la science nautique d'Apollonios de Rhodes', *Revue internationale de l'enseignement* 30.230—85.
Leach, Edmund R. 1966a. *Rethinking Anthropology*. 2 ed. LSE Monographs in Social Anthropology 22. London.
Leach, Edmund R. 1966b. 'Frazer and Malinowski: on the "Founding Fathers" ', *Current Anthropology* 7.360—7. [Repr. from *Encounter*, 25 May 1964, 24—36.]
Le Goff, Jacques, and Le Roy Ladurie, Emmanuel. 1971. 'Mélusine maternelle et défricheuse', *Annales ESC* 26.587—622.
Le Goff, J., and Vidal-Naquet, P. 1979. 'Lévi-Strauss en Brocéliande', in *Claude Lévi-Strauss* (edd. R. Bellour and C. Clément), pp. 265—319. Paris.
Lemay, E. 1976. 'Histoire de l'antiquité et découverte du Nouveau Monde chez deux auteurs du XVIIIe siècle', *Studies on Voltaire and the Eighteenth Century* 151—5, pp. 1313—28.
Lerat, Lucien. 1952. *Les Locriens de l'Ouest*. 2 parts. BEFAR 176. Paris.
Lévêque, Pierre, and Vidal-Naquet, Pierre. 1964. *Clisthène l'Athénien: essai sur la représentation de l'espace et du temps dans la pensée politique grecque de la fin du VIe siècle à la mort de Platon*. Annales littéraires de l'Université de Besançon 65. Paris.
Lévi-Strauss, Claude. 1966a. *The Savage Mind*. London and New York. [ET of *La Pensée sauvage*, Paris, 1962.]
Lévi-Strauss, Claude. 1966b. 'Le triangle culinaire', *L'Arc* 26.19—30.
Lévi-Strauss, Claude. 1970. *The Raw and the Cooked*. London and New York. [ET of *Le Cru et le cuit* (Mythologiques 1), Paris, 1964.]
Lévi-Strauss, Claude. 1971. *L'Homme nu*. Mythologiques 4. Paris.
Lévi-Strauss, Claude. 1973. *From Honey to Ashes*. London and New York. [ET of *Du Miel au cendres* Mythologiques 2), Paris, 1966.]
Lévi-Strauss, Claude. 1977. 'Comparative religions of non-literate peoples', in *Structural Anthropology* 2, pp. 60—7. Harmondsworth and New York (1976). [ET of *Anthropologie structurale* 2, Paris, 1973.]
Lévy-Bruhl, Henri. 1947. *Nouvelles études sur le très ancien droit romain*. Publications de l'institut de Droit romain de l'Université de Paris 1. Paris.
Lindsay, Jack. 1965. *The Clashing Rocks. A study of early Greek religion and culture and the origins of drama*. London.
Lloyd, Geoffrey E.R. 1966. *Polarity and Analogy: two types of argumentation in early Greek thought*. Cambridge.
Lloyd, Geoffrey E.R. 1979. *Magic, Reason and Experience. Studies in the Origin and Development of Greek Science*. Cambridge.

Lloyd-Jones, Hugh. 1973. 'Modern interpretations of Pindar: the Second Pythian and Seventh Nemean Odes', *JHS* 93.108—37.
Loraux, Nicole. 1975. '*Hébè* et *andreia*. Deux versions de la mort du combattant athénien', *Ancient Society* 6.1—31.
Loraux, Nicole. 1977. 'La belle mort spartiate', *Ktema* 2.105—20.
Loraux, Nicole. 1978. 'Mourir devant Troie, tomber pour Athènes. De la gloire du héros à l'idée de la cité', *Information sur les sciences sociales* 17.801—17.
Loraux, Nicole. 1980a. *L'invention d'Athènes. Histoire de l'oraison funèbre dans la 'cité classique'*. Paris.
Loraux, Nicole. 1980b. 'L'Acropole comique', *Ancient Society* 11 (forthcoming).
Lord, Albert B. 1960. *The Singer of Tales*. Harvard Studies in Comparative Literature, no. 24. Cambridge, Mass., and London.
Lotze, Detleff. 1959. μεταξὺ ἐλευθέρων καὶ δούλων: *Studien zur Rechsstellung unfreier Landbevölkerungen in Griechenland bis zum 4 Jhdt. vor Christ.* Deutsche Akademie der Wissenschaften zu Berlin, Schriften der Sektion für Altertumswissenschaft 17. Berlin.
Lovejoy, Arthur O. and Boas, George. 1935. *A documentary history of Primitivism and Related Ideas*, 1: *Primitivism and related ideas in Antiquity*. Baltimore. [Repr. New York, 1965.]
Luccioni, J. 1959. 'Platon et la mer', *REA* 61.15—47.
Luce, John V. 1978. 'The sources and literary form of Plato's Atlantis narrative', in Ramage, E.S. (1978), pp. 49—78.
Luria, Salomo. 1933. 'Frauenpatriotismus und Sklavenemancipation in Argos', *Klio* 26 (NF 8).210—28.
Maass, Ernest. 1889. Review of Joh. Töpffer, *Attische Genealogie*, Berlin, 1889. GGA, 1 October, no. 20.801—32.
MacDonald, Sir George. 1905. *Coin-types: their origin and development*. (Rhind Lectures, 1905.) Glasgow.
Maffre, Jean-Jacques. 1972. 'Deux pélikai attiques à figures rouges trouvées à Thasos', *BCH* 96.327—61.
Malten, Ludolf. 1925. 'Bellerophontes', *JdAI* 40.121—60.
Manns, Otto. 1888—90. *Über die Jagd bei der Griechen.* Königliches-Wilhelms-Gymnasium zu Cassel, Jahresbericht: 3 parts (1888: 7—38; 1889: 3—20; 1890: 3—21). Also published together. Cassel.
Marett, Robert R. (ed.) 1908. *Anthropology and the Classics*. Oxford.
Margarido, A. 1971. 'Proposiçõs teoricas para a leitura de textos iniciaticos.' *Correio de Povo* [Porto Alegre, Rio Grande del Sol, Brazil] for 21 August.
Marienstras, R. 1965. 'Prospère ou le machiavelisme du bien', *Bulletin de la Faculté des Lettres de Strasbourg* 43.899—917.
Marinatos, S. 1950. 'Περὶ τὸν θρῦλον τῆς Ἀτλαντίδος', *Kretika Chronika* 195—213.
Marinatos, S. 1971. *Some words about the legend of Atlantis*. 2 ed. Athens.
Marrou, Henri-Irenée. 1956. *History of education in Antiquity*. London. [ET of *Histoire de l'éducation dans l'Antiquité*, Paris, 3 ed. Latest: 4 ed. 1948, repr. 1965.]
Martin, Thomas-Henri. 1841. 'Dissertation sur l'Atlantide', in *Études sur le Timée de Platon* (2 vols. in 1), 1, pp. 257—333. Paris.
Marx, Karl. 1964. *Precapitalist economic formations*. Edition of sections of the *Grundrisse*, with an introduction, by Eric J. Hobsbawm. London.
Mauss, Marcel. 1921. 'Une forme ancienne de contrat chez les Thraces', *REG* 34. 388—97.
Mauss, Marcel. 1970. *The Gift: forms and functions of exchange in archaic societies.* [ET by Ian Cunnison of 'Essai sur le don', first printed in *L'Année sociologique*, n.s. 1, 1 (1923—4) [1925], 30—186, reprinted in Mauss, *Sociologie et anthropologie* (Paris, 1950, ed. 4, 1968), 145—270.] London.

Works cited

Maxwell-Stuart, P.G. 1970. 'Remarks on the black coats of the Ephebes', *PCPhS* 196 [= n.s. 16], 113—16.
Mazon, Paul. 1944. *Hésiode. Théogonie, Travaux et les Jours, Le Bouclier.* (ed. and trans.) Collection des Universités de France (Budé). (1st ed. 1928.) Paris.
Méautis, Georges. 1922. *Recherches sur le pythagorisme.* Université de Neuchâtel: Recueil de travaux publiés par la Faculté des Lettres, 9. Neuchâtel.
Meek, Ronald L. 1976. *Social science and the ignoble savage.* Cambridge Studies in the History and Theory of Politics. Cambridge.
Meiggs, Russell, and Lewis, David M. (eds.) 1969. *A Selection of Greek Historical Inscriptions to the end of the fifth century BC.* Oxford.
Mélèze-Modrzejewski, J. 1975. 'Hommes libres et bêtes dans les droits antiques', in *Hommes et bêtes: entretiens sur le racisme* (ed. Léon Poliakov), pp. 75—102. Paris.
Mercier, Paul. 1971. *Histoire de l'anthropologie.* 2 ed. Le sociologue 5. Paris. (1 ed. 1966.)
Mestre, Édouard. 1937. 'Monnaies métalliques et valeurs d'échange en Chine', *Annales sociologiques,* sér. D (Sociologie économique) 2.33—61.
Meuli, Karl. 1921. *Odyssee und Argonautika: Untersuchungen zur griechischen Sagengeschichte und zum Epos.* Berlin.
Meyerson, Ignace. 1948. *Les fonctions psychologiques et les oeuvres.* Études de psychologie et de philosophie 9. Paris.
Mihailov, G. 1955. *La légende de Terée.* Annuaire de l'Université de Sofia 50,2. 77—208.
Mitchell, F.W. 1975. 'The so-called earliest ephebic inscription', *ZPE* 19.233—43.
Mitsos, M. Th. 1975. 'ἐπὶ Νικθφήμ[ο ἄρχοντος].' Ἀρχαιολογικὴ Ἐφήμερις, Ἀρχαιολ. Χρον., 39—40.
Momigliano, Arnaldo D. 1966. *Studies in Historiography.* London.
Mommsen, August. 1898. *Feste der Stadt Athen im Altertum, geordnet nach attischem Kalender.* Leipzig.
Moraux, Paul. 1957. *À la Recherche de l'Aristote perdu. Le dialogue 'Sur la Justice'.* Aristote: traductions et études. Paris—Louvain.
Morel, J.-P. 1969. 'Pantomimus allectus inter iuvenes', *Hommages à M. Renard* 2, pp. 526—35. Collection Latomus 102 (ed. J. Bibaux). Bruxelles.
Morel, J.-P. 1976. 'Sur quelques aspects de la jeunesse à Rome', *Mélanges Jacques Heurgon,* pp. 663—83. Paris.
Moreux, Bernard. 1967. 'La nuit, l'ombre et la mort chez Homère', *Phoenix* 21.237—72.
Morgan, Lewis Henry. 1857. 'Laws of descent of the Iroquois', *Proceedings of the American Association for the Advancement of Science* 11,2.132—48.
Morgan, Lewis Henry. 1877. *Ancient Society, or Researches in the lines of human progress through barbarism to civilization.* Chicago and London. [Repr., ed. Leslie White, Cambridge, Mass., 1964.]
Morin, Edgar. 1965. *Introduction à une politique de l'homme,* suivi de *Arguments politiques.* L'Histoire immédiate. Paris.
Mossé, Claude. 1961. 'Le rôle des esclaves dans les troubles politiques du monde grecque à la fin de l'époque classique', *Cahiers d'histoire* 6.353—60.
Mühll, P. Von der. 1940. Art. 'Odyssee.' *RE Suppl.* 7, cols. 696—768.
Müller, Karl Otfried. 1844. *Geschichten Hellenischer Stämme und Städte.* 2 ed., by F.W. Schneidewin, 3 vols. Vols. 2—3, *Die Dorier.* [1 ed. 1820—24.]
Mumford, Lewis. 1965. 'Utopia, the City and the Machine', *Daedalus* (Journal of the American Academy of Arts and Sciences), 94. 271—92.
Nilsson, N.M.P. 1906. *Griechische Feste von religiöser Bedeutung, mit Ausschluss der attischen.* Leipzig.
Nilsson, N.M.P. 1951. *Cults, Myths, Oracles and Politics in Ancient Greece* (with two appendices: the Ionian phylae; the phratries). Skrifter utgivna av Svenska Institutet i Athen, 8°, 1. Lund.

Nilsson, N.M.P. 1951—60. *Opuscula selecta*. 3 vols. Skrifter utgivna av Svenska Institutet i Athen, 8°, 2. Lund.

Nilsson, N.M.P. 1951—60a. 'Der Ursprung der Tragödie', in *Opuscula Selecta* 1.61—145. [Repr. from *Neue Jahrbücher für klassischen Altertum* 27 (1911), 609—96.]

Nilsson, N.M.P. 1951—60b. 'Die Grundlage des Spartanischen Lebens', *Opuscula Selecta* 2, pp. 826—69. Lund. [Repr. from *Klio* 12 (1912), 308—40.]

Nilsson, N.M.P. 1951—60c. 'Die *traditio per terram* im griechischen Rechtsbrauch', in *Opuscula selecta* 1.330—5. [Repr. from *ARW* 20/21 (1920), 232—6.]

Nilsson, N.M.P. 1951—60d. 'Der Flammentod des Herakles auf dem Oita', in *Opuscula selecta* 1.348—54. [Repr. from *ARW* 22 (1922), 310—16.]

Nilsson, N.M.P. 1951—60e. 'The new inscription of the Salaminioi', in *Opuscula selecta* 2.731—41. [Repr. from *AJPh* 59 (1938), 385—93.]

Nilsson, N.M.P. 1967. *Geschichte der Griechischen Religion*, vol. 1. 3 ed. Iwan Müllers Handbuch der Altertumswissenschaft 5,2. München.

Norden, Eduard. 1966. 'Orpheus und Eurydice: ein nachträgliches Gedenkblatt, für Vergil', in *Kleine Schriften zum klassischen Altertum*, pp. 468—532. Berlin. [Repr. from *SB der Preussischen Akademie der Wissenschaften*, 1934, 626—83.]

Orlandos, Anastasios K. 1966—8. *Les Matériaux de construction et la technique architecturale des anciens Grecs*. 2 vols. École Française d'Athènes. Travaux et mémoires des anciens membres étrangers de l'école et divers savants 16, 16bis. [French translation by K. Laumonier and V. Hadjimichali of part of Ἡ ἀρχαία ἑλληνικὴ ἀρχιτεκτονική, Athens, 1955— .]

Orth, F. 1914. Art. 'Jagd.' *RE*, cols. 558—604.

Osthoff, Hermann. 1905. 'Etymologische Beiträge zur Mythologie und Religionsgeschichte, 2', *ARW* 8.52—68.

Page, Denys L. 1955. *The Homeric Odyssey*. Mary Flexner Lectures, Bryn Mawr. Oxford. [Repr. 1966.]

Pallottino, Massimo. 1952. 'Atlantide.' *Arch. Class.* 4.22—40.

Panoff, Michel. 1972. *Bronislaw Malinowski*. Petite bibliothèque Payot 195. Paris.

Panofsky, Erwin. 1962. *Studies in Iconology: humanistic themes in the art of the Renaissance*. New York. (1 ed. 1939).

Papathomopoulos, Manolis. 1968. *Antoninus Liberalis, Metamorphôseôn Synagôgē (Les Métamorphoses)* (ed. and trans.). Budé edition. Paris.

Parry, Adam. 1967. 'Have we Homer's Iliad?', *YCS* 20.175—215.

Passmore, John. 1975. 'The treatment of animals', *JHI* 36.195—218.

Payne, Humfry. 1931. *Necrocorinthia: a study of Corinthian art in the Archaic period*. Oxford.

Pease, A.S. 1937. Art. 'Oelbaum.' *RE*, cols. 1998—2022.

Pélékidis, Chrysis. 1962. *Histoire de l'éphébie attique. Des origines à 31 avant J.-C.* École française d'Athènes: Travaux et mémoires des anciens membres étrangers de l'école et de divers savants 13. Paris.

Pembroke, Simon G. 1965. 'The last of the Matriarchs: a study in the inscriptions of Lycia', *JESHO* 8.217—47.

Pembroke, Simon G. 1967. 'Women in Charge: the function of alternatives in early Greek tradition and the ancient idea of matriarchy', *JWCI* 30.1—35.

Pembroke, Simon G. 1970. 'Locres et Tarente: le rôle des femmes dans la fondation de deux colonies grecques', *Annales ESC* 25,5.1240—70.

Pépin, Jean. 1954. 'À propos du symbolisme de la mer chez Platon et dans le néoplatonisme.' Résumé of paper in *Actes du Congrès de l'Association Budé, de Tours et de Poitiers, 3—9 Sept. 1953*, pp. 257—9. Paris.

Pfister, Friedrich. 1909. *Der Reliquienkult im Altertum*. (2 parts.) RGVV 5. Giessen.

Picard, Charles. 1931. 'Les Néréides funéraires du monument de Xanthos (Lycie).' *RHR* 103, 5—28.

Works cited

Picard, Charles. 1939. *Manuel d'archéologie grecque: la sculpture*. II. *Période classique*. 2 vols. Paris.

Picard, Charles. 1940. 'L'Héroôn de Phrontis au Sounion', *RA*, sér. 6,16.5—28.

Picard, Charles. 1958. 'L'Athéna "Horia" et les "Bornes de la Patrie" (Musée Acropole Athènes no. 695)', *RA*, n.s. 1.95—8.

Piccaluga, Giulia. 1968. *Lykaon: un tema mitico*. Quaderni di SMSR 5, pp. 5—245. Roma.

Pisani, Vittore. 1929. 'Miscellanea etimologica, nos. 19—34', *Rendiconti della Reale nazionale Accademia dei Lincei, Classe di scienze morali, storiche e filologiche*, Ser. 6, no. 5.3—18.

Pisani, Vittore. 1943—4. 'Glottica parerga, 7. Graeca minora', *Rendiconti del' Istituto Lombardo di Scienze e Lettere, Classe di Lettere*, Ser. III, 8.1. 529—70.

Pleket, Henri Willy. 1969. '*Collegium Iuvenum Nemesiorum*: a note on ancient youth organisation', *Mnemosyne*, ser. 4, 22.281—98.

Pley, Jakob. 1911. *De lanae in antiquorum ritibus usu*. RGVV 11, 2. Giessen.

Poliakov, Léon. 1974. *The Aryan myth: a history of racist and nationalist ideas in Europe*. Columbus Centre Series. London. [ET of *Le Mythe aryen*, Paris, 1972.]

Popp, Harald. 1959. *Die Einwirkung von Vorzeichen, Opfern und Festen auf die Kriegführung der Griechen im 5. und 4. Jahrhundert vor Christ*. Diss. Erlangen. Neustadt an der Aisch.

Propp, Vladimir. 1968. *The Morphology of the Folk-tale*. (Trans. L. Scott, rev. ed. by Louis Wagner.) Publications of the American Folklore Society, Bibliographical and Special Series, vol. 9. Austin and London. [ET of *Morphologia skazke*.]

Pugliese-Carratelli, Giovanni. 1970. 'Ὀλύμπιος καιρός', *PP* 25.248—9.

Pugliese-Carratelli, Giovanni. 1971. 'Fraintendimente ed errore: a proposito di Olympios Kairos e de Sepolcro di San Pietro', *PP* 26.347—53.

Radermacher, Ludwig. 1938. *Mythos und Sage bei den Griechen*. Baden-bei-Wien/ Leipzig.

Radke, Gerhard. 1936. *Die Bedeutung der weissen und der schwarzen Farbe im Kult und Brauch der Griechen und Römern*. Diss., Berlin.

Ramage, Edwin S. (ed.) 1978. *Atlantis, fact or fiction?* Bloomington, Indiana and London.

Rawson, Elizabeth. 1969. *The Spartan Tradition in European thought*. Oxford.

Rayet, Olivier, and Collignon, Max. 1888. *Histoire de la céramique grecque*. Paris.

Rehm, Albert. 1919. Art. 'Kanopos', *RE*, cols. 1881—3.

Reinach, A.-J. 1910. 'Itanos et l'*inventio scuti*: étude sur l'hoplolatrie primitive en Grèce, 3', *RHR* 61.197—237.

Reinmuth, Oscar W. 1971. *The Ephebic Inscriptions of the fourth century BC*. Mnemosyne Supplements 14. Leiden.

Reisch, Emil. 1905. Art. 'Dreifuss.' *RE*, cols. 1669—96.

Resek, Carl. 1960. *Lewis Henry Morgan, American scholar*. Chicago.

Richter, Will. 1968. *Die Landwirtschaft im homerischen Zeitalter*. Mit einem Beitrag von Wolfgang Schiering. Archaeologia homerica Bd. 2. Göttingen.

Ridder, André Henri P. de. 1912. 'L'Athéna mélancholique, 1', *BCH* 36.523—8.

Rivaud, Albert. 1925. *Timée. Critias*. Platon: Collection des Universités de France (Budé), vol. 10. Translation and notes. Paris.

Robert, Carl. 1909. 'Die Iasonsage in der *Hypsipyle* des Euripides', *Hermes* 44. 376—402.

Robert, Carl. 1915. *Oidipus. Geschichte eines poetischen Stoffs im griechischen Altertum*. 2 vols. Berlin.

Robert, Carl. 1920—26. *Die griechische Heldensage*. 5 vols. (Constituting Part 2 of Ludwig Preller's *Griechische Mythologie*.) Berlin.

Robert, Louis. 1938. *Études épigraphiques et philologiques.* Bibliothèque de l'École des Hautes Études: Sciences historiques et philologiques, fasc. 272. Paris.

Robert, Louis. 1940. 'Ἀμφιθαλής.' Athenian Studies presented to William S. Ferguson, pp. 509—19. Harvard Studies in Class. Philology 1. Cambridge, Mass.

Robert, Louis. 1955. *Hellenica. Recueil d'épigraphie, de numismatique et d'antiquités grecques* 10. Paris.

Robert, Louis. 1960. 'Recherches épigraphiques', *REA* 62.278—361.

Robert, Louis. 1962. *Villes d'Asie mineure: études de géographie anc.* 2 ed. Paris.

Robert, Jeanne and Louis. 1966. 'Bulletin épigraphique', *REG* 79.335—449.

Robert, Jeanne and Louis. 1967. 'Bulletin épigraphique', *REG* 80.453—573.

Robert, Jeanne and Louis. 1973. 'Bulletin épigraphique', *REG* 86.48—211.

Robert, Jeanne and Louis. 1976. 'Bulletin épigraphique', *REG* 89.415—595.

Robertson, D.M. 1931. 'Bouzyges and the first plough on a krater by the painter of the Naples Hephaistos', *AJA* 35.152—60.

Röder, Günther. 1919. Art. 'Kanobus' (2). *RE*, cols. 1870—3.

Rolley, Claude. 1974. 'Fouilles à Eretrie. Archéologie, histoire et religion' (review article). *RA*, n.s. 307—11.

Rose, Herbert J. 1951. *Andrew Lang: his place in anthropology.* Edinburgh.

Rose, Herbert J. 1961. *A Handbook of Greek Literature, from Homer to the age of Lucian.* London and New York. [Repr. of 4 ed. 1950, with corrections. 1 ed. 1934.]

Rosellini, Michèle, and Saïd, Suzanne. 1978. 'Usage de femmes et autres *nomoi* chez les "sauvages" d'Hérodote: essai de lecture structurale', *ASNP*, ser. 3, 8.3.949—1005.

Rouse, W.H.D. 1902. *Greek votive offerings. An essay on the history of Greek religion.* Cambridge.

Roussel, Pierre, 1921. Review of Alice Brenot, *Recherches sur l'éphébie attique et en particulier sur la date de l'institution (Paris, 1920). REG* 34.459—60.

Roussel, Pierre, 1941. 'Les chlamydes noires des éphèbes athéniens', *REA* 43. 163—5.

Roussel, Pierre. 1951. 'Essai sur le principe d'ancienneté dans le monde hellénique du 5e siècle avant J.-C. à l'époque romaine', *Mémoires de l'Académie des Inscriptions et Belles-Lettres* 43,2.123—228. [True date, 1941.]

Roux, René. 1949. *Le Problème des Argonautes. Recherches sur les aspects religieux de la légende.* Paris.

Rudbeck, Olaf (Rudbek, Olf). 1689—98. *Atland eller Manheim, dedan Japhetz afkomne, de förnämste keyserlige och kungelige Slechter ... ;* (in Latin) *Atlantica sive Manheim, Vera Japheti posterorum sedes ac patria ...* [Latin text by Andreas Norcopensis]. 3 vols. in 4. Uppsala.

Rudberg, G. 1956. *Platonica selecta.* Stockholm.

Rudhardt, Jean. 1958. *Notions fondamentales de la pensée religieuse et actes constitutifs du culte dans la Grèce classique.* Genève.

Rudhardt, Jean. 1971. *Le thème de l'eau primordiale dans la mythologie grecque.* Travaux publiés par la Société Suisse des Sciences Humaines 12. Berne.

Ruschenbusch, Eberhard. 1958. 'Πάτριος πολιτεία. Theseus, Drakon, Solon und Kleisthenes in Publizistik und Geschichtsschreibung des 5. und 4. Jhrdts. vor Chr.', *Historia* 7.398—424.

Rutgers van der Loeff, A. 1915. 'De Oschophoriis', *Mnemosyne*, ser. 2.404—15.

Saintyves, P. 1912. 'L'anneau de Polycrate: essai sur l'origine liturgique du thème de l'anneau jeté à la mer et retrouvé dans le ventre d'un poisson', *RHR* 66.49—80.

Sakellariou, Michel. 1958. *La Migration grecque en Ionie.* Collection du Centre d'Études d'Asie mineure: Institut français d'Athènes. Athens.

Saussure, Ferdinand de. 1966. *Course in general linguistics.* [ET of *Cours de linguistique générale*, 1915, ed. Charles Bally and A. Sechehaye. New York.

Works cited

Schachermeyr, Friedrich [Fritz]. 1950. *Poseidon und die Enstehung des Griechischen Götterglaubens*. Bern.

Schaerer, René. 1948. *La question platonicienne*. Neuchâtel.

Schmidt, Joanna. 1939. Art. 'Omophagia', *RE*, cols. 380—2.

Schmitt, Hatto H. 1969. *Die Staatsverträge des Altertums*, vol. 3: *Die Verträge der griechisch-römischen Welt von 338 bis 200 v. Chr.* Kommission für alte Geschichte und Epigraphik, München. München.

Schmitt, Pauline. 1977. 'Athena Apatouria et la ceinture: les aspects féminins des Apatouries à Athènes', *Annales ESC* 32,6.1059—73.

Schmitt, Pauline. 1979. 'Histoire de tyran ou comment la cité grecque construit ses marges', in *Les marginaux et les exclus dans l'histoire* (edited by B. Vincent), pp. 217—31. Paris.

Schnapp, Alain. 1973. 'Les Représentations de la chasse dans les textes littéraires et la céramique.' Thèse 3ème Cycle, Paris. Unpublished.

Schuhl, Pierre-Maxime. 1968a. *La fabulation platonicienne*. 2 ed. Paris.

Schuhl, Pierre-Maxime (dir.). 1968b. *Aristote: De la Richesse etc. Fragments et témoignages*. (Edited by Jean Aubonnet, Janine Bertier, Jacques Brunschwig, Pierre Hadot, Jean Pépin, Pierre Thillet.) Publications de la Faculté des Lettres et Sciences Humaines de Paris — Sorbonne: Série 'Textes et Documents' 17. Paris.

Schwabl, Hans. 1966. *Hesiods Theogonie: eine unitarische Analyse*. Österreichische Akademie der Wissenschaften, Phil.-hist. Klasse, Sitzungsberichte 250 no. 5. Wien.

Schwartz, Jacques. 1960. *Pseudo-Hesiodea. Recherches sur la composition, la diffusion et la disparition ancienne d'oeuvres attribuées à Hésiode*. Leiden.

Schwendemann, K. 1921. 'Der Dreifuss: ein formen- und religionsgeschichtlicher Versuch', *JdAI* 36.98—185.

Schwyzer, Eduard. 1928. 'Zu griechischen Inschriften, 3', *RhM* 77.225—61.

Scranton, R.L. 1949. 'Lost Atlantis found again?' *Archaeology* 2, 3.159—62.

Seeliger, K. 1884—86. Art. 'Athamas.' *LGRM* 1, cols. 669—75.

Segal, Charles P. 1962. 'The Phaeacians and the symbolism of Odysseus's return', *Arion* 1,4.17—63.

Segal, Charles P. 1966. 'Orpheus and the Fourth Georgic. Vergil on Nature', *AJPh* 87.307—25.

Segal, Charles P. 1967. 'Transition and ritual in Odysseus's return', *PP* 116.321—42.

Segal, Charles P. 1968. 'Circean temptations: Homer, Vergil, Ovid', *TAPhA* 99. 419—42.

Severyns, Albert. 1938. *Recherches sur la Chrestomathie de Proclus*: 1. *Le Codex 239 de Photius*. 2 vols. Bibliothèque de la Faculté de Philosophie et Lettres de l'Université de Liège 78, 79. Paris.

Severyns, Albert. 1966. *Les Dieux d'Homère*. Mythe et Religions 57. Paris.

Sharpe, Eric J. 1975. *Comparative religion: a history*. London.

Shmueli, E. 1970. 'Modern hippies and ancient Cynics: a comparison of philosophical and political developments and its lessons', *CHM* 12.490—514.

Siewert, P. 1977. 'The ephebic oath in fifth-century Athens', *JHS* 97.102—11.

Simiand, François. 1934. 'La monnaie, realité sociale', *Annales sociologiques*, sér. D (Sociologie économique), 1.1—58 (followed by a discussion, pp. 59—86).

Simon, Erica. 1960. *Réveil national et culture populaire en Scandinavie; la genèse de la højskole nordique, 1844—78*. Paris.

Siska, Heinz W. 1933. *De Mercurio ceterisque deis ad artem gymnicam pertinentibus*. Diss., Halle.

Snodgrass, Antony M. 1977. *Archaeology and the rise of the Greek state*. Inaugural lecture. Cambridge.

Sofri, G. 1969. *Il modo di produzione asiatico. Storia di una controversia marxista*. Torino.

Sokolowski, Franciszek. 1962. *Lois sacrées des cités grecques: Supplement* ... École française d'Athènes. Travaux et mémoires des anciens membres étrangers de l'école et de divers savants, fasc. 11. Paris.

Sokolowski, Franciszek. 1969. *Lois sacrées des cités grecques.* École française d'Athènes. Travaux et mémoires des anciens membres étrangers de l'École et de divers savants, fasc. 18. Paris.

Solmsen, Friedrich (ed.). 1970. *Hesiodi Theogonia, Opera et Dies, Scutum* (with Fragment Selecta). Oxford.

Sourvinou-Inwood, Christiane. 1971a. Review of Angelo Brelich, 1969. *JHS* 91. 172–7.

Sourvinou[-Inwood], Christiane. 1971b. 'Aristophanes, *Lysistrata,* 641–647', *CQ* n.s. 21. 339–42.

Sourvinou-Inwood, Christiane. 1974. 'The votum of 477/6 BC and the foundation legend of Locri Epizephyrii', *CQ* n.s. 24.186–98.

Spanuth, Jürgen. 1953. *Das enträtselte Atlantis.* 2 ed. Stuttgart.

Sperber, Dan. 1968. *Le Structuralisme en anthropologie,* in *Qu'est-ce que le structuralisme?,* ed. François Wahl, pp. 167–238 (and separately). Paris.

Stanford, William B. 1963. *The Ulysses theme. A study in the adaptability of a traditional hero.* 2 ed. Oxford. (1 ed. 1954.)

Steier, August. 1932. Art. 'Möwe.' *RE,* cols. 2412–18.

Stengel, Paul. 1905. 'Ἀίδης Κλυτόπωλος', *ARW* 8.203–13.

Stengel, Paul. 1920. *Die griechischen Kultusaltertümer.* 3 ed. (Müller's Handbuch der klassischen Altertumswissenschaft 5,3.) München.

Strohm, Hans. 1944. *Tyche. Zur Schicksalsauffassung bei Pindar und die frühgriechischen Dichtern.* Stuttgart.

Taillardat, J. 1968. 'La trière athénienne et la guerre sur mer', in Vernant, J.-P., 1968, pp. 183–205.

Tannery, Paul. 1925. 'Sur Diodore d'Aspende [1896]', in *Mémoires scientifiques* (edited by J.L. Heiberg and H.-G. Zeuthen): Philosophie ancienne, pp. 201–10. Paris–Toulouse.

Taylor, A.E. 1928. *A commentary on Plato's Timaeus.* Oxford.

Thompson, D'Arcy Wentworth. 1936. *A Glossary of Greek Birds.* 2 ed. Oxford. (1 ed. 1895.) [Repr. Hildesheim, 1966.]

Thompson, D'Arcy Wentworth. 1938. 'Was ist αἴθυια?', *Sudhoffs Archiv für Geschichte des Medizin und der Naturwissenschaften* 30.335–9.

Thompson, Homer A., and Wycherley, Richard E. 1972. *The Agora of Athens; the history, shape and uses of an ancient city center.* American School of Classical Studies at Athens: Athenian Agora 14. Princeton, N.J.

Thomson, George D. 1941. *Aeschylus and Athens. A study in the social origins of drama.* London. [Repr. 1946, 1966.]

Tigerstedt, Eugène Napoleon. 1965–74. *The legend of Sparta in classical antiquity.* 2 vols. Stockholm Studies in the history of literature, nos. 9, 15. Stockholm.

Todorov, Tzvetan. 1967. 'Le récit primitif', *Tel Quel* 30.47–55.

Töpffer, Johannes Alexander F. 1889. *Attische Genealogie.* Berlin. [Repr. New York, 1973.]

Trumpf, Jürgen. 1960. 'Kydonische Äpfel (Ibykos, fr. 6D)', *Hermes* 88.14–22.

Tylor, Edward B. 1903. *Primitive Culture: researches into the development of mythology, philosophy, religion, art and custom.* 4 ed., 2 vols. London. [Other editions: 1871; 1873; 1891; abridgement, ed. Leslie White, Ann Arbor, 1960.]

Ure, Percy N. 1922. *The origin of tyranny.* Cambridge.

Usener, Hermann. 1887. *Epicurea.* Leipzig. [Repr. Roma, 1963.]

Usener, Hermann. 1899. *Die Sintfluthsagen.* Religionsgeschichtliche Untersuchungen, vol. 3 [3 vols. in all, 1889–99]. Bonn. [Repr. Hildesheim, 1972.]

Works cited

Usener, Hermann. 1907. 'Mythologie', in *Vorträge und Aufsätze* (ed. A. Dieterich), pp. 37—65. Leipzig—Berlin. [Repr. from *ARW* 7 (1904), 6—32.]

Usener, Hermann. 1912—13a. 'Göttliche Synonyme', in *Kleine Schriften*, 4 vols., 4, pp. 259—206. Leipzig—Berlin. [Repr. from *RhM* 53 (1898), 329—79.]

Usener, Hermann. 1912—13b. 'Heilige Handlung', in *Kleine Schriften*, 4 vols., 4, pp. 422—67. [Repr. from *ARW* 7 (1904), 281—339.]

Valenza Mele, Nazarena. 1977. 'Hera ed Apollo nella colonizzazione euboica d'occidente', *MEFR* 89,2.493—524.

Vallet, Georges. 1958. *Rhégion et Zancle. Histoire, commerce et civilisation des cités chalcidiennes du détroit de Messine*. BEFAR 189. Paris.

Van Compernolle, René. 1975. 'Le mythe de la gynécocratie-doulocratie argienne', in *Le Monde grec: pensée, littérature, histoire, documents. Hommages à Claire Préaux* (edited Jean Bingen et al.), pp. 355—64. Université Libre de Bruxelles: Faculté de Philosophie et Lettres, vol. 52. Bruxelles.

Van Groningen, Bernhard (ed.) 1966. *Theognis: le premier livre édité avec un commentaire*. Verhandelingen der Koninklijke Nederlandse Akademie van Wetenschappen, Afd. Letterkunde, nieuwe reeks, dl. 72, 1. Amsterdam.

Van Nes, Dirk. 1963. *Die maritime Bildersprache des Aischylos*. [Proefschrift.] Groningen.

Verdenius, Willem Jacob. 1964. ''Ανω καὶ κάτω', *Mnemosyne* ser. 4.17.387.

Vernant, Jean-Pierre. 1962. *Les Origines de la pensée grecque*. Collection Mythes et Religions 45. Paris.

Vernant, Jean-Pierre. 1963. 'Sur le Vieux de la mer chez Hésiode (*Théog.* 233—37)', *REG* 76.xvii—xviii.

Vernant, Jean-Pierre (ed.). 1968. *Problèmes de la guerre en Grèce ancienne*. École pratique des Hautes Études, 6e section: Civilisations et sociétés 11. Paris—The Hague.

Vernant, Jean-Pierre. 1971. *Mythe et pensée chez les Grecs*. 3 ed., 2 vols. (4 ed. 1974.) Paris.

Vernant, Jean-Pierre. 1972. 'Les troupeaux du Soleil et la Table du Soleil', *REG* 85.xiv—xvii. (Revised in Detienne and Vernant, 1979: 239—49.)

Vernant, Jean-Pierre. 1974. *Mythe et société en Grèce ancienne*. Paris. [ET 1980.]

Vernant, Jean-Pierre and Vidal-Naquet, Pierre. 1972. *Mythe et tragédie en Grèce ancienne*. Paris. [ET 1981.]

Veyne, Paul. 1971. *Comment on écrit l'histoire. Essai d'epistémologie*. Univers historique. Paris.

Vian, Francis. 1960. 'Le mythe de Typhée et le problème de ses origines orientales', in *Éléments orientaux dans la religion grecque ancienne*, pp. 17—37. Travaux du Centre d'Études d'Histoire des Religions de Strasbourg. Paris.

Vian, Francis. 1968. 'La fonction guerrière dans la mythologie grecque', in J.-P. Vernant, 1968, 53—68.

Vidal-Naquet, Pierre. 1964. Foreword to K.A. Wittfogel, *Le Despotisme oriental* [French translation of Wittfogel, *Oriental Despotism: a comparative study of total power*, New Haven, 1957.] Paris.

Vidal-Naquet, Pierre. 1965. 'Économie et société dans la Grèce ancienne: l'oeuvre de Moses I. Finley'. *Archives Européennes de Sociologie* 6,111—48.

Vidal-Naquet, Pierre. 1968. 'La tradition de l'hoplite athénien', in J.-P. Vernant, 1968, 161—81.

Vidal-Naquet, Pierre. 1972. 'Le *Philoctète* de Sophocle et l'éphébie', in J.-P. Vernant and P. Vidal-Naquet, 1972, 161—84. Paris. [Repr. with alterations from *Annales ESC* 26 (1971), 623—38.]

Vidal-Naquet, Pierre. 1973a. 'Les esclaves grecques étaient-ils une classe?' in *Ordre et Classes* (edited D. Roche), pp. 29—36. The Hague—Paris. [Reprinted from *Raison présente* 6 (1968), 103—12.]

Vidal-Naquet, Pierre. 1973b. 'Réflexions sur l'historiographie grecque de l'esclavage', in *Actes du Colloque de Besançon sur l'esclavage* (1971), pp. 23—42. Besançon—Paris.

Vidal-Naquet, Pierre, 1975a. 'Bêtes, hommes et dieux chez les Grecs', in *Hommes et bêtes: entretiens sur le racisme* (ed. Léon Poliakov), pp. 129—42. Paris.

Vidal-Naquet, Pierre. 1975b. 'Les esclaves immortels d'Athéna Ilias', in *Le Monde grec: pensée, littérature, histoire, documents. Hommages à Claire Préaux* (edited Jean Bingen *et al.*), pp. 496—507. Université Libre de Bruxelles: Faculté de Philosophie et Lettres, vol. 52. Bruxelles.

Vidal-Naquet, Pierre. 1978. 'Plato's myth of the statesman, the ambiguities of the Golden Age and of history', *JHS* 98.132—41.

Vidal-Naquet, Pierre. 1981. 'Étude d'une ambiguité: le statut des artisans dans la cité platonicienne', in *Le Chasseur noir — Formes de pensée et formes de société dans le monde grec*. Paris.

Vincent, A. 1940. 'Essai sur le sacrifice de communion des rois Atlantes', *Mémorial M.-J. Lagrange* (Cinquantenaire de l'école biblique et archéologique française de Jérusalem), pp. 81—96. Paris.

Visscher, Fernand de. 1931. 'Ducere dona iube: Énéide 5, 385', in *Études de droit romain*, pp. 353—7. Paris. [Repr. from *RBPH* 7 (1928), 579—83.]

Voelke, A.J. 1966. 'Un point de vue nouveau sur Posidonius' (review of Laffranque, 1964). *ASSPh* 26.281—9.

Wachsmuth, Ernst W.G. 1846. *Hellenische Altertumskunde aus dem Gesichtspunkt des Staates*. 2 ed., 2 vols. Halle. (1 ed. 2 vols., Halle, 1826—30.)

Wachsmuth, D. 1967. Πόμπιμος ὁ δαίμων: *Untersuchung zu den antiken Sakralhandlung bei Seereisen*. Diss., Berlin.

Wachtel, Nathan. 1971. 'Pensée sauvage et acculturation: l'espace et le temps chez Felipe Guaman Poma de Ayala et l'Inca Garcilaso de la Vega'. *Annales ESC* 26.793—840.

Walbank, Frank W. 1957—79. *A Historical Commentary on Polybius*. 3 vols. Oxford.

Walcot, Peter D. 1966. *Hesiod and the Near East*. Cardiff.

Waltzing, Jean-Pierre. 1925. 'Le crime rituel reproché aux chrétiens du IIe siècle', *BARB*, sér. 5, 11.205—39.

Waser, Otto. 1901. Art. 'Danaos' (1). *RE*, cols. 2094—8.

Waszink, J.H. 1950. 'The dreaming Kronos in the *Corpus Hermeticum*', *AIPH* 10 [= *Mélanges offerts à Henri Gregoire*, II].639—63.

Weil, Raymond. 1959. *L'"Archéologie" de Platon. Commentaire du Livre III des Lois*. Études et commentaires 32. Paris.

Weiss, Egon. 1923. *Griechisches Privatrecht auf rechtsvergleichender Grundlage*: 1. *Allgemeine Lehren*. Leipzig. [Repr. Aalen, 1965.]

Welwei, Karl-Wilhelm. 1974. *Unfreie im antiken Kriegsdienst*, 1. Forschungen zur antiken Sklaverei 5,8. Wiesbaden. [Vol. 2, 1977.]

West, Martin L. 1966. *Hesiod's Theogony* (ed. and comm.). Oxford.

Westrup, C.W. 1934—54. *Introduction to Early Roman Law. Comparative sociological studies. The patriarchal joint family*. 5 vols. Vol. 2: *The joint family and family property* (1934). Copenhagen—Oxford.

Wide, Samuel Carl Anders. 1893. *Lakonische Kulte*. Leipzig. [Repr. Stuttgart, 1973.]

Wilamowitz-Moellendorff, Ulrich von. 1893. *Aristoteles und Athen*. 2 vols. Berlin. [Repr. Zürich, 1966.]

Wilamowitz-Moellendorff, Ulrich von (ed.). 1927. *Aristophanes: Lysistrate*. Berlin. [Repr. Berlin, 1958.]

Wilamowitz-Moellendorff, Ulrich von. 1935—37. 'Oropos und die Graer', in *Kleine Schriften*, 5 vols. in 6 (ed. Paul Maas *et al.*), 5.1, pp. 1—25. [Repr. from *Hermes* 21 (1886), 91—115.]

Works cited

Wilamowitz-Moellendorff, Ulrich von. 1955. *Der Glaube der Hellenen*. 2 vols. 2 ed. Basel. [1 ed. 1931–2; repr. Darmstadt, 1959.]
Wilhelm, Adolf. 1911. 'Die Lokrische Mädcheninschrift', *JÖAI* 14.163–256.
Wilkinson, Lionel Patrick. 1969. *The Georgics of Virgil. A critical survey*. Cambridge.
Will, Édouard. 1955. *Korinthiaka. Recherches sur l'histoire et la civilisation de Corinthe des origines aux guerres médiques*. Paris.
Willetts, Ronald F. 1955. *Aristocratic Society in Ancient Crete*. London.
Willetts, Ronald F. 1959. 'The servile interregnum at Argos', *Hermes* 87.495–506.
Willetts, Ronald F. 1962. *Cretan Cults and Festivals*. London.
Willetts, Ronald F. 1967. *The Law Code of Gortyn*. Kadmos Supplement 1. Berlin.
Wolska, Wanda. 1962. *La topographie chrétienne de Cosmas Indicopleustès: théologie et science au VIe siècle*. Bibliothèque byzantine, Études 3. Paris.
Wuilleumier, Pierre. 1939. *Tarente, des origines à la conquête romaine*. Paris.
Yalman, Nur. 1967. 'The Raw : the Cooked :: Nature : Culture. Observations on *Le Cru et le cuit*', in *The Structural Study of Myth and Totemism* (ed. E.R. Leach), pp. 71–89. ASA Monographs 5. London.
Yalouris, Nikolaos. 1950. 'Athena als Herrin der Pferde', *Museum Helveticum* 7. 19–101.
Zeitlin, Froma I. 1978. 'The dynamics of misogyny: myth and myth-making in the *Oresteia*', *Arethusa* 11,1–2.149–89.
Ziehen, Ludwig. 1939. Art. 'Opfer'. *RE*, cols. 579–627.
Zuidema, Rainer T. 1971. *Ethnologia e storia: Cuzco e le strutture dell'impero inca* (with a preface by N. Wachtel). Torino. [Italian translation by H. Marazzi and M.V. Malvano of Zuidema's *The Ceque system of Cuzco: The Social organization of the capital of the Inca*. International Archives of Ethnography 50 [Supplement], Leiden, 1964.]

Index

Abaris, 139—40

Abioi (= *Gabioi*), 86

abstinence: from sexual pollution, 98, 101; from food etc., 102; from bloodshed, 104; from meat, 221—3

Achilles, 75—6, 85; hunts by running, 159

adolescence: and *ephebeia*, 147—52, 156—60, 174—8; and *krypteia*, 153—5, 181—4; of Spartan girls, 184—5; of Athenian girls, 178—80; in Crete, 157—8, 177; marked in funerary practice, 173—4; and hunting, 160—2; Telemachus, 90; the Huskanaw in Virginia, 171; *see also* age-classes; childhood; masquerade; rites of passage

Adonia, 101—2

Aegis, 86, 136—7

Aeolus (Master of Winds), 40, 246 n. 24; and incest, 87, 92—3

Aeschylus: *Agamemnon*, 120—1, 190; *Choephoroi*, 190—1; *Eumenides*, 140; on Typhon, 9; navigation, 24; incest, 198; Parthenopaeus, 161 n. 40; significance of fire (*Prometheus*), 54, 74

agalma: as precious object, 114ff, 119, 123, 126, 128, 130, 141—2

Agave (mother of Pentheus), 224

age-classes, 173, 178—84, 255 n. 5; city cancels opposition between, 178; *see also* adolescence; hoplite

age of Cronus; age of gold, *see* Golden Age

agela, in Crete, 155, 157, 177, 183

agogē, in Sparta, 181, 182ff

agon, 44, 157—8, 184; *see also* Eris/*eris*

agora, 68, 84, 94, 132—3; absent in proto-Athens (Plato), 207; at Sparta, 24—5; in Phaeacia, 34

agriculture: defines the human condition, 49, 54, 71—4, 78—9, 80—3, 89—91; in proto-Athens (Plato), 206—7; invented by Cecrops and Bouzyges, 82; excluded from world of Odysseus's stories, 84, 86—7; and

the ephebic oath, 149, 162; and slaves, 192—3, 194, 200; sacred ploughing, 134—5; *see also* bios; plough; women

agronomos, in Plato, 148, 158; *see also peripolos*

aidōs, 100, 121, 242 n. 20

Aietes (king of Colchis), 134, 137, 139, 140

Aigipan, 10

Aisa, 231 n. 2 (in Alcman)

Ajax, son of Oileus, 25—6

Alcibiades, 178 (opposes Nicias)

Alcinous, 34, 91—4; palace of, 89, 204; as perfect *oikos*, 93—4

Alcmaeon, 121 (murders mother)

Alcman: on *Aisa* and *Poros*, 231 n. 2; on *Tyche*, 22

Alexander the Great, 125—6 (sacrifice to sea)

Amalthea, 136—7

Amazons, 190 (topsy-turvy world)

ambiguity: of the human condition, 50, 53, 55, 63—5; of Promethean fire, 49, 59, 75; of Pandora, 51, 55, 81; of Elpis (Hope), 55—6; of *eris*, 68—9; of flour, 78; of objects, 120—3, 138—9, 142; of *Aithuia*, 17—18; of bees, 98; of *numphē*, 102—3; of status of Giants, 13; of *Tyche* and *Kairos*, 21ff; of Golden Age with gods, 86; of cannibalism in Dionysiac cult, 225; of ephebe, 147ff, 149—50 (double); of Jason, 149; of Scheria, 91—2

ambrosia, 14, 15, 72, cf. 54

Amphiaraus, 121—2

Amphitrite, 122, 130

Andropompos, 152

Androphagoi, 220, 247 n. 39

Anesidora, 53, 245 n. 8

animal skin: wearing of (sheepskin), 136; (leopard-skin), 149; (sealskin), 232 n. 11; (goatskin (aegis)), 136; golden fleece, 131ff; hide of sacrificial animal, 136—7; bull's hide as bag, 87